D0202737

Encyclopedia of
Body Adornment

Encyclopedia of
BODY ADORNMENT

MARGO DeMELLO

GREENWOOD PRESS
Westport, Connecticut • London

Library of Congress Cataloging-in-Publication Data

DeMello, Margo.
Encyclopedia of body adornment / Margo DeMello.
    p. cm.
   Includes bibliographical references and index.
   ISBN-13: 978–0–313–33695–9 (alk. paper)
   1. Body marking—Encyclopedias.   2. Tattooing—Encyclopedias.   3. Body
   piercing—Encyclopedias.   4. Scarification (Body marking)—Encyclopedias.
   5. Body, Human—Social aspects—Encyclopedias.   I. Title.
  GN419.15. D46   2007
   391.6′503—dc22   2007016304

British Library Cataloguing in Publication Data is available.

Library of Congress Catalog Card Number: 2007016304
ISBN-13: 978–0–313–33695–9

First published in 2007

Greenwood Press, 88 Post Road West, Westport, CT 06881
An imprint of Greenwood Publishing Group, Inc.
www.greenwood.com

Printed in the United States of America

The paper used in this book complies with the
Permanent Paper Standard issued by the National
Information Standards Organization (Z39.48–1984).

10 9 8 7 6 5 4 3 2

Contents

List of Entries

Guide to Related Topics

ACCEPTABILITY OF PRACTICES

Criminality
Freaks
Legislation and Regulation

Spanner Case
Stigmata

ANIMALS

Animal Branding
Animality
Animal Surgical Procedures
Animal Tattooing

Genetic Engineering
Sprague, Eric
Stalking Cat
Wildenstein, Jocelyn

BODY IMAGE

Anorexia and Bulimia
Apotemnophilia
Beauty
Bodybuilding
Body Dysmorphic Disorder
Body Hair

Breast Augmentation and Reduction
Cosmetic Surgery
Facial Hair
Obesity
Plastic Surgery
Sex Reassignment Surgery

BODY PLAY

Body Play
Spanner Case

Suspensions

COERCIVE BODY MODIFICATION

Auschwitz
Breast Ironing
Castration
Clitoridectomy

Female Genital Mutilation
Prisoners
Slavery
Torture

CULTURES

Australia
Borneo
Brazil
Celts
Chicanos
China

Easter Island
Egypt
England
Ethiopia
Greco-Roman World
Hawaii

India
Inuit
Ivory Coast
Japan
Maori
Marquesas
Marshall Islands
Meso-America
Native Americans
New Guinea
New Zealand

Nigeria
Pacific Northwest Indians
Philippines
Russia
Samoa
Sudan
Tahiti
Thailand
Tonga
Zaire

HEALTH AND MEDICINE

Acupuncture
Amputation
Anorexia and Bulimia
Association of Professional Tattooists
Bariatric Surgery
Body Dysmorphic Disorder
Breast Augmentation and Reduction
Breast Reconstruction
Cosmetic Dentistry

Cosmetic Surgery
Health Issues
Intersexuality
Medical Tattooing
Obesity
Plastic Surgery
Sex Reassigment Surgery
Trepanation

HISTORY

Barnum, P. T.
Bible
Circus
Cook, Captain James

Egypt
Freak Shows
Greco-Roman World
Meso-America

INDIVIDUALS

Barnum, P. T.
Broadbent, Betty
Collins, Sailor Jerry
Enigma, The
Great Omi, The
Hardy, Don Ed
Haworth, Steve
Lazonga, Vyvyn
Musafar, Fakir

Sprague, Eric
Stalking Cat
Tuttle, Lyle
Wagner, Charlie
Ward, Jim
Wildenstein, Jocelyn
Zeis, Milton
Zulueta, Leo

MEDIA

BMEZine.com
Dances Sacred and Profane
Modern Primitives

PFIQ
Tattoo Magazines
TattooTime

NONINVASIVE BODY ADORNMENT

Bodybuilding
Body Hair
Body Painting
Corsets
Cosmetics
Facial Hair
Fingernails
Hair Cutting and Head Shaving

Hairstyles
Hair Treatments
Henna
Jewelry
Makeup
Skin Whitening
Tanning

OTHER BODY MODIFICATIONS

Amputation
Branding
Breast Ironing
Castration
Circumcision
Cosmetic Surgery
Cutting
Dermal Anchoring
Ear Shaping
Ear Stretching
Encumberments
Foot Binding
Genetic Engineering

Genital Mutilation
Head Binding
Implants
Infibulation
Labrets
Scalpelling
Scarification
Self-Mutilation
Silicone Injections
Stretching
Super/Subincision
Tongue Splitting

PIERCING

Body Piercing
Clitoral Piercing
Ear Piercing
Facial Piercing
Gauntlet
Genital Piercing
Hand Piercing
Lip Plates

Navel Piercing
Nipple Piercing
Nose Piercing
Oral Piercing
Penis Piercing
PFIQ
Piercing
Surface Piercing

RELIGION

Christianity
Islam
Judaism
Magic

Neo-Paganism
Rites of Passage
Stigmata

SEX AND SEXUALITY

Asceticism
BDSM
Body Play

Bondage
Cross-Gender
Genital Piercing

Intersexuality
Pain
Spanner Case

Transgender
Transsexuals
Tranvestites

SUBCULTURES

BDSM
Biker Tattooing
Fraternities
Gang Members
Hijras
Military Tattoos
Modern Primitives

Prison Tattooing
Punk
Transgender
Transsexuals
Transvestites
Yakuza

SURGICAL PRACTICES

Amputation
Bariatric Surgery
Circumcision

Cosmetic Surgery
Plastic Surgery
Sex Reassignment Surgery

TATTOOING

Alliance of Professional Tattooists
American Tattooing
Association of Professional Piercers
Biker Tattooing
Contemporary Tattooing
Cosmetic Tattooing
Facial Tattoos
Flash
Genital Tattooing
Medical Tattooing
Military Tattoos
Moko
National Tattoo Association

Pe'a
Prison Tattooing
Tattoo Community
Tattooed Attractions
Tattooed "Natives"
Tattooing
Tattoo Magazines
Tattoo Reality Shows
Tattoo Removal
Tattoo Shows
Tattoo Technology
TattooTime

THEORETICAL ISSUES

Animality
Bakhtin, Mikhail
Bio-Power
Bourdieu, Pierre

Class and Status
Foucault, Michel
Gender
Primitivism

Preface

Body adornment and body modification have been important topics for scholars in the social sciences as well as the humanities for the past twenty years. Currently, there is not a single overall reference book that covers the breadth and scope of the field. This encyclopedia is the first of its kind to take a comprehensive look at body modifications and body adornments around the world and throughout history. It addresses the major adornments and modifications, their historical and cross-cultural locations, and the major cultural groups and places in which body modification has been central to social and cultural practices. This encyclopedia also includes background information on some of the central figures involved in creating and popularizing tattooing, piercing, and other body modifications in the modern world. Finally, the book addresses some of the major theoretical issues surrounding the temporary and permanent modification of the body, the laws and customs regarding the marking of the body, and the social movements that have influenced or embraced body modification, and those which have been affected by it.

This volume is aimed at general readers with an interest in the modification and adornment of the body, as well as students and scholars who are doing more in-depth work on the social and cultural uses of the body. Most entries include a list of further reading on the subject for readers who desire more information, and there is as well a list of resources (including magazines, organizations, Web sites, and museums devoted to body modification) at the end of the book, as well as a comprehensive bibliography.

There are 207 entries in this encyclopedia, which cover the major adornments and modifications to the body, the groups associated with them, the movements involved with them, and the laws and norms which have dealt with them over time. Major organizations and people involved in the modern body modification movement have been included, with a special emphasis on North America, but for the most part, the book covers societies spanning the world, and going back into prehistory.

Entries are listed in alphabetical order, and when a subject has multiple names for it, the most commonly used name (i.e., castration) will be the name used for the entry, and other names (i.e., orchiectomy) will include a note directing the reader to the full entry. Additionally, each entry contains cross-referenced items in bold type, as well as a list of related subjects at the end of each entry.

Each entry explains the term, gives an overview, and provides any historical or cross-cultural significance. Because of the speed with which the modern body modification movement changes, there will doubtless be new types of modifications that have come out that are not included in this encyclopedia.

Nevertheless, all attempts have been made to include the most relevant and up-to-date information.

ACKNOWLEDGMENTS

Every book, regardless of the author, includes the work and assistance of a great many people. I owe my first thanks to Clinton Sanders who recommended me to my editor at Greenwood, Sarah Colwell; without the confidence of these two individuals, I would not have produced this book.

A number of people helped secure images for the book, including Jeff Hayes of Rival Tattoo Art Studio in Albuquerque, New Mexico. Jeff not only provided many of the beautiful images included in this book from his own portfolio; he is also my tattooist and his work on my own body over the year that I worked on this book, and his insight into the tattooing and piercing community greatly enriched this work. Most of the historical images in the book are from the Library of Congress Prints and Photographs Division, and a few are from the National Library of Medicine. I am also grateful for the photo I received from Nels Akerlund. Steve Truitt of Stay Gold Tattoo & Body Modification and Ascension Studios, both in Albuquerque, provided the contemporary piercing, cutting, and other body modification photos in the book.

Chuck Eldridge of the Tattoo Archive in Berkeley, California, provided a number of the archival photos used in the book, and I want to thank him for his generosity in lending me these images, as well as his work in preserving the history of tattooing. Chuck was also my very first tattooist, and provided a great deal of support and guidance when I was writing my first book.

I am also grateful for the support I received from Erin Williams, my coauthor on another book I worked on this year, and her friendship, hard work, and support has been and is very precious to me.

Finally, I want to thank my husband, Tom Young, who endured my increasing levels of stress during the last, frantic months of this project, and set me up with a new computer when my last one crashed two months before deadline, and my parents, Bill DeMello and Robin Montgomery, who have always given me love and support throughout all of my projects.

Introduction

Humans have been adorning and modifying the human (and animal) body for thousands of years, and most likely, since humans became human. All cultures everywhere have attempted to change their body in an attempt to meet their cultural standards of beauty, as well as their religious and/or social obligations. In addition, people modify and adorn their bodies as part of the complex process of creating and recreating their personal and social identities.

Body adornment refers to the practice of physically enhancing the body by styling and decorating the hair, painting and embellishing the fingernails, wearing makeup, painting the body, wearing jewelry, and the use of clothing. Body adornments are by definition temporary. Body modification, on the other hand, refers to the physical alteration of the body through the use of surgery, tattooing, piercing, scarification, branding, genital mutilation, implants, and other practices. Body modifications can be permanent or temporary, although most are permanent and alter the body forever.

Body painting has probably been practiced since the Paleolithic as archaeological evidence indicates, and the earliest human evidence of tattooing goes back to the Neolithic with mummies found in Europe, Central Asia, the Andes, and the Middle East. Adornments such as jewelry have been found in the earliest human graves and bodies unearthed from five thousand years ago show signs of intentional head shaping. It is clear that adorning and modifying the body is a central human practice.

Today, tattooing, scarification, piercing, body painting, and other forms of permanent and temporary body modification are found in every culture around the world, and are seen by anthropologists as visible markers of age, social status, family position, tribal affiliation, and other social features. Scholars who have studied the ways in which humans mark their bodies note that bodily displays create, communicate, and maintain status and identity. This has been found not only in traditional societies, but in state-level societies as well. Succinctly put, the modification of the body is the simplest means by which human beings are turned into social beings—they move from "raw" to "cooked" as the body goes from naked to marked. According to theorist Michel Thevoz, "there is no body but the painted body," because the body must always be stamped with the mark of culture and society; without marking, the body cannot move within the channels of social exchange.

But in reality, human bodies are never "blank" or unmarked, even when not explicitly marked through adornment or modification. Bodies can be fat or thin, dark or light, male or female, young or old. In these ways, too, social position is marked onto even naked bodies, in every society. Even then, however, societies dictate that the body needs more in terms of marking in order to make them truly culturally and socially intelligible.

Many cultures that practice piercing, scarification, tattooing, and other permanent body modifications believe that one is not fully human if the body is not properly adorned or modified. In fact, even the wearing of makeup and the styling of hair can be seen as ways in which the human body is distinguished from the animal body. Permanent and temporary, all of the ways in which the human body has been altered historically can be seen as markers of civilization, of culture, and of humanity. The more altered the body, often the more human and civilized. Body adornments and modifications are symbolic as well, symbolizing a great many subtle and not-so-subtle social features about the wearer.

Because the body has always been used as a means of expression and self-construction, it is not surprising that we find in both the archaeological record and among the practices of people around the world, an enormous variety of techniques and procedures by which the human body is transformed. In every society, each individual marks off his or her social position by clothing, adornments, and modifications to the body. Most are temporary, but some are permanent, and many involve quite a bit of pain. Temporary markings, such as body painting, are often used in a ritual context to make the individual different, extraordinary, and is often used to celebrate or mark a specific cultural or ritual event. Permanent markings, on the other hand, such as tattooing, scarification, and genital mutilation, are generally used to mark a permanent status onto the body, such as adulthood, marriageability, or class or caste status.

In traditional societies such as foraging bands and pastoral or horticultural tribes, the marking of the body was a sign of inclusion in the community, but with the development of agriculture and the state, markings like tattooing, scarring, and branding became signs of exclusion and stigmatization, while in modern state-level societies, these same markings have become a means to individuate the self from the social group.

In traditional societies, for example, the use of body paint, tattooing, scarification, piercing, head flattening, lip and ear stretching, and genital modifications like circumcision are quite common. These practices have multiple purposes, but the most central among them include decoration and the marking of social position. Temporary adornments are most typically used to mark transitional statuses or for specific social events, whereas permanent modifications are more commonly used to mark permanent changes in status, permanent affiliations, and cultural concepts of beauty.

In early state-level societies, we see for the first time the state and elites marking power onto individual bodies. Through the use of tattoos and brands to punish criminals, denote slave status, or mark ownership of animals, these are examples of state power being inscribed directly onto the body, as a way to control unruly or criminal bodies. At the same time, elites used very different adornments and modifications—such as elaborate hairstyles, jewelry made of precious stones, beautiful clothing, and cosmetic surgery—to demonstrate their elevated status.

The differential marking of criminals and the lower classes continued into the twentieth century in many societies, and of course the use of specialized adornments among the elites to distinguish themselves from the other classes continues as well.

In modern society, we see that the desire to mold the body as a sign of social status is unchanged, with men and women using makeup, jewelry, hairstyles, cosmetic surgery, dieting, and fashion to transform their bodies in accordance with the current dictates of style. Fashionable bodies are young, thin, and beautiful, and when commonly practiced forms of adornment and modification (such as dieting, makeup, and hairstyling) cannot achieve these characteristics, more extreme modifications are available to those who can afford them. Full face, hair, and body makeovers are purchased by the wealthy and are also seen on television shows like "The Swan" and "Extreme Makeover," and rely on modern surgical procedures such as bariatric surgery, cosmetic surgery, cosmetic dentistry, cosmetic dermatology, and hair implants and weaves.

Also in modern societies, we have seen the development of nonnormative body modifications such as tattooing, piercing, stretching, branding, scarification, and genital modifications, which allow individuals to step outside of the bounds of the normal social order, and mark membership in alternative subcultures, such as bikers, punks, convicts, gang members, or among those who practice alternative sexualities. Also in the twentieth century we saw the development of a movement that not only uses nonnormative and often extreme body modifications but relies on them for aesthetic, spiritual, sexual, and personal growth. This movement, known as the modern primitives movement, borrows body modification techniques and religious and cultural beliefs from non-Western societies to resist and challenge modern social practices. Ironically, however, while the traditions borrowed in the modern primitives movement generally serve to mark traditional peoples as belonging to the social order, those practices, when used in the contemporary West, serve instead to separate the wearers from society, rather than integrate them. Even more ironic, perhaps, is the fact that many of these traditional forms of body modification have now disappeared from the societies in which they were practiced, often stamped out through Western imperialism, and only exist now in cannibalized form among modern primitives.

According to theorist Michel Foucault, in state-level societies, power is inscribed on bodies through modes of social supervision and discipline as well as self-regulation. But at the same time, bodies also can be sites of resistance as they always entail the possibility of counterinscription, of being self-marked. Thus the use of body modifications in ways that are not only not socially sanctioned but are explicitly antisocial can be seen as a way in which disaffected or marginalized bodies can mark themselves in accordance with their owners' self-image.

Contemporary members of the body modification movement who use extreme modifications in nonnormative ways see themselves as taking control of their own bodies and expressing their individual identities. Proponents see these modifications as ways in which they actively transform the self. However, mainstream society typically views them in a very different light, and sees them as a disfigurement or mutilation. Extreme modifications such as heavy tattooing and highly visible tattoos (i.e., on the face, hands, or head), multiple piercings as well as genital and nonnormative facial piercings, brands, intentional scars, and especially the use of implants, genital modifications, or voluntary amputations, are seen by some as a symptom of body dsymorphic disorder, and are generally frowned upon and are often criminalized or heavily regulated.

This encyclopedia aims to make a wide variety of adornment and modification practices intelligible to the reader.

Further Reading: Brain, Robert. *The Decorated Body*. New York: Harper and Row, 1979; Thevóz, Michel. *The Painted Body*. New York: Rizzoli International, 1984; Turner, Terence. "Social Body and Embodied Subject: Bodiliness, Subjectivity and Sociality among the Kayapo." *Current Anthropology* 10(2) (1995): 143–170.

A

ACUPUNCTURE

Acupuncture is an ancient Eastern medical technique that uses the insertion of needles into the body to cure illness.

In **China**, where acupuncture is thought to have originated, it has been known as far back as the first millenium BCE. It has also been practiced for thousands of years in Korea and **Japan**, and was possibly practiced in Eurasia in the Bronze Age. It was first described in a 4,700-year-old Chinese medical text, *Yellow Emperor's Classic of Internal Medicine.*

Acupuncture is the practice of inserting very fine needles into the body at points called acupuncture points, or acupoints, in order to influence physiological or emotional health of the body. Shen Nung, a third millenium BCE medical and agricultural scholar, came up with the theories that form the basis of modern acupuncture. He postulated that the body had an energy force running through it known as Qi, which includes spiritual, emotional, physical, and mental aspects. The Qi travels through the body along special pathways or meridians, and if the Qi is unbalanced or lacks strength, or its travels are disrupted, ill health can occur. Shen Nung felt that the Meridians come to the surface at specific locations in the body, which allowed them to be accessed in order to repair the Qi. These points of access are the acupoints, and can be accessed via the use of needles, as well as through acupressure and moxibustion, the burning of herbs over the skin. By balancing and repairing the Qi, the patient can be healed.

Acupuncture, as well as other forms of Chinese medicine, are based on a very different understanding of health and the human body than Western medicine. The Western approach, for example, is oriented toward disease, with treatments aimed at eliminating or controlling disease, and sees diseases of the mind and body as being separate in origin and nature (and thus in treatment), resulting in a reductionist approach that views the body and mind as constituting a series of parts that can be healthy or sick. Chinese medicine, on the other hand, is a holistic approach that focuses not on disease or pathology but on wellness and balance. It sees the body as divided into several systems of function that correspond to physical organs, and illness is a result of systems being out of balance or harmony. The diagnosis of illness, then, is not associated with a certain organ or part being diseased, but of a systemic disorder, which must be treated on that basis.

Acupuncture experienced a decline in China during the Ching Dynasty (from the eighteenth to the early twentieth century), as China became influenced by Western medical practices such as surgery and the bacteria theory of disease. With the rise of communism in late 1920s, acupuncture continued to fall from favor as the early communist leadership felt that acupuncture was superstitious and irrational, and conflicted with the Communist party's aims of scientific progress. Chairman Mao, however, later supported the use of acupuncture to help keep Chinese troops healthy using inexpensive methods during the civil war. He also saw traditional Chinese medical techniques as an important cultural tradition to be cherished and documented. Now known as Traditional Chinese Medicine, it was incorporated into medical school curriculum in the 1950s, and was taught as a science.

With a more scientific approach, and later a blending of Western and Eastern practices, new methods developed including the use of acupuncture as anesthesia, the injection of fluids into joints to treat arthritis, and the development of new sites for acupuncture such as the scalp. Electro-acupuncture is also practiced today, which involves stimulating needles with electrical currents during insertion.

Today, acupuncture is practiced not only throughout Asia but throughout the Western world as well, by practitioners who either combine acupuncture with traditional Western methods (in this case, the use of acupuncture is known as a complementary therapy), or those who practice only traditional Chinese techniques.

Because acupuncture, like **tattooing, piercing**, and other forms of decorative body modification, uses needles and is an invasive practice, most localities in the United States have regulations governing the licensing and training of acupuncturists, as well as regulations pertaining to infection control and waste disposal.

Practitioners who specialize in acupuncture are known as licensed acupuncturists, and do not need medical licenses or medical training, but must receive anywhere from 2,500 to 4,000 hours of training at one of a few dozen schools in the United States, and, in order to receive a certificate to practice, must take a test provided by the National Certification Commission for Acupuncture and Oriental Medicine. While many states require this test for licensing, some states do not. Doctors, nurses, dentists, and other medical personnel who use acupuncture as a complementary therapy, receive training in acupuncture, although their training is more limited than licensed acupuncturists. The American Academy of Medical Acupuncture provides training and develops standards for doctors who practice acupuncture alongside Western therapies, and has 1,500 members.

The Food and Drug Administration defines acupuncture needles as safe when used appropriately by licensed professionals. Appropriate use includes the size and type of needle, the depth of insertion, and sterilization of needles. All states with regulations pertaining to acupuncture require the use of single-use, presterilized stainless steel needles which are discarded after each use.

According to a National Health Interview survey in 2002, 8.2 million Americans have used acupuncture. As a complementary therapy, it is used for **pain** control, anxiety, drug detoxification, stroke and palsy symptoms, muscle spasms, gastrointestinal disorders, headache, arthritis, and bone pain. Some veterinarians also use acupuncture to treat back and muscle pain, arthritis, epilepsy, nervous conditions, and gastrointestinal disorders.

Many Western doctors reject the efficacy of acupuncture, and explain the apparent successes to the fact that some diseases and conditions will naturally go away on their own, some diseases are cyclical, and to the fact that patients who seek

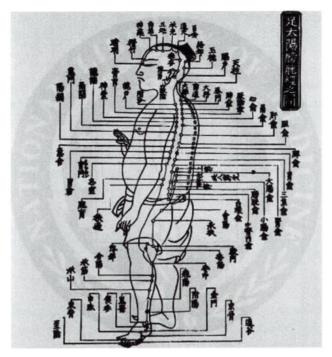

Human figure with acupuncture points indicated. Illustration from early Chinese Medical Textbook, World Health Organization Photo, No. A013734. Courtesy of the National Library of Medicine.

alternative treatments may be more invested in their health and in feeling better. In addition, some patients will "hedge their bets," using acupuncture alongside of Western treatments, and thus they cannot tell which treatment provided the cure.

Acupuncture is linked to contemporary body modifications beyond the shared use of needles. Acupuncture needles are often used in **body piercing** in which the needles are left in the body, and permanent piercings are also sometimes done on acupuncture points. Some piercers use piercings to help treat chronic pain, and women in **India** have been said to pierce their noses to induce a state of submissiveness, by locating the piercing on an acupoint.

See also: Body Piercing; Legislation and Regulation

Further Reading: Beijing College of Traditional Chinese Medicine. *Essentials of Chinese Acupuncture*. New York: Pergamon Press, Inc., 1981; Ellis, Andrew, Nigel Wiseman, and Ken Boss. *Fundamentals of Chinese Acupuncture*. Brookline, MA: Paradigm Publications, 1991; Maciocia, Giovanni. *The Foundations of Chinese Medicine: A Comprehensive Text for Acupuncturists and Herbalists*. Oxford: Churchill Livingstone, 2005.

ALLIANCE OF PROFESSIONAL TATTOOISTS

The Alliance of Professional Tattooists, Inc. (APT), was founded in 1992 as a nonprofit organization focused on the development and promotion of health and safety standards within **tattooing**. This is important from a legal perspective, as there is increasing pressure in many states to regulate tattooing, ostensibly for health reasons. APT's position is that it is better to be regulated internally rather than by county or state health officials; thus they are concerned that all member tattooists use modern sterilization practices.

Today, virtually all professional tattooists are aware of the risks of transmitting diseases like Hepatitis through tattooing (HIV is much less easily transmitted this way), and now autoclave their tattoo equipment, wear rubber gloves, dispose of paper towels, used needles and other contaminated items safely, and use individual portions of ink and ointment. Most as well use new needles and tubes for each client, and will disinfect the entire work area between clients with an approved cleanser that kills bacteria and viruses. APT can certainly take credit for many of these innovations.

By educating tattooists on health issues, and by assuring the general public that tattooing is practiced in a safe and professional manner, APT helps to ensure that the industry is not threatened by over-regulation, and that tattooing will win favor with a wider constituency. APT has a visible presence at tattoo conventions around the country every year, by tabling, distributing educational information both to tattooists and to the public, and holding seminars on disease prevention and sanitation in conformance with Occupational Safety and Health Administration (OSHA's) regulations on blood-born pathogens.

See also: Health Issues; Legislation and Regulation; National Tattoo Association

Further Reading: Graves, Bonnie. *Tattooing and Body Piercing: Perspectives on Physical Health*. Mankato, MN: Life Matters Press, 2000. Sanders, Clinton. *Customizing the Body: The Art and Culture of Tattooing*. Philadelphia, PA: Temple University Press, 1989.

AMERICAN TATTOOING

Tattooing had been practiced in the United States by a number of **Native American** tribes since before Europeans arrived in America. For instance, many California coastal Indians tattooed decorative marks on women, often on the face; a common design was a series of lines extending from the lips down to the chin. Many Plains and Southwest Indians practiced tattooing as did a number of Southern and Eastern tribes.

Native American tattooing, however, probably had very little impact on the development of tattooing among Euro-Americans. Instead, tattooing in the United States can trace its origins to two related phenomena: the practice, started by Europeans, of sailors and other explorers bringing back from their explorations descriptions of tattoos, tattoos on their own bodies, and tattooed native peoples; and the display of **tattooed natives** and later, tattooed Europeans, at festivals and carnivals.

From at least the eighteenth century, and perhaps as early as the fifteenth century, European explorers brought home with them information about tattooing as it was practiced by many of the peoples that they encountered during their travels. These sailors began to get tattooed, probably influencing soldiers at home to get tattoos as well. In the United States, certainly since at least the Civil War, tattoos were an acceptable means for soldiers and sailors to demonstrate their love of their country as well as their feelings for the loved ones left behind. The first professional tattoo artist in the United States, Martin Hildebrandt, who opened his shop in New York City in 1846, tattooed many soldiers and sailors on both sides of that war. Hildebrandt also tattooed a number of **tattooed attractions**, such as his daughter Nora, who was said to have 365 tattoos (one for each day of the year).

Tattooed attractions were, alongside soldiers and sailors, the other major conduit for tattooing to enter mainstream American society. As American and European citizens clamored to see the tattooed natives being displayed at festivals and later World's Fairs and carnivals, Europeans, and later Americans, got into the act, becoming tattooed themselves and traveling from place to place to earn money as an attraction. Starting in the 1870s, **P. T. Barnum** brought tattooed attractions into the American **circus**, and beginning in the first decade of the twentieth century, tattooed people moved onto the carnival midway. Circuses and carnivals brought tattooed people from the cities (where they were previously displayed at dime museums) into the country, where most people had never seen a tattoo, influencing countless men and women to leave their towns, join the circus, and become tattooed.

> [Being tattooed] separates me from anybody else, no one else has anything like what I have. I feel a little bit different from Joe Shmoe on the street, and I guess inside it makes me feel special.
>
> ANONYMOUS

With Samuel O'Reilly's invention of the electric tattoo machine, the process of tattooing became faster and less painful. This development played a huge role in the rise of the American circus attraction, as more men and women clamored to tattooists like O'Reilly to get a full-body tattoo in order to earn a living. Through the circus, many tattooists were able to travel the country tattooing, making tattoos more common, if not more popular among respectable citizens.

With O'Reilly's invention, which allowed the artist to use a number of needles at once for outlining as well as for shading (as opposed to the single needle used in old-fashioned American pricking), the true Americana style of tattooing was born: strong black lines, typically made with five (or more) needles, heavy black shading, and a dab of color (first black and red, and later, green and blue became available).

While tattoo forms were European, consisting of many badge-like designs arranged on the body with no obvious relationship between them, the designs themselves were influenced both by what was popular with European clients (military insignia, hearts, banners, roses, etc.), and by what was specifically relevant to U.S. citizens (primarily patriotic imagery). Asian designs (dragons, Chinese characters, "Suzy Wongs," tigers, etc.) also became popular in the West as sailors received tattoos at Chinese and Japanese tattoo parlors before the Second World War.

American tattooists in the nineteenth and early twentieth centuries were typically working-class men with no artistic training. Some were sign painters, some learned to tattoo on the circus or carnival circuit, and many answered ads in men's magazines which promised easy money ("$500 in 5 days") for tattooing. Other tattooists learned their trade by paying an older tattooist to teach them. Some artist/suppliers would sell poor quality machines to unsuspecting buyers only to then charge them extra to teach them how to properly fix and use the machines. Percy Waters, a tattooist and supplier from the early part of the century, offered not only instructions on tattooing for a dollar ("a dollar well spent") but offered to help locate the new tattooist in a carnival or circus. And finally, new tattooists could learn to tattoo by serving an apprenticeship with a tattooist. For little to no pay, the apprentice would trace **flash**, cut stencils, clean equipment, fix machines, make needles, and run errands.

I always wanted one so I got one fairly small one, it was a bug (I was already an entomologist), shortly after I finished my PhD ... I've kind of kidded people that the cicada is just like me because it's small, harmless and makes a really big noise cause I'm always stirring up trouble.

ANONYMOUS

Tattooing evolved in twentieth-century North America in small spaces located alongside barbershops, in dirty corners of arcades, under circus tents, or on carnival boardwalks. While hidden away at the margins of society, the shops were nevertheless a home away from home for large numbers of men: sailors, carneys, drunks, laborers, as well as younger boys who would hang around hoping to learn the trade.

The classic American tattoo, whether the eagle or anchor of the sailor or the more universal vow tattoo ("mom" or a girlfriend or wife's name), is a literal tattoo, or one whose meaning is readily understood and agreed to by members of the community who are literate in the system. The images were derived from popular culture, the placement was visible, the lines and color were bold, and the liberal use of alphabetic script in tattoos (the "word tattoo") made them extremely easy to read.

Tattooing began to lose its popularity in the United States after World War II. The Pacific Ocean was no longer a hub of North American military activity, and many of the new enlistees were not planning on a career in the military. In addition, it was in the post–World War II period that saw many new restrictions placed on tattooing around the country, and in some areas, tattooing was banned because of concerns about Hepatitis and other **health issues**. The circus sideshow, too, which played such a major role in promoting tattooing to the American public, faded as well during this time, leaving heavily tattooed people without an occupation and removing the venue through which tattooists traveled the country.

As the nation's military men returned to civilian life after World War II, the popularity of tattoos continued to decline as did the powerful influence that the military had on the forms of North American tattoos. While the new middle class busied themselves with marrying, having children, and moving to the suburbs, inner city and port town tattooing fell to its lowest levels of popularity. Traditional American tattooing was still practiced among many working-class men in most tattoo parlors, but a new form of confrontational, biker-style tattooing was developing on the streets. Tattooing in this period became a form of defiance, a challenge to both emerging mainstream middle-class values, as well as to the traditional form of patriotic and love-inspired working-class tattoo. Not only were tattooed outlaw bikers emerging as a subcultural group to be viewed with fear by the middle class in the late 1940s, but prisoners and **Chicano** gang members, already practicing homemade tattooing, moved into the public eye (especially after the zoot suit riots of the 1940s brought so much media attention to the tattooed *pachuco* culture), contributing not only to an increasingly negative image of tattooing, but also to a splintering of the practice, wherein imagery, styles, and social practices became adapted to the individual subgroups.

As marginal groups began to wear tattoos in greater numbers (including, as well, hippies in the 1960s and punks in the 1970s and 1980s), tattoos themselves became the mark of marginality, a situation that would not change until the 1970s with the renaissance of American tattooing. This renaissance was led by **Don Ed Hardy, Leo Zulueta,** and a number of other influential artists (many of whom were influenced by the work of **Sailor Jerry Collins**), and aided by the spread of non-Western tattoo styles from **Japan, Borneo**, and other places, as well as the increasing professionalism of the trade.

See also: Military Tattoos; Tattooed Attractions; Tattooed Natives; Tattoo Technology

Further Reading: DeMello, Margo. *Bodies of Inscription: A Cultural History of the Modern Tattoo Community*. Durham, NC: Duke University Press, 2000; Ebenstein, Hanns. *Pierced Hearts and True Love: The History of Tattooing*. London: Derek Verschoyle, 1953; Govenar, Alan. "The Changing Image of Tattooing in American Culture." In Jane Caplan, ed., *Written on the Body: The Tattoo in European and American History*. London: Reaktion Books, 2000; Parry, Albert. *Tattoo: Secrets of a Strange Art Practiced by the Natives of the United States*. New York: Collier, 1971; Sanders, Clinton. *Customizing the Body: The Art and Culture of Tattooing*. Philadelphia, PA: Temple University Press, 1989; St. Clair, Leonard, and Alan Govenar. *Stoney Knows How: Life as a Tattoo Artist*. Lexington: University of Kentucky Press, 1981; Steward, Samuel. *Bad Boys and Tough Tattoos: A Social History of the Tattoo with Gangs, Sailors and Street-Corner Punks, 1950–1965*. New York: Harrington Park Press, 1990.

AMPUTATION

Amputation refers to the removal or loss of a limb through trauma or surgery, or for purposes of punishment. Amputation as a surgical technique used to stop the spread of cancer or gangrene or other disease, as well as when a limb has been crushed beyond repair, has been used by medical or sometimes religious specialists for thousands of years. Individuals have sometimes had to amputate their own limbs when a leg or an arm has been trapped, and the film *Saw*'s premise is that two men must saw off their own legs in order to escape death.

Prior to the modern era, amputation was also the main treatment for leprosy, frostbite, animal bites, and infectious diseases. Tools used included knives and saws for cutting, pliers and sometimes a crow bar for removal of the limbs, and hot iron to cauterize the blood vessels and stop the bleeding. Today, amputation techniques (when medically administered) are much more sophisticated and use a wide range of tools, as well as more sophisticated techniques to control bleeding.

Prosthetic devices which replace the missing limb have also grown more sophisticated in the last century, and have moved from simple pegs of wood strapped to a leg or an arm stump to modern lightweight metal and plastic prostheses which not only replace the missing limb but allow for a wide range of mobility as well.

Amputation is also a form of extreme body modification and is related to a psychiatric disorder called Body Integrity Identity Disorder, Amputee Identity Disorder, or Apotemnophilia in which a person has the desire to remove a healthy limb. Many people who have this condition experience a strong drive, which often began in childhood (sometimes with feelings of jealousy aimed at a person with a missing limb), to have a limb removed, and will know exactly which limb must be removed in order to achieve satisfaction. Most individuals with this condition do not sexualize their amputation drives, although others do fetishize the loss of limbs, either on themselves or others. However, because of the deep dissatisfaction with the body in its complete state, apotemnophiliacs often are sexually dysfunctional or have unsatisfying relationships, which is why it is classified as a paraphilia by the American Psychiatric Association. The desire to have a limb amputated can also be characterized as a type of **body dysmorphic disorder**, which is a condition in which an individual obsesses, sometimes compulsively, about imagined or minor defects or flaws in the body.

Of men and women with this condition, a few convince a doctor to remove their limbs, but most doctors will not intentionally remove a healthy limb, although there are a handful of underground doctors who will perform these surgeries, even though they may or may not be licensed to do so, and could face censure or worse from the medical establishment.

Many apotemnophiliacs, however, either intentionally damage their limbs enough so that they will have to be surgically removed in order to save their lives or because the limbs are damaged beyond repair. A great many remove their own limbs themselves (although this is most commonly done when it is a small appendage like a finger or toe), and some convince sympathetic friends to do it for them. A wannabe, on the other hand, is a person who desires the removal of one of their limbs, but has either not yet achieved their goal, or will never go as far as to achieve it. "Wannabes" will often pretend as if their limb is removed, for instance by wearing a sling or taping up a limb, either in private or in public. "Pretenders" are those who do not wish to remove a limb themselves yet pretend that they are disabled, either by hiding a limb or by using a wheelchair, brace or crutches, in order to get attention or some other psychological satisfaction. Finally, amputee fetishists are known as devotees, and are sexually attracted to people with amputated limbs. The Web site "Ampulove" is a place for amputees, wannabees, and devotees to share stories, photos, and experiences.

For some wannabes, having the limb removed "cures" the problem, and the individual becomes happier and better adjusted. In these cases, as with transexualism, the individual feels that their external body does not match their internal view of themselves, and only through modifying the external body can the two selves be aligned. Individuals like this resist the medicalization of their condition, and do not see it as a psychiatric disorder at all. The problem, instead, lies with their physical body and any mental or emotional distress simply derives from having a body that is not right. For others, however, the condition is simply a sign of a deeper mental illness and the amputation does not solve the patient's problems.

The most common limbs removed by do-it-yourselfers appear to be fingers, which are either sawed, chopped, or sliced off, although arms and legs appear to be the most common target limbs for sufferers as a whole. Because do-it-yourself surgery is so dangerous, and the few doctors who are willing to perform such nonmedical amputations are often unlicensed or unqualified, a number of deaths have occurred as a result of this disorder. In 1999, for instance, a man from New York who wanted his leg removed died in a Tijuana motel room after his surgery by an unlicensed doctor.

Finally, some men are characterized by an intense desire to have their penis or scrotum and testicles removed, and sometimes all of the external genitalia. A nullo, for instance, is a man who has all of his genitalia removed for sexual and/or aesthetic reasons. While male to female transsexuals have their genitals removed as part of their transition, a nullo's desires are more complicated and people with this desire make up a very small percentage of the extreme body modification community, and even within that community, many people find them difficult to comprehend.

See also: Body Dysmorphic Disorder; Castration; Genital Mutilation; Health Issues

Further Reading: Bruno, Richard L. "Devotees, Pretenders and Wannabes: Two Cases of Factitious Disability Disorder," *Journal of Sexuality and Disability* 15 (1997): 243–260; Furth, G. and R. Smith. *Amputee Identity Disorder: Information, Questions, Answers and Recomendations about Self-Demand Amputation*. London: Authorhouse, 2000; Money, J., R. Jobaris, and G. Furth. "Apotemnophilia: Two Cases of Self-Demand Amputation as a Paraphilia." *The Journal of Sex Research* 13(2) (1977): 115–125; Thomas, C. "The 'Disabled' Body." In Mary Evans and Ellie Lee, eds., *Real Bodies: A Sociological Introduction*. Basingstoke: Palgrave, 2002.

ANIMAL BRANDING

The tradition of **branding** livestock is as the keeping of livestock and the development of iron. In fact, animals and slaves were both branded by ancient Egyptians, throughout the **Greco-Roman world**, and by the ancient Hebrews in order to mark ownership, deter theft, and sometimes to punish runaway slaves. Branding was brought to the United States by the Spanish, and dates back to the days of Spanish livestock ranchers, or vaqueros, in the southwest.

Originally the word brand meant anything hot or burning, such as a burning stick, but later became used to denote the process of burning an identifying mark into an animal (or human) to mark ownership. In the United States, a branding iron is an iron rod with a seal in the form of a symbol or series of symbols at the end, which is heated in a fire. Once the brand turns red-hot, the brand is pressed against the animal's hide and, ideally, should burn through the hair and outer layer of skin, leaving a permanent mark that can be seen through the hair or fur.

An older style of brand used in the United States was called a "running iron" and consisted of a heated straight or curved iron that was used to draw the design on the animal.

In the United States, brands were both used to prevent theft, to identify lost animals, and to identify ownership when cattle from multiple owners are grazing together. (Unbranded animals are called "slicks" and are very difficult to legally identify.) In addition to the ownership brands, ranchers and horse owners also use branding to identify individual animals, usually with simple numbers that are not registered with the state or the county. While these marks are not considered proof of ownership, they can help the rancher medicate individual animals or choose specific animals for breeding.

Many western states have their own laws that mandate branding, as well as mandate recording the brand with the county clerk, agriculture department, or livestock agency. And even if government regulations don't mandate it, banks often require branding to insure loans when cattle are posted as collateral. Without recording or registering one's brand, which is like a fingerprint in that no two brands can be identical, there is no evidence to use in court if the animals are stolen. Under some laws, individuals can register new brands, can transfer brands to another person, or they can apply to use brands that have not been used for five years (because brands will expire if not reregistered to keep them active). The brand will be rejected if that particular design has already been registered, or if the brand is too small. (Cattle brands should be at least 3/8 inches wide and 4 inches in height.) Some states will also prohibit the defacing or branding of another person's animal or brand. Both the symbols of the brand and the location of the brand are used to identify the owner of the animals, and brands can be registered for various parts of the animals's body.

Cattle are not the only animals marked with brands. Wild mustangs living on Bureau of Land Management land wear freeze brands on the left side of their neck to mark them as federally protected. Registered Arabian horses have a similar brand on the right side of the neck, and thoroughbred horses have registration numbers tattooed inside their upper lips. The most popular locations for brands on horses are the left or right hip or the left or right shoulder. Other less common locations are ribs, stifles, and jaws. Owners of expensive horses will also often have photographs of their animals and detailed records noting all identifying marks, the brand or tattoo is considered the only solid way that an owner can stop an animal from being sold or slaughtered.

Because each owner must register a unique brand, choosing the combination of letters, symbols, and numbers is of utmost importance. Brands are typically made up of capital letters, numerals, pictures, and symbols such as slash, circle, half-circle, cross, bar, and the like, with a huge variety of combinations. Most brands today include at least three characters because of the number of brands that have already been registered. Characters can be vertical, horizontal, connected, combined, or reversed.

Reading brands is like reading tattoos: with the right knowledge, the complex symbols begin to make sense. Being able to read a brand is referred to as "callin' the brand," and brands can be read from left to right, from top to bottom, and when the brand is enclosed, it is read from outside to inside. How a brand is read also differs from locality to locality, with Mexican brands, for instance (which derive from the original Spanish brands of the southwest), being hard to read for many Americans.

Traditionally, ranchers branded their own animals, but today many have a livestock veterinarian do the branding. Brands today include the traditional hot iron brands and the newer freeze brands. Freeze branding does not burn the skin, but rather kills the pigment-producing cells in the hair follicle so that when the hair regrows where the brand was applied, it is white. Freeze branding works best on black, dark red, or red animals, and is applied with copper or bronze irons which are cooled to between $-100°$ and $-300°$ F.

There are other ways in which livestock owners mark their animals. Ear tags, which are made of metal or plastic and pierce the ear, locking the tag onto the ear, is one method and dates back to the early twentieth century. Tattoos, which are applied to the ears with a pliers-like device that punches the ink into the skin, is another way that individual animals can be marked, but ear tags can fall off and tattoos can be hard to read from afar. Microchips provide a third new method, but are not that convenient for most ranchers because they have to be read by a machine.

Branding is opposed by the animal rights community, because of the fact that animal branding is done without anesthesia and causes a considerable amount of pain. Face branding of cattle had already been banned in this country in 1995, and many hope that other forms of branding without anesthesia will be banned as well.

In recent years, agricultural industry groups have been facing increasing levels of protest over the treatment of food animals, including the branding of livestock without anesthesia, not only from animal rights groups but from mainstream organizations like the American Veterinary Medical Association. One 1997 study measured the behaviors associated with pain in cattle as well as escape behaviors, and found that heat-branded animals showed more pain and escape behaviors than freeze-branded animals. Ranchers and the industry groups that support them, on the other hand, say the pain is temporary and minimal and that no better alternative exists, and cattle rustling remains a problem even in modern America.

One new alternative might be inexpensive DNA testing (not yet available), which could be used to fingerprint individual animals, and individual animals, and their owners, could be tracked via computer.

Today the United States is moving toward a national animal identification system, which would be run by the Animal and Plant Health Inspection Service of the USDA, and would track the births, movement, and deaths of all livestock in the United States, primarily for disease control purposes. Once this system is in place, all livestock will be identified via a fifteen-character animal identification number, with a technology that has yet to be chosen, but could include DNA tracking or radio frequency ear tags.

Branding calves on roundup. Photo by John C. H. Grabill 1888. Courtesy of Library of Congress Prints and Photographs Division, Washington, DC, No. LC-USZ62-15909.

See also: Branding

Further Reading: Benson, John G. *The Well-Being of Farm Animals: Challenges and Solutions*. Oxford: Blackwell Publishers, 2004; Elofson, Warren M. *Cowboys, Gentlemen and Cattle Thieves: Ranching on the Western Frontier*. Montreal: McGill-Queens University Press, 2000; Steele, Christy. *Cattle Ranching in the American West*. Milwaukee, WI: World Almanac Library, 2005.

ANIMALITY

Animality refers to the practice of "becoming animal" through body modification. Typically, humans throughout cultures and history have needed to differentiate themselves from animals via human culture and ritual. Animality, or the desire to become animal-like, totally subverts this practice.

The very act of body modification is of course a centrally human act. No other animal can change their bodies in the ways that we can, and we have not seen any evidence to suggest that animals would want to change the appearance of their bodies. So body modification through piercing, tattooing, implants, scarification, and the like, could be seen as an attempt to make the human body more human, and less animal.

Animality, on the other hand, goes in the opposite direction, as humans use ancient and modern modification and adornment techniques to attempt to transform themselves into animals.

Animality in body modification is linked to the rise of primitivism as a philosophy, which posits that humans, and especially Westerners, are out of touch with the environment, physically destructive, violent, and represent all that is wrong with the world. Non-Western peoples or "primitives" are seen as providing the antidote to destructive Western behaviors. In some circles, however, all humans are seen as bad and the only way to rectify the damage caused by humans is to emulate animals which are seen as good, balanced, sane, in touch with nature, etc. Just as primitive people are seen by modern primitives as representatives of a pure, peaceful, environmentally correct world, animals are now, for some, the highest ideal to aspire to: the ultimate authentic creature.

Animality can be seen as more than just the human emulation of the animal. It can also be seen in the ways that animal bodies and human bodies are overlapping in ways that blur the line, between human and animal. Developments such as xeno transplanation, in which animal organs are transplanted into human bodies, and genetic engineering, which changes the genetic makeup of an animal or human by manipulating and transferring selected genes from one animal to the next, are both frontiers for the development of scientific animality.

Examples of the desire to change from human to animal include **Lizard Man** (Eric Sprague), **Stalking Cat** (Dennis Avner), and **Jocelyn Wildenstein**, all of whom have, through various surgical, tattooing, and piercing techniques, attempted to become more animal-like. All, not surprisingly, are considered **freaks** by modern society (in the case of Lizard Man, he actually does make his living as a sideshow freak). Freaks in fact have always challenged the human–animal border; classic American freaks like lobster boys, dog girls, elephant men, and monkey girls were labeled and billed as human/animal combinations, or sometimes "missing links" between animals and humans.

Animality in body modification goes back to the days of the **Great Omi,** who transformed himself into a zebra man via tattoos, tooth filing, and piercings, and who was typically displayed in the sideshows alongside either wild animals or native peoples.

See also: Freaks; The Great Omi; Sprague, Eric Stalking Cat; Wildenstein, Jocelyn

Further Reading: Potts, Annie. "The Mark of the Beast: Inscribing 'Animality' through Extreme Body Modification." In P. Armstrong and L. Simmons, eds., *Knowing Animals*. Leiden: Brill, 2007.

ANIMAL SURGICAL PROCEDURES

Ever since animals were first domesticated between ten and fifteen thousand years ago, humans have been modifying animal bodies. Traditionally, that modification has primarily occurred through selective breeding of livestock, and later, companion animals, in order to produce the most useful or aesthetically pleasing combination of physical and behavioral traits, and making today's domestic animals very different from their wild ancestors.

Through domestication, behavioral traits like curiosity, lack of fear, willingness to try new things, food begging, and submissiveness—which are found among the juveniles of species like dogs or cattle—were originally selected for, along with youthful physical traits like shorter faces, excess fat, smaller brains, and smaller teeth. This has led to the creation of modern domesticates who are essentially perpetual juveniles.

Once humans began selectively breeding domestic animals in order to emphasize or discourage certain physical or behavioral traits, the animals changed even further, resulting today in animals that are, for the most part, smaller, rounder, more colorful, and with more variations in fur and hair type as well as ear and tail appearance. Today, when we look at modern livestock, the changes are even more dramatic as modern pigs, turkeys, and chickens can barely hold up the weight of their fleshy bodies, thanks to selective breeding, intensive husbandry conditions, the use of hormones, and **genetic engineering**. Companion animals, too, suffer a whole host of genetic disorders that are linked to their breeding, and are an accepted side effect of the process of creating purebred dogs and cats.

But surgical procedures have also played a critical role in the human reshaping of animal bodies.

Because the control of animal reproduction is critical to keeping domestic animals, **castration** has been used for thousands of years to ensure that undesirable animals cannot breed, or to increase the size or control the temperament of certain animals. Castration was traditionally performed via banding (in which a tight band is placed around the base of the testicles, constricting blood flow and eventually causing the scrotum to die and fall off after about two weeks), crushing (this method uses a clamping tool called a Burdizzo, which crushes the spermatic cords), and surgery (in which the testicles are removed from the scrotum by opening the scrotum with a knife or scalpel). For centuries, and even today among some ranchers, surgical castration was not done by veterinarians or medical professionals and did not include anesthesia; instead the individual animal owner simply cut open the tissue and performed the procedure.

Today, on the other hand, surgical castration, now known as neutering, is commonly performed on most companion animals in the West, in a veterinary office with modern anesthesia and painkillers. In the twentieth century, with the keeping of companion animals rising in popularity, surgical techniques to remove the uterus and ovaries of female animals were developed, and spaying is now an extremely common surgery for companion animals, although it is very rarely performed on livestock.

Today, millions of companion animals are spayed and neutered annually to control individual reproduction as well as the population of the species, to protect health (reproductive cancers in unspayed female animals like dogs and rabbits are extremely common and testicular cancer is linked to unneutered dogs), and to control temperament (as spaying or neutering reduces aggression and other negative behaviors). Livestock such as pigs are still routinely castrated in order to produce more meat.

Modifying animal bodies in other ways has also been common for years, particularly in livestock and purebred companion animals. The increasing reliance on cosmetic surgery for dogs is one result of the focus, common among animal fanciers, on breed perfection. Certain breeds of dogs require, in order to conform to standards, docked tails (in which the tail is removed or shortened), cropped ears (the removal of the ear flap), or both. Although veterinarians, who normally perform the procedure, did not provide pain medication for years, and some still do not, the use of pain medication is becoming more common today.

Companion animals also undergo forms of modification that are for behavioral, rather than aesthetic reasons. For instance, some dog owners have their dogs debarked (by cutting their vocal cords) in order to reduce barking, and many cat owners elect to have their cats declawed (which involves amputating the the front portions of a cat's toes) in order to prevent harm to their furniture.

Livestock body modifications, on the other hand, are primarily done today to alleviate the problems associated with intensive confinement operations (also known as factory farms). The debeaking of chickens (amputating, without anesthesia, the front of the chicken's beak) and the removal of pigs' tails are both common procedures in the livestock industry in which chickens and pigs both are so intensively confined that they will cannibalize each other out of stress and overcrowding. Cattle are often dehorned in order to make them easier to handle and to reduce injuries within a group of cattle.

And finally, horses undergo a variety of procedures which are done to produce a desired style of horsemanship (e.g. tail and tongue myotomies to produce a limp tail and flaccid tongue for the show ring) or to produce a requisite appearance for equine sales and auctions (e.g. scleral tattooing to minimize the appearance of the white-ringed eye and surgical thinning of the throatlatch area).

See also: Animal Tattooing; Castration

Further Reading: Miller, Lila and Stephen Zawistowski, eds., *Shelter Medicine for Veterinarians and Staff*. London: Blackwell Publishing, 2004.

ANIMAL TATTOOING

Tattoos are one of the most common ways today that nonhuman animals are permanently identified. Tattoos are used in the biomedical industry to tattoo laboratory animals, in the agricultural industry to identify livestock, and by some pet breeders and 4-H clubs to mark individual purebred animals. They are also used by veterinarians and animal rescue groups to denote that a rescued animal has been spayed. Many pet owners, as well as owners of thoroughbred horses, will also have their animals tattooed so that they can be identified if they are lost or stolen.

The American Kennel Club also mandates that anyone giving away or selling an AKC registered dog must ensure that the dog is identifiable via a collar tag, microchip, or tattoo. Because tags can be lost and microchips aren't always reliable (plus various microchip companies have a variety of technologies), tattoos are a widely used method to do this. Tattoos are also used today to ensure that companion animals don't show up in research labs; the labs must scan the animal for either a microchip or tattoo to make sure there are no other claims of ownership. And light colored animals are occasionally tattooed to prevent sunburn (on the nose, for example).

Tattoos have to be registered in order for a lost or stolen pet to be returned to their caretaker. The best-known registries, Tattoo-A-Pet, I.D. Pet, and National Dog Registry, have both been in operation since the mid-1960s. Each industry has its own requirements and procedures. For livestock, cattle are often tattooed on the ears and tattoos must be registered with a livestock board or agency. Horses are usually tattooed inside of their lips, and dogs and cats are generally tattooed on their ear. In many locations, dogs and cats will also be tattooed on an ear, or on the stomach or inner thigh, to indicate that they have been spayed.

Some veterinarians and breeders use an electric tattoo machine to tattoo animals, but others use a hand-device that punches the ink into the animal's skin via metal numbers on the tool. When performed by a veterinarian with an electric machine, the animal is typically under anesthesia during the procedure.

Finally, some people have tattooed animals for decorative purposes. Some **circuses** and sideshows, for example, had tattooed families as exhibits, including a tattooed dog, and the Web site **BMEZine.com** includes photos, submitted by readers, of their own pets with decorative tattoos (although the Web site carries a disclaimer saying they do not condone it).

See also: Animal Branding

Further Reading: United States Congress, House Committee on Agriculture, Subcommittee on Livestock and Horticulture. The Development of USDA's National Animal Identification Program: Hearings Before the Committee on Agriculture. United States Congress, 2004.

ANOREXIA AND BULIMIA

Anorexia nervosa is an eating disorder in which the sufferer has a distorted image of their body leading them to undereat and sometimes overexercise, sometimes to the point of starvation and death. Anorexics often also struggle with perfectionism, obsessive compulsive disorder and have obsessive thoughts about food and weight. Anorexics also may utilize diet pills or diuretic drugs in order to lose or control weight. Purging through vomiting, exercise, laxatives, or spitting is generally classified as bulimia, and many people suffer from both conditions. Anorexia and bulimia primarily affect adolescent girls in the Western world, with perhaps as much as 10 percent of all victims dying from the disease.

While the disease was first described at the end of the seventeenth century, it has only become a common condition in the twentieth century, thanks to standards of **beauty** in the West that emphasize an extremely thin ideal, combined with a growing and powerful diet and exercise industry and the mass media's heavy focus on the human (and particularly the female) body. Many feminists feel that the thin ideal is a thinly disguised way to keep women decorative, feminine, and to ensure that they do not take up too much space—literally or figuratively.

Anorexia can be seen as more than a psychiatric and physical disorder, however, and can be viewed as an intentional form of body modification. While some sufferers do want help for their conditions and recognize that they are threatening their health and lives by refusing to eat, others reject the label and the stigma that comes with having a psychiatric disorder. Many anorexics and bulimics have formed "pro-ana" communities (often online) in which they support each other's choices and swap weight loss tips as well as advice on how to hide one's condition from family, friends, and medical professionals. For these people, anorexia is a lifestyle choice and they are intentionally molding their bodies in a way that shows that they are able to control them.

While the pro-ana movement is not as popular now as it once was (the height of it as measured by pro-ana Web sites was between 2001 and 2003) it still remains true that anorexia is seen by many young women as an alternative lifestyle and that by modifying their bodies in the extreme way they do, it is their choice. For these people, anorexia, or extreme dieting, is not about having a psychiatric disorder or a problem with one's body image; instead, it is about exercising control and pushing one's body's limits. In addition, some feel that it is a form of self-expression, but even within the body modification community, self-starvation is seen as an unhealthy disorder.

See also: Body Dysmorphic Disorder; Health Issues

Further Reading: Bordo, Susan. "Reading the Slender Body." In Mary Jacobus, Evelyn Fox Keller, and Sally Shuttleworth, eds., *Body Politics: Women and the Discourses of Science*. New York: Routledge, 1990; Bordo, Susan. *Unbearable Weight: Feminism, Western Culture, and the Body*. Berkeley: University of California Press, 1993; Fallon, P., M. Katzman, and S. Wooley, eds. *Feminist Perspectives on Eating Disorders*. New York: Guilford, 1994; Gremillion, Helen. *Feeding Anorexia: Gender and Power at a Treatment Center*. Durham, NC: Duke University Press, 2003; Levenkron, Steven. *Anatomy of Anorexia*. New York: W.W. Norton & Co., 2001; Girard, Rene. "Hunger Artists." In Tobin Siebers, ed., *The Body Aesthetic: From Fine Art to Body Modification*. Ann Arbor: University of Michigan Press, 2000.

APOTEMNOPHILIA *See* Amputation

ASCETICISM

Asceticism refers to a life that is characterized by abstaining from worldly and bodily pleasures, through self denial and often **self-mortification**. The goal of the ascetic is to strengthen one's spiritual life through distancing oneself from the profane world. Asceticism is a part of a number of religious traditions including Christianity, Judaism, and Islam as well as Buddhism and Hinduism. Because not all members of a religious tradition can life an ascetic life, asceticism is usually practiced by monks, nuns, yogis, and other especially devoted adherents.

Fasting is a form of self-denial, and is the most common practice associated with asceticism, and involves the temporary abstaining from food in order to punish oneself, atone for one's sins, or to produce visions. Fasting and other forms of spiritual purification is often a step in the process of communicating with God or the gods. Other forms of self-denial include refraining from sexual contact (either temporarily or permanently), dressing in old clothing or rags, and giving up all personal possessions, all of which are used to release one's connection to the profane world and also to purify the soul.

Fasting is often used in conjunction with forms of self-mortification like flagellation, a form of whipping in which the individual is whipped or whips themselves as a form of penance or, in the case of Christians, to imitate the suffering of Christ. Early Christians also wore a hair shirt, a very coarse item of clothing meant to disturb the skin, and some carried iron chains with them wherever they went.

Indian holy men called Sadhus, for example, engage in extreme practices of self-denial and mortification in order to attain spiritual liberation. Some may stand in one place for years upon end, never use a leg or refrain from speaking.

Self-mutilation is another form of mortification, and often involves the cutting or piercing of the skin, either as a form of sacrifice, penance, or extreme devotion.

See also: Christianity; Self-Mortification; Self-Mutilation; Stigmata

Further Reading: Grimm, Veronika. *From Feasting to Fasting, the Evolution of a Sin: The Development of Early Christian Asceticism*. New York: Routledge, 1996; Kaelber, Walter. *Tapta Marga: Asceticism and Initiation in Vedic India*. Albany: State University of New York Press, 1989; Sheils, W. J., ed. *Monks, Hermits and the Ascetic Tradition*. London: Basil Blackwell, 1985; Zysk, Kenneth G. *Asceticism and Healing in Ancient India*. New York: Oxford University Press, 1991.

ASSOCIATION OF PROFESSIONAL PIERCERS

The Association of Professional Piercers is the first and largest organization of professional piercers in the world, founded in the 1970s by Michaela Grey, former Master Piercer and trainer at the **Gauntlet** and a former coeditor of *PFIQ*.

Grey's relatively cautious views on **piercing** (she, like **Jim Ward**, founder of Gauntlet, opposed the use of anesthesia for piercings, dermal punches, scalpels, and implants), influenced the organization that she founded and also alienated her from the more extreme members of the body modification community. Like the **Alliance of Professional Tattooists**, Grey saw a need in the piercing community for a professional organization which would provide guidelines on safety and health issues, in order to keep the industry safe and prevent undue government oversight and control. During the 1990s, as piercing experienced an explosion of interest, hundreds of piercers with very little, if any, training, set up shop around the country, attracting a great deal of public attention, not all of it good.

Since its founding, APP, a nonprofit organization, has member piercers around the world, and offers piercing procedure manuals to piercers, educational brochures to the public on subjects such as picking a piercer, piercing aftercare, and health and safety information posters to hang in piercing studios or public health offices. APP also acts as a media and political liaison group, and its members have helped in drafting piercing guidelines around the world. They hold several conventions yearly. APP member studios are "certified" as meeting a variety of minimum standards of safety, so that customers can feel safe in being pierced at an APP shop. Today, most piercers and piercing studios are not members of APP.

See also: Alliance of Professional Tattooists; Health Issues; Legislation and Regulation; *PFIQ*; Piercing; Ward, Jim

Further Reading: Graves, Bonnie. *Tattooing and Body Piercing: Perspectives on Physical Health*. Mankato, MN: Life Matters Press, 2000.

AUSCHWITZ

Concentration camp prisoners in the Auschwitz Complex (which included Auschwitz 1, Auschwitz Birkenau, and Monowitz) were tattooed with identifying marks during the Holocaust. While **tattooing** of Jews during World War II was commonly thought to occur throughout Germany, this complex was the only location where tattooing of this kind occurred. Outside of the concentration camps, and prior to the implementation of Hitler's "final solution," Jews had been forced to wear a cloth star (first white, and then later yellow) inscribed with the word "Jude" starting in 1939 in Poland, and in 1941 in Germany.

In the concentration camps, however, other means of identification became necessary to appease the Nazis' obsession with order and control. In the Auschwitz complex, when new prisoners arrived at the camp, they were issued serial numbers which were then sewn onto their prison uniforms, along with different characters that represented the prisoner's status, nationality, or religion. Once prisoners began to die in very high numbers, it became difficult to identify all of the corpses, especially once clothes had been removed from the bodies. This led to staff starting to write prisoners' identification numbers directly onto the bodies of sick prisoners, and by 1941, when the camp began exterminating large numbers of Russian prisoners of war, tattooing was adopted instead, first for Russian prisoners, and, by 1943, for everyone.

Tattoos were initially given using a device that stamped numbers made out of needles directly onto the chest, followed by rubbing ink into the wounds. Later, camp officials began hand-tattooing identifying numbers (and sometimes symbols) on prisoners' arms using needles dipped into ink. Jewish prisoners often received a triangle, and Gypsies a Z; starting in 1944, Jews also began receiving an A or a B with their identification number, representing the series of numbers being used at the time. Men and women had separate numbering systems, and prisoners who were gassed immediately upon arrival were not tattooed at all. At Birkenau, the bodies of the dead were laid out so that the prisoner's left arm and tattooed identification numbers were visible.

While **Judaism** prohibits tattooing, Jews who were tattooed in the Holocaust under these conditions are obviously exempt from blame, and are allowed to be buried in Jewish cemeteries and to take part in all other aspects of Jewish life. Since the end of the Holocaust, the biblical prohibition against tattooing was strengthened for many Jews, who now associate tattooing with the Nazi practices outlined here. On the other hand, some Jews today proudly wear tattoos, some with Jewish symbols, in order to display pride in their heritage or even as a reminder of the Holocaust.

See also: Criminality; Judaism; Tattooing

Further Reading: Levi, Primo. *Survival in Auschwitz: The Nazi Assault on Humanity*. New York: Pocket Books, 1995; Rees, Laurence. *Auschwitz: A New History*. New York: Public Affair, 2006.

AUSTRALIA

Aboriginal Australians are known for a number of body adornment and modification practices, including **scarification, body painting, piercing, circumcision,** and other forms of **genital mutilation** such as **subincision.**

In Australia, scarification was practised among a number of bands, but is very rarely practiced now, and is restricted almost entirely to parts of Arnhem Land. Traditionally, however, scarification was seen as a language inscribed on the body, which represented social and personal identity, courage and endurance, and beauty. Men and women underwent scarification prior to marriage, at the age of 16 or 17, and in fact were not considered marriageable without scars. In addition, scarification was necessary for a person to be able to trade items with other people. In addition, scarification allowed one to be able to perform ceremonial songs, or blow the didgeridoo at ceremonies. Clearly, scarification made a person a social member of society. Without a scar, one was clean-skinned or unbranded, and could not do anything at all.

Wardaman men and women received two cuts on each shoulder, two on the chest, and four on the belly. Jawoyn people got one cut on the shoulder, one on the chest, and a long cut on the belly. Other band members had three cuts on the shoulder and many on the belly.

The traditional scarification technique was simple: with a very sharp stone knife, an elder would cut into the recipient's skin, and then rub ashes into the wound with a stick, to stop bleeding and allow the scar to form. The wearer had to keep the stick on the cut until the skin healed and the stick fell off.

Many Australian Aboriginal communities have been painting their bodies for thousands of years as a social marker that demonstrates important social facts such as one's totem. Body painting is also a means of communication, and when used in traditional dances, can tell a story. Because traditional paints were made out of earth, and Aboriginal religions center around the earth, using body paints was and is a sacred activity.

Australians have also used genital modifications as part of male initiation rituals for hundreds or thousands of years. In central Australia, circumcision is the primary operation to define male adulthood, and it may be accompanied by tooth evulsion (in which a front incisor is knocked out with a rock), the piercing of the septum, scarification, and, usually later, subincision.

Rites of passage for adolescent boys typically occur from the ages of 10 to 12, and last for weeks, during which initiates are separated from their mothers. They traditionally do not speak nor are they spoken to, observe a number of food taboos, and must remain in seclusion until the end of the ritual when they are allowed to rejoin society as a man. After that time, he can also receive a wife.

During the circumcision ritual, the initiate was often required to swallow his foreskin, and sometime after the ritual, many boys additionally underwent subincision. In all of these rituals, the boys are not allowed to show pain. The participants in a boy's circumcision include his father, paternal uncles, and, if he is engaged, his future father-in-law and brothers-in-law. By shedding his blood and undergoing pain with the important men in his family (both blood relatives and future conjugal relatives), he reinforces his solidarity with them, and also sheds the polluting influences of femininity.

Among the groups who practice circumcision, the ritual marks the beginning of a boy's entry into the men's secret ceremonial life, during which he witnesses ceremonies that he later, as an adult, will perform. Some time later, the boy may also undergo subincision, which is the splitting of the underside of the penis, in a way that is thought to resemble the vulva. The bleeding following the subincision is seen as a form of menstruation and further rids the boy of any remaining femininity. Subincision has been most common among the Yiwara, Arrernte, Luritja, and Pidjandara bands. Among the Lardil people, men who underwent subincision would continue, at ceremonial occasions, to open up the wound as a form of ritual bloodletting.

Aboriginal Australians did not practice **tattooing**, but because Australia was used by Great Britain as a repository of English criminals during the nineteenth century, with convicts at that time making up most of the English population of Australia, tattooing became a common feature of Australian society from that time on. British criminals sent to Australia often tattooed themselves on their passage overseas with symbols signifying their condition. (The criminals were relatively unsupervised while on the ship, and, probably because of the boredom, collective trauma, and proximity to sailors who were most likely tattooed, it makes sense that they would have tattooed themselves.) Anchors were a common theme for the prisoners, in that they symbolized hope (Hebrews 6:19 said "Which hope we have as an anchor for the soul, both sure and steadfast, and which entereth into that within the veil."), and tattoos of the virtue hope were common as well, and usually depicted a woman clutching an anchor. Biblical passages were also common tattoos, as well as images of Jesus on the cross, often with the convict's initials next to the crucifixion, suggesting a parallel in the convict's treatment to Jesus.

See also: Body Painting; Circumcision; Criminality; Prison Tattooing; Rites of Passage; Scarification; Subincision

Further Reading: Davis, Geoffrey V., and Dieter Riemenschneider. *Aratjara: Aboriginal Culture and Literature in Australia*. Amsterdam/Atlanta: Rodopi, 1997; Meggitt, M. J. *Desert People: A Study of the Walbiri Aborigines of Central Australia*. Sydney: Angus and Robertson, 1986; Stewart, Hamish Maxwell, and Ian Duffield, "Skin Deep Devotions: Religious Tattoos and Convict Transportation to Australia." In Jane Caplan, ed., *Written on the Body: The Tattoo in European and American History*. London: Reaktion Books, 2000.

B

BAKHTIN, MIKHAIL

Mikhail Bakhtin (1895–1975) was a Russian philosopher and literary scholar, whose work on the French renaissance poet François Rabelais is useful to understanding many current body modification practices.

Born in Russia, Bakhtin attended St. Petersburg University during the time of the Russian Revolution and, in 1941, submitted a dissertation on the French Renaissance poet François Rabelais while at the Institute of World Literature in Moscow. Because his professors found his ideas too controversial, he was denied a doctorate (he instead received the degree of Candidate), and his dissertation, *Rabelais and Folk Culture of the Middle Ages and Renaissance* was not published until 1965 (renamed *Rabelais and His World*).

Two of the focuses of *Rabelais and His World* are carnival and grotesque realism.

For Bakhtin, European carnival represented for peasants an arena in which the styles and values of high culture could be inverted, thrown on their head, and ultimately debased. Carnival is marked by drunkenness, rowdiness, and bawdy sexuality, all of which lie outside of and threaten the dominant social order. More importantly, carnival is free and utopian, in marked contrast to the increasingly regimented morality of the Renaissance, with participants feeling part of a larger collectivity. Bakhtin also demonstrated that the utopian elements found in popular-festive forms are always expressed in material bodily form, thus such festivals are marked by images of sexuality, birth, feasts, slaughter, cursing, violence, and defecation; what he called "material bodily affluence." Bakhtin writes further, "in the atmosphere of Mardi Gras, reveling, dancing, music were all closely combined with slaughter, dismemberment, bowels, excrement, and other images of the material bodily lower stratum."

The combination of sexuality and excrement, and death and renewal, is a primary feature of what Bakhtin calls the grotesque concept of the body. The grotesque body—which is open, secreting, protruding, and unfinished—is everywhere present in the world of body modifications. Tattooed bodies, pierced bodies, and surgically altered bodies can be seen as always in progress, their borders open and extended, and through the acquisition of more tattoos, **piercings**, or surgery, they are literally bodies in the act of becoming.

Because much of contemporary body modification is either oppositional in nature, or at the very least contrary to socially accepted ways that the body can be used, Bakhtin's work can be used to understand how the types of bodies that are acceptable within the contemporary Western social order—clean, white, unaltered, and unmarked—are opposed to the stretched, tattooed, pierced, and scarred, and entirely excessive bodies of many of its citizens. The heavily modified body, then, is a grotesque body, a body out of bounds, a body no longer controlled by society.

Bakhtin writes of a transcoding between bodily and social topography which sets up a homology between the lower bodily stratum and the lower social classes—the reference to the body being invariably a reference to the social. Control over the body has long been associated with bourgeois political control. So the body becomes, according to this ideology, a privileged trope of the lower social classes, and through which bodily grossness operates as a critique of dominant ideology. So both dominant ideology and its challenge maintain this distinction. The very highness of dominant culture is structured through the obsessive banishment of the low, through the suppressing of the grotesque body in favor of what Bakhtin calls the classical body, a refined orificeless, laminated surface which is homologous to high culture. Certainly, in the West, marginalized cultural groups have always been at the forefront of body modifications: bikers, **gang members**, and sailors and soldiers, as well as members of the gay **BDSM** movement.

See also: Bourdieu, Pierre; Foucault, Michel

Further Reading: Bakhtin, Mikhael. *Rabelais and His World*. Bloomington: Indiana University Press, 1984; Clark, Katerina, and Michael Holquist. *Mikhail Bakhtin*. Cambridge: Harvard University Press, 1984.

BARIATRIC SURGERY

Bariatric surgery, also known as **obesity** surgery, is surgery to combat obesity. It is typically used by individuals defined as morbidly obese, such as those with a body mass index of 40 or more, who are over 80–100 pounds overweight, and/or those with life-threatening issues related to their weight. Bariatric surgery is now a recognized subinterest in the field of general surgery.

Bariatric surgery is becoming far more popular for people who can afford it (the cost runs from $10,000 to $40,000), or whose insurance policies will cover the procedures. Thus it is beginning to become the first choice for weight loss, especially for overweight celebrities, over the conventional weight loss methods of dieting and exercise. In fact, it has become so common that any time an overweight celebrity loses a large amount of weight in a relatively short time, it is assumed that that person lost the weight via surgery.

Besides the costs, there are a great many risks involved in such surgeries, such as infections, stomach and gastrointestinal leaks, ulcers, excessive bleeding, pulmonary problems, and, in a small percentage of cases, mortality.

The most common types of surgeries are stomach stapling, the lap band, and gastric bypass surgery, all of which are gastric restrictive procedures, meaning that the patient's volume of food intake after surgery is restricted. Bariatric surgery does not involve liposuction or tummy tucks or other cosmetic surgery procedures. Instead, through stapling, banding, or other methods, the patient's stomach is made much smaller than it was previously, leaving the patient unable to consume large quantities of food in a single sitting. In gastric bypass surgery, the stomach size is decreased and the first part of the small intenstine is bypassed so that fewer calories are absorbed into the body.

Through obesity surgery, large numbers of elite overweight individuals like Star Jones, Al Roker, and Carnie Wilson have been able to modify their bodies in a very short period of time in order to conform to Western society's standards of beauty. While it could be considered an extreme form of body modification in that it can radically change the shape and look of a person's body, it is not considered that in modern society because it makes the body conform to social norms.

See also: Beauty; Obesity

Further Reading: Martin, Louis F. *Obesity Surgery*. New York: McGraw-Hill, 2004.

BARNUM, P. T.

Phineas Taylor Barnum (1810–1891) was the best-known circus showman in American history. He is most well known for founding the circus that eventually became Ringling Brothers and Barnum and Bailey **Circus**, but also for introducing the world to marvels like Jumbo the elephant and the little person Tom Thumb.

Barnum began his career as a storekeeper and a newspaperman, but in 1835, saw the rise of dime museums and the public fascination with **freaks**. He began his career as a showman that year with his purchase and display of a blind and disabled slave named Joice Heth, who Barnum said was the 160-year-old nurse of George Washington, although she was no more than 70 years old. It was Barnum who brought men and women who were physically or mentally disabled, exotic animals, native peoples, and other "freaks" from the fairground into the city, and later the circus sideshow. He made being a freak a legitimate profession for some, and helped **tattooing** develop as a profession in the United States.

In 1841, Barnum purchased a dime museum called Scudder's American Museum in New York City and renamed it Barnum's American Museum. Some of his most well-loved attractions were Charles Stratton, whom he renamed General Tom Thumb, in 1842, as well as the Fiji Mermaid, a hoax mummy made up of various parts of fish, monkeys, and other animals. He also displayed the original Siamese twins, Chang and Eng, During 1844–1845 Barnum toured with Tom Thumb in Europe and met with Queen Victoria.

Barnum briefly retired from show business in 1855, but, after his American Museum burned down, established in 1871 P. T. Barnum's Grand Traveling Museum, Menagerie, Caravan & Hippodrome, a traveling circus and sideshow which by 1872 was billing itself as "The Greatest Show on Earth." After an 1881 merger with James Bailey, it later became the Barnum & Bailey Greatest Show On Earth. The show's primary attraction at that time was Jumbo, an African elephant he purchased in 1882 from the London Zoo.

In 1873, Barnum brought Alexandrino, known as Prince Constantine, to the United States, who became the most flamboyant and best known of all tattooed attractions until he retired in the 1880s. He had 388 tattoos, mostly of animals in the Burmese style, and he sold pamphlets describing them and his forced abduction and torture by Chinese "tartars." Barnum said that he paid Constantine $1,000 per week, although this was probably not the case.

Besides Barnum's talent in finding exotic attractions that the American and European public would pay to see, Barnum is most well known for his skill in promotion. Barnum saw nothing wrong in entertainers or vendors using exaggeration in their promotional material, just as long as the public was getting good value for its money. Barnum was elected to the Connecticut legislature in 1865 as the Republican representative for Fairfield and served two successful terms. In 1875, Barnum was elected mayor of Bridgeport, Connecticut for a one-year term and worked vigorously to improve the city water supply, bring gaslighting to the streets, and strictly enforce liquor and prostitution laws. Barnum was instrumental in starting Bridgeport Hospital, founded in 1878, and served as its first president.

See also: Circus; Freak Shows; Freaks

Further Reading: Adams, Bluford. *E Pluribus Barnum: The Great Showman and the Making of U.S. Popular Culture*. Minneapolis: University of Minnesota Press, 1997; Reiss, Benjamin. *The Showman and the Slave: Race, Death, and Memory in Barnum's America*. Cambridge: Harvard University Press, 2001; Saxon, Arthur H. *P.T. Barnum: The Legend and the Man*. New York: Columbia University Press, 1995; Cook, James W., ed. *The Colossal P.T. Barnum Reader: Nothing Else Like It in the Universe*. Champaign: University of Illinois Press, 2005.

BDSM

BDSM, or Bondage Discipline Domination Submission, refers to a number of sexual behaviors that include the use of consensual pain, submission, or dominance. The BDSM community can be regarded as a sexual subculture within mainstream society, but has primarily been associated with the gay leather community. Being involved in BDSM or dominant/submissive relationships on a regular basis is often referred to as being "in the lifestyle."

BDSM often involves dominance and submission. A dominant person enjoys controlling his or her sexual partner. A submissive person is one who seeks out a partner to dominate them. Partners can also be tops and bottoms without formally being in a dominance/submission relationship. A top is the person who, when performing sexual acts that include bondage, humiliation, or **pain**, is the person who controls the activities; bottoms would be the partners to whom the acts are being done, and unless the partners are in a formal dominance relationship, they often will switch roles.

While men and women have most likely enjoyed enduring pain with sex for centuries, like pornography, it was probably not seen as a special category of sexual behavior until the eighteenth century when European society began categorizing (and stigmatizing) certain sexual practices.

In the twentieth century, BDSM has most been associated with the gay leather scene that emerged from of a group of gay soldiers after World War II. These early sexual pioneers not only experimented with a variety of nonmainstream sexual

practices such as erotic spanking, flogging, sex toys, paddling, sensory deprivation, and movement restriction, but were the first group of Westerners to really
experiment with **body piercing, facial piercing, branding**, and **genital piercing**.
In addition, they pioneered many of the play piercing and **suspension** methods
now used by many in the **modern primitives** community, and members of the
BDSM community were the first Westerners to acquire genital tattoos and tattoos
of a sexual nature.

The BDSM community originated a set of ideas that go beyond the erotic. BDSM
(with or without body modifications) is seen as a vehicle for personal transformation, a basis for greater spiritual awareness, and a way for participants to reconnect
with their physical bodies.

Many if not most of BDSM activities involve pain. Sensation play is one way that
one person will inflict pain on the other, without actually injuring them. Participants enjoy the release of endorphins that occurs during these activities. Another
motivation is that sensation play is about exploring and pushing one's personal
limits, physically and emotionally.

Play piercing, which is piercing without jewelry and for no decorative purpose, is an example of sensation play, and could involve a partner putting needles
or other sharp objects into his or her partner's skin, often for hours, and often
their genitals. In some participants, this can induce orgasm. Using clothespins
and clamps to pinch nipples, skin, or genitals is another common practice, as is
cutting. A more extreme form of play piercing is flesh hook suspension where a
person is suspended by metal hooks through their flesh.

Branding and ownership tattoos are often used by dominant partners to mark
ownership of their submissives, and some submissives will go to the extreme step
of having some or all of their genitals removed.

The influence that this community has had on the development of modern
primitivism in the West and transformation of the modern **tattoo community**, as
a whole, cannot be overstated. Not only had this community used cutting, scarification, and piercing as rites of passage but also as a means of gaining self-awareness
and self-acceptance for decades prior to their emergence in the West. In fact, since
at least the 1960s, the BDSM scene (with or without other forms of body modification) has itself been seen as a path to enlightenment and a transformation of the
self, and thus predated by at least twenty years modern primitivism's evolution. It
is clear that many of the spiritual and therapeutic uses of tattooing, piercing, and
other practices that the body modification community later popularized actually
originated much earlier within this subculture.

See also: Body Piercing; Body Play; Musafar, Fakir; Pain; Suspensions; Ward, Jim

Further Reading: Brame, Gloria William, and Jon Jacobs. *Different Loving: An Exploration
of the World of Sexual Dominance and Submission*. New York: Villard Books, 1993; Thomp-
son, Mark. *Leatherfolk: Radical Sex, People, Politics, and Practice*. Los Angeles, CA: Daedalus
Publishing, 1991; Phillips, Anita. *A Defence of Masochism*. London: Faber & Faber, 1999;
Weinberg, Thomas S. *S&M: Studies in Dominance & Submission*. New York: Prometheus
Books, 1995; Wiseman, Jay. *SM 101: A Realistic Introduction*. Emeryville, CA: Greenery
Press, 2000.

BEAUTY

Beauty has both biological and cultural characteristics in that what humans consider beautiful in people may be evolutionary adaptations that help the species' survival, yet what we consider beautiful differs greatly historically and cross culturally.

Because of the importance of beauty, people in every culture around the world make attempts to artificially beautify the body via the use of clothing, headgear and footwear, the styling of hair, the use of **cosmetics**, various body modifications such as tattoos and **piercings**, and adornments such as **jewelry**.

According to evolutionary psychologists, there are a number of physical features that both men and women are programmed to find beautiful, including smooth skin, thick shiny hair, and symmetrical faces and bodies. These features are considered beautiful because they signify good health and good genes. In addition, according to evolutionary theory, men are programmed to find women with hourglass figures attractive because women with such figures are potentially more fertile than other women; similarly full lips and narrow jaws signify low testosterone and high estrogen, which are, again, indicators of fertility. Women are thought to look for indicators of high testosterone in men such as strong jaws, broad shoulders, tall stature, and other masculine features. On the other hand, women may forfeit some or all of these indicators of genetic health and reproductive fitness in exchange for men with financial resources, which are necessary to help a woman to raise her offspring.

On the other hand, there is a tremendous variety in the types of bodies, faces, and types of adornments and body modifications that societies around the world find beautiful, indicating that beauty is also culturally constructed.

> A tattoo is more valuable than jewelry. You can't steal a tattoo. Nobody can steal it. You can't lose a tattoo as long as you keep your arm out from under freight trains.
>
> LEONARD "STONEY" ST. CLAIR, tattooist

One aspect of culture that plays a strong role in standards of beauty is economics. In many societies, a body that signifies elite status is considered the most beautiful. So very light skin would be considered beautiful when darker skin is a sign of working outdoors; conversely, darker skin became beautiful as wealthy people could afford to travel to warmer climates during the winter. Plumper bodies, especially on women, would be considered beautiful when working people and the poor were thin; on the other hand, in contemporary Western culture, thinness is considered beautiful whereas plumper bodies are associated with the poor who cannot afford healthy diets, nutritionists and trainers, and do not have the time for exercise. Because sugar was so expensive in Renaissance Europe, the wealthy not only could afford to consume sugar—which was known to rot the teeth—but intentionally blackened their teeth to simulate tooth decay.

Because of the dominance of Western media, some Western standards of beauty—such as large eyes—are now becoming highly sought after in other cultures. Because of this, some Asian cultures now value large Caucasian-looking eyes, making cosmetic surgery to remove the epicanthal folds a very popular procedure in some East Asian countries today. Similarly, in India, the features associated with high castes, that is fairer skin and long, straight noses, are considered as signs of attractiveness and are still sought after in potential brides while darker skin is considered undesirable.

Whether beauty is biologically programmed or culturally constructed, beauty is important in human societies, and not only plays a role in whether a man or a woman achieves a mate, but in contemporary Western society, beauty plays a role in how much money a person earns in their lifetime, and whether they will be experience other benefits based on their physical appearance. Because of the importance of beauty, **cosmetic surgery** has become much more popular in contemporary society.

Beauty is also gendered, in that not only are there different standards of beauty for men and women, but women, especially in modern society, are held to a much higher and difficult (some would say impossible) to attain standard than men.

As women in the past few decades have experienced unprecedented levels of financial, political, and social independence and clout, they have also been assaulted by increasing numbers of images and messages about their appearance. As the messages increase and the standards of beauty became harder to attain, numbers of eating disorders skyrocket, the diet industry balloons, cosmetic surgery rates take off, and girls' and women's self esteem plummets. Today, being deemed unattractive or overweight has very real consequences, as women who don't meet certain beauty standards find that they earn less, will get promoted less, and will get hired less often, than thinner or more attractive women. Beauty continues to be a major standard by which women are judged, and is associated with a woman's self-esteem, chances of happiness, and upward mobility.

See also: Cosmetics; Cosmetic Surgery; Gender; Hairstyles; Jewelry; Piercing; Tattooing

Further Reading: Banner, Lois. *American Beauty*. Chicago: University of Chicago Press, 1983; Jeffreys, Sheila. *Beauty And Misogyny: Harmful Cultural Practices in the West*. London: Routledge, 2005; Sullivan, Deborah. *Cosmetic Surgery: The Cutting Edge of Commercial Medicine in America*. New Brunswick, NJ: Rutgers University Press, 2001; Wolf, Naomi. *The Beauty Myth: How Images of Beauty Are Used Against Women*. New York: Harper Perennial, 2002.

BIBLE

The Bible, and in particular the Old Testament or Hebrew Bible, mention a number of body modifications that were practiced by the ancient Hebrews and their contemporaries, including **tattooing, piercing**, and **circumcision**.

For example, **nose piercing** and **ear piercing** are mentioned in the Old Testament. In Genesis 24:22, for instance, Abraham's servant gave a nose ring and bracelets to Rebekah when he knew he found the right bride for Abraham's son, Isaac, demonstrating the use of both forms of **jewelry** as adornment, as well as the use of **nose piercing**. In Exodus 32, Aaron makes the golden calf from melted earrings, which were commonly worn by women in biblical times. Deuteronomy 15:12-17 mandates the use of ear piercing for slaves, which was a common practice at that time, and Exodus 21:5-6 notes that slaves who loved their masters would request that their ears be pierced as a permanent sign of servitude.

Tattooing is mentioned a number of times in the Bible, most notably in Leviticus 19:28, which reads: "You shall not make gashes in your flesh for the dead, or incise any marks on yourselves: I am the Lord." Because other cultures surrounding the ancient Jews did tattoo themselves, sometimes for mourning, the writers of the Bible probably prohibited it as a way of differentiating the Hebrews from other tribes, and solidifying their own sense of solidarity.

On the other hand, Isaiah 44:23, reads, "One shall say, 'I am the Lord's,' and another shall use the name of Jacob, and another shall mark his arm 'of the Lord' and adopt the name of Israel." Perhaps some among the Jews did tattoo themselves (either literally or symbolically) as God's servants as a sign of their devotion.

While tattooing is not mentioned in the New Testament, early Christians in the **Roman** world may have begun tattooing themselves as a way of mimicking the **stigmata** of Christ, whose death by crucifixion is detailed in the Gospels. In addition, because Christianity was criminalized in the Roman Empire until the time of Constantine, Christians were often tattooed as a form of punishment. The prophet Paul in fact writes in Galatians 6.17, "I carry the marks of Jesus tattooed (stigmata) on my body." While this was a metaphorical usage as Paul was probably not tattooed, he is invoking the practice of punitive tattooing.

Circumcision is prescribed for Jews in the Bible. In Genesis 17:10-14, God told Abraham to circumcise himself, his household, his descendents, and his slaves as an everlasting covenant in their flesh. Those who were not circumcised were to be cut off from their people. Apart from slaves, circumcision was intended for the children of God, and not other people, and Christians, who use the Old Testament as the first book of their Bible, do not recognize this mandate as applying to them. To many Christians, Leviticus is not literally about law or regulations for worship, but instead a prophecy prefiguring Jesus, regarding in particular, his crucifixion as a sin offering.

See also: Christianity; Judaism; Piercing; Slavery; Stigmata; Tattooing

Further Reading: Browning, W.R.F. *A Dictionary of the Bible* (Oxford Paperback Reference). Oxford: Oxford University Press, 2004.

BIKER TATTOOING

Bikers have been associated with **tattooing** since the end of the Second World War. As the nation's military men, who until that time were among the most dedicated wearers of tattoos in the United States, returned to civilian life after the war, the popularity of tattoos began to decline as did the powerful influence that the military had on the forms of North American tattoos. With this change, a new form of confrontational, biker-style tattooing was developing on the streets which used the tattoo as a form of defiance to mainstream middle-class values, as well as to the traditional form of patriotic and love-inspired working-class tattoo.

Since the 1960s, bikers have emerged as possibly the group most associated with tattoos in this country. The style and content of biker tattoos is radically different from traditional tattoos, in that the tattoos are almost exclusively black and are done in the fine line, single-needle style usually associated with **Chicano** and convict tattoos. This is no accident as many outlaw bikers acquired their first tattoos in prison, and took the prison style—either done by hand through picking or with single-needle rotary setups—with them to the outside.

The imagery is also very different from traditional working-class imagery. It is not patriotic and is often explicitly antisocial. Classic biker tattoos include Harley Davidson motorcycles and emblems, V-twin engines, club logos, marijuana leaves, swastikas, skulls, and logos such as "FTW," "Born to Lose,"

> Show me a man with a tattoo and I'll show you a man with an interesting past.
>
> JACK LONDON, author, 1883

"Live to Ride, Ride to Live," and "Property of . . ." on the women. For men and women, biker tattoos are located on public areas of the body, as they are not private expressions so much as public commentary. Men's tattoos will be located on the arms (the goal is to be fully "sleeved out"), back, chest, hands, and head (very little on the legs, as bikers wear jeans when riding), while women's tattoos will be found on the breasts, hips, arms, and back, and are easily exposed via halter and tank tops or by simply going topless at bike runs and other community events. Biker tattooing comprises a highly literal system of communication within the biker community, and, for those who recognize the imagery and slogans, it can extend outside of the community as well. (Most people recognize the antisocial sentiments behind, for example, a "Fuck the World" tattoo.) Furthermore, tattoos are an indispensable part of the biker image and can serve as a passport into the culture, even for nonbikers who wear tattoos.

See also: Chicanos; Criminality; Prison Tattooing

Further Reading: DeMello, Margo. *Bodies of Inscription: A Cultural History of the Modern Tattoo Community*. Durham, NC: Duke University Press, 2000.

BIO-POWER

Bio-power is a term developed by French philosopher **Michel Foucault** that refers to the way in which the modern state controls and regulates their citizens' bodies.

Foucault discusses the term in his work on the history of sexuality as a way of understanding the normalizing, coercive strategies by which the government manages and controls the individual body, as well as the entire population.

We can see the ways that states exercise control over bodies when we look at the history of population control, policies and regulations surrounding birth control and abortion, laws prohibiting various forms of sexual acts, laws governing marriages or relationships between racial or caste groups, and a whole host of other locations. Even the entire medical profession, which is set up ostensibly to protect human health, serves the interests of the state in the way that doctors attempt to control human behavior via nutritional advice, sex education, and the like. **Cosmetic surgery**, while not mandated for anyone, is one way in which hegemonic standards of **beauty** that are not possible for most people to attain, are made available to the wealthy via the surgical transformation of the body.

Intersexuality is another place in which the medical profession exercises an enormous degree of control over the shape and even sex of individual bodies. Because the medical establishment, and society in general, does not accept the presence of sexes beyond biological male and female, those who are born with bodies that do not conform to one or the other sex will be surgically modified, usually in infancy, and without the individual's consent, in order to conform to social standards.

In this way, bio-power can also be seen as a way of controlling unruly bodies, or bodies which do not conform to social norms.

When individuals choose to take their own bodies into their own hands, and modify them themselves via **piercing, tattooing**, and surgical and pseudo-surgical practices such as **amputations, implants**, and the like, it is not surprising that, for the most part, the state reacts by either banning those practices or regulating them. **Sex reassignment surgery** is another practice over which the medical establishment exercises a huge degree of power, so much so that individuals desiring surgery who are not considered to be suitable candidates often take their lives in their hands by seeking out surgery from unqualified or unlicensed doctors. This also occurs with those who want to have a limb amputated.

See also: Foucault, Michel; Intersexuality

Further Reading: Foucault, M. *Discipline and Punish*. Harmondsworth, UK: Penguin, 1979; Foucault, M. *Power/Knowledge: Selected Interviews and Other Writings, 1972–1977*. Brighton, UK: Harvester, 1980.

BMEZINE.COM

BMEZine.com (Body Modification Ezine) is an online magazine devoted to the documentation of body modification practices. The Web site contains photos and stories about, and information on, a diverse range of body modifications practiced primarily by Americans. Piercing enthusiast Shannon Larratt started the Web site in 1994, and today it is an extremely popular site for body modification practitioners as well as those interested in learning about the practices.

BMEZine is primarily aimed at those who have modified their bodies, and those thinking about doing so. Its goals are to give body modification practitioners a safe place to share stories and photos of their modifications, to educate the public on body modification, to encourage the growth of body modification and manipulation, to increase the acceptance of these activities among the mainstream public, and to create a community for body modification and manipulation users to support each other.

BMEZine's focus is reader stories and photos. The site allows readers a forum for sharing their personal stories about how they got a particular modification, why they got it, the process that they underwent, and the impact on their life since they received it.

Users can post their photos as well, and stories, educational articles, and photos are categorized on the basis of type of modification, that is, **piercing** (ear, tongue, nose, etc.), **scarification**, **tattooing** (artist photos, user photos, convention photos, and flash), photos and stories of ritual activities (such as blood play, **suspensions**, ball dances, and the like), extreme and erotic body modifications, and "culture" which includes stories and photos related to the body modification scene.

The Web site hosts a comprehensive encyclopedia of body modifications, as well as a comprehensive FAQ (Frequently Asked Questions) section which covers topics such as information for parents, piercing do-it-yourself information, elective home **surgery**, and information on suspensions and hooking. There is also a news section that includes reader editorials and guest articles, interviews, and articles about legal issues, a blog, and the BME Risks encyclopedia, which catalogues the various health and safety risks associated with all of the practices.

Because a primary purpose of the site is to encourage the development of community, there are personal ads, event listings, and IAM.bmezine community. The Web site is geared to adults as it contains sexually explicit materials, as well as photos of dangerous or life threatening activities.

See also: BDSM; Body Play; Piercing; Tattooing; Scarification

Further Reading: Pitts, Victoria. *In the Flesh: The Cultural Politics of Body Modification*. New York: Palgrave Macmillan, 2003.

BODYBUILDING

Bodybuilding is the process of developing large muscles through a combination of weight training, increased caloric intake, and rest.

Bodybuilding is also an organized sport dating to the end of the nineteenth century, with competitions, judges, and rules, but unlike other sports, bodybuilding competitions are not arenas in which competitors demonstrate or use physical skills or talents, but instead, they allow the display of the heavily muscled body. Thus the skills that lead to a bodybuilder's success are skills that are developed outside of the competition. The only actual skill at the competition itself is the act of posing.

As a sport, bodybuilding is similar to the **freak shows** of the nineteenth and early twentieth centuries, in which paying audiences gawk at people with bodily deformities of all kinds. In fact, bodybuilding as a performative sport developed in the nineteenth century and in early bodybuilding performances, audiences gaped as overly muscular men engaged in "muscle display performances." Sometimes performers, known at that time as strong men (and sometimes strong women), wrestled or displayed their strength by lifting heavy objects or bending iron bars, activities which have now been separated completely from bodybuilding. They were often displayed alongside other freaks in **circus** and carnival **sideshows**, and dressed in revealing and outlandish costumes. Eugen Sandow, known as the father of bodybuilding, was one of these strong men, and displayed himself beginning in the 1890s.

Eugen Sandow, the father of modern bodybuilding, 1893. Photo by Napoleon Sarony. Courtesy of Library of Congress Prints and Photographs Division, Washington, DC, No. LC-USZ62-97474.

In the early years of the sport in the nineteenth century, bodybuilders worked to attain a Grecian ideal of masculine beauty, and were judged by how closely they matched these ideal proportions. After World War II, many young men were inspired to be bigger, stronger, and more aggressive, and thus the physical ideal for the bodybuilder changed as well as the techniques to achieve the body. The late twentieth century saw improvements in training techniques, better nutrition, and more effective equipment, as well as the use of hormonal steroids to aid in muscle growth.

Today, the strategy used by most bodybuilders is to build muscle for most of the year and, a few months prior to competition, work to eliminate body fat (which is known as cutting), by radically cutting calories and increasing workouts. Finally, a week before a competition, competitors will drink more water and increase sodium intake, and then drastically cut sodium and water just prior to the event, adding carbohydrates back into the diet to expand the muscles.

To prepare for the competition, bodybuilders will usually administer a self-tanner and apply oils to the skin to make their muscles appear even more defined, and will lift weights in order to force blood into their muscles.

Bodybuilding is similar to the **self-mortification** practices of many religious believers in that it relies on the deliberate denial of the flesh through a carefully controlled diet, as well as extreme physical damage to the flesh in order to increase body size. Unlike other practices, however, it is not done for religious reasons or for penance, but for aesthetic reasons, to overcome physical limitations, and to feel a sense of accomplishment.

Bodybuilding can also be seen as an extreme body modification in that, unlike **piercing** and **tattooing**, which can be one-time activities, body building is an intense, physically challenging activity that can take eight or more hours per week of direct devotion to the body plus the rest of the time the bodybuilder is also extremely sensitive to the body in terms of the diet, nutrition, water, and medications that are used. Rituals are often used, and the "correct frame of mind" is needed to achieve the level of bodily perfection that is sought. Like other extreme activities such as **suspensions**, it's also about overcoming the body's physical limitations and stretching them to new limits. And like anorexia, bodybuilding involves an intense degree of control and discipline, through which the bodybuilder gains a sense of power.

While audiences have been drawn to bodybuilding since the days when strong men traveled with freak shows in order to see the extraordinary and grotesque body, it is also true that the bodybuilder's body is simply an extreme version of the masculine ideal. For that reason, female bodybuilders have always been seen as even more freakish, as their bodies are not only extraordinary but do not in any way conform to dominant notions of female **beauty**. In fact, female bodybuilders must overcome the stigma associated with being a woman with a strong, masculine body, and even bodybuilding judges typically do not allow women who are too muscular to win; the female bodybuilder must, ultimately, retain her soft, feminine appearance.

See also: Corsets

Further Reading: Bolin, Anne. "Vandalized Vanity: Feminine Physiques Betrayed and Portrayed." In Frances Mascia-Lees and Patricia Sharpe, eds., *Tattoo, Torture, Mutilation, and Adornment: The Denaturalization of the Body in Culture and Text*. Albany: State University of New York Press, 1992; Heywood, Leslie. *Bodymakers: A Cultural Anatomy of Women's Body Building*. New Brunswick, NJ: Rutgers University Press, 1998; Klein, Alan. *Little Big Men: Bodybuilding Subculture and Gender Construction*. Albany: State University of New York Press, 1993; Lindsay, Cecile. "Body Building: A Postmodern Freak Show." In Rosemary Garland Thompson, ed., *Freakery: Cultural Spectacles of the Extraordinary Body*. New York: New York University Press, 1996; Lowe, Maria R. *Women of Steel: Female Bodybuilders and the Struggle for Self-Definition*. New York: New York University Press, 1998; Mansfield, Alan and Barbara McGinn. "Pumping Irony: The Muscular and the Feminine." In S. Scott and D. Morgan, eds., *Body Matters*. London: Falmer Press, 1993; St Martin, L. and N. Gavey. "Women's Bodybuilding: Feminist Resistance and/or Femininity's Recuperation." *Body & Society* 2(4) (1996): 45–57.

BODY DYSMORPHIC DISORDER

Body dysmorphic disorder is a psychological disorder in which an individual is perpetually unhappy with his or her own body, and often sees their body in a way that is totally disconnected from reality.

Generally, people with BDD think that there is something wrong with their appearance, often based on some perceived minor defect, and will seek repeated **cosmetic surgery** or perhaps nonmainstream body alterations in an effort to change the appearance of their bodies to match their expectations. However, because there really isn't a problem with the person's appearance and the disorder is of a psychological or emotional nature, the individual is never satisfied, even after the surgery. Instead, they will assume that the surgery didn't work or will begin to obsess on a new physical defect.

BDD is often associated with eating disorders such as **anorexia** or bulimia, and is so disabling to sufferers that many cannot leave the house or have normal interactions with other people. BDD sufferers often exhibit obsessive-compulsive behaviors such as mirror checking, excessive grooming behaviors like constant hair combing or eyebrow plucking, or even physically harmful activities like **cutting**.

Women (and sometimes men) who undergo multiple sessions of plastic surgery in order to achieve their ideal notion of **beauty** are often thought to suffer from BDD. People who undergo extreme body modifications in order to transform their bodies into something else are thought by some doctors to suffer from this as well, such as **Stalking Cat** or **Jocelyn Wildenstein.**

See also: Amputation; Anorexia and Bulimia; Cosmetic Surgery; Health Issues

Further Reading: Phillips, Katharine A. *The Broken Mirror: Understanding and Treating Body Dysmorphic Disorder*. Oxford: Oxford University Press, 2005.

BODY HAIR

Human body hair is much less dense than that of most other mammals, whose bodies are covered in hair or fur.

Most of the human body is covered with a type of hair that is much finer, and often lighter, than the hair on the head, and is often known as peach fuzz. In addition, men and women, after puberty, each possess patches of thicker, coarser body hair as well, known as androgenic hair. For men, the areas on which androgenic hair grow include the face, the chest, the underarms, the belly, and the pubic region, as well as, in lesser concentrations, the arms, legs, and sometimes back. For women, androgenic hair grows on the pubic region and under the arms, and women also possess hair on their legs and lower arms.

Body hair, like the hair that grows on the head, is significant to most societies and relays important information about the person's sexual and social status. The presence of androgenic hair in particular is generally seen as a sign of masculinity in men, and femininity in women when in the "right" place, and as a sign of effeminacy in men and masculinity in women when in the "wrong" place. Women who for genetic reasons grow hair in the male pattern are known to have hirsutism, a condition that was once seen frequently in **freak shows**.

Where the right and wrong places for body hair growth are differ from one culture to another, however. While an abundance of chest hair on men is often seen as a sign of masculinity and virility, some cultures prefer men to be bare-chested as a sign of youth, or hygiene. Most cultures, in fact, recognize a normative amount of hair for males and females, and people whose body hair growth violates those norms may experience social ostracism or rejection.

Because of the broad cultural concern with body hair, body hair removal has been practiced in some form or another in most cultures. One reason that so many cultures are concerned with body hair, or excess body hair, could be the link between human body hair and **animality**. Because mammals have hair or fur covering most of their bodies, a hairy human body can be seen as somewhat animalistic. Thus removing, or even styling, body hair is one way of separating human and animal, and ensuring that the human body is marked by culture, via waxing, shaving, or plucking.

In ancient **Egypt**, a completely smooth, hairless body was considered to be the standard of beauty for women. Elite Egyptian women removed all of their body hair including their pubic hair, and many removed the hair on their heads as well, which they replaced with a wig. (Egyptian priests also removed all of their body hair, facial hair, and head hair as a sign of purity.) Greeks and Romans also considered a hairless body to be an ideal for both men and women, as a smooth body represented a youthful body. It's not surprising to find that these cultures preferred hairless bodies given the hot desert climate. Waxing with sugar, lemon, and oils was the preferred method for hair removal.

In the modern West, body hair removal did not become popular until the twentieth century, when women's clothing became more revealing, and as the sexualized female body became a mainstay of advertising, television, and film. Most women in the United States now wax or shave their lower legs, underneath their armpits, and the "bikini area" on their upper thighs. In the 1970s, it was common for women involved in the developing women's liberation movement to stop shaving their legs and armpits, and countercultural groups like hippies often resisted shaving as well. Today, however, women who do not remove much of their body hair often find themselves as the objects of scorn or ridicule, although some people find armpit hair on women to be erotic.

In the late twentieth century, many women in the United States and other Western countries also began removing or shaping their pubic hair, a trend that began in Brazil among women who wanted to wear thong bikinis but did not want their pubic hair to be seen. In some groups, natural pubic hair is seen as unhygienic or messy. The need to remove or contain pubic hair has resulted in the development of a new industry devoted to the waxing of pubic hair, as well as the development of new pubic hair "styles" such as the Brazilian, in which all hair in the pubic region is removed except for a small line of hair on the vulva, and styles named after the shape that the pubic hair has been trimmed into, like the triangle, landing strip, or heart. The preference for hairless genitalia is known as acomoclitism.

A concern with pubic hair has been seen in other cultures and long predates modern America's obsession with it. For example, in Islamic societies in the arid Middle East and Eastern Europe, female pubic hair is thought to be unclean, and has been removed for millennia.

In the late twentieth century, young fashionable men in the United States and some European countries began removing (usually via waxing) their chest hair, a trend that may have started in beach areas in California. Male body hair removal, trimming, or styling is often known as "manscaping" but has not become popular with most men. Many Westerners still see body hair as a sign of masculinity, and some groups, such as the bear subculture within the gay community, prefer men with abundant body hair. In the gay community, on the other hand, genital waxing has been popular since the late twentieth century and is now becoming more common among other men.

The methods used to remove hair vary among times and regions, but shaving with a sharp blade or razor has historically been the most common method of hair removal. The other popular method of hair removal is waxing, which uses bees' wax, honey, or sugar, often combined with oils and a strip of cloth to strip off the hair from the body.

See also: Facial Hair; Hair Cutting and Head Shaving.

Further Reading: Rosenthal, M. Sara. *Women and Unwanted Hair*. Toronto: Your Health Press, 2001; Younger, John G. *Sex in the Ancient World from A to Z*. London: Routledge, 2005.

BODY PAINTING

Body painting is a temporary body adornment in which part or all of the human body or face is painted with nontoxic paint, clay, **henna**, or dyes.

Body and face painting has been practiced around the world as evidence from Paleolithic burial sites have revealed. In traditional societies, body and face painting is typically used during the performance of certain rituals or ceremonies, during important hunts, and at other important times. The patterns used often demonstrated group affiliation in that each tribe or group uses different colors and designs, but they are not primarily used to mark social position or group membership. In this sense, body painting is unlike many of the other body modifications and adornments practiced around the world in that it is used to make the wearer different from his or her normal appearance, rather than to permanently mark their social position on their body.

Body painting is commonly used in **rites of passage**, such as initiation rituals marking the passage of boyhood to manhood in traditional societies. In these rituals, boys are often painted to demonstrate their liminal status, and sometimes are painted (and adorned) to resemble animals, or spirits, and the body paint is often seen as a form of temporary protection until the initiate completes the ritual and reemerges as a man. The dead are also often painted as a way to help them transition from the world of the living into the afterworld.

Body painting is also unusual in that, while it is often quite artistic, and in fact has the capacity to transform the wearer into a (temporary) work of art, it is not used primarily as a form of decoration or adornment.

Body paints are typically made from clay and pigments found in leaves, fruits, and berries, sometimes mixed with oils, fats, or other liquids. The most common colors include white, red, and black, but can include any color found in the natural world.

The colors used in body paint are often symbolic: red is typically used to symbolize blood, or death, or fertility, for example, and others are seen to have protective qualities.

Today, body painting is practiced among the indigenous people of **Australia**, Polynesia, Melanesia, and parts of Africa, and many Native American tribes once practiced it as well. Mehndi, which uses dyes made from the leaves of the henna plant, is a form of decorative body painting used in India and the Middle East, especially on brides and bridal guests.

In **Papua New Guinea**, most tribes use body painting for ceremonial purposes. During bridewealth ceremonies prior to a marriage, the bride and relatives of both the bride and the groom often paint themselves to celebrate the occasion, and to signify good fortune. Papuans use body painting at other ceremonies as well as a means of reinforcing group membership.

Many Native American dancers traditionally painted their bodies and faces for dance performances with designs

Last Horse, wearing body paint and feathers in his hair. Photo by Herman Heyn, 1899. Courtesy of Library of Congress Prints and Photographs Division, Washington, DC, No. LC-USZ62-94940.

such as arrows, lightning, stars, and lines. Some tribes used body paint in conjunction with permanent tattoos. It is speculated that the term "redskin" may have derived from the practices of certain Native communities to cover much of their bodies with red pigment.

Many Australian Aboriginal communities have been painting their bodies for thousands of years, as a way of demonstrating important social positions such as one's totem. It is also a means of communication, and when used in traditional dances, can tell a story. Because traditional paints were made out of earth, and aboriginal religion centers around the earth, using body paints was a sacred activity.

Many Northwest Indians used face painting, again primarily for ceremonial activities, such as attending potlatches. Some groups used stamps which were dipped into paint and them stamped onto the face, to mark clan emblems. Young men of the Nuba and the Masai tribes, both pastoral groups in Africa, wear body painting at ceremonies and rituals to demonstrate their strength and attractiveness.

While body painting has never been commonly practiced in the West, since the 1960s (when social taboos surrounding nudity began to lessen) it has become a unique artistic form practiced by some people. In the West today, body painting is practiced by artists who specialize in body or face painting, as well as makeup artists and fine artists. These artists display their work on models at festivals and competitions around the world, as well as in magazines such as the *Face and Body Art Magazine*, and body painting is often seen in television and movies. Body painting in the West is not linked to social identification nor is it used as part of ritual activities, but instead, it is seen as a form of art as well as individual expression.

Actors and clowns around the world have painted their faces and sometimes bodies for centuries, and continue to do so today. Face painting is also used as camouflage in the military and among hunters. Face painting is also popular at secular festivals, theme parks, and carnivals, especially for children, and is used by some sports fans to demonstrate their allegiance to their home team. More subdued form of face paints for everyday occasions evolved into the **cosmetics** we know today.

See also: Australia; Henna; Makeup; Papua New Guinea

Further Reading: Kupka, Karel. *Dawn of Art: Painting and Sculpture of Australian Aborigines*. Sydney: Angus and Robertson, 1965; Thevóz, Michel. *The Painted Body*. New York: Rizzoli International, 1984.

BODY PIERCING

Body piercing refers to the practice of using a needle to pierce the body, generally for the purposes of wearing **jewelry**, and piercing refers as well to the pierced part of the body, and sometimes to the jewelry worn. Body piercing can also refer to the practice of play piercings, in which parts of the body are pierced for ritual or sexual purposes, or even bloodletting, which was practiced, for example, by the ancient Mayans as well as a number of American Northwest Indians.

Body piercings include those done on the earlobe and ear cartilage, the nostril and septum, the lips and mouth, the face, the genitals, the nipples, and other areas of the body.

Piercing has been practiced for thousands of years by people all over the world. Ancient mummies have been found with pierced ears, jewelry dating back hundreds and thousands of years has been found in archaeological digs, and ancient paintings, sculptures, and other artifacts testify to the practice of piercing, most typically the ears, nose, and lips.

The ancient Hebrews wore **nose piercings** and **ear piercings**, both for decorative purposes and also to mark slaves, the Centurions of ancient Rome are thought to have worn nipple piercings, Egyptians from the New Kingdom had pierced ears, nose piercing has been common in **India** since at least the sixteenth century, and ancient Meso-Americans wore jewelry in their ears, noses, and lower lips, and such decorations continue to be popular amongst indigenous peoples in these regions. A number of African tribes, including the Berber and Beja, as well as the Bedouins of the Middle East and North Africa, have worn nose piercings.

In **Australia** and **Papua New Guinea**, some tribesmen had their septums pierced, and wore tusks and other ornaments through their nose in order to make themselves appear more fierce when fighting. In **Borneo**, some men had their penises pierced for adornment, and lip plates and stretched ears have been worn in cultures ranging from **Ethiopia** to **Brazil** to Alaska to **China**.

Ritual piercing, in which the body is pierced and must endure being weighted with **encumberments**, has been practiced among a number of Native American societies including the Sioux, as well as by ascetics in India.

In the West, pierced ears have been common for women for hundreds of years, and **nipple piercing** may have been practiced by some men in Europe as early as the nineteenth century.

Piercing is often a decorative act, as the jewelry worn in pierced ears, noses, and lips is often highly elaborate and decorative. On the other hand, piercing is often a part of initiation rituals and other **rites of passage**, and is used to mark an individual's social position or their transition from one life stage to another. Piercing is also sometimes, especially in the modern West, used for sexual purposes, especially **genital piercings**, nipple piercings and tongue piercings, which are often worn by members of the **BDSM** community. Gay men have also historically worn piercings more than other Americans, both for sexual and decorative reasons.

In the West, while ear piercing has been a normative decorative practice for centuries, other forms of piercing are less widely accepted. Nose piercings are perhaps the next most common piercing in the West, but most other piercings are seen by most mainstream Americans as unconventional at best, and deviant at worst. Body piercing in the West began to grow in the 1970s in California thanks to the work of piercer and Gauntlet founder **Jim Ward**, who, along with a handful of other piercing afficionados, began to develop and refine piercing technologies and jewelry, and offer them to the gay and leather community in West Hollywood that made up the initial community of piercing advocates. Later, piercing spread to punks, mainstream gay men and lesbians, and later youth in general.

Body piercing in the West today is typically practiced at body piercing studios, and sometimes tattoo studios, and in the United States, most piercings are done with a hollow medical needle. The needle is partially inserted into the part of the body being pierced, and, while still in the body, the jewelry, usually stainless steel or titanium, is pushed through the opening and the needle is removed. In some parts of the world, the piercer uses a cannula, which is a hollow plastic tube placed at the end of the needle, into which the jewelry is inserted. Piercing guns are only recommended to pierce ears, specifically the earlobe. Professionally created piercings can take anywhere from two weeks to eight months to heal, depending on the type of piercing and the placement on the body. Once the piercing has healed, jewelry other than the starter jewelry can be worn.

Piercing studios, like tattoo studios, are generally regulated by the state health department, and practice the same types of sanitation and sterilization procedures taken by tattoo studios. Tools and jewelry are sterilised in autoclaves, piercers wear single-use gloves, and working areas are cleaned with antiseptic cleansers.

See also: Bible; Body Play; Clitoral Piercing; Ear Piercing; Facial Piercing; Genital Piercing; Hand Piercing; Navel Piercing; Nipple Piercing; Nose Piercing; Oral Piercing; Penis Piercing; Surface Piercing

Further Reading: Gans, Eric. "The Body Sacrificial." In Tobin Siebers, ed., *The Body Aesthetic: From Fine Art to Body Modification*. Ann Arbor: University of Michigan Press, 2000; Gay, Kathlyn. *Body Marks: Tattooing, Piercing, and Scarification*. New York: Millbrook Press, 2002; Myers, James. "Nonmainstream Body Modification: Genital Piercing, Branding, Burning and Cutting." *Journal of Contemporary Ethnography* 21(3) (October 1992): 267–306; Pitts, Victoria. *In the Flesh: The Cultural Politics of Body Modification*. New York: Palgrave Macmillan, 2003; Swift, B. "Body Art and Modification." In Guy N. Rutty, ed., *Essentials of Autopsy Practice: Current Methods and Modern Trends*. New York: Spring Publishing, 2001.

BODY PLAY

Body play refers to rituals in which participants perform various body modifications on themselves or others, usually of a temporary nature, for sexual, religious, or personal reasons. It generally includes the use of **piercing, tattooing, cutting, branding**, contortions, corsetting, and other (often extreme) practices.

Body play is primarily associated with the **modern primitives** movement as well as the **BDSM** scene and was largely popularized in the United States by **Fakir Musafar** starting in the 1970s, and really became popular after the publication of Re/Search Publication's *Modern Primitives* in 1989.

The philosophy embraces the use of Native American and other non-Western body techniques in order to bring about a heightened state of awareness or elevated consciousness via enduring **pain** and overcoming one's personal limits. It is also used to create a sense of "body awareness." According to proponents, participants learn to transcend the pain involved in the practices and transform it into feelings of ecstasy and empowerment. For many advocates, the purpose of body play is to use physical and emotional sensations to influence consciousness, and lead to altered states of awareness.

According to Fakir Musafar, body play can be achieved via contortion, constriction, deprivation, **encumberment**, fire, penetration, or **suspension**. **Foot binding**, for example, would be a form of contortion, and the wearing of corsets would be a form of constriction. Fasting or abstinence from sex would be an example of deprivation. Electric shock, branding, and burning would all be examples of body play by fire. Hanging weights from hooks inserted into pierced holes in the flesh would be an example of encumberment, as would hanging weights from the testicles or penis, and hanging the body from flesh hooks would be an example of suspension. Finally, inserting large objects into the anus would be an example of body play via penetration.

Play piercing refers to the use of body piercing in order to experience the sensations of the piercing, and no jewelry is involved. It is also a form of body play by penetration. In a play piercing session, a person may have needles, skewers, sharpened bones, or knives inserted into their bodies, usually in a specific configuration, which are then removed at the end of the session, letting the holes heal. Sometimes small or large weights (such as bells, lead balls, or other objects) are attached to the piercings, as a form of encumberment. As with other forms of body play, participants feel that play piercing allows for self-discovery, sexual pleasure, or the overcoming of personal obstacles. Suspensions are also examples of play piercing, in which the body is suspended from the ceiling via hooks in the flesh attached to ropes or chains.

See also: BDSM, *Modern Primitives*; Musafar, Fakir; Primitivism; Suspensions

Further Reading: Vale, V. and Andrea Juno. *Modern Primitives*. San Francisco, CA: Re/Search Publications, 1989.

BONDAGE *See* BDSM

BORNEO

Borneo is a tropical island in Southeast Asia, which is divided into three administrative and political units, controlled by Indonesia, Malaysia, and the Sultanate of Brunei. The third largest island in the world, it was controlled by the Malay Brunei Sultanate Empire from the fifteenth to the seventeenth centuries, and by the nineteenth century, was primarily under the control of the British and the Dutch. By the end of World War II, Indonesia gained its independence from the Dutch and later, Malaysia from the British; both countries now control the bulk of the island. Today, the population of Borneo consists of Javanese, Sundanese, Malays, Dayaks (which includes Ibans, Kayans, Kenyahs, and other indigenous tribes), as well as Chinese and Europeans.

Tattooing has long been practiced by many of the indigenous Dayaks, and for most, are spiritual and magical in nature; today, however, traditional tattooing is largely dying out in Borneo. A myth explains the origin of tattooing in Borneo by telling of a bird which fell into a bowl of ink and began to peck at a warrior, until his body was covered with tattoo designs.

Borneo tattoo techniques resemble Samoan techniques in that pins are attached to the end of a stick in a perpendicular fashion and are rested on the skin; a mallet drives the needles in at high speed. The ink is made of powdered charcoal or soot, and is thought to ward off evil spirits, especially when other sacred substances are mixed into the pigment. The tattooists could be men or women—among the Kayan, the women are the artists and inherit the position from their mothers, but among the Iban, men are the tattooists. In both cases, spirits govern the act of tattooing and the artist must call on the spirits for guidance. Some tribes use pattern blocks made out of wood to imprint the design onto the body before tattooing, whereas other tribes freehand the design. Design elements include plants and animals which have curative or protective powers, such as dogs, pigs, birds, flowers, and ancestral spirits.

A man without tattoos is invisible to the gods.

IBAN proverb

Tattoos were worn by both men and women on shoulders, arms, hands (especially the fingers), legs, and feet, and were able to protect the wearer from harmful spirits, illness, and harm. In addition, like tattoos worn by many tribal peoples, they indicate social rank, as only the elites could wear certain designs, and in general, tattoos, because they had to be paid for with beads or pigs, were not easily affordable by all. They also represented prestige earned by head hunting for men, or weaving, dancing, and singing for women. Iban men who had participated in a headhunt could have their fingers tattooed with spirits, and women received geometric patterns on the fingers, and images of spirits on her wrists. Men also received tattoos—which also symbolize new beginnings—as a sign of manhood, during a **rite of passage** attended by other men in the community. Tattoos were also decorative.

Older Ngaju men who had attained wealth and stature were able to receive the most complete tattoo, which used images from nature such as palm fronds to cover the shoulder and arms and a great tree to cover the torso, and took days or weeks to complete, leaving the wearer, according to tribesmen, perfect, sacred, and complete.

See also: Modern Primitives; Tribalism

Further Reading: Graham, P. *Iban Shamanism: An Analysis of the Ethnographic Literature*. Canberra: Research School in Pacific Studies, Australian National University, 1987; Scharer, H. *Ngaju Religion: The Conception of God among a South Borneo People*. The Hague: Martinus Nijhoff, 1963.

BOURDIEU, PIERRE

Pierre Bourdieu (1930–2002) was a French sociologist whose work, especially his 1984 book *Distinction: A Social Critique of the Judgement of Taste*, is useful in developing an understanding of how social class is marked on the body.

How we walk, eat, or blow our noses, according to Bourdieu, reflect our class position, and the social divisions present in modern society. Bourdieu noted that we embody not only our class position but the entire social structure, via our physical size, shape, or color (wealthy bodies, for example, tend to be both thin and light-skinned), as well as the differential tastes, appearance, habits, and lifestyles of each class. Because members of each class operate from a different "habitus," or internalized form of class condition which informs the ways that one inhabits one's body, it is to be expected that their tastes in clothing, food, or sports will differ. Bourdieu's position is that the body is the embodiment of class. Thus in the West, prior to the modern renaissance of **tattooing**, tattooed bodies were very clearly poor or working-class bodies, as only sailors, soldiers, convicts, and other members of the working classes or underclasses wore tattoos. Even today, the types of tattoos worn by modern Westerners demonstrate to a large extent their class position, as tattoo styles such as biker tattoos betray one's working-class roots, whereas elaborate full-body Japanese tattoos, as worn by Westerners, typically are limited to middle-class people who can afford them and have the artistic sensibilities to desire them.

Bourdieu's work is also useful in contrasting the types of body adornments and modifications that different classes might appreciate. For Bourdieu, middle-class cultural forms are characterized by distance and critical appreciation, while working-class forms are characterized by intense involvement, explaining the preference for tattooing among the underclasses in the West. Those body modifications that have traditionally been practiced by elites tend to be limited to those that are expensive, that conform to social norms and standards of beauty, and that are procured through professionals, such as **cosmetic surgery**. The consumption of these very different practices—tattooing and cosmetic surgery, for instance—reinforces and legitimates social differences.

See also: Class and Status

Further Reading: Bourdieu, Pierre. *Distinction: A Social Critique of the Judgement of Taste.* London: Routledge, 1984.

BRANDING

Branding humans is a tradition that goes back to at least ancient **Egypt** and Rome when wealthy elites branded their livestock and their slaves with a hot iron. The symbols branded onto the slaves indicated their ownership by their owners, and were the same symbols used on that family's cattle. On the other hand, branding has also been used in some African and Native American societies as part of **rites of passage** marking the transition of young men into warriors or elders. More recently it has been used as a form of punishment in the West, but today is a widely practiced form of body modification for some communities.

The origin of human branding in the West is to mark the ownership of slaves. It was seen in the **Greco-Roman world**, and also was used by European slave traders. The Greeks branded slaves with a Delta for doulos or slave. Runaway slaves were marked by the Romans with the letter F (for *fugitivus*). Robbers, like runaway slaves, were marked by the Romans with the letter F (fur); and men sentenced to work in the mines, and convicts condemned to fight in gladiatorial shows, were branded (or perhaps tattooed) on the forehead for identification. Under Constantine I the face was not permitted to be disfigured, so any punitive marks, be they tattoos or brands, were put onto the hand, arm, or calf.

Throughout Europe branding was used to mark criminals, combining physical punishment, as burns are very painful, with public humiliation (which is greatest if marked on a normally visible part of the body), and the permanent marking of criminal status. Anglo-Saxons marked gypsies, vagabonds, and brawlers with a brand. In Europe, and later the New World colonies in America and the Carribean, the branding of slaves was common till the nineteenth century. British

Army deserters were branded with a D, and, beginning in the eighteenth century, the British started using cold iron brands for high-status criminals. Theft and many other offenses were punished with a brand, often with the letter T. In France galley slaves and convicts could be branded TF for forced labor (*travaux forcés*) until 1832. In Germany, branding was used in the seventeenth and eighteenth centuries. Canada too branded military prisoners: D for Desertion and BC for Bad Character.

After the establishment of Australia as a penal colony in the eighteenth century, a great many criminals arrived from England, many with brands or tattoos. Branding was prohibited throughout the West in the nineteenth century and replaced by other methods of corporeal punishment. Branding was also used in **India** to mark and punish criminals.

Today, in the West, branding is no longer used to mark slaves or criminals but continues to be used to mark the ownership of animals. It is also now used as a form of voluntary body modification that involves burning an image or symbol onto a person's skin.

Today branding is often used as a form of initiation for groups like **fraternities**, street gangs, and even in prison. It serves as a test of endurance as well as a demonstration of loyalty and group solidarity, and provides a rite of passage for new group members. It's a lifetime reminder of what their brotherhood means to them. In the fraternity context, the brand is usually the Greek letter of the organization.

It is rumored that George W. Bush, while president of the Delta Kappa Epsilon chapter at Yale, may have helped introduce an initiation ritual for pledges that involved branding a D onto the buttocks with a heated wire coat hanger.

Wilson Chinn, a branded slave from Louisiana. Photograph by Kimball, 1863. Courtesy of Library of Congress Prints and Photographs Division, Washington, DC, No. LC-USZ62-90345.

In fraternities, branding is used in African American fraternities, although it is not officially sanctioned by any. (In fact, some Greek organizations feel that branding is a form of hazing and have prohibited it.) The practice probably started in the 1950s and is a way in which fraternity members not only visibly mark themselves with a permanent badge of fraternity status and loyalty, but reclaim a practice that had been used against their ancestors during slavery. These students have subverted the understanding of branding as a mark of ownership and slavery, and have taken control of their bodies for themselves.

While fraternity members may simply use a hot coat hanger for branding, other methods have been developed, such as the use of a pen-like instrument (known as the cautery method), which allows for much more precision on the design than is possible with a heated iron brand.

Branding, like **scarification**, is unpredictable and can result in raised scars for some and very faint images for others. Most branding results in a second-degree burn, but third-degree burns are common as well. There are ways to interrupt the healing process in order to get the desired scar (for instance, by picking off scabs or by repeatedly cleaning the wound), but how one scars is almost entirely genetically determined.

Of late, branding has also become a practice associated with **primitivism**. Body modification guru **Fakir Musafar** had been practicing branding since the 1960s, practicing on his own body starting at about 17. Through his experiments, he found that complex brands were not suitable for human skin, and eventually created methods of branding that he later taught to others at his seminars. He recommends using stainless steel strips (he calls strikers) ranging from .010 to .015 inches thick and heated with a propane torch to about 2400 degrees Fahrenheit. He calls it multistrike branding.

Branding is widely used today in the **BDSM** community. For instance, in extreme BDSM dominance and submission relationships, a consensual slave may desire or accept a brand as a permanent mark of belonging and commitment to one's master.

See also: Animal Branding; Criminality; Fraternities; Musafar, Fakir; Primitivism; Slavery

Further Reading: Mizumoto Posey, Sandra. "Burning Messages: Interpreting African American Fraternity Brands and Their Bearers." *Voices, the Journal of New York Folklore* 30 (Fall–Winter 2004): 42–44; Musafar, Fakir. "Kiss of Fire: The Abc's of Branding." *Body Play* (1) (1992).

BRAZIL

Brazil is a large country in South America, originally colonized by Portugal in the sixteenth century, and made up of a variety of tribes living in both the coastal and interior regions of the country. Native Brazilians of many tribes once adorned their bodies with feathers, paint, and natural fibers. For example, the Kayapo, hunter-gatherers and horticulturalists who still live in the Amazon Basin, paint their bodies with vegetable dye and charcoal and wear headdresses of macaw feathers for ritual occasions. They also wear large **lip plates** and plugs as a form of decoration.

The men and women of the Suya tribe, horticulturalists who live in the Indigenous Park of the Xingu, as well, wore lip plates and earplugs in ear openings stretched up to 8 centimeters. Like other Brazilian Indians, the Suya call the piercing of the ears "opening" and this ritual occurs at adolescence when a boy is expected to open his ears and listen to his elders. Eventually, he will wear, on ceremonial occasions, large ear discs made of wood or palm leaves, painted white, in his stretched earlobes. Lips are pierced several years later, at 15 or 20, as confirmation of adulthood, and men will not go out in public without the lip plate, which is painted with red and black dye. Whereas ear discs are associated with hearing, lip discs are associated with oration and song. The Suya haven't practiced these modifications since the 1950s.

Among the Canela, hunter-gatherers who live in central Brazil, body modifications are also performed in order to signal changes in social identity, and express culturally prescribed values. They are also decorative. Like the Suya, Canela men must have their ears opened at adolescence. The piercing is performed by a ritual piercing specialist who pierces the ear with a hardwood awl, and then places wooden pins into the holes. Over the next few weeks, the boy replaces the first wooden pins with a series of larger pins which will enlarge the hole.

Tattooing has also been practiced by some Brazilian tribes. A Jesuit priest in the sixteenth century reported that some of the natives used the teeth of rodents to make crossed patterns into their skin, into which they rub a fluid consisting of coal powder mixed with the juice of a herb.

Tribes used many different instruments for tattooing: diamonds, palm tree thorns, fish teeth, and mammals' teeth. Members of the Munducuru, horticulturalists and hunters living in the Amazon forest, used a piece of wood set with rodents' teeth that created a line in the skin, into which dye would be rubbed.

While most of these practices are no longer practiced in Brazil, some tribes do still maintain their ancient traditions of body modification.

See also: Body Painting; Ear Stretching; Lip Plates; Tattooing

Further Reading: Crocker, William H. "The Canela (Eastern Timbira), I: An Ethnographic Introduction." In *Smithsonian Contributions to Anthropology*, No. 33. Washington, DC: Smithsonian Institution Press, 1990; Turner, Terence S. "The Social Skin." In Jeremy Cherfas and Roger Lewin, eds., *Not Work Alone: A Cross-Cultural View of Activities Superfluous to Survival*. Beverly Hills, CA: Sage Publications, 1980; Turner, Terence S. "Social Body and Embodied Subject: Bodiliness, Subjectivity and Sociality among the Kayapo." *Current Anthropology* 10(2) (1995): 143–170.

BREAST AUGMENTATION AND REDUCTION

Breast augmentation surgery is the third most common form of **cosmetic surgery** in the United States, with almost 300,000 surgeries performed each year, and over two and a half million surgeries over the past fifteen years. Breast augmentation surgery involves the insertion of a saline or silicone implant into a woman's chest in order to increase the size of her breasts. Breast augmentation surgery is also performed on male to female **transsexuals** as part of **sex reassignment surgery**.

In societies in which breast size is positively correlated with female beauty of sexual appeal, women have used a variety of means to increase the breast size. Surveys have shown that a large percentage of American women are dissatisfied with their bodies, and that 30 percent of survey respondents are unhappy with the size or shape of their breasts. Because breast size cannot be changed by diet or exercise (unless one is extremely overweight or underweight), women who have been unhappy with their breasts have resorted to a great variety of ways to fix what they perceive to be their problem. The most common, and the simplest way to do this, is by wearing breast pads made of cotton, synthetic materials, rubber, or silicone gel. This, however, is a temporary solution. Over the years a number of products have been marketed to women that promise a permanent increase in breast size, including creams, pills, and a pump that sucks at the breast using a vacuum, but all have proven ineffective.

Since the late nineteenth century, women interested in permanently increasing the size of their breasts have turned to surgery, with mixed results. The earliest methods involved the injection of paraffin, silicone, rubber, as well as implants made of polyethylene, rubber, foam, and sponge.

In the 1960s, breast implants made from a silicone shell filled with silicone gel were developed, and, were used by millions of women. After a number of health problems and lawsuits in the 1990s related to leakages, ruptures, hardening of the breasts, and cancer, their use was restricted by the FDA, although new silicone models may be allowed again. Saline-filled implants, since the 1990s, have become the most commonly used implant in the United States, and have caused fewer health problems, although the cosmetic appearance of saline implants is often not as good as the silicone implants.

Breast implants are inserted into the breast after an incision is made either below the breast, along the areola, in the navel, or in the armpit, and are either placed in front of or behind the pectoral muscles.

Many women, after receiving a breast implant, find that they cannot breastfeed their babies, and some women report a loss of sensation in the breasts. Other women must replace their implants as the material hardens or changes consistency and appearance.

Breast lifts are becoming increasingly common surgical procedures as women of all ages attempt to achieve or maintain a youthful body for as long as possible. Breast lifts are used by women who feel that their breasts are drooping, and are sometimes combined with a breast implant. With or without an implant, breasts are lifted through the surgical removal of excess skin and breast tissue, and the elevation of reshaping of the remaining breast tissue. Breast lifts, however, will never be permanent as the breasts will continue to droop with age, necessitating for many repeated surgeries over time.

Some women seek breast reduction surgery when they feel that their breasts are too large, either for cosmetic or health reasons, and sometimes as part of liposuction, tummy tucks, or other cosmetic surgeries aimed at eliminating excess body fat. Breast reduction surgery involves an incision around the areola and down the breast, exposing breast tissue, which is then removed and the nipple and areola are moved into a new position on the smaller breast.

See also: Beauty; Breast Reconstruction; Cosmetic Surgery; Implants

Further Reading: Freud, Robert Michael, and Alex Van Dyne. *Cosmetic Breast Surgery: A Complete Guide to Making the Right Decision—From A to Double D*. New York: Marlow & Company, 2004; Lynch, Wilfred. *Implants: Reconstructing the Human Body*. New York: Van Nostrand Reinhold Company, 1982.

BREAST IRONING

Breast ironing is a body modification practiced among some tribes in Cameroon, in which adolescent girls' breasts are artificially flattened.

In Cameroon, as in many countries, large breasts are seen as sexually attractive to men and a girl's breasts are a sign of maturing sexuality. So in order to protect daughters from rape or early marriages, mothers will pound or massage their growing daughters' breasts in order to make them disappear, allowing the girls to finish school without interruption. Some girls will also pound their own breasts in order to protect themselves from the advances of men.

According to some studies, a quarter of all Cameroonian girls, primarily in the southern region of the country, have had their breasts flattened with tools like wooden pestles, rocks, spatulas, coconut shells, and other hard implements, which are then heated. The force of the pounding combined with the heat make this quite a painful procedure, according to girls and women who have undergone it. Sadly, it has not worked to prevent sexual activity among girls and many girls with flattened breasts still have sex, many becoming pregnant.

Some Cameroonians are working to fight the practice, and groups like the Association of Aunties is educating men and women about birth control, HIV prevention, and abstinence, and the health problems associated with ironing. While the practice is illegal and punishable by up to three years in jail, it continues today.

See also: Breast Augmentation and Reduction; Female Genital Mutilation

Further Reading: Curry, Ginette, ed., *Awakening African Women: The Dynamics of Change*. Cambridge: Cambridge Scholars Press Ltd, 2004.

BREAST RECONSTRUCTION

Breast reconstruction is the rebuilding of a breast, generally after a masectomy due to breast cancer, or, in some women, as a preventative measure against cancer. It generally involves the insertion of a saline implant, or sometimes relocated tissue from the woman's own body, and often includes the reformation of an areola and nipple.

Some women elect to have the initial part of their reconstructive surgery during the same surgery in which their breast was removed, while others wait until a later date for the surgery, but because the procedure is complex, it is usually accomplished in multiple operations.

The insertion of the implant necessitates first expanding the tissue in which the new implant will sit, and is most often done through the insertion of a temporary tissue expander into which the surgeon will inject saline over a period of weeks or months in order to create a cavity large enough for the new implant. After the permanent implant has been inserted, the nipple and areola must be reconstructed. Nipples and areola can be created through skin grafts from a donor or by using a flap of skin from the patient in order to create a mound. Once the shape of the new nipple and areola is finalized the skin in the region is generally tattooed a darker color than the surrounding skin.

Some women do not elect to have breast reconstruction after a masectomy, and some choose to have the scars associated with their surgery tattooed. Many women report that **tattooing** their surgical scars is empowering and transforms the negative memories into something positive. For others, the tattoo serves as a powerful reminder of the cancer.

See also: Beauty; Breast Augmentation and Reduction; Cosmetic Surgery; Implants

Further Reading: Berger, Karen J., and John Bostwick Berger. *A Woman's Decision: Breast Care, Treatment & Reconstruction*. St. Louis, MO: Quality Medical Publishing, 1998.

BROADBENT, BETTY

Betty Broadbent (1909–1983) was the most famous female **tattooed attraction** of all time. In 1923, when she was 14, she moved from Orlando, Florida to Atlantic City to take a baby-sitting job, and saw a tattooed man exhibited on the Boardwalk. Betty originally wanted to be an artist, but as she needed money, she decided to become herself a work of art, and got tattooed instead. Prior to that time, she had rode horses in the rodeo and her rodeo money ended up paying for her tattoos. She took her savings to New York and got her work done by **Charlie Wagner** and Joe Van Hart over a two-year period. She got her first job in 1927 as the youngest tattooed woman in the world (she was called the "Tattooed Venus") with Ringling Brothers and Barnum and Bailey **Circus**. (Unlike many of the tattooed ladies at the time, Betty resisted the "native capture" narratives that were used to draw patrons to her act, and hated being called the Tattooed Venus.) Betty estimated that she had 365 tattoos.

She began her performance in a floor-length satin or velvet robe, depending on the weather. The platform lecturer would announce, "And now, ladies and gentlemen, the lady who's different!" She would then unzip her rope and underneath, she had a long bathing suit on that came four inches above her knees—Betty said that hers was a respectable act, "not like those carnival floozies with one or two tattoos who would bump and grind."

> decided to get tattooed. I wanted
> to be independent and to take care
> of myself.
>
> BETTY BROADBENT, tattooed lady

Betty wore Pancho Villa on her left leg, Charles Lindbergh on her right leg, and had a Madonna and child portrait on her back. When women were allowed to show more of their bodies, Bert Grimm tattooed Betty's upper legs, and her bathing suit was shortened to

Betty Broadbent, known as the Tattooed Venus, the most famous American tattooed lady. Courtesy of Tattoo Archive.

display her thighs. In interviews with Betty and stories about her published after her death, her respectability and ladylike behavior is always emphasized. Betty was said, for example, to like flowers and breeding fancy birds. Like the other tattooed ladies, Betty was presented as feminine, classy, and refined. She left the sideshow for a few years and worked as a rider in Harry Carey's Wild West Show. During the off season she was often tattooed in San Francisco at one of the arcades on Market.

Betty was one of the last working tattooed ladies in the country, only retiring in 1967 from the Clyde Beatty Circus. She was the first person to be entered into the Tattoo Hall of Fame in August of 1981. She died two years later.

See also: Freak Shows; Tattooed Attractions

Further Reading: Aurre, Judy. "Meet Betty Broadbent." *Tattoo Historian* 1 (1982): 21–23; Beal, George Brinton. "TheTattooed Lady." *Tattoo Archive* (Fall 1989): 44; Eldridge, Chuck. "TABC." *Tattoo Historian* 2 (1983): 9–10.

C

CASTRATION

Castration generally refers to the surgical removal of the testicles in humans and animals. Castration is also used to refer to the use of chemicals in the human or animal male in order to stop the production of testosterone and sperm.

In nonhuman animals, castration is performed in order to render the animal sterile, and sometimes to control an animal's behavior, as castrated (also known as neutered) animals are known to be more docile than nonneutered animals. Some meat animals are also castrated in order to fatten them. Castration is the most commonly performed **animal surgical procedure**, and has been practiced since the early days of animal agriculture, going back as far as 6,500 years.

Companion animals are generally castrated surgically, by a veterinarian, under anesthesia, via an incision, made with either a scalpel or laser, in front of the scrotum. Livestock are often castrated scrotally by either a veterinarian or farmer, often without anesthesia. Castration methods for livestock include the use of an elastrator tool which secures a band around the testicles that disrupts the blood supply, or the use of a Burdizzo tool or other emasculators to crush the spermatic cords and disrupt the blood supply.

Castrated animals often are referred by different names than intact males, such as ox, bullock, or steer for cattle, barrow or hog for pig, wether for sheep, and gelding for horse. Gelding also refers to the practice of neutering or castrating an animal.

Castration in humans most certainly developed after the rise of agriculture and animal domestication, which both provided the impetus for the development of state-level civilization as well as the technology for castration itself. Human castration has a long history throughout many of the early states and has primarily been used for punitive purposes, religious reasons, and to control certain categories of slaves and servants. While castration technically refers to the removal of the testicles, in some ancient states like **China** it was not just the testicles that were removed but the penis, testicles, and scrotum. (Chinese eunuchs kept their organs in a jar to be buried with the man when he died, so that he would be reborn as a whole man.)

In humans, the results of the removal of the testicles include sterility, reduced or eliminated libido, sometimes a loss of body strength, feelings of calmness and sometimes depression, weight gain or fat redistribution, and softer body hair. Many men also experience similar symptoms to female menopause such as loss of bone density, hot flashes, and mood swings. Castrated men will not get male pattern baldness and generally have a lower incidence of prostate cancer than other men. Historically, the reasons for castrating men were primarily to reduce their sexual appetite, to destroy their reproductive ability, and to make them calmer.

Early states often used castration as a punishment for criminals. In the civilizations of the Mediterranean and Middle East, for instance, as well as in China and Medieval Europe, castration was often used as a punishment for rape, homosexuality, or adultery. In more modern times, the Nazis sometimes used castration as a punishment and as a way of controlling the reproduction of "unfit" populations.

Castration has also been used throughout history during wartime; invading armies would castrate either their captives or the corpses of the defeated, in order to demonstrate their victory over the conquered people, as a form of ethnic cleansing, and sometimes as a method of **torture**; castration of men was often used alongside the rape of women during war. This has been seen in ancient Persia, **Egypt**, Assyria, **Ethiopia**, and among the ancient Hebrews, as well as among the Normans, the Chinese, and in modern times, the Vietcong were rumored to have castrated prisoners and dissidents, and the Janjaweed in the ongoing Sudanese conflict castrate men and rape women.

Also found only in state societies is the use of castrated men—often prisoners of war—as slaves and servants. In societies in which elite men kept multiple wives, such as throughout the Middle East, castrated men, known as eunuchs, were used to guard those women. Eunuchs were preferred as harem guards because one of the side effects of castration, especially when it is performed prior to puberty, is the loss of sexual appetite. (Although some eunuchs could still have and enjoy sex, making them popular, and sterile, sexual partners for the women.) Other societies, such as ancient Rome, Egypt, and the Incan Empire also castrated slaves, as a way to make those servants more docile, and obedient, as well as to prevent them from having sexual relations with female members of the household.

Eunuchs were sometimes also accorded a high social class, even when acting as servants. Some eunuchs in Assyria, Egypt, Persia, the Byzantine Ottoman Empires, and China served in the court and were able to wield a considerable amount of power.

Castration has also been used in a number of religious cults, as a way of **self-mortification** used to deny the person sexual pleasure. While some religions mandated castration only for monks and other serious devotees, other cults demanded castration for all members. Others did not require it at all but especially devoted adherents chose it as a sign of devotion and loyalty. Members of the Roman cult of Cybele were castrated, as were some early Christians, as well as a number of members of the twentieth century Heaven's Gate cult prior to their mass suicide.

Because women were not allowed to sing or perform in the Catholic Church, and sometimes elsewhere, in Renaissance Europe, boys were often castrated prior to puberty to enable them to take on the female vocal roles, since prepubescent castration would prevent their voices from deepening. Castrati, as they were known, were often castrated by their parents as a way to achieve upward mobility for themselves, via their sons, because some castrati in the seventeenth and eighteenth centuries achieved a high degree of fame and wealth. Castrati whose voices were not good enough for the stage often ended up working in the Church.

While castration as a method of punishment and control became less common after the nineteenth century, and castrati were no longer allowed to sing in the Catholic Church beginning in the twentieth century, it is still practiced in some groups today.

Male-to-female **transsexuals**, as well as some transgendered people, undergo physical castration as part of their transition from one gender to the other. In some transsexuals, castration is performed prior to the major **sex reassignment surgery**. For some it is performed at the same time that the penis is removed, and for others, castration is the only surgical procedure performed. Indian **Hijras** still practice the total removal of the male genitalia for most members. And while rare, some nontransgendered men also seek castration to control their libido if they masturbate excessively or their sexual appetite causes them other problems.

Most transsexuals are taking female hormones when they obtain their castration, which means that the effects of hormones will have already caused many of the effects of castration. Others, however, undergo their castrations first, in order to more quickly feel the effects of feminization on their bodies, or to avoid the side effects that can come with taking female hormones.

Many people who are born intersex will also undergo castration, as well as removal of the penis or reduction of the clitoris, as a way of transforming ambiguous genitalia into female genitalia.

While involuntary castration is very rare in the modern world, some American and European states do allow for the voluntary chemical castration of sex offenders. Testosterone depletion treatment, often in the form of Depo-Provera injections (a hormonal birth control method used by women), is a way of temporarily reducing the sex drive of sex offenders, although the success rates of these procedures are questionable, and injections must be ongoing. While surgical castration is more effective in eliminating sexual drive than chemical castration, in both cases there are still problems, as postpubescent men often retain sexual drive even after castration, and the drive to rape is not an exclusively (or even primarily) sexual drive.

Voluntary castration is also used today as an extreme body modification and for the purposes of sexual excitement. Some men, for example, feel sexually aroused by the thought of having their genitals mutilated or removed, and **BDSM** fantasies often revolve around the removal of one partner's testicles. Some men want to be castrated in order to put an end to the sexual side of themselves, and plan to remain celibate after their testicles have been removed. A nullo is a man who chooses to have all of his genitalia removed for aesthetic and sexual purposes.

Men who seek voluntary castration today can get castrated by a medical doctor, although most doctors will not castrate a man unless he is undergoing sex reassignment therapy. When unable to find (or afford) a doctor, some men will turn to a cutter, a friend, or will do the procedure themselves. Using a cutter or a friend is risky because they may not possess the skills, knowledge, or equipment to do a castration safely and hygienically, especially in the case of complications, but self-castration is the most risky, and is often used as the last resort by those who are desperate for the procedure.

Some in the extreme body modification community use a Burdizzo for castration, rather than surgery. The Burdizzo is a tool that looks like a walnut cracker, and is used to castrate livestock by crushing the blood vessels which run through the testicles. Once the vessels are destroyed, the testicles will shrink and eventually disappear. While quick, castration via Burdizzo is evidently extremely painful.

See also: Amputation; Criminality; Genital Mutilation; Hijras; Slavery; Torture; Transsexuals

Further Reading: Taylor, Gary. *Castration: An Abbreviated History of Western Manhood.* New York: Routledge, 2000.

CELTS

The terms Celtic or Celt generally refer to the cultures and languages of Ireland, Scotland, Wales, Cornwall, the Isle of Man, and Brittany.

The origin of insular (i.e., found on the British Isles) Celtic peoples and languages is controversial but most scholars feel that Celts are not indigenous to the British Isles but instead arrived from the European continent through centuries of trade and other contact, starting around the ninth century BCE. By the **Roman** period, however, most of the inhabitants of the isles of Ireland and Great Britain were Celtic in terms of language and culture.

> The tribal [tattoo] ties back into the old ways, the back to nature kind of thing. The first people, the Celts, were into tattooing, and I'm going to get a Celtic cross over my heart that'll separate and divide my rain forest. I'm just heavy into nature, I guess I'm almost pagan, that's why I'm getting all this stuff.
>
> ANONYMOUS

Prior to the arrival of the Romans, some tribes of insular Celts most likely used **tattooing** to mark tribal affiliation and other salient social features. Caesar, for example, in 55 BCE, referred to **body painting** with woad among the Celts, but it may have been tattooing rather than painting that he saw. A quote from Herodian, a first-century Roman historian, noted that the Celts, who wore no clothing, "punctured" their bodies with pictures of animals. There is also evidence that contemporary cultures to the Celts, like the Scythians, who were known to have influenced Celtic culture, practiced tattooing.

The Picts, another Celtic tribe, are thought to have been given their Roman name (which means painted people) from the practice of painting or dying their bodies, or from the iron tool used to tattoo. In addition, "Briton" means painted in various colors. Roman conquerors describe the Britons that they encountered as having their bodies, faces, and, hands painted. But, again, painting could also refer to the practice of tattooing.

The Roman occupation of Britain led to a merging of Roman and Celtic cultural practices. Once the Celts came under Roman control and became Christianized, they soon adopted the wearing of Christian tattoos, as in the style of the Jerusalem souvenir tattoos. These tattoos were referred to in Medieval Celtic texts as **stig-mata**, the term used to describe tattoos in the Christianized Roman world. This practice may also have been associated, as with the Roman practice, with the marking of slaves and criminals, but it was certainly used by Celtic Christians to mark devotion.

By about the fifth century as the Roman Empire collapsed, the Celts were pushed westwards by Germanic invaders, although it is unclear how much of Celtic culture survived to influence modern English culture (and the English practice of tattooing).

See also: Body Painting; Christianity; Greco-Roman World; Stigmata; Tattooing

Further Reading: Charles MacQuarrie, "Insular Celtic Tattooing: History, Myth and Metaphor." In Jane Caplan, ed., *Written on the Body: The Tattoo in European and American History*. London: Reaktion Books, 2000.

CHICANOS

Chicano refers to people of Mexican descent who live in the Southwestern states of the United States, primarily California.

Chicano **tattooing** began with the *pachuco* gang culture of the 1940s and 1950s in the barrios of California, Texas, New Mexico, and Arizona. Tattooing in this context was originally done by hand with a sewing needle wrapped with thread and dipped in India ink. Classic Chicano tattooing utilizes exclusively black ink, fine lines (because of the use of a single needle), and bold shading. Chicano and Mexican tattooists use color and professional machines for their tattoos, but many Chicano youth, prisoners, and gang members still wear the monochromatic, hand-picked tattoos. Whether by hand or by machine, classic Chicano tattoos are immediately distinguishable from classic American tattooing by the thin lines, lack of color, and different imagery used. Images popular in Chicano tattooing include religious iconography like the Virgin of Guadelupe or Christ with a crown of thorns, long-haired sexy women, low-riders and other period cars, Aztec warriors and imagery, and the Old English lettered-*loca*, or gang or neighborhood of origin, usually tattooed across the back or the chest.

Chicano tattoo art is very similar to other forms of Chicano art such as mural and low-rider art, although certain images are limited to tattoos. Without a doubt the most classic Chicano tattoo is the small "*pachuco* cross" tattooed on the hand between forefinger and thumb. It was once used to identify members of gangs and to assert the solidarity of the group; to outsiders the cross represented crime and violence. To insiders, however, Chicano tattoos tend to represent loyalty to community, family, women, and God—very similar in theme to the nationalist designs seen among sailors, but stylistically, a world apart.

Freddy Negrete and Jack Rudy, two East Los Angeles tattooists, were possibly the first professional tattooists working in this style in the late 1970s. They, along with tattooist Charlie Cartright, perfected this technically difficult style, bringing it to mainstream prominence. Because of the use of single needles, this type of work was more finely detailed than traditional American tattoos, allowing the creation of finely shaded, "photo realistic," portraits on the skin. **Ed Hardy** was impressed by the work that these men were doing, and bought Good Time Charlie's Tattooland after Cartright quit tattooing. Later, Rudy and Negrete moved into a different shop together, still with Hardy's support. Hardy liked the style so much that he opened Tattoo City in San Francisco's (predominantly Latino) Mission District in 1975 in order to focus on just this kind of work. Rudy, who now runs the Tattooland chain, has since become world famous for his portraits, and is one of a number of "tattooists' tattooists," that is, tattooists who are sought out for work by other tattooists.

Today, because of the influence of Chicano tattooing, it is rare for a tattooist to use heavy needles for outlines, unless he or she is specifically trying to create an old-fashioned, traditional look (or a tribal tattoo). Chicano-style tattooing, and its fine-lined technique, now serves as the basis for many newer trends in mainstream U.S. tattooing. Indeed, it has made possible many of these newer styles of tattoo like circuitry-based tattoos. The only places where fine-lined tattooing is still not popular is in street shops that cater to military clientele. Most sailors and soldiers do not want this sort of work, and many old-time tattooists refuse to do it because they do not feel that it holds up over time.

Not only have the technical elements of Chicano tattooing been embraced by the middle class, but the imagery now has as well. The Virgin of Guadeloupe and the head of Christ have become favored motifs among the young middle class, and even the *loca* has been adopted by middle-class white patrons and is translated onto their chests, necks, and stomachs in a simulation of Chicano street life.

See also: Biker Tattooing, Gang Members; Hardy, Don Ed

Further Readings: Govenar, Alan. "The Variable Context of Chicano Tattooing." In Arnold Rubin, ed., *Marks of Civilization: Artistic Transformations of the Human Body*. Los Angeles: Museum of Cultural History, UCLA, 1988.

CHINA

The Chinese have for centuries used multiple body modification and adornment techniques, including **acupuncture**, **tattooing**, **foot binding**, and **ear piercing** and **ear stretching**. The Chinese also castrated defeated enemy soldiers, and Imperial Chinese royalty employed men who had their genitals removed.

Foot binding is the modification most associated with China. Foot binding—in which a young girl's feet were bound in tight bandages in order to deform them, keeping them small—was practiced in China for centuries, only ending in the twentieth century. Having bound feet was a sign of status for Chinese women as it implied that they could not work (given the pain of even standing on bound feet). Not only was it popular among elite women but lower class women as well, as a sign of status and beauty.

The medical practice of acupuncture is thought to have originated in China almost five thousand years ago. Acupuncture is the practice of inserting very fine needles into the body at points called acupuncture points, or acupoints, in order to influence physiological or emotional health of the body by manipulating the Qi, or the body's energy force. While not a body adornment, acupuncture is linked to a number of other body modification practices such as **piercing**.

Both Chinese women and men wore earrings and it was very common to stretch the earlobes, as can be seen by illustrations of ancient emperors as well as the large number of illustrations and statues of the Buddha with stretched ears. The length of the stretched ears may have been associated with rank, and perhaps as well with health and longevity.

Tattooing has also been practiced in China, particularly among ethnic minorities such as the Drung and the Dai. Drung girls were tattooed with geometric designs on the face at puberty as a sign of maturity. Women, who did the tattooing, would draw the design onto the cheeks, around the mouth, on the chin, and between the eyes, with bamboo dipped into ink made of ash and water. The tattooing implement was made up of thorns or other sharp implements attached to an instrument; like the Polynesian method, the implement would then be hammered into the skin with another wooden tool. More soot would be rubbed into the wounds in order to create the permanent image. Dai men and women were also tattooed, men on the body and women on the hand, face, or arms, and also as a sign of maturity, protection against evil spirits, and a sign of strength in men and beauty in women. Tigers, dragons, and flowers are popular designs.

Imperial Chinese also used tattooing, along with banishment, as a mode of punishment for criminals. (The punishment was known as *ci pei* or tattoo/exile.) It was China's association with tattooing and criminality that led to their influence on the Japanese practice of tattooing being associated with the underclasses, criminals, along with banishment. The tattoo on the face permanently marks the person as a criminal.

Chinese characters and designs have been popular as Western tattoos for at least two centuries, when sailors began picking up Chinese tattoos when visiting those ports of call. Today, Asian tattoos in general are associated with the exotic for many Americans, making them very popular designs. Unfortunately for the wearers, many tattoos made up of Chinese characters have no real meaning in Chinese, or else the meaning is not what was intended in the original design.

See also: Ear Stretching; Foot Binding

Further Reading: Hong, Fan. *Foot Binding, Feminism and Freedom: The Liberation of Women's Bodies in Modern China*. London: Frank Cass & Co., 1997; Ko, Dorothy. *Cinderella's Sisters: A Revisionist History of Foot binding*. Los Angeles: University of California Press, 2005; Peers, C.J., and Michael Perry (illustrator). *Imperial Chinese Armies: 200 BC–589 AD* (*Men-At-Arms Series, 284*). Oxford: Osprey Publishing, 1995.

CHRISTIANITY

Christianity is associated with tattooing through the biblical prohibition against tattooing, as well as through the practice of Christian tattooing which began in **Roman** times and is still commonly practiced in Christian nations today.

Tattooing, or "marking," or "gashing" the flesh, is explicitly prohibited in the Old Testament, which is both the first book of the Christian **Bible** as well as the Jewish Torah. However, most Christians do not follow any of the prohibitions enumerated in the Book of Leviticus, so Christians do not see tattooing as prohibited.

In fact, Christian tattoos are one of the earliest forms of tattoos used in the West. In Roman times, criminals were tattooed on the forehead with a word or symbol indicating their crime, and because Christianity was prohibited throughout much of the Roman Empire, Christians were arrested, tattooed, and often sent to work in the gold, silver, and lead mines.

Other Christians, particularly after the rise of Christianity in the Roman Empire, gave themselves voluntary tattoos, which were modeled after the wounds of Christ (or **stigmata**, which also was the Roman word for tattoo) as a sign of their faith, and as a mark of group membership into the Christian religion. Slaves were also tattooed by the Romans, and because many Christians saw themselves as slaves of God, wearing a tattoo marking one's slave status would also be a sign of extreme piety.

Paul's statement in Galatians 6:17, "I carry the marks of Jesus tattooed (stigmata) on my body," was probably also used as a justification for this practice. While this was a metaphorical usage as Paul was probably not tattooed (and there is no proof that he was encouraging tattooing among the faithful), he is invoking the practice of punitive tattooing, as well as the suffering of Christ. Given that many Christians were tattooed and punished simply for being Christian, it makes sense that the stigma of tattoos would transform into a badge of honor for Christians, and as a sign of group membership.

I got this tattoo of a cross because when I got confirmed in the Catholic Church I wanted to represent it.

ANONYMOUS

When Constantine became Emperor of Rome and embraced Christianity in the fourth century, he banned the practice of tattooing criminals on the face, because he believed that the human face was a representation of the image of God and should not be disfigured or defiled. He did allow criminals to continue to be tattooed on the legs, however, although Christians were no longer punitively tattooed. The Council of Northumberland in 787 noted that Christian tattoos, unlike "pagan" tattoos, were worthy of praise.

Later, as the Roman influence spread throughout Europe and European pilgrims began journeying to the Holy Land, many received tattoos as both a souvenir and as a sign of faith. Images for these tattoos include the Jerusalem cross, the crown of Jesus, the word "Jerusalem," the date of one's pilgrimage, and sometimes Jesus's name. The tattoos themselves, which were and still are composed of individual designs placed on a small part of the body, probably influenced the badge-style of tattoos used by Europeans and Americans through the modern period. Jerusalem tattoos were made with sharp needles bound together with string, piercing the skin, with black powder rubbed in. Some tattooists providing souvenir tattoos to Christian pilgrims charged a small fee; others provided it for free as a sign of devotion. Many Holy Land tattooists were Coptic Christians, who passed down their tattoo designs over the centuries, and used wood blocks as templates for the designs. The most common Coptic tattoo for pilgrims was a small cross on the inside of the wrist. Medieval crusaders often were also tattooed with a cross on their arms to ensure a Christian burial. Pilgrims during the Middle Ages also received souvenir tattoos when visiting other holy sites such as Loreta in Italy or Santiago de Compostela in Spain.

Since Christianity arrived in **Egypt** in the form of Coptic Christianity in the first century, Coptic Christians in Egypt, **Ethiopia,** and Eritrea have gotten Coptic tattoos to demonstrate their faith, such as the cross on the forehead. Christians in the Balkans and other areas of the Christian world also use tattooing as a sign of faith, and sometimes to protect the wearer from evil.

Since Roman times, Christianity has served as a rich source of imagery for religious tattoos, a practice that continues today. Common Christian tattoo images include crucifixes (including the ancient Jerusalem cross as well as Celtic crosses and other designs), figures of the Virgin Mary (the Virgin of Guadelupe is an especially popular image among **Chicanos**), the Sacred Heart, images of Jesus himself, often on the cross, and representations of the Rock of Ages and other images taken from non-biblical sources.

The Rock of Ages design stems from a 1775 hymn which

The Rock of Ages is a classic Christian tattoo image. Engraving by Currier and Ives, 1868. Courtesy of Library of Congress Prints and Photographs Division, Washington, DC, No. LC-USZ62-4668.

refers to Isaiah 26:4 "For in the Lord Jehovah is the Rock of Ages." Rock of Ages tattoos, like artwork based on the design, show a large stone crucifix rising out of a stormy sea, with a woman desperately clinging to its surface; during the early decades of the twentieth century it was a common American tattoo.

See also: Bible; Criminality; Ethiopia; Stigmata

Further Readings: Carswell, John. *Coptic Tattoo Designs*. Beirut: American University of Beirut Press, 1957; Hardy, Don Ed. *Rocks of Ages*. Honolulu, HI: Hardy Marks Publications,

1992; Jones, C. P. "Stigma and Tattoo." In Jane Caplan, ed., *Written on the Body: The Tattoo in European and American History*. Princeton, NJ: Princeton University Press, 2000.

CIRCUMCISION

Circumcision refers to the surgical removal of the foreskin of the penis. It is practiced primarily as a **rite of passage** for adolescent males in traditional societies all over the world, but is also performed for health and social reasons in the West, and as a religious ritual for Jewish infants. Circumcision has been practiced for thousands of years around most of the world.

In the ancient Middle East, circumcision was practiced by the Hebrews, Egyptians, Edomites, Ammonites, Moabites, Ethiopians, Phoenicians, and Syrians. Egyptian boys, for example, were circumcised between the ages of 6 and 12, and artwork found in Egyptian tombs shows circumcised boys and men. The Greeks, however, did not circumcise and as the Greek Empire spread, circumcision became less popular in much of the ancient world.

Circumcision is commonly practiced today throughout Africa and **Australia** to mark tribal membership, and as part of initiation rituals into manhood. Circumcision was also commonly practiced in Melanesia and Polynesia.

For instance, among the Okiek of Kenya, boys (as well as girls) undergo a circumcision ritual between the ages of 14 and 16, after which they are excluded from the world of adults and the opposite sex for a number of weeks. Following Arthur Van Gennep's three-part description of a rite of passage, the Okiek are first separated from the tribe, kept in isolation with members of their sex and age cohort (during which time they wear white body paint and are given secret tribal knowledge), and are reintroduced to society as adult men. Because circumcision in situations like this is done without anesthesia, it is painful, which is one of the important aspects of a male initiation ceremony—to test or challenge the boys to ensure that they are strong enough to attain adulthood.

The Gisu of Uganda also practice circumcision in order to make boys into men. One part of the ritual demands that the boy's younger sister act as his symbolic wife throughout the ritual, until she is married and her brideprice is used to purchase the brother his own wife.

Bantu boys are also separated from society along with other boys in their age-group, in preparation for their circumcision ritual. Shaved, stripped, ritually bathed, and covered in white powder, boys are physically, ceremonially, and emotionally stripped of their previous identities as boys and undergo a liminal state in which they are neither boy nor man. As with most other groups that practice circumcision, the initiate is expected to demonstrate bravery during the procedure, and must also continue to live in isolation during recovery, while they fast, observe a number of taboos, and are instructed in the knowledge of adult males. Upon reintroduction, the young men once again get to rejoin the world of women, and feast to celebrate their adulthood.

Some groups practice circumcision on individual boys at a time; others do the ceremony once a year, and still others, like the Maasai, wait many years until there are enough boys in the right age-group to undergo the ritual together. (The Maasai also do not remove the foreskin entirely, but instead remove some and leave the rest as a flap.) And in some African societies, boys are now circumcised at birth in a hospital, as in the West.

Among Australian Aboriginals, circumcision is also used to mark male adulthood. For Australians, as with Africans, both **pain** and physical transformation are critical aspects of the ritual, and as with African examples, boys are expected to demonstrate strength and courage and not flinch under the pain. Some Australian groups who practice circumcision also use other practices to transform boys into men, including tooth evulsion (in which a boy's front tooth is knocked out with a rock), **scarification**, and, a year or two after the circumcision, **subincision**, in which the penis itself is split.

As a rite of passage, Australian circumcision marks the beginning of a boy's introduction to adult male ceremonial life. During the boys' separation from society, they witness secret religious ceremonies and are given information about the origins of the universe; because they are separated from their mothers, their relationship with other boys and men is solidified as well, a relationship that may also involve ritual homosexuality, and which also bonds a boy to the men of the family to whom he will ultimately be married.

In both Africa and Australia circumcision makes a boy into a man, through physically transforming his body and not coincidentally, shedding blood which is often seen as symbolically female and polluting. The rest of the ceremony, including the isolation from community (especially women), the bonding with other men, and the transmission of secret knowledge, all play an important role alongside of the circumcision in making a boy into a man. And while many African societies do also perform a similar operation on women, known in some circles as female circumcision and in others as **female genital mutilation** or **clitoridectomy**, these practices are very different in terms of the physical transformation of the body and the meanings associated with it.

While circumcision is painful, the practice does not harm or impede the man's sexual function, and, in fact, is seen as an improvement on sexual function to many. It shows as well his strength and courage, both important attributes of masculinity. Female circumcision, on the other hand, is used to control female sexuality, to ensure that women do not engage in premarital or extramarital sex, all of which make the girl more marriageable and ensure that she does not bring shame onto her family. More to the point, female circumcision as it is most commonly practiced does not just remove the clitoral hood (which would be analogous to male circumcision) but removes the clitoris itself, removing the source of female sexual pleasure.

Circumcision is practiced very differently in the Semitic world, among Muslims, Jews, and some Christians, all of whom circumcise in infancy, rather than as a rite of puberty.

For Jews, circumcision is biblically ordained. In Genesis 17:10-14, God told Abraham to circumcise himself, his family, and his slaves as a contract, in the flesh, with God; those who were uncircumsed were to be excluded from the community of the faithful. Apart from the slaves of Jews, circumcision as it is laid out in the Bible was never meant for people outside the Jewish faith. Circumcision, then, was one way in which the ancient Hebrews distinguished themselves from unbelievers. (Many Jews under Greek and Roman rule were persecuted for being circumcised, and for that reason tried to hide their circumcision or developed more subtle forms of circumcision like blistering, rather than removing, the foreskin in order to appear physically similar to the surrounding peoples.)

Christians, who do not observe a great many of the prohibitions (including **tattooing**) and commandments in the Bible, are said to be freed from the Law of Moses, which explains why they do not practice circumcision. Formalized in the first Church Council in Jerusalem, St. Paul warned Christians not to adopt the practice. For early Christians, circumcision was seen as a sign of slavery and was thus rejected, although other Christians chose to be tattooed, which was also a sign of slavery at that time.

Coptic Christians, Ethiopian Orthodox, and Eritrean Orthodox churches on the other hand, do observe the ordainment, and circumcise their sons anywhere from the first week of life to the first few years.

Circumcision remains a rite of passage within **Judaism**, although it marks Jews' acceptance of the contract with God rather than their transformation into adulthood, and continues to be used to set Jews apart from non-Jews, (and, according to some, to demonstrate the superiority of Jewish males over Jewish females). Jewish boys are generally circumcised on the eighth day after their birth by a professional circumciser known as a *mohel*. Traditionally, during the circumcision, which is known as a *Brit milah* or *bris*, the boy's blood must be sucked from the wound either by mouth or, today, through a suction pump. Converts to Judaism must typically also undergo circumcision, although the Reform tradition no longer demands this.

Muslims also circumcise their sons, typically on the seventh day after birth, but often within the first few years of life or even up to adolescence. While not mandated in the Quran, it is seen as a requirement for marriage and for Muslim converts. Some Muslim cultures such as in Turkey, the Balkans, Central and South Asia, and rural Egypt follow a practice that merges Semitic circumcision with tribal practices, in that their boys are circumcised during or before adolescence as part of a rite of passage, followed by a major celebration. In other Muslim societies, however, especially in urban contexts, Muslims are circumcised in the hospital at birth with no celebration or ritual at all, as in the United States.

Today, infant circumcision is widely practiced in the United States among Jews and non-Jews, although non-Jews have only been circumcised in great numbers in this country since the turn of the twentieth century. Today anywhere from 55 to 75 percent of infants in the United States undergo the operation, but the rest of the Western world practices circumcision in far fewer numbers. Canada, Australia, New Zealand, and Great Britain also practice routine circumcision for infants, as well as countries in which the United States has had a strong cultural presence, such as South Korea. Circumcision is the most widely performed surgical practice in the United States.

Circumcision in the United States, when performed on non-Jews, differs from circumcision rituals surveyed around the world. In the United States, circumcision emerged in the nineteenth century as a solution to the problem of male adolescent masturbation; it was thought that by removing what was thought to be the most sensitive part of the male sexual anatomy, boys would stop touching themselves. Later, circumcision was linked to hygiene and health care, and was seen as a form of preventative medicine; by removing the foreskin doctors felt that any dangerous secretions which would normally develop would be eliminated, keeping the body cleaner and safer. As hospital births became more common in the twentieth century, circumcision became more routine, especially among the middle- and upper classes, and the lack of circumcision became associated with lower class status. Today, circumcision is routine for many American parents, both because it is seen as normative and because a circumcised penis is seen as aesthetically more pleasing.

Today, circumcision is widely debated among medical groups, children's advocacy groups, and parents. For instance, the major medical organizations in every English-speaking country except the United States do not advocate routine infant circumcision. American groups like the American Academy of Pediatrics, on the other hand, while not necessarily recommending the practice for all parents, do see circumcision as a means to reduce urinary tract infection. In addition, in recent years circumcision in Africa is thought to reduce the transmission of AIDS, adding to its potential health benefits.

On the other hand, the genital integrity movement is a movement that opposed infant circumcision on the grounds that it is a human rights violation, given the lack of consent on the part of the patients. Some circumcised adults report that they feel an emotional impact from the loss of their foreskin and some men also feel that their sexual response has been impacted. Until recently, anesthesia was not common for infants, and many feel that the pain is not justifiable for what is essentially an aesthetic procedure.

See also: Australia; Bible; Christianity; Clitoridectomy; Health Issues; Judaism

Further Reading: Cohen, Shaye J. D. "Why Aren't Jewish Women Circumcised?" *Gender & History* 9(3) (1997): 560–578; Meggitt, M. J. *Desert People: A Study of the Walbiri Aborigines of Central Australia*. Sydney: Angus and Robertson, 1986; Turner, Victor. "Three Symbols of Passage in Ndembu Circumcision Ritual: An Interpretation." In Max Gluckman, ed., *Essays on the Ritual of Social Relations*. New York: The Humanities Press, 1962; Wallerstein, Edward. *Circumcision: An American Health Fallacy*. New York: Springer Publishing Company, 1980.

CIRCUS

While circuses as we know them today are an American invention, they have their roots in two different historical phenomena: **Roman** public exhibitions and Medieval European traveling shows.

Ancient Romans enjoyed attending a variety of public games and festivals, including horse and chariot races, gladiator competitions, and other human–animal events held in open-air arenas; the first such entertainment venue in Rome was the Circus Maximus, but these attractions, while popular, did not migrate with Roman culture to Europe. Instead, European elites entertained themselves with hunting, feasts, music, poetry, and athletic competitions. Commoners entertained themselves with bear-baiting (in which a pack of dogs attacks an imported bear), cockfighting, as well as nonanimal sports, plays, fortune-telling, magic acts, and traveling minstrel shows of all kinds. At the same time, commoners enjoyed the traveling shows that came to their towns, bringing with them exotic animals, the physically disabled, the mentally disabled, and beginning around the eighteenth century, native peoples. Traveling acts such as these were popular for centuries in Europe and in the end of the eighteenth century, moved to America in the form of "dime museums," while at the same time England developed early versions of stationary circuses that combined equestrian activities with other entertainment in spaces such as the London Hippodrome.

American dime museums were started by men who called themselves scientists and ostensibly viewed these venues as education, or more properly, education through entertainment. In 1840, **P. T. Barnum** became the proprietor of the American Museum, bringing wild animal acts to prominence. These early dime museums exhibited animals alongside people with disabilities, tattooed people, native people, and "gaffes," or manufactured fakes. Since people had never before seen any of these curiosities, the managers and showmen were able to concoct bizarre explanations for their origins, stories that were morally and socially uplifting, as well as educational. These exhibits told tales of cannibalism, savagery, and the man/"beast" connection seen in both native people and the disabled. At the end of the nineteenth century, the dime museum began to decline, but the acts themselves starting in about 1840 became the sideshow in the newly developing American circuses.

In the early days, American circuses were relatively small affairs, primarily based upon equestrian shows. The first true circus in the United States was held in 1793 in Philadelphia, but it wasn't until 1825 that the big top tent arrived, and in the 1880s circuses began traveling by railcar. Starting in the 1920s circuses added more acts, growing into the large tent shows that we know today, performing for thousands of visitors at each show.

P. T. Barnum, founder of the first American circus, specialized originally in the display of human oddities or **freaks**, and later moved to animal acts. His first attraction was a blind, mostly paralyzed slave he purchased for $1,000 in 1835; he claimed that she was 161 years old and served as George Washington's maid, and he earned $750 per week through showing her off. Later, after opening what would become Ringling Brothers and Barnum & Bailey Circus, his first major animal act was Jumbo, an african elephant, whom he purchased from the London Zoo in 1882 for $10,000.

For over seventy years every major circus employed several **tattooed attractions**, who worked in sideshows, doing other circus acts like juggling, or serving as tattooists. Many tattooists in the early twentieth century traveled with the circus during the season (spring and summer) and worked at home, usually in the South, in the winter.

See also: Freak Shows; Freaks; Tattooed Attractions

Further Reading: Bogdan, Robert. *Freak Show*. Chicago: University of Chicago Press, 1988; DeMello, Margo. *Bodies of Inscription: A Cultural History of the Modern Tattoo Community*. Durham, NC: Duke University Press, 2000; St. Clair, Leonard, and Alan Govenar. *Stoney Knows How: Life as a Tattoo Artist*. Lexington: University of Kentucky Press, 1981.

CLASS AND STATUS

Body adornments and modifications have always signified class position in strati-fied societies, and in nonstratified societies, they have often signified rank or status as well. In that sense, **tattooing, scarification**, and **branding**, as well as **cosmetics, hairstyles**, and **jewelry** are all literal marks of social position.

In hunter-gatherer, pastoral, and horticultural societies which lack a system of stratification, men and women are differentiated from each other, and in pastoral and horticultural societies, individuals are also differentiated on the basis of status and rank. We see these differences play out on the bodies in many societies. For instance, the Nyangatom wear large bead necklaces to indicate status and wealth, and only high status Tlingit girls were able to wear **labrets**. **Lip plates** often in-dicate status as the size of the lip plate increases with the wealth of the woman. Some societies restricted tattoos only to the elites, such as among the **Maori** at one time, while in other cases, the type of tattoo worn represented status or rank, as among the Marquesans and the Hawaiians. In societies in which body fat or even **obesity** is a sign of status, such as among the Ibo, wealthy girls are fattened prior to marriage, and thin girls have less value.

In stratified societies, the differences are greater. Wealthy men in **China** wore hat buttons and women wore gold and gems on their foreheads, both of which demonstrated social rank. In some cultures, such as ancient Rome and throughout pre-Colombian **MesoAmerica**, only the elites were allowed to wear certain items of jewelry, such as the large ear spools worn by the Mayans and Incans. Shaped heads also indicated high rank among the Mayans, and even skin color demon-strates rank, with light skin usually being associated with the wealthy and dark skin (until the mid-twentieth century) with the poor. Makeup and the use of wigs and hair products too can be seen as a way in which elite men and women dif-ferentiate themselves from their poorer counterparts by disguising imperfections, highlighting features considered beautiful, and in general making themselves de-sirable to those at the top of the social system. **Cosmetic surgery** perhaps rep-resents the apex of this system by which only those with wealth can afford to purchase **beauty**.

Bodies, then, display in their shape and on their skin the social structure to which they belong. How they are used is also an indicator of class and status. Through the use of tattooing, **torture**, confinement, and branding, the state has been able to control poor, marginal, or criminal bodies—slaves and convict bod-ies in particular. Since the ancient Persians, criminals, slaves, and other undesir-ables have been permanently marked by the state to demonstrate their low status. As a form of identification, a corporal punishment, and a signification of the crime, the criminal tattoo and brand has been for thousands of years one of the most significant ways that class status is inscribed on the body.

But because the body is not simply the target of power, but the source of power as well, bodies can resist control as well, thus the development of a whole host of bodily practices specifically used by the lower classes to resist state control. Power, then, operates differently on different bodies.

For example, criminals who have been punitively tattooed have often creatively remarked or reinscribed their bodies to either erase the stigmatic signs of their punishment, or have, as in the case of tattooing in prison, taken back the inscriptions and reinvested them with new meaning, creating a badge of honor and affiliation.

Tattooing in the West since the time of the Greeks has been associated with state control over criminal and slave bodies. Thanks to that legacy, tattooing throughout much of European and later American history was associated with the underclasses, even as sailors and soldiers also began to get tattooed, and tattooed attractions (both third world and European) began to be displayed at fairs and carnivals. The medical and criminological literature looking at tattoos in Europe in the nineteenth century, for instance, largely associated tattoos with criminals, soldiers, and sailors: all members of the underclasses.

On the other hand, in the late nineteenth century, there existed for a time a tattoo fad in England where upper-class men and women began receiving tattoos. While the fad was shortlived, it did contribute to a refinement of the art of tattooing during that time, especially among English but also American tattooists, which was later taken up in the late twentieth century when middle-class, fine art trained artists began to practice tattooing, bringing with them a whole new middle-class clientele. The tattooing fad of the 1880s also demonstrated that tattooing, no matter who uses it, can always be used as a marker of class difference. Upper-class tattoos were received in a comfortable, hygienic studio by tattooists using the newest technology—the tattoo machine—which allowed them to create finely detailed, sophisticated artwork, while at the same time, the lower classes were still receiving hand-pricked tattoos.

In the twentieth century in the United States, new underclass groups began to use tattooing to mark themselves. Gang members, bikers, and **Chicanos** all adopted the tattoo as a mark of affiliation for themselves, and all three populations developed tattoo styles and techniques that were both distinctive to those groups, and which also borrowed heavily from (and influenced) American prison tattoo styles.

See also: Bakhtin, Mikhail; Bourdieu, Pierre; Foucault, Michel

Further Reading: Bakhtin, Mikhail. *Rabelais and His World*. Bloomington: Indiana University Press, 1984; Bourdieu, Pierre. *Distinction: A Social Critique of the Judgement of Taste*. London: Routledge, 1984; Bradley, James. "Body Commodification? Class and Tattoos in Victorian Britain." In Jane Caplan, ed., *Written on the Body: The Tattoo in European and American History*. Princeton: Princeton University Press, 2000; Clark, Katerina, and Michael Holquist. *Mikhail Bakhtin*. Cambridge: Harvard University Press, 1984; DeMello, Margo. *Bodies of Inscription: A Cultural History of the Modern Tattoo Community*. Durham, NC: Duke University Press, 2000.

CLITORAL PIERCING

Generally, the term clitoral piercing refers to a **piercing** on the hood of the clitoris, rather than the clitoris per se. Clitoral hood piercings are a relatively common piercing in the body modification community, and are both used to adorn the female genitals and to provide extra stimulation, both during sex and at other times as well.

Choices for clitoral hood piercings include the vertical hood piercing, which is the most common, in which the piercing is placed vertically above the clitoris. The piercing itself goes through the thin bit of clitoral hood tissue, and the jewelry, usually a barbell or curved barbell, will stimulate the clitoris—sometimes so much that some women report irritation.

The horizontal hood piercing is done more for aesthetic reasons than sexual reasons as the jewelry does not have direct contact with the clitoris, since the piercing is done on top of the hood, rather than through it. Jewelry is also a barbell, ring, or circular barbell.

The triangle piercing is performed at the base of the clitoral hood, leaving the jewelry, usually a captive bead ring, situated immediately behind the nerve endings of the clitoris, increasing sensation. The triangle piercing can also be combined with the vertical piercing in which the piercing, usually a flexible or curved barbell, enters the skin under the clitoris and exits through the clitoral hood.

If a woman has a large enough clitoris, some do choose to get the clitoris itself pierced, although this is rare. Because of the danger of harming the nerve endings, many piercers will not perform the piercing. Clitoral piercings, like other genital piercings, are used to enhance the appearance of the genitals as well as to enhance sexual pleasure. The jewelry used is usually a very small barbell or captive bead ring.

See also: Genital Piercing

Further Reading: Vale, V., and Andrea Juno. *Modern Primitives*. San Francisco, CA: Re/Search Publications, 1989.

CLITORIDECTOMY

Clitoridectomy refers to the partial or full removal of the clitoris. While it sometimes goes by the name of female **circumcision**, this is a misnomer, and technically refers to the practice of removing the clitoral hood. Many opponents of the practice of clitoridectomies refer to it as female genital mutilation (FGM).

While clitoridectomies were performed by doctors during the late nineteenth and early twentieth centuries to control masturbation and other signs of "excessive" sexuality in women, the practice is most associated with Arab, Muslim, and North African countries.

Today, clitoridectomies and **infibulation**, in which the clitoris and labia minora are removed and the labia majora is sewn together, are commonly performed on young girls around the world. West Africa, North Africa, East Africa, and the Arab Peninsula are the areas in which it is most commonly practiced, although it is also found in any country with large immigrant populations from these areas, such as

France or the United States. Among the Muslim populations in Somalia, **Egypt, Sudan, Ethiopia,** and Mali, as many as 95 percent of all women are reported to have undergone the procedure, and in Saudi Arabia, Jordan, and Iraq, it is also common. It is more commonly practiced in Sunni Muslim cultures than in Shia communities; Shia Muslims often remove instead a piece of the clitoral hood.

In total, the World Health Organization estimates that 100 million women have undergone genital mutilation procedures while Amnesty International estimates that 130 million women have been operated on, over 2 million each year.

Girls are typically operated on during their early childhoods, and always prior to the onset of puberty. By removing the clitoris, the mothers and grandmothers who typically perform the surgeries ensure that their daughters can experience no sexual pleasure; this is done to ensure that they will be virgins upon marriage and will remain faithful to their husbands after marriage. A girl who has had her clitoris removed is considered to be a good candidate for marriage, whereas one who has not is often considered unmarriageable, or at the very least, she will not fetch a very high brideprice.

In many Arab and Muslim cultures, women are said to be sexually dangerous, and female genital mutilation is a way to control their sexuality. Because a woman's behavior can bring shame or honor on her family and her husband's family, by ensuring that she does not stray there is no danger of her shaming her family. In addition, a woman who does not stray in marriage will only bear children who are legitimate heirs to her husband's lineage, which is also critical in the patrilineal societies in which clitoridectomy is practiced. Finally, the clitoris is seen as a masculine organ in some cultures so a girl with a clitoris is seen as masculine, not to mention dirty.

In Africa, the practice is often associated with traditional initiation rites, and sometimes occurs at the same time that boys' circumcision rituals do, and in some non-Muslim cultures, such as among the Masai, it is not intended to control female sexuality, but simply to mark a girl as a woman, although the result is the same.

The surgery itself is performed typically outside of a hospital and by women who are not medical practitioners. Tools include scissors, knives, or pieces of glass, and sterilization is not practiced, nor is anesthesia used. Because of the conditions, the practice, which is quite painful, commonly results in infections, excessive bleeding, scarring, and sometimes death, and long-term problems include urinary and reproductive difficulties, including, ironically, sterility. The most common result, however, is the intended one, which is the elimination of a woman's main organ of sexual pleasure, and thus is opposed by feminists as a human rights violation.

While Western and non-Western feminists as well as health and human rights organizations are opposed to female genital mutilation, women continue to perform the procedure on their daughters and granddaughters. For them, there are a great many benefits. When women's only opportunity in life, for example, is tied to getting married, then a procedure that ensures marriageability and increases the odds of finding a higher status husband will certainly be a powerful force. Also in countries where adultery for a woman is punishable by death, or at the very least where a woman who strays from her marriage is ostracized forever, then ensuring chastity by any means is certainly an important concern. A promiscuous girl in these cultures is often a girl who is risking her life.

In African countries without as great a focus on a girl's sexuality, clitoridectomies are performed as part of a **rite of passage** that makes a girl a woman, raising her status and demonstrating her maturity, submissiveness, and ability to withstand **pain** (which will be needed in childbirth). It is also often seen as an important community ritual in which the girl receives moral instruction from her elders and is bonded to the generations before her who have undergone the procedure.

Advocates also note that girls who undergo the procedure will have a stronger bond with their husbands since there will be no risk of her cheating on him, that he will treat her better knowing that she will not stray, and that she will love him even more because her love will not be based on sexual passion.

Female genital mutilation is prohibited throughout the West, and some African countries prohibit it as well, such as the Central African Republic, the Ivory Coast, Ghana, Guinea, Senegal, Tanzania, and many countries, such as Indonesia and Egypt, have been attempting to eradicate it through education. Others are trying to ensure that the procedure is only done in a hospital. Thanks to outreach work by health officials and to the United Nations' condemnation of the practice, many countries have seen a drop in the practice.

In 2006, the United States saw its first criminal case against female genital mutilation go to court, when an Ethiopian immigrant was charged and convicted with cutting off his 5-year-old daughter's clitoris with a pair of scissors. There are well over one hundred thousand girls living in the United States whose parents come from countries that practice female genital mutilation, so this will no doubt not be the last case.

Some African and Arab feminists who oppose female genital mutilation also oppose Western attempts to abolish it, and instead are working to educate women and to create alternative initiation rituals for girls. Women's health organizations in Kenya, for example, have come up with a ritual called *Ntanira Na Mugambo*, which means circumcision by words, as a replacement for traditional rituals. Another issue which would need to be addressed is to change the economic circumstances that only allow a woman economic and social mobility through marriage.

In the West, a small number of modern body modification practitioners choose to have their clitorises removed in order to negate their sexuality. Some women elect to have their clitorises removed, and others remove the clitoral hood and often the labia as well, resulting in just a vaginal and urethral opening.

See also: Circumcision; Infibulation

Further Reading: Adams, K. E. "What's 'Normal': Female Genital Mutilation, Psychology, and Body Image." *Journal of the American Medical Women's Association* 59 (2004): 168–170; Althaus, Frances A. "Female Circumcision: Rite of Passage or Violation of Rights?"

International Family Planning Perspectives 23(3) (1997): 130–133; Salecl, Renata. "Cut in the Body: From Clitoridectomy to Body Art." In S. Ahmed and J. Stacey, eds., *Thinking through the Skin*. New York: Routledge, 2001.

COLLINS, SAILOR JERRY

Sailor Jerry Collins (1911–1973) was born Norman Keith Collins and started **tattooing** as a teenager, originally using the hand-pricking method. In the late 1920s, Collins met Chicago tattooist Tatts Thomas who taught him how to use a tattoo machine. Under the tutelage of Thomas, Collins practiced on drunks brought in from Skid Row. He made his home in **Hawaii** in the 1930s, where he opened his first tattoo parlor, and also worked as a dockworker.

Collins developed an early interest in Asian imagery during his travels through the Far East (he served as a merchant marine in World War II and often tattooed at his ports of call), and through his peacetime exposure to other sailors' tattoos, and incorporated dragons and other designs into his flash. He also had a strong interest in improving tattooing as an art form, and felt that most U.S. tattooists were greedy, talentless copycats. Early on he sought out and began a correspondence with tattooists like Paul Rogers and Brooklyn Joe Lieber who shared his interest in improving the art. At the same time, he spoke out against those who he saw as hurting the field through their shady business practices and lack of talent.

But it was not until 1960, when he opened his final tattoo shop in Honolulu's Chinatown that his interest in the "Oriental style" of tattooing really blossomed. He developed a trade relationship with Japanese tattooist Horihide, and Hong Kong tattooist Pinky Yun, whereby he would exchange American machines and needles for designs and advice. He was especially impressed by the Japanese use of colors, shading, and their focus on the entire body as a canvas for sophisticated artistic expression. Ironically, while Collins developed a close business friendship with tattooists Horihide, Horiyoshi II, and Horisada, he also never forgave the Japanese for bombing Pearl Harbor and for what he saw as their economic takeover of Hawaii. In fact, by his own admission, Collins wanted to "beat them at their own game": to create an American style that was based on what he called the "Jap style of tattoo," yet one that reflected imagery from the United States.

What he did was borrow the Japanese aesthetic style—wind bars, finger waves, full-body tattoos—to represent the history and pop culture of Americana: General Custer at Little Big Horn, the Alamo, the Spirit of '76, Rock of Ages, big busted mermaids, and other images inspired by the North American imagination. This was extremely innovative, and reflected Collins' belief that what was exceptional about Japanese tattooing was not the central image, but the background. While other old-time tattooists had been doing large-scale pieces since at least the 1940s, Jerry was the first to achieve the unified look of the Japanese tattoo in the West, through the use of the wind and water in the background.

While most tattooists in the United States did not show an interest in Jerry's work, resisting the Oriental influence, a few did. Cliff Raven and **Ed Hardy**, who would both be critical in the transformations of North American tattooing in the 1970s and 1980s, noticed his work in the late 1960s through tattooist Don Nolan, and all three developed important relationships with Collins aimed at learning more about the Japanese style of tattoo and incorporating it into their own work.

See also: Contemporary Tattooing; Japan

Further Readings: Hardy, D. E. *Sailor Jerry Collins: American Tattoo Master*. Honolulu, HI: Hardy Marks Publications, 1994; Rubin, Arnold. "Tattoo Renaissance." In Arnold Rubin, ed., *Marks of Civilization: Artistic Transformations of the Human Body*. Los Angeles: Museum of Cultural History, UCLA, 1988.

CONTEMPORARY TATTOOING

Contemporary **tattooing** in the West can be traced to the period beginning in the 1970s when members of the counterculture began to wear tattoos as a sign of resistance to straight, white, middle-class values, new tattoo artists with different types of training emerged, and new tattoo images began to appear which appealed to this younger, hipper audience.

Beginning in the 1970s, American tattooists began to change, as young men and women with fine art backgrounds began to enter the profession alongside the older, traditionally trained tattooists. These newer tattooists took their artistic inspiration from "exotic" cultures (initially **Japan,** later **Borneo, Samoa,** and Native America) rather than from traditional North American or European designs, and in the process, began to appeal to a middle-class audience. By demonstrating that tattooing, long stigmatized in the West, can be traced to cultural traditions in which tattooing is used in a positive way, and in which tattooing is embedded within important social institutions, modern tattooists and promoters of tattooing have been attempting to reintegrate tattooing into modern Western society.

How tattooists enter the profession has also changed a great deal. While it once was typical for new tattooists to apprentice with an experienced tattooist, learning the trade the slow way, many young tattooists today order a machine and some basic equipment from a tattoo supplier and get started on their own. One of the reasons for this is the proliferation of young wanna-be tattooists, and a shortage of older tattooists to train with. Additionally, many young tattooists come out of art school thinking that since they can already draw (or paint or sculpt), they do not need to learn how to tattoo, and certainly not from an old-timer. Contemporary tattooing also developed as the field itself began to be professionalized as new health and hygiene standards were developed alongside of the new design elements brought in by the new artists.

New tattoo discourses also developed during this time that borrowed from popular social movements of the 1970s such as the New Age movement, the peace movement, self-help, environmentalism, feminism, the men's movement, and gay liberation. During this time, tattoos began to move from a mark of stigma used by bikers, gang members, and the military to a mark of individualism, using the language from transformational social movements, all of which provided a symbolic and discursive context for the artistic changes occurring within tattooing.

I designed my own tattoo and it consists of religious symbols from around the world, it's an armband that goes around my arm. There's an Egyptian hieroglyph, a Mayan hieroglyph, the Venus of Wellendorf, a cave painting called "the sorcerer," an African drum, a cave painting of a dancer. I wanted to feel that I was part of an earth-tribe-clan-thing. I felt like I was connecting to more ancient cultures.

ANONYMOUS

Tattooing has changed not only in terms of the artists, the professionalism, and the meanings behind the designs. The designs themselves have changed as well. Tattoos have moved from the badge-like designs common for hundreds of years in the West to designs, again, borrowed from non-Western cultures, which use the whole body or large portions of it. Designs have also moved from simple cartoonish representations of pop culture icons to abstract representations, created on a custom basis for the individual client, rather than pulled off of the wall in a tattooist's studio.

Contemporary tattooists prefer to do custom work, that is, work that was created by them, usually with the help of the client, rather than taken directly off of the wall. While there are still far more street shops than custom-only shops in this country, most tattooists who have started tattooing since the 1980s try to do as little **flash** work as possible and strongly encourage their customers to design their own tattoos.

Tattooing today is a youth-driven field, dominated by young artists with fine art training and a high degree of technical skill and creativity, and their young clients, with bold designs on their arms, heads, legs, and bodies, and often with multiple piercings as well. While many of older tattoo customers choose to hide their tattoos, many of the younger generation, without the white-collar jobs of middle-class boomers, proudly display their tattoos on highly visible parts of their bodies.

Within this context, tattoos have been partially transformed into fine art by a process of redefinition and framing based on formal qualities (i.e., the skill of the artist, the iconic content of the tattoo, the style in which the tattoo is executed, etc.) and ideological qualities (the discourses that surround "artistic" tattoos, discourses that point to some higher reality on which the tattoo is based). Moreover, certain tattoos, like those that mimic the styles of Japan, Micronesia, or Melanesia, are seen as paradigmatic—as the fine art tattoos against which all others are compared, and which, in fact, define the genre for many Americans. This transformation of meaning is only possible because of tattoo's historic position in western societies: as a stigmatized sign, traditionally used to mark negative status (such as convict status), it has never occupied a regular role in the West, thus its meanings have never been fixed, and are now more easily changeable.

The traditional American tattoo designs (such as "Mother" inscribed alongside a heart) are no longer the bread and butter of the contemporary tattooist. Such tattoos are now seen by modern tattoo artists and fans as too literal, too transparently obvious, and too grounded in everyday experience and social life to qualify as art. The modern, artistic tattoos that have increasingly gained favor are less "readable," and no longer have an easily recognizable function. These artistic tattoos are no longer part of a collectively understood system of inscription in which people communicate information about themselves to others. Some are purely decorative, and those that are intended to signify meaning often do so only for the individual or those in his or her intimate circle.

> Learning to tattoo from a book is just about as successfully accomplished as learning to swim from a book in your living room.
>
> SAMUEL STEWARD
> (aka Phil Sparrow), tattooist

Where the baby boomers who transformed tattooing into a practice suitable for the middle classes entered tattooing through hippies and the idealistic social movements of the early 1970s, the younger generations entered through punk rock and the megaconsumerism that has marked the 1980s. Not only are the aesthetics substantially different, but the attitudes about tattooing are different as well, leading to a more cynical, less idealistic notion of tattooing for the younger generation, and one which rejects modern society and its values to a much greater extent than that of the older generation. Tattooing, for many of the younger generation, can be seen as a means to both challenge the commodification of their generation, as well as to participate in that commodification, via the consumption of trendy, expensive tattoos—the ultimate consumer item.

See also: Hardy, Don Ed; Primitivism

Further Readings: Atkinson, Michael. *Tattooed: The Sociogenesis of a Body Art.* Toronto: University of Toronto Press, 2003; DeMello, Margo. *Bodies of Inscription: A Cultural History of the Modern Tattoo Community.* Durham, NC: Duke University Press, 2000; Rubin, Arnold. "Tattoo Renaissance." In Arnold Rubin, ed., *Marks of Civilization: Artistic Transformations of the Human Body.* Los Angeles: Museum of Cultural History, UCLA, 1988; Sanders, Clinton. *Customizing the Body: The Art and Culture of Tattooing.* Philadelphia, PA: Temple University Press, 1989; Sweetman, Paul. "Anchoring the (Postmodern) Self? Body Modification, Fashion and Identity." In Mike Featherstone, ed., *Body Modification.* London: Sage Publications, 2000.

COOK, CAPTAIN JAMES

Captain James Cook (1728–1779) was an English explorer who made three voyages to the Pacific Ocean. He was the first European who explored **Australia** and **Hawaii** and circumnavigated Newfoundland and New Zealand.

Cook's first voyage to the Pacific was in 1766 when the Royal Society hired him to observe and record the transit of Venus across the Sun. He arrived in **Tahiti** in 1769 and brought a Tahitian named Tupaia with him who helped him reach New Zealand later that year. In 1770 he first reached Australia and had contact with Australian Aborigines.

Cook's second voyage began in 1772 and was again commissioned by the Royal Society, this time to search for the mythical *Terra Australis,* which the Society felt lay further south than the actual island of Australia which he had already encountered. On this leg of the voyage the captain of one of his ships, Captain Furneaux, brought back with him a young tattooed Tahitian man named Omai. Another crew member, Joseph Banks, later displayed Omai as a human oddity throughout Europe. In 1774 on his return trip, Cook also visited Tonga (which he named the Friendly Island) and Easter Island (which he named because he landed on Easter Sunday).

Cook made a third voyage in 1776 to locate the Northwest Passage, and to return Omai, bearing European gifts, to Tahiti. After returning Omai, Cook became the first European to visit Hawaii in 1778. From Hawaii, Cook traveled to Vancouver in North America, and returned to Hawaii in 1779, where he met his death at the hands of the Hawaiians.

The universality of tattooing is a curious subject for speculation.

CAPTAIN JAMES COOK, 1779

It was thanks to Captain Cook that Polynesian tattooing was brought to Europe and later America, igniting a resurgence of Western tattooing. While tattooing had existed in Europe prior to the colonial encounters in Polynesia (Christian pilgrims, for example, had been receiving tattoos as souvenirs of their faith on pilgrimages to the Holy Land for centuries, the Celts had practiced tattooing prior to the Roman conquest, and tattooing was used as a form of punishment), it was through the early explorations of the Pacific that tattooing came into modern European consciousness, and eventually began its transformation from a mark of the underclasses.

It was Cook who gave the first accounts of Polynesian tattooing, first, in 1769 upon his stay in Tahiti. Also that year he visited New Zealand where he and his crew were the first Europeans to describe the Moko, and in 1778, when he first encountered Hawaiians and Hawaiian tattooing. Cook and his crew wrote and drew about the practice on subsequent voyages, and Cook was the first Westerner to use the Tahitian word ta-tu or tatau when describing the practice (prior to that time, tattoos were known in Europe as "pricks" or "marks"). Cook's crew noted that Polynesian tattoos included lines, stars, and other geometric designs, as well as figures of animals and humans, and were worn by both men and women. In addition, at least as far back as 1784, Cook's own crewmen started getting tattooed by the native people, and thus played a major part in bringing the tattoo to Europe.

Cook's crew also played a major role in changing indigenous Polynesian tattoos. At the time of European contact, tattoos in Tahiti, for instance, were primarily linear and included as well representations of plants and animals. By the nineteenth century, later voyagers noted that the designs included, in addition to the animals and plants found earlier, rifles and cannons and dates and words commemorating the origin and death of chiefs. These newer designs were probably introduced to the Polynesians by Cook's crew. Also by this time, Western ship artists, using native technology, were tattooing the Polynesians, again with introduced designs.

After the native people adopted Western weapons, their tattoos, now influenced by Westerners, probably became solely decorative, as tattoos would no longer need to serve their original magical and protective functions.

See also: Hawaii; Moko; Tahiti; Tattooed Natives

Further Reading: Douglas, Bronwen, Nicholas Thomas, and Anna Cole, eds., *Tattoo: Bodies, Art and Exchange in the Pacific and the West*. Durham, NC: Duke University Press, 2005; Kaeppler, Adrienne."Hawaiian Tattoo: A Conjunction of Genealogy and Aesthetics." In Arnold Rubin, ed., *Marks of Civilization: Artistic Transformations of the Human Body*. Los Angeles: Museum of Cultural History, UCLA, 1988.

CORSETS

A corset is an item of clothing, typically made of cloth as well as bone, wood, or other stiffening material, that is worn in order to constrict the torso. Corsets have been worn primarily by women in order to create the effect of a small waist, but have also been worn by both men and women for medical reasons, and today, for fetishistic purposes.

The shaping of the body through the use of **encumberments** has been practiced in societies throughout the world, typically as a manner of beautification, and include using heavy metal rings to lengthen the neck, the use of metal bands to constrict a portion of the arm or leg, binding the feet with cloth in order to make them appear small, and binding the head with bandages in order to elongate or flatten it. Some cultures also used belts to constrict the waist, such as the Ibitoe of **New Guinea**. The corset is the Western version of these practices, and originated in the fifteenth century as an item worn outside of the clothing, by both men and women, in order to stiffen one's posture. Early corsets were made of a wooden busk in front combined with vertical whalebone ribs all around. Early corsets, like later versions, pushed the breasts upward and pressed torso flesh downward, creating a narrower waist and an hourglass figure.

In the early years, corsets were worn primarily by upper-class women who competed with one another for the most feminine shape; by the nineteenth century, and especially after the Industrial Revolution which allowed for more inexpensive corsets to be produced, corsets were commonly worn by European and American women of all classes, although the narrow waist and hourglass figure were still seen as emblematic of the upper classes. Attaining the hourglass figure was so important, in fact, that baby girls wore a belt around their waist and young girls wore training corsets. In addition, an upright posture, for both men and women, was associated during the Victorian era with virtue and discipline, while women who let their bodies loose were seen as immoral and lazy. (Men too often wore corsets to narrow the figure and improve posture, and, for a period in the early nineteenth century, upper-class men also used corsets to achieve an hourglass figure.)

As corsets developed, a variety of types emerged that either covered the entire torso, extended from the torso down to the knees, or only covered the waist (known as a waist cincher). In all cases, the body of the corset was generally made of cloth with verticle ribs made of bone, wire, wood, or metal, which provided the stiffening. The corset was typically fastened on the body by laces in the back; the tighter the corset was laced, the more extreme the effect on the body.

Woman wearing corset, showing off her very tiny waist, 1899. Courtesy of Library of Congress Prints and Photographic Division, Washington DC, No. LC-USZ62-101143.

Besides the aesthetic aim, corsets were also used to strengthen the muscles in the back and pelvis, especially after childbirth, and are sometimes worn by people with injuries to the spine or the internal organs who need extra support in the back. For the most part, however, corseting was not known to be a healthy practice. The tighter the lacing, the more restricted the body, which sometimes resulted in damage to ribs or internal organs. Many women who wore tight corsets had trouble breathing, and prolonged corset wearing permanently changes the shape of the skeleton. In addition, wearing corsets over a prolonged period of time could result in the back muscles atrophying due to disuse. Of greater concern to the medical establishment, however, was the dangers the corset could bring to a woman's fertility or to the health of her unborn offspring (there were even corsets to be worn during pregnancy). Women wearing corsets could eat very little, denying themselves food in exchange for beauty, a practice which continues to this day.

Even with the dangers, however, women were the primary advocates for corset wearing for hundreds of years, a practice that did not disappear until the mid-twentieth century, thanks to changes in fashion, technology (such as the use of Lycra in clothing, leading to the development of the girdle), and, by the 1970s, the rise of the feminist movement. However, the narrow-waisted **beauty** ideal has not disappeared, and for most women, the corset has been replaced by diet, exercise, and **cosmetic surgery**.

While the wearing of corsets was typically not associated with sexuality, today, many fetishists find corsets to be extremely erotic, and they play a major role in some **BDSM** practices, in which the lacing itself, performed by the partner, is seen as erotic as the result.

In addition, tightlacing, in which corsets are worn very tightly over long periods of time—sometimes all day, for months at a time—in order to achieve permanent changes to the body, is practiced by men and women in the modern body modification community, who aim to achieve very small waists. **Fakir Musafar** was an early proponent of tightlacing, inspired by pictures in National Geographic of the Ibitoe of New Guinea, who used belts to constrict their waists. Fakir borrowed their methods and was able to shrink his own waist to 19 inches; many modern tightlacers aim for 16- or 17-inch waists, which generally results in a shifting of the organs within the body and a change in the skeleton itself. Other results of prolonged tightlacing are difficulty in breathing, difficulty eating certain foods or large quantities of foods, and even damage to the ribs.

See also: Beauty; Encumberments; Gender

Further Reading: Fee, E., T. M. Brown, J. Lazarus, and P. Theerman. "The Effects of the Corset." *Am J Publ Health* 92 (2002): 1085; Kunzle, David. *Fashion and Fetishism: A Social History of the Corset, Tight-Lacing and Other Forms of Body Sculpture in the West*. New York: Rowman & Littlefield, 1982; Steele, Valerie. *Fashion and Eroticism*. New York: Oxford University Press, 1985; Steele, Valerie. *The Corset: A Cultural History*. New Haven, CT: Yale University Press, 2001.

COSMETIC DENTISTRY

Cosmetic dentistry refers to a specialty within the field of dentistry that deals with improving the appearance of the teeth.

Altering the teeth for aesthetic reasons is a practice that has been found in cultures around the world. Some Australian Aboriginals practice tooth evulsion in which one or both of the front incisors are chipped in such a way as to be aesthetically pleasing, a practice also found among some Vietnamese tribes. Other cultures file their teeth into sharp points, such as the Mentawai of Sumatra or the Dinka of **Sudan**. In Bali, teeth are filed not for decorative reasons but because teeth symbolize negative emotions like anger, jealousy, and greed, which can be controlled through filing the teeth. Teeth filing for the Balinese is also an important **rite of passage** for adolescents, and helps to ease their transition into adulthood. Upper-class Mayans also filed their teeth, and sometimes etched designs onto the surface of the teeth as well, a tradition that has also been found in Africa and Central America. The Mayans also drilled holes into the teeth for the purposes of inserting jewels, a practice which would have been limited to the elites. Some cultures also stained the teeth to make them more beautiful; in Vietnam, for example, black teeth were once preferred to white, and the Iban of **Borneo** not only blackened their teeth, but filed them and inserted a brass stud into a drilled hole.

In the West, especially in the United States, white, straight, even teeth are desired for both men and women, and cosmetic dentistry practices are geared toward achieving this ideal. Boys and girls with crooked teeth often wear metal braces for a period of months or years in order to straighten their teeth, and some adults in recent years have taken to wearing braces as well, especially since clear plastic braces were developed. Other common treatments include tooth whitening (which can be done at a dentist's office or at home using home-whitening kits), tooth bonding, and veneers, both of which cover one's natural teeth with an artificial surface, and dental implants and bridges which replace missing teeth with artificial teeth. Teeth can also be reshaped in order to achieve a more pleasing appearance, and gums can also be operated in order to change the shape and appearance of the gums and teeth.

Today in the contemporary body modification community, teeth sharpening is a relatively rare practice, but is used by some people, including those who want to mimic the look of an animal, such as **Eric Sprague** or **Stalking** Cat. Tooth filing is done at a dentist's office, although some people have filed their own teeth at considerable risk.

Many African Americans, especially those involved in the hip hop culture, wear gold crowns over a tooth, typically an incisor, as a sign of status. More popular in recent years is the practice of having diamonds and other jewels inserted into the incisors. For those who do not want to make the permanent commitment, some dentists offer removable appliances which offer the look of gold teeth with or without implants.

See also: Meso-America

Further Reading: Alt, K., and Pichler, S. "Artificial Modifications of Human Teeth." In K. Alt, F. Rosing, and M. Teschler-Nicola, eds., *Dental Anthropology Fundamentals, Limits and Prospects.* New York: SpringerWien, 1998; Hillson, S. *Dental Anthropology.* New York: Cambridge University Press, 1996; Milner, G., and C. S. Larsen. "Teeth as Artifacts of Human Behavior: Intentional Mutilation and Accidental Modification." In Marc Kelley and Clark Spencer Larson, eds., *Advances in Dental Anthropology.* New York: Wiley-Liss, 1991.

COSMETICS

Cosmetics, or makeup, refers to the application of temporary dyes and powders to the skin, usually the face, for decorative purposes. As with so many body adornments, makeup is used differently in different cultures, depending on that society's standards of **beauty**. Because unlike men, women are judged around the world by their appearance, it is not surprising that most cosmetics are worn by women. Makeup, in fact, is one way in which men and women are differentiated, making women appear more feminine and men, by comparison, more masculine.

Skin is the primary focus of cosmetics around the world, but hair, eyelashes, lips, **fingernails,** and teeth are also areas for which cosmetics have been developed. Cosmetics include products to color and shape the lips; foundation, concealers, powders, and blush to change the appearance of the skin; eyeliners, eye shadow, mascara, and eyebrow liners to define the eyes; and nail polish and nail art to decorate the fingernails and toenails.

The appearance of the skin is a common focus in societies around the world. Clear, clean, healthy skin is considered beautiful in many cultures, but many other cultures use **body paint** to make people more beautiful, powerful, or to convey important social information about the person. Artificially lightened skin is considered attractive in many cultures, especially where light skin is associated with the upper classes, and dark skin with working people. For that reason, one of the earliest forms of makeup found in many stratified societies is white face powder. Both the ancient Greeks and **Romans** used lead-based makeup to lighten their faces, and Europeans in the Middle Ages used arsenic to lighten the skin, and even painted blue lines on their foreheads to make their skin appear translucent. Japanese Geishas use a heavy white powder to whiten their skin, because, again, white skin is associated with beauty and social status. **Skin whitening** creams and powders remain popular throughout the world today, wherever white skin is associated with status and beauty.

On the other hand, rouges and powders have been used for centuries in order to add a sun-kissed or flushed appearance to the face. While products to darken the skin such as artificial bronzers did not become popular until the twentieth century, when sun-tanned skin became fashionable, powders and creams to provide color to certain parts of the skin—usually the cheeks—have long been popular. Rosy cheeks are associated with youth and also with sexual arousal, making red cheeks very desirable—especially when contrasted with powdered white skin, as in the case of the Geishas as well as European women during the Renaissance.

Many cultures are also concerned with keeping the skin moist, and a range of oils, fats, and other products have been used in order to combat dryness, which is associated with aging. Many Sub-Saharan African cultures, such as the Nuba of **Sudan,** rub oil or fat

Two geishas in full costume. Courtesy of library of Congress Prints and Photographs Division, Washington, DC, No. LC-DIG-GCBAIN-24690.

onto their skin to keep it moist and shiny, and women will not go out if they do not have oil for their skin. The ancient Egyptians, too, used oils to keep their skin soft, and oils also served as the basis for a number of other important products like perfume and eye makeup. Cosmetics of all kinds have been used throughout the Middle East, but today, in areas controlled by fundamentalist Muslims, makeup is often prohibited.

The lips are another area of the face on which cosmetics have been focused. Because plump lips are associated with youth and high levels of estrogen, women have often worn products aimed at accentuating the lips, usually by coloring them red or pink, but also often by enlarging them, either through lip liners, or through various types of lip plumpers. Other cultures, on the other hand, favored small lips.

The eyes are the other major area of the face that is addressed by makeup. While many cultures associate large eyes with beauty and youth, developing mascaras, lip liners, and eye shadows which make the eyes seem bigger, many East Asian cultures at one time saw large eyes as barbaric, and found the less open eyes common among Eastern and Northern Asian cultures more beautiful. Today, however, "Western" looking eyes are sought after in Japan, **China** and Korea, and many women now undergo **cosmetic surgery** to make their eyes look rounder. The ancient Egyptians were known for their heavy use of eye makeup, using kohl to line their eyes, and green malachite to shadow them, creating the distinctive cat eye seen in Egyptian art.

White teeth is seen as normative in much of the world today, but this has not always been the case. For many centuries, for example, Japanese women blackened their teeth because black teeth were thought to be beautiful, as did women in Renaissance Europe, as a way to simulate the appearance of rotted teeth (which were a sign of status because only those who could afford sugar would typically have rotten teeth).

Makeup has often been used to distinguish the classes in stratified societies. In Medieval Europe, only the upper classes wore makeup, for example, although by the modern period, women of all class groups could afford to wear makeup. Even so, makeup can only go so far in terms of making a woman beautiful, and where makeup fails, cosmetic surgery is available to the wealthy to achieve results that working class and poor women could never achieve.

See also: Beauty; Cosmetic Surgery

Further Reading: Wykes-Joyce, Max. *Cosmetics and Adornment: Ancient and Contemporary Usage*. New York: Philosopical Library, Inc., 1961.

COSMETIC SURGERY

Cosmetic surgery is a surgical discipline that is intended to improve the appearance of a person, although some procedures, such as breast reductions, can be done for medical reasons as well.

Cosmetic surgery developed during World War I, when doctors needed to develop new techniques to repair the bodies and faces of soldiers who were wounded in the war. Today, cosmetic surgery generally refers to procedures that have been developed to repair congenital birth defects such as cleft palates, or disfigurements caused by accidents or injury, such as burns, scars, and severe body and facial trauma, as well as to those voluntary procedures which are aimed at making a person look younger or more beautiful. And while it's difficult to imagine comparing a club foot with an "A" cup breast, women with small breasts often feel that their condition needs correcting just as much as those with a club foot.

Of the voluntary procedures, the most common today include tummy tucks, breast implants, breast lifts, eyelid surgery, butt implants, chemical peels, nose jobs, facelifts, chin augmentations, collagen injections, liposuction, and botulism injections. In almost all of these procedures, the aim is to make the patient appear younger and slimmer, and therefore more beautiful. Because the standard of **beauty** in Western society demands youth and slenderness as the feminine ideal, it is not surprising that these procedures would be so popular with women, with over 700,000 procedures performed on women in 2002 in the United States alone. On the other hand, in recent years, the number of men seeking cosmetic surgery—including "masculine" procedures like pectoral and calf implants—has been increasing as well, with 150,000 men undergoing surgery in 2002.

Cosmetic surgery is not typically covered by health insurance, so beauty is becoming increasingly a sign of upper-class status, as only the wealthy can afford to undergo these procedures. Furthermore, as beauty is becoming a commodity that can be purchased by the wealthy, men and women whose faces and bodies are not naturally beautiful, but who cannot afford to change their appearance, find themselves at a disadvantage, given the preferential treatment that the genetically and surgically endowed receive in almost every aspect of social and economic life.

And while it was at one time the case that only older women underwent facelifts and other procedures to make them appear younger, young women are now getting Botox injections as well as lip plumping procedures at very early ages, in order to "prevent" aging (in 2002, 18% of all patients were under 25). Indeed, the prevalence of cosmetic surgery in the United States today indicates an increasing need to deny the inevitable; as the physical signs of aging are being pushed further and further into the future, the wealthy can pretend that the biological rules do not apply to them.

A new problem that has developed in those who can afford it is a condition where men and women become addicted to cosmetic surgery, having procedure upon procedure performed on their body. Multiple surgeries to the same part of the body often weaken and damage tissue, as in the case of Michael Jackson's nose, which often leads to further surgeries to correct the damage. Typically referred to as **body dysmorphic disorder**, a psychological disorder in which an individual is desperately unhappy with his or her own body, patients cannot stop getting surgeries because regardless of the results, they are never happy with their appearance. (Cosmetic surgery, in fact, relies on the patient's unhappiness with their appearance. The patients, after all, are not sick, and if they were not unhappy with their looks, would not need surgery at all.) On the other hand, the overwhelming demand for youth and beauty, which is fueled by our obsession with celebrities, no doubt plays a major role in this condition as well.

See also: Beauty; Body Dysmorphic Disorder; Gender

Further Readings: Alam, M. and J. S. Dover. "On Beauty: Evolution, Psychosocial Considerations, and Surgical Enhancement." *Arch Dermatol* 137 (2001): 795–807; Balsamo, Anne. "On the Cutting Edge: Cosmetic Surgery and the Technological Production of the Gendered Body." *Camera Obscura* 28 (1992): 206–237; Brush, Pippa. "Metaphors of

Inscription: Discipline, Plasticity and the Rhetoric of Choice." *Feminist Review* 58 (1998): 22–43; Capozzi, Angelo. *Change of Face: What You Should Know if You Should Choose Cosmetic Surgery* New York: Kampmann Publishing Company, 1984; Davis, Kathy. *Reshaping the Female Body: The Dilemma of Cosmetic Surgery*. London: Routledge, 1995; Davis, Kathy. "'My Body Is My Art.' Cosmetic Surgery as Feminist Utopia?" *The European Journal of Women's Studies* 4(1) (February 1997): 23–37; Gilman, Sander. "Imagined Ugliness." In Tobin Siebers, ed., *The Body Aesthetic: From Fine Art to Body Modification*. Ann Arbor: University of Michigan Press, 2000; Morini, Simona. *Body Sculpture: Plastic Surgery From Head to Toe*. New York: Delacorte Press, 1972; Rose, Christine. "The Democratization of Beauty." *The New Atlantis* (5) (Spring 2004): 19–35; Stark, Richard B. *Aesthetic Plastic Surgery*. Boston, MA: Little, Brown and Company, 1992; Sullivan, Deborah. *Cosmetic Surgery: The Cutting Edge of Commercial Medicine in America*. New Brunswick, NJ: Rutgers University Press, 2001.

COSMETIC TATTOOING *See* Permanent Makeup

CRIMINALITY

In societies around the world, but especially in state-level societies, criminals have commonly been marked in some way by the state either as punishment for their crime, to identify them as a criminal, or to stigmatize them throughout their lives. In addition, corporal punishment, in which the body is the site of the punishment via whipping, the removal of a limb, or even death, is another way that punishment is literally "marked" on the body.

Some trace the evolution of this practice to the biblical story in which God places a mark on Cain, the first murderer, to brand him as a criminal and social outcast, but corporal punishment had been practiced throughout the **Greco-Roman** and Egyptian world. In addition, all those cultures used **tattooing** and **branding** as a form of punishment and identification for criminals, practices which were continued throughout Western civilization in Europe and the Americas.

The first known societies to use tattoos in a punitive fashion were the Thracians, Persians, Greeks, and Romans, all of whom marked runaway slaves and criminals. The Persians tattooed slaves and prisoners with the name of their captor, master, and sometimes the emperor, and Roman slaves were marked on the face with either the crime or the punishment (which was commonly being sent to the mines), until Constantine outlawed facial tattooing in the fourth century. The Greeks and Romans both called these tattoos **stigmata**, and punitive tattooing remained in the Roman world through ninth century.

Punitive tattooing and branding traveled through the Roman world to Europe where both practices were used in Germany, England, and France to mark slaves, prisoners, adulterers, army deserters, and the like. The American colonies inherited the practices as well. Slave masters in American and West Indian colonies also used tattooing and branding for the identification of slaves and to punish runaway or insubordinate slaves.

In **India**, another European colony, after 1797, criminals had their criminal status tattooed on them. The word for tattooing in Hindi later came to mean the marking of criminals in the nineteenth century. Indian criminals were sometimes also branded with the English word for thug. Many Indian criminals attempted to cover, remove, or change their markings via wearing their hair longer or turbans over their faces. The Japanese used punitive tattooing as well. In **Japan**, tattoos moved from punitive to decorative as people developed elaborate designs to mask criminal tattoos. In fact, the modern practice of prisoners tattooing themselves in prison probably derived from punitive tattooing, when convicts turned their mark of criminality into a badge of honor.

Tattoos and brands were a preferred form of punishment in all of these cases because it was a dual-purpose punishment: one purpose was to inflict **pain**, but another was to permanently, and often very publicly proclaim the crime, either through the words or letters used, or simply the fact that forehead tattoos were associated with criminality.

Criminality is associated with the body in another way as well. European criminal scholars once thought that certain forms of body modification, particularly tattoos, could be linked to a tendency toward criminal behavior, and a great many books were written and

> Tattooing is most common among criminals.
>
> CESARE LOMBROSO,
> criminologist, 1895

studies conducted in order to test the link between tattooing and criminal behavior. These theories can be drawn from biological approaches popular in the nineteenth century that saw crime as being caused by inheritance, and that furthermore, a person's physical appearance could indicate their disposition to crime.

The idea that a person's character can be interpreted by looking at his or her face is derived from ancient times, but was codified into a scientific theory in the nineteenth century called phrenology, which postulated that the shape of the brain and the skull could reveal an individual's personality and psychological development.

An Italian doctor named Cesare Lombroso was an advocate of this approach and examined the bodies of hundreds of criminals in the nineteenth century in order to ascertain the physical characteristics shared by criminals. Not surprisingly, he found that a number of traits, such as broad noses or fleshy lips, were found more commonly in criminals, and came up with a theory that said that these traits were associated with "primitive man." Of course these traits were also found more commonly among Africans, a group he knew to be inferior to whites.

Lombroso also wrote about tattooing, which he associated with criminality. Again, this association is not surprising given the practice, since Roman times, of tattooing criminals. After conducting a study of prisoners, Lombroso felt that wearing tattoos would predispose a person to commit crime, and that criminals and tattooed people both had a higher tolerance for pain than others.

This association between tattooing and criminal behavior extends well beyond Lombroso. In India, for instance, in the nineteenth and twentieth centuries, British colonial authorities noted the use of tattoos among many of the tribal groups. They also shared Lombroso's theories that criminality was inherent and they thought that they could chart the use of tattoos by different groups in India to show their propensity toward criminality. Tribal groups were seen as especially crime-prone so their tattoos were especially scrutinized.

In **Australia** in the nineteenth century, convicts sent from England to the penal colonies there had their tattoos catalogued prior to leaving England, and again upon reaching Australia, as a way of identifying convicts in the days before fingerprinting, and as a way of apprehending escaped convicts. Because the convicts often tattooed themselves on the ship en route to Australia, perhaps out of boredom or collective suffering (and probably due to the proximity of tattooed sailors around them), their new tattoos were a way of subverting English authority in that their body markings would now differ from when they left England. This demonstrates a practice that was also seen in Roman times: of criminals self-marking themselves in order to erase or cover the criminal marks given to them, or even to highlight them, seeing them as a badge of honor.

Today, law enforcement agencies continue to track the tattoos on former criminals, **gang members**, and those who have been arrested for a crime.

See also: Bio-Power; Branding; Foucault, Michel; Greco-Roman World; Prison Tattooing; Slavery; Stigmata

Further Reading: Anderson, Clare. "Godna: Inscribing Indian Convicts in the Nineteenth Century." In Jane Caplan, ed., *Written on the Body: The Tattoo in European and American History*. London: Reaktion Books, 2000; Burma, John. "Self-Tattooing among Delinquents: A Research Note." In M. E. Roach and J. B. Eicher, eds., *Dress, Adornment and the Social Order*. New York: Wiley, 1965; Gustafson, Mark. "The Tattoo in the Later Roman Empire and Beyond." In Jane Caplan, ed., *Written on the Body: The Tattoo in European and American History*. Princeton, NJ: Princeton University Press, 2000; Lombroso, Cesare. *Criminal Man*. Raleigh: Duke University Press, May 2006; Maxwell Stewart, Hamish, and Ian Duffield, "Skin Deep Devotions: Religious Tattoos and Convict Transportation to Australia." In Jane Caplan, ed., *Written on the Body: The Tattoo in European and American History*. London: Reaktion Books, 2000; Roberts, T. A., and S. A. Ryan. "Tattooing and High-Risk Behavior in Adolescents." *Pediatrics* 110 (2002): 1058–1063; Sanders, Clinton. *Customizing the Body: The Art and Culture of Tattooing*. Philadelphia, PA: Temple University Press, 1989.

CROSS-DRESSERS *See* Tranvestites

CUTTING

The term cutting refers to at least two body modification practices. One use of the term refers to a method of **scarification** which uses a blade to create cuts into the body, and it also refers to the **self-mutilation** of the body via the cutting of the skin. Both forms of cutting leave a scar, but while the former is decorative and intentional, the latter is seen as a sign of a mental or emotional disorder, although people who cut themselves may well disagree with this assessment.

When used for scarification, cutting consists of etching a predefined design on the skin with a surgical blade or scalpel. Unlike many forms of scarification practiced in Africa, the skin is not first raised with a hook in order to create a raised welt. Instead, the cuts tend to leave recessed scars in the skin, in the form of the design drawn. And because cutting uses a blade that cuts a continuous line into the skin, the resulting design can be very precise.

Sometimes the cutter will cut a thin line on the skin, but larger pieces of skin can be removed as well, leaving a wider, and sometimes deeper, scar. In addition, tattoo pigment can be rubbed into the open wound, resulting in a colored scar.

Cutting as a symptom of a mental or emotional disorder is generally quite different. In this case, the individual takes a blade and cuts their own skin, generally without a plan or decorative intent, and often obsessively, in order to try to cope with their emotional problems. For many who cut themselves, they feel that the pain of the cutting relieves the emotional pain that they are feeling, although the relief is generally temporary, and the person must cut again, since the underlying problem has not been solved. For others, cutting oneself is a way of exercising control over one's body, when they feel that other aspects of their life are out of control. Still others do their own cuttings in a ritual-

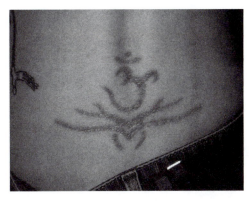

Cutting on back by Steve Truitt of Stay Gold Tattoo & Body Modification and Ascension Studios, Albuquerque, NM.

istic fashion, and feel that it, like so many other body modification practices, is a form of self-transformation and empowerment. Cutting, unfortunately, because of the scars that it leaves (self-cutters usually cut themselves on the wrists and arms, and sometimes other places as well), marks the individual as being unstable, whether or not that is the case.

See also: Health Issues; Scarification; Self-Mutilation

Further Reading: Myers, James. "Nonmainstream Body Modification: Genital Piercing, Branding, Burning and Cutting." *Journal of Contemporary Ethnography* 21(3) (October 1992): 267–306; Pitts, Victoria. "Body Modification, Self-Mutilation and Agency in Media Accounts of a Subculture." In Mike Featherstone, ed., *Body Modification*. London: Sage Publications, 2000.

D

DANCES SACRED AND PROFANE

Dances Sacred and Profane is a 1987 film directed by Mark Jury that not only documented a number of extreme body modification and **body play** techniques, but helped to popularize and promote these practices to a wider audience.

The film features the work of fetish and body modification photographer Charles Gatewood, and covers a whole host of extreme and nonmainstream practices that Gatewood had been documenting. Shot over three years, *Dances* includes footage of Mardi Gras festivities, New York **BDSM** clubs, nudist events, and a tattoo convention.

The film introduced **Fakir Musafar**, known as the Father of the **Modern Primitive** movement, to the world, and showcased his philosophy and body modification practices, including **branding, piercing**, play piercing, **suspensions**, and the use of **encumberments** for emotional and physical transformation.

The highlight of the film is the performance (and evidently the first filming) of the Sun Dance ritual in South Dakota with Musafar and piercer and **Gauntlet** founder **Jim Ward**. The Sun Dance is a ceremony once practiced differently by several Native American groups, but known especially among the Sioux, which usually include dancing, singing, and drumming, as well as fasting and in some cases, self-torture. Lasting for days, the highlight of the dance (at least as interpreted by modern primitives), has the dancers attaching themselves to a pole (similar to a May Pole), via ropes attached to bone or wood skewers, which are inserted into pre-pierced holes in the chest. Then, dancing around in a circle to the beat of drums and prayers, the particpants pull against the pole to tear the skewers out.

Dances also includes a scene of Fakir taking a Kavadi. The Kavadi is a lengthy, ecstatic trance-inducing dance ritual done while enduring some form of physical hardship. Generally, the hardship involves carrying heavy weights up a steep hill. The form of Kavadi that is of most interest to the body modification world is where a steel frame is held (supported by the shoulders and/or hips) by the participant, through which long weighted skewers are passed, which are then pierced into the skin of the back and chest. In the film, Fakir has eighty steel spears piercing his torso.

The *Kavadi* is a Hindu ritual normally performed during the Thaipusam festival in **India**. Bearing Kavadi means to bear a large basket or other container filled with items to be offered to the god Muruga, as a form of penance. Some participants wear a spear inserted through their tongue and others through their cheeks, and still others on other parts of the body, and some also walk through burning coals during the ceremony. The form of Kavadi that Musafar reenacted was the form in which the basket itself is suspended from the body with hooks and spears.

Dances has served as an inspiration to many in the body modification community who have reenacted the rituals themselves, borrowing Musafar's philosophy. It was rereleased in the 1990s with the name *Bizarre Rituals*, and the filmmaker has recently released an updated version called *Dances Sacred and Profane Redux* on DVD.

See also: Body Play; Musafar, Fakir; Native Americans; Ward, Jim

Further Reading:: Vale, V., and Andrea Juno. *Modern Primitives*. San Francisco, CA: Re/Search Publications, 1989.

DERMAL ANCHORING

Dermal anchoring is a relatively new **piercing** technique that creates the appearance of a bead floating on the surface of the skin. It is similar to pocketing, in which the ends of the jewelry are under the skin, and the middle—where the decorative bead is—is exposed in a small pocket in the skin. Dermal anchoring, however, uses a needle to create a single point on the skin, rather than the two points used in pocketing. Except for the bead, the **jewelry** lies hidden under the skin, similar to a transdermal implant, **surface piercing**, or a **nose piercing**. Dermal anchoring differs from transdermal implants, however, in that implants are permanently embedded in the skin, and surface piercing, which uses a technique that is not appropriate for all skin types or body locations. Dermal anchoring can be done almost anywhere on the body since the jewelry is relatively small, but healing will differ based on body area. Locations such as between the eyes (to simulate the Hindu *pottu*), on the outside corner of the eye (as in a beauty mark), on the chest, and on the fingers (worn like a ring) are popular.

The most common way of performing a dermal anchoring utilizes the dermal punch technique used for surface piercing, in which a hole punch (known as a dermal punch) is used to remove flesh under the skin, and a device called a taper is used to elevate some of the skin around it to allow for jewelry insertion. Another method is to just use a normal piercing needle, inserting it partway into the skin, followed by the insertion of the jewelry once the needle is turned sideways. The jewelry in a dermal anchoring consists of a straight bar, a curved part of the bar that holds the jewelry under the skin, and a bead that sits on the skin.

See also: Body Piercing; Pocketing and Stapling; Surface Piercing; Implants

Further Reading: www.BMEZine.com.

E

EAR PIERCING

Ear piercing refers to putting a hole in the ear, usually the lobe, in order to wear **jewelry** through the ear. It is one of the oldest and most common forms of body modification in the world, and is perhaps the oldest form of **piercing**. In the West, the piercing of the earlobe has long been the most acceptable and popular form of facial or body piercing. Today, many people also have the upper and outer cartilage parts of the ear pierced as well. And while pierced ears are associated primarily with women in the modern West, men and women have both worn earrings in cultures around the world, as well as in European and Western history.

Pierced ears and earrings for pierced ears have been found on every continent throughout history. Evidence from the earliest civilizations in the Middle East show that pierced ears were worn at least six thousand years ago, but given the popularity of pierced ears in nonstate-level societies, they certainly must predate the archaeological record. Multiple ear piercings were used in some cultures, such as ancient Mesopotamia, pre-Colombian **Meso-America**, and the **Greco-Roman world**. Many cultures have also stretched the ear holes and worn earplugs. Earplugs were worn by ancient Egyptians, Mayans, and Aztecs, by the Chinese, as well as by traditional cultures around the world.

Pierced ears have primarily been used as a form of adornment, and, for cultures which carry wealth in the form of jewelry, as a form of displaying wealth as well, such as among nomadic tribes like the Fulani of West Africa, the Tuareg of the Sahara, and the Bedouins of the Sinai Peninsula. The types of earrings worn also have been, in many cultures, an indication of rank and status, and some societies as well pierce the ears for religious purposes or magical purposes; in some societies, spirits are thought to enter the body through the ear, but the wearing of earrings repels them. Among many Northwest Coast Indians, such as the Tlingit, ear piercing is used to mark individual rank. Because paying for an ear piercing was costly, the number of holes in one's ear show the amount of wealth in one's family.

In many cultures young girls have their ears pierced a short time after birth; in some communities in **India**, Hindus pierce a girl's ears and nose twelve days after birth when she is given her name. The Tchikrin of central **Brazil** pierced boys' and girls' ears at birth, and immediately inserted wooden earplugs, which would be exchanged as the ear holes grew larger.

In other societies, ears are pierced as part of a **rite of passage**, usually at adolescence, or just prior to marriage. In **Borneo**, for example, parents pierce a child's ears to represent the child's dependence on the parents. The Fulani also use ear piercing to mark the life stages of their members.

The Bible mentions pierced ears and earrings in a number of places. From those references we know that earrings were worn by Hebrews as a form of adornment, and that gold earrings represented wealth, but also that slaves' ears were pierced as a mark of servitude; Exodus 21:5-6 tells that freed slaves who want to continue to serve their master could have their ears pierced in court as a sign of permanent service. Just as Roman Christians chose to use the stigma of tattooing to mark themselves as slaves of God, other Christians use pierced ears as a way to show this same commitment.

Elsewhere in the Middle East, Romans, Greeks, and Egyptians all wore earrings, as a sign of **beauty** and wealth, and both men and women wore earrings. The finer the materials and the more elaborate the design, the wealthier the wearer. In Europe, the Middle Ages saw a decline in the wearing of earrings, but jewelry of all kinds became popular again in the Renaissance, when elite men and women wore earrings to demonstrate their status and wealth.

In the United States, ear piercing began to lose popularity in the 1920s with the advent of clip-on earrings, but became popular again beginning in the 1960s, primarily with women and girls. Most ear piercings at that time were done at home, generally by sticking a sterilized or heated sewing needle through the ear into a piece of cork or other object, followed by the earring itself. This is very similar to how ears are pierced around the world. Also available since the 1960s were spring-loaded earrings in the shape of a ring with the ends sharpened to a point. By placing the earring around the earlobe, and squeezing, over a period of days or weeks the ear will eventually be pierced through.

By the 1970s, one could get one's ears pierced in a doctor's office or at department stores, in events were sponsored by earring manufacturers. Ear piercing guns were developed in 1970, and quickly became the most popular way to get one's ears pierced, at mall jewelry or accessory stores.

While it has primarily been women in the United States to wear pierced ears, men in some groups have worn them as well. Sailors, for instance, used a pierced earlobe to indicate that the sailor had sailed around the world or had crossed the equator; another legend says that a pierced ear would improve a sailor's eyesight, and that if a sailor was found washed up on a shore, his gold earring would pay for his burial.

In the late 1960s, men began to wear earrings thanks to the influence of the gay community and the hippies. In the 1970s, punks began piercing their own ears and later, other male musicians began wearing earrings as well, leading to a fashion among rock stars, rappers, and basketball players. For a time in the 1980s and 1990s, it was thought that when a man pierced just one of his ears, it meant he was gay, although this is no longer recognized.

Earring types include stud earrings in which a stud made of either metal or stone sits on the front part of the earlobe, which is connected through the lobe to a backpiece holding the earring on in the back. Hoop earrings generally pierce through the ear with a wire or post, and then encircle the bottom of the earlobe.

And dangling earrings attach to the earlobe with a post or a hook and include a longer portion of metal, beads, and/or stones that flow from the bottom of the earlobe. In the West, when men wear earrings, it is usually a stud or a small hoop.

In the end of the twentieth century, newer ways of wearing earrings developed. First, multiple holes in the earlobe, and later the cartilage, developed. And while the earlobe is still by far the most common place historically and cross culturally to find a piercing, in the modern body modification scene, a variety of specialized cartilage piercings have since become popular. These include the tragus piercing, antitragus piercing, rook piercing, industrial piercing, helix piercing, orbital piercing, daith piercing, and conch piercing.

The inner conch piercing is a piercing that goes through the inner part of the ear, near the ear canal. Piercings through the outer part are called outer conch piercings. The tragus piercing pierces the small piece of cartilage that projects immediately in front of the ear canal. The antitragus piercing is

Massai girls with large ear ornaments, 1936. Courtesy of Library of Congress Prints and Photographs Division, Washington, DC, No. LC-DIG-MATPC-00418.

a piercing on the small pierce of cartilage in the inner ear, directly opposite the tragus. A daith piercing passes through the ear's innermost cartilage fold, above the ear canal.

A helix piercing is a piercing of the upper ear cartilage. A rook or antihelix piercing is a piercing on the outer portion of the inner ear. A helix piercing together with an antihelix piercing can be connected with a single straight piece of jewelry, usually an extended barbell, and is called an industrial piercing; in this piercing, the straight bar of the jewelry extends from the top of the ear to the outer edge. On the other hand, an orbital piercing is defined as any two piercings that are connected by a hoop, usually in the ear.

See also: Ear Spools and Earplugs; Ear Stretching; Jewelry

Further Reading: Mascetti, Daniela, and Amanda Triossi. *Earrings: From Antiquity to the Present*. London: Thames and Hudson, 1999; McNab, Nan. *Body Bizarre Body Beautiful*.

New York: Fireside, 2001; Ostier, Marianne. *Jewels and Women; The Romance, Magic and Art of Feminine Adornment.* New York: Horizon Press, 1958; Van Cutsem, Anne. *A World of Earrings: Africa, Asia, America.* New York: Skira International, 2001.

EAR SHAPING

Humans have shaped dogs' ears for centuries. Certain breeds of dogs require, in order to conform to breed standards, cropped ears such as Great Danes, American

Pit Bull Terriers, Boxers, Doberman Pincers, Miniature Pincers, and Schnauzers. A veterinarian normally crops the ears a few weeks after the puppy's birth. Although veterinarians did not provide pain medication for years, and some still do not, it is much more common today, and some veterinarians refuse to crop ears altogether. On the other hand, some breeders and dog owners continue to perform these surgeries themselves, without anesthesia, which can result in infection and blood loss, not to mention considerable pain. Because of these concerns, a number of localities have now banned or restricted the procedure.

In the contemporary body modification scene, human ears are also the focus of shaping and modification. For instance, ear cropping or ear pointing refer to the reshaping of the ear via the removal of

Ear pointing and ear coil by Steve Truitt of Stay Gold Tattoo & Body Modification and Ascension Studios, Albuquerque, NM.

part of the cartilage (and sometimes the sewing up of the resultant ear), in order to create a specific ear shape such as the Vulcan ears on Star Trek, or an elfin ear. Some people also choose to have their earlobes removed for aesthetic reasons or to remove a stretched earlobe. Because most surgeons will not crop human ears, most people who seek to have their ears shaped turn to cutters, piercers, and sometimes will do the procedure themselves.

See also: Ear Spools And Earplugs; Ear Stretching

EAR SPOOLS AND EARPLUGS

Ear spools and earplugs refer to the jewelry worn in stretched ear holes. Ear spools and plugs were commonly used throughout much of pre-Columbian America, and are still worn by some tribes today.

An earplug is a cylindrical piece of jewelry that fits into a large hole in the ear, and is sometimes flared at both ends to keep it in place. These are one of the most common forms of jewelry worn by modern body modification advocates with stretched ears. Earplugs can be made of wood, bone, stone, or even glass.

Ear spool is the term used to describe the jewelry worn in the ears in many Meso-American cultures. A spool is a large cylinder that fits through the ears with a large disk or decorative sheet on the front side. It is thought that ear spools were inserted into the ear by first slicing the ear open, inserting the spool, and as the wound heals, the spool is sealed into place. Other theories hold that the ears were pierced and then stretched to accommodate the jewelry.

Ancient Meso-Americans not only wore earrings, but stretched their earlobes and wore gold, jade, shell, and obsidian earplugs and ear spools. Archaeologists have unearthed masks from the Olmec civilization which show large holes in stretched earlobes for ear spools; ancient ear spools themselves have also been found. The Mayans were also well known for wearing ear spools; only elites could wear the larger and more elaborately decorated spools. In fact, throughout the Americas, large and decorated ear spools and earplugs were used as a sign of high status. The ancient Incans also wore engraved ear spools of gold, silver, copper, sometimes inset with stone or shells, and these were most likely reserved for the elites. Ear spools have also been found in Guatemala and Panama.

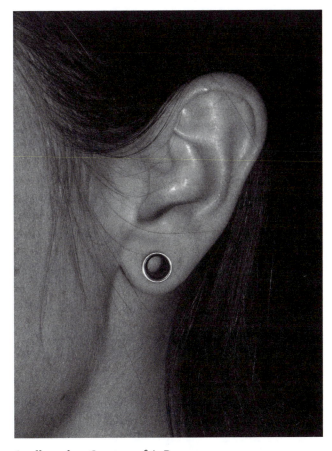

Small earplug. Courtesy of A. Page.

Mississippian Indians also wore earplugs, made of clay, shell, stone, feldspar, and wood covered with copper. The earplugs found by archaeologists measure only a half inch or so in diameter but up to 5 inches in length, which means that they emerged from the ears for quite a distance. Earplugs were most likely worn by both commoners and elites. The Indians most likely inserted feathers into their ears as well. Ear spools made of stone were also found among tribes in Oklahoma, Ohio, and other eastern Native American sites.

Today, earplugs are becoming a more common body modification, although they are not yet mainstream. **Flesh tunnels** are a modern form of earplugs and ear spools. They are a hollowed-out version of a plug, and resemble an empty spool of thread, and can be worn with another decorative item running through the middle.

See also: Ear Piercing; Ear Stretching; Meso-America

Further Reading: Bray, Warwick. *Everyday Life of the Aztecs*. New York: Dorset Press, 1968; Meskell, Lynn, and Rosemary Joyce. *Embodied Lives: Figuring Ancient Maya and Egyptian Experience*. London: Routledge, 2003.

EAR STRETCHING

While almost any **piercing** can be stretched, one of the most popular parts of the body in which to stretch a piercing is the earlobe. Earlobe stretching, like other body modification practices, has been around for thousands of years, but only in the last few years has it become widespread in the United States. Ears are typically stretched so that they can wear jewelry, but sometimes stretched ear holes are worn by themselves.

Kenyan man with stretched ears, 1880–1925. Courtesy of Library of Congress Prints and Photographic Division, Washington, DC, No. LC-USZ62-92557.

In the West, the most common way to stretch an ear hole is to begin with a conventional pierced hole in the ear. Once the piercing has healed, there are a number of ways of stretching the hole, which usually involve stretching it a little bit at a time in order to minimize tissue damage and pain.

Tapering is the most common technique used for stretching, and involves the use of a conical metal rod known as a taper, which is pushed through the hole until the widest part of the taper is even with the skin; larger jewelry is then pushed through, parallel to the back of the taper. Larger tapers, and then jewelry, will be substituted over time as the hole gets bigger. Dead stretching is the practice of simply stretching a hole in the skin until it is big enough to accommodate the desired jewelry. A piercing can also be stretched via the hanging of weights onto the jewelry. This is a common way that people in traditional societies stretched ears in the past, although it can result in tissue tearing and thinning. A more modern way of stretching is via **scalpelling**, or using a scalpel to cut a large hole around a piercing, removing a piece of flesh.

Stretched piercings allow for a wider variety of jewelry than can be worn in many more conventional piercings, although the most commonly worn jewelry is known as an **earplug**. An earplug is a cylindrical piece of jewelry that fits into a large hole, and is sometimes flared at both ends to keep it in place. **Flesh tunnels** are a hollowed-out version of a plug, and resemble an empty spool of thread, and can be worn with another decorative item, like a feather, running through the middle. Ear spirals are another option, which are spiral-shaped coils that are inserted into the ear. Ear spools were worn in the ears in many Meso-American cultures, and are large cylinders that fits through the ears with a large disk or decorative sheet on the front side.

From statues, mummies, and other evidence, we know that stretched ears have been worn in major civilizations around the world, including **Egypt**, **China**, and by the Olmecs, Mayans, Aztecs, and Incans. Tutankhamen, for example, had a stretched ear piercing. Small Scale societies, too, have practiced ear stretching. The men of the Marshall Islands, for example, used to stretch their earlobes and wear large gauge earrings through the holes.

In all cases, stretched ears, and the elaborate jewelry worn in them, seem to be associated with elite or royal status and rank. In many cases, we know that the ears were stretched intentionally to wear earplugs, ear spools, and the like. But in other cases, as in China, the ears may have been stretched through the wearing of heavy hanging earrings in regular pierced ears. Today, stretched ears are still worn among some South American and African tribes, and often serves as a **rite of passage** and a mark of cultural identity for young boys or girls.

> I got my ears pierced because I was always attracted to them but my parents would never let me. So when I turned 18, I got them done. I didn't plan on gauging them but when I did it for the first time, the pain I got from stretching my ears was amazing so I just kept doing it.
>
> ANONYMOUS

Today, thanks to the **modern primitive** movement, stretched ears have become popular for many young people, who both like the way that stretched earlobes look, appreciate the variety of jewelry that can be worn in them, and in some cases, want to mimic the practices of "primitive" people around the world.

See also: Ear Piercing; Ear Spools and Earplugs; Stretching

Further Reading: Pitts, Victoria. *In the Flesh: The Cultural Politics of Body Modification*. New York: Palgrave Macmillan, 2003.

EASTER ISLAND

Easter Island, known as Rapanui to its inhabitants, is a Polynesian island which is controlled by the country of Chile. The island was mostly settled between 300 and 600 CE by people who may have arrived from the **Marquesas** Islands. The first European explorer to arrive was Dutch navigator Jacob Roggeveen who arrived on Easter in 1772. **Captain James Cook** arrived in 1774. From 1860 to the late nineteenth century, the island's population was decimated, thanks to the islanders' overexploitation of native resources, and later, to the export of the native people to Peruvian slave traders. Those few hundred remaining islanders were forced, after slavery, to live on a reservation until the 1960s, because the island was rented to a sheep company that grazed their sheep over the island. Since that time, the people have been rebuilding their traditional culture.

Easter Island is famous for the giant stone statues, or *moai*, that cover the island—over 800 in all. These statues, which represent the heads and torsos of deceased ancestors and perhaps living chiefs, were carved between the twelfth and seventeenth centuries, and most were knocked over by the time Europeans arrived in the eighteenth century.

Prior to the decimation of local traditions, Easter Island practiced a form of **tattooing** closely related to Marquesan tattooing, which was described by the early explorers, and is also seen on the *moai*, many of which have detailed designs on their back which appear to represent tattoo motifs of stripes, circles, squares, triangles, and other abstract designs. By the twentieth century, tattooing, however, had all but disappeared.

Both men and women wore tattoos, and tattoos were done on the face and head, which were considered to be the most sacred part of the body, but also included shoulders, upper back, arms, buttocks, and thighs. Facial tattoos for both men and women generally consisted of very heavy curved and straight lines combined with dots, which appear somewhat like Maori *moko*. Some of the facial markings on women may have been related to fertility, and facial tattoo marks are also seen on the barkcloth figures made by the native peoples.

As with other Polynesian cultures, tattoos demonstrated kinship and rank, and the chiefly and warrior classes wore tattoos most commonly. Tattooing was done in the classic Polynesian style, with a tool known as *ta kona*, carved out of bird bone into teeth, which was connected to a longer handled wooden implement and, after dipping it into pigment, was tapped into the skin with a mallet.

Further Reading: Allen, Tricia. "European Explorers and Marquesan Tattooing: The Wildest Island Style." *TattooTime* 5 (1991): 86–101; Diamond, Jared. *Collapse: How Societies Choose to Fail or Succeed*. New York: Viking Press, 2004; Métraux, Alfred. *Ethnology of Easter Island*. Bulletin 160. Honolulu, HI: Bernice Bishop Museum, 1940.

EGYPT

The ancient Egyptians, and especially the elites, devoted a great deal of time and energy to the adornment and modification of the body. The types of adornments and modifications worn by an individual represented a great deal about their status, wealth, and social or political roles. Because the Egyptians left such a wealth of artwork, statuary, funerary materials, and mummies, we know a tremendous amount of how they treated their bodies and what the standards of **beauty** were.

Ancient Egyptian mummies, artwork, and artifacts provide information on many of their practices, which range from the decorative—**makeup, henna**, wigs and **hairstyles, jewelry, scarification,** and **tattooing**—to the punitive (**branding**) and encompass as well **circumcision**, which marks social status for boys.

Branding humans is a tradition that goes back to at least ancient Egypt and Rome when wealthy elites branded both livestock and slaves with a hot iron. As one of the earliest state-level societies, it is not surprising that the Egyptians would have used branding for both purposes.

Circumcision, too, was found in Egypt, and may have spread from Africa. Egyptian circumcision practices may have then spread to other nearby lands, eventually leading to the biblical commandment to circumcise.

Egyptian boys were generally circumcised with sharpened copper blades between the ages of 6 and 12, although evidence from mummies indicates that not all boys were circumcised. In fact, some feel that only priests were circumcised, and that prepubescent, virginal boys were selected to be priests, and were at that time circumcised at Thebes in order to serve the gods. Circumcised penises were signs of fertility; one myth has God circumcising himself and his blood created the universe. Others, however, feel that circumcision was almost universally practiced among Egyptians; artwork shows regular men who were clearly circumcised. In any case, circumcision for priests was certainly mandatory, and was combined with a number of other proscriptions for priests that were enacted to maintain their purity, such as mandated head shaving (indeed, priests shaved their entire bodies), regular ritual washing, and the wearing of only linen clothing.

In terms of adornment, Egyptians spent a great deal of time, energy, and money on hair. Egyptian hairstyles varied with age, gender, and social status, with elites being able to hire professional hairdressers, afford the most expensive wigs, and use the richest oils, dyes, and scents for their hair.

Boys and girls until puberty wore their hair shaved except for a side lock left on the side of their head. Many adults—both men and women—also shaved their hair as a way of coping with the heat and lice. However, adults did not go about bald, and instead wore wigs in public and in private. Slaves and servants wore their hair simply, often tied back from the head.

Men who did wear their own hair generally wore it short, with the ears exposed. Women, on the other hand, wore a variety of hairstyles (and wig styles) from long to short, but generally favored waves or curls. Many women used henna to dye their hair or cover their gray hair. Women also decorated their hair and wigs with flowers, ribbons, and jewels, with wealthier women being able to afford more elaborate decorations.

Wigs were initially only worn by the elites, but later were worn by women of all classes, although those who could not afford quality wigs made of human hair wore cheaper wigs, made of vegetable fibers or wool, or hair extensions. Even certain wig styles were limited to the wealthy, and the wealthy could also afford the oils needed to properly maintain wigs.

Egyptians also used makeup from a very early period, with evidence dating back 6,000 years. Oils were used to soften the skin and hair, henna and other natural dyes were used to color the hair, **fingernails**, face, and body, the scents of plants like rose or peppermint were used to perfume the hair and body, and minerals like ochre and malachite were ground up to create face and eye makeup. Men and women both lined their eyes and darkened their brows with kohl, and elites, again, had a wide variety of products to use to enhance their appearance.

Jewelry too was used by all classes to adorn the body. The wealthy wore elaborate pendants, necklaces, earrings for pierced ears, and bracelets made of fine metals, ivory, and precious stones as both adornment and status indicators. Some mummies and artwork show evidence of stretched ears, which may have been caused by the wearing of heavy jewelry. Tutankhamen, for example, had stretched ears.

Tattooing was practiced in Egypt, but appears to have been limited to women, and was used as a primarily decorative practice, although there may have been ritual significance as well. The practice was probably introduced by the Nubians sometime during the Middle Kingdom. Female tattooed mummies have been uncovered dating back 4,000 years. The earliest tattooed mummy found was Amunet, Priestess of Hathor, who wore parallel lines made up of dots and dashes on her arms and thighs and an oval pattern on her belly. The tattoos on the belly may have been related to fertility or sexuality. Artwork and mummies from the New Kingdom show the development of representational tattoos, in particular images of the god Bes on the thighs of a number of women. Female mummies have also been found with scarification patterns across their bellies.

Today, Coptic Christians living in Egypt continue to wear Coptic tattoos as a sign of their faith, the most prominent being a cross on the forehead.

See also: Branding; Circumcision; Hairstyles; Henna; Makeup

Further Reading: Bianchi, Robert. "Tattoo in Ancient Egypt." In Arnold Rubin, ed., *Marks of Civilization: Artistic Transformations of the Human Body*. Los Angeles: Museum of Cultural History, UCLA, 1988; Budge, E. A. *The Gods of the Egyptians*. New York: Dover Publications, 1969; Strouhal, Eugen. *Life of the Ancient Egyptians*. Norman: University of Oklahoma Press, 1992.

ENCUMBERMENTS

Encumberments refer to hanging or wearing weights on the body in order to restrict and often reshape the body, for aesthetic, sexual, or personal reasons.

The wearing of tight metal armbands and legbands in some tribal societies would be an example of an encumberment, in that they not only act as a form of **jewelry** but will, when worn tightly enough and over enough time, reshape the body by compressing that section of the arm or leg into a narrower shape.

Corsetting is also a form of encumberment. Wearing a very tightly laced corset on a regular basis, especially when started at a young age, will also result in a waist that is artificially, and permanently, smaller than the waist normally would have been.

The most extreme form of encumberments practiced around the world is probably the practice of wearing heavy metal neck coils found in some African tribes or among the Padaung and Kayan tribes of Myanmar (formerly Burma). Padaung girls traditionally had large golden rings placed around their necks and their calves from about 5 years old. Over the years, more rings are added, until an adult Padaung woman's neck carries over 20 pounds of rings, which compress the collarbone and upper ribs, in turn lengthening the neck by 10–15 inches. The girls are known as giraffe necks and it is often thought that without the support of the rings, the girls' heads would no longer be supported by their bodies, which is not true. In fact, the women periodically remove the rings in order to wash their necks.

In the modern primitive community, encumberments are often worn for ritual or performative purposes, and are often combined with play piercing, **suspensions**, and other **body play** activities. For instance, a person may allow

Padaung girls from Myanmar with golden neck coils, 1887–1890. Courtesy of Library of Congress Prints and Photographic Division, Washington, DC, No. LC-USZ62-132761.

themselves to be pierced on the chest, legs, genitals, or face, and then have hooks hung in the holes, which are weighted with bells, metal balls, and other weights. Sometimes the weights are worn for a certain amount of time in order to produce sensations of ecstasy in the wearer, and other times the participants will dance with the weights until they tear themselves from the flesh.

See also: Body Play; Corsets; Musafar, Fakir; Suspension

Further Reading: Vale, V., and Andrea Juno. *Modern Primitives*. San Francisco, CA: Re/Search Publications, 1989.

ENGLAND

Tattooing has been practiced on the island of Great Britain for perhaps two thousand years, starting with the Celts, one of the island's earliest inhabitants. The term "Briton," in fact, is derived from a word meaning "painted in various colors." Caesar, for instance, noted that the Britons "dyed" their bodies with woad; he may in fact have been referring to tattooing. A quote from Herodian, a first-century Roman historian, noted that the Celts, who wore no clothing, "punctured" their bodies with pictures of animals. There is also evidence that contemporary cultures to the Celts, like the Scythians, who were known to have influenced Celtic culture, practiced tattooing.

Once the Celts came under Roman control and became Christianized, they soon adopted the wearing of Christian tattoos, as in the style of the Jerusalem souvenir tattoos. This practice may also have been associated, as with the Roman practice, with the marking of slaves and criminals, but it was certainly used by Celtic Christians to mark devotion.

After the fifth century when the Roman Empire collapsed, the Celts were pushed westwards, and it is unclear whether Celtic tattooing continued and was able to influence the English practice of tattooing. However, by the Middle Ages, we do know that tattooing was still being practiced in some quarters.

For example, Anglo-Saxons continued to practice tattooing, at least among the nobility and warrior classes. Pilgrims, for instance, received tattoos during their travels to the Holy Land, but religious tattoos were not the only tattoos that the English wore. Following the Battle of Hastings in the eleventh century, for example, King Harold's body was identified only because he had "Edith" tattooed over his heart.

Also in the Middle Ages, tattooing was associated with occult practices. Some people tattooed astrological symbols by at least the seventeenth century in England. Temporary or permanent writing on the body was common in magical, medical, and religious practices in Europe, although it's unclear how much of this involved tattooing rather than temporary marks on the skin. Corporal magic of this kind was seen as especially effective because it may not always be easy to get the rare ingredients needed for some magical spells. In that case, one can use the symbol of the ingredient or the symbol of the corresponding planet, and mark it on the body.

Tattooing in England was perhaps more prominent than it was in other parts of Europe because of the long tradition of sea exploration associated with the country. Since the early sixteenth century, British sailors and explorers had been traveling around the world on voyages of exploration, bringing back with them stories and illustrations of tattooing from Polynesia, the Americas, **India**, and elsewhere. They also brought back with them tattooed peoples and very early on started getting tattooed themselves. The explorations of **Captain James Cook** in the late eighteenth century were especially notable in the attention that they brought to tattooing in

Europe (the word "tattoo" was brought back by Cook from his visit to **Tahiti**), but Cook was not the first explorer to uncover tattooing. Sailors would have had to be tattooed prior to Cook's trip to Polynesia based on how prevalent tattoos were among sailors by the end of the eighteenth century; by the century's end, British ports had tattooists providing their services to sailors. Sailors continued for centuries to wear tattoos, a practice that began in England and later spread to the United States.

Criminals too were being punitively tattooed in England, starting perhaps in the sixteenth and certainly by the seventeenth century, which led, as it has in other societies in which tattooing is a form of punishment, to self-tattooing among criminals. By the nineteenth century when England was exporting convicts to penal colonies in **Australia**, criminals and the underclasses in general were becoming tattooed, and were tattooing themselves, in increasing numbers.

The first documented professional tattooist in England was D. W. Purdy, who worked in North London in the 1870s. In the late 1880s fashionable folks in England started getting tattooed. English tattooist George Burchett saw the trend beginning with Edward, Prince of Wales, who was tattoed in the Holy Land in 1862 with a Jerusalem Cross. Later, as King Edward VII, he acquired still more tattoos, and his sons (one of whom later became King George V) were also tattooed, both in **Japan** in 1882 and later in Jerusalem. After this, a great many elite men and women of English society began to acquire tattoos, both from the Japanese, who were widely acknowledged to possess the most sophisticated tattoo art in the world, as well as from local tattooists like Burchett.

A great many media reports at that time noted how fashionable Londoners (and later Americans) were getting tattoed, but tattooing never spread to the middle classes. Elites were tattooed by Japanese fine artists as well as newly professional British tattooists like Burchett, who provided a comfortable and relaxing studio for his customers. Burchett also used topical anesthetic and the newly invented tattoo machine to make the process less painful, and to create more detailed designs, often based on Asian images. Yet at the same time, sailors continued to get hand-pricked tattoos from port tattooists, which were crude, painful, and unsophisticated.

By the end of the ninteenth century, the upper-class tattoo fad notwithstanding, tattoos in England mostly were associated with criminals and sailors, as well as soldiers. In fact, in the nineteenth century, doctors noted a connection between tattooing and syphyllis, thinking the disease may have been passed in the military by infected tattooists spitting on the needles to mix in the ink.

Starting in the 1970s, as the English **punk** movement developed, tattoos began to gain prominence again. As the stylistic trappings of punk were appropriated and spread into mainstream society via fashion and music, tattoos began to move into the middle class, a process enabled by the renaissance of tattooing in the United States during that same period. In the twentieth century, tattooing continues to be prominently practiced among a variety of social classes throughout England.

See also: Celts; Cook, Captain James; Magic and the Occult

Further Reading: Bradley, James."Body Commodification? Class and Tattoos in Victorian Britain." In Jane Caplan, ed., *Written on the Body: The Tattoo in European and American History*. London: Reaktion Books, 2000; Burchett, George, and Peter Leighton. *Memoirs of a Tattooist*. London: Oldbourne Book Company, 1958; Rosecrans, Jennifer Allen. "Wearing the Universe: Symbolic Markings in Early Modern England." In Jane Caplan, ed., *Written on the Body: The Tattoo in European and American History*. London: Reaktion Books, 2000.

THE ENIGMA

The Enigma (born as Paul Lawrence) works as a **sideshow** performer and musician, and has built his career on his extreme body modifications, including extensive **tattooing** in the manner of a jigsaw puzzle, subdermal implants shaped like horns, and **body piercings**.

Raised in Seattle, Lawrence began studying piano when he was 6 years old and later took lessons in singing, flute, and dancing. He was also interested in magic as a child, and began teaching himself how to do magic acts, including sword swallowing and fire eating. Performing music and novelty acts at street festivals and fairs, Lawrence heard about Jim Rose, who at that time in the early 1990s was performing on a bed of nails. Rose founded the Jim Rose Circus, a modern **freak show** made up of people who used their bodies to entertain and shock the crowd. Lawrence, working as the Slug (because he ate slugs and other small creatures) ended up being one of the original members; besides the sword swallowing and fire eating and slug eating, he also learned to lift weights with his eyelids.

The Jim Rose Circus and Enigma attained national fame when they performed at Lollapolooza in 1992. In the meantime, he also decided to transform his appearance, and chose a jigsaw pattern that would eventually cover his whole body. Because he had no money for such a procedure, his first tattooist was fellow performer Katzen (and later girlfriend), who began tattooing all of his puzzle piece outlines in late 1992. Later he had many more tattooists work on his puzzle pieces, and says now that he's been worked on by approximately 200 artists, sometimes a few at a time. While from afar it seems as if his body is covered with blue jigsaw puzzle pieces, from up close one can see that there are multiple other tattoos underneath the puzzle pieces, including a number of circus freaks.

Since leaving the Circus, the Enigma has been playing music and doing sideshow performances either solo with his band, Human Marvels, of which Katzen is a member, or with a band called Pigface. He has also appeared in films, magazines, and on television, with his most notable appearance being a 1995 episode of "The X-Files" in which he played a character known as the "Condundrum."

The Enigma is not only the recipient of tattoos, he is also willing to do some tattooing himself—as long as it's a blue puzzle piece, since that's the only thing he'll tattoo.

See also: Circus; Freak Shows; Freaks; Implants

Further Reading: Adams, Rachel. *Sideshow USA: Freaks and the American Cultural Imagination*. Chicago: University of Chicago Press, 2001; Hill, Dee J. *Freaks and Fire: The Underground Reinvention of Circus Art*. Brooklyn, NY: Soft Skull Press, 2005.

ETHIOPIA

Ethiopia is a Northeast African country with cultural influences from traditional East Africa, **Islam,** and **Christianity.** Unlike other African nations with a large Christian population, Christianity in Ethiopia goes back to the fourth century, when King Ezana converted. Because of the mix of Christianity, Islam, and indigenous religions and traditions, Ethiopia has a wide variety of body modification and body adornment practices.

The Christianity practiced by the vast majority of Ethiopia's Christians (and the majority of Ethiopians as well) is Coptic Christianity, an early Egyptian form of Christianity established in the first century by the Apostle Mark. Tattoos are worn by Coptic Christians in Egypt and Ethiopia and are usually found on the face, neck, and back of hands and consist of Coptic designs. The most popular tattoo is the Coptic cross, often tattooed on the face. Ethiopia also had a large population of Jews, many of whom tattooed themselves with Coptic tattoos in order to blend in with Ethiopian society; after they moved to Israel in the 1980s and 1990s, they sought to have their tattoos removed so as to conform to **Judaism**'s ban on tattooing.

Tribal people in Ethiopia have also practiced **scarification, body painting,** and other forms of body adornment for hundreds or thousands of years. The Karo tribe, for example, a farming and pastoral community living in Southern Ethiopia, use scarification to beautify women, and as an indication of a man's success in warfare. Women have scars on their chests and torsos, and men get a line carved into his chest for each man that he has killed during war. Scars are made through slicing the skin and rubbing in ash to accentuate the scar. The Karo also use body painting to distinguish themselves from neighboring tribes, and unlike most groups who use body painting, they use it as a regular, rather than a ceremonial, adornment. Karo people also wear heavy metal armbands and pierced ears.

The Nyangatom are another southern Ethiopian tribe that practices scarification. For women, as in many other parts of Africa, scars are seen as a way of beautifying the body and making it more sensual, and women are scarred with dots and straight and curved designs on the cheekbones, arms, abdomens, backs, and torsos. Men are scarred on their arms, shoulders, back, and chest to commend them for bravery in fighting. The Nyangatom also wear large bead necklaces to indicate status and wealth. Women in the tribe pierce their labia and wear decorative jewelry in the holes as adornment, and both men and women of the Nyangatom wear lip plugs in their lower lips.

Elaborate hairstyles and headdressings made with clay, feathers, and other natural materials are also worn by a number of Ethiopian tribes like the Karo and the Hamar, and signify rank, beauty, and bravery. The more elaborate headware indicates that a man has had success in hunting or fighting and can be worn for as long as a year.

Muslim Ethiopians have borrowed practices from other Islamic countries, such as the use of **henna** to decorate the hands of brides before their weddings.

See also: Christianity; Scarification

Further Reading: Fisher, Angela. *Africa Adorned*. New York: Harry Abrams, 1984; Carswell, John. *Coptic Tattoo Designs*. Beirut: American University of Beirut Press, 1957.

F

FACIAL HAIR

Facial hair refers to both the light hair found on the bodies and faces of men and women, and also the androgenic hair found on men. Androgenic hair is a secondary sex characteristic of men, developing after puberty. Women tend to have very light and fine hair on the face, but genetic makeup will influence the color and thickness of facial hair in women. In addition, postmenopausal women will often develop thicker facial hair. Eyebrows and eyelashes, on the other hand, represent the areas of the face in which darker and thicker hair grows on both sexes of any age.

Because women naturally do not have a great deal of hair on their faces, it is considered a sign of femininity to have as little facial hair (except for eyebrows and eyelashes) as possible. Because of this, most women in Western cultures shave or wax and sometimes bleach the hair that grows on their upper lip, chin, and sometimes elsewhere, and carefully tweeze the hair on their eyebrows in order to keep the eyebrows controlled and to conform to current style. On the other hand, eyelashes are considered a sign of femininity and are encouraged, via **makeup** and other products, to grow as long and thick as possible.

Because of the social stigma associated with facial hair in women, women who do have what would be considered "excess" facial hair are generally considered to lack femininity or to appear mannish. Excessive hairiness on a woman is known as hirsutism, and "bearded ladies" were once common attractions at **freak shows**.

For men, the presence or lack of facial hair can represent high or low status, conformity or rebellion, youth or age, and growing a beard or mustache is an indicator of social position, and, often, individual preference. Facial hair, or the ability to grow facial hair, most commonly represents masculinity however, and men who cannot grow a mustache or a beard are often seen as less masculine than other men.

While Romans and Egyptians considered the clean shaven face to be the norm (although Roman servants and slaves wore beards), other cultures embraced beards for men. The Greeks, for example, grew beards, as do many Arab and Asian countries.

Wearing a beard is often culturally associated with wisdom and virility, and it is common in some cultures for older men to allow their beards to grow quite long. On the other hand, wearing a beard, moustache, goatee, or other form of facial hair is often a stylistic choice, and some men go back and forth between being clean shaven and wearing facial hair. Some cultures dictated that during mourning, facial hair be removed, as with the Greeks, while the Romans would grow their hair and beards when mourning.

In Western culture, however, most men do not wear facial hair. Facial hair fell out of fashion during the seventeenth century, but became fashionable again in the nineteenth century, and, since the twentieth century are associated with old men and hippies, who popularized the look again in the 1960s. Removing the hair via shaving with a razor is the most common form of hair removal today, and is used by most men in the West to control their hair growth. Most men who shave do so every day, in order to appear clean shaven, as it generally takes only a day for stubble to appear through the skin after shaving.

Some professions and social statuses require men to be clean shaven, or to wear facial hair. For example, Egyptian priests were required to shave their faces, bodies, and heads, and many countries' military branches require their soldiers to be clean shaven. On the other hand, moustaches are often worn by men in the military, with higher ranked officers wearing larger moustaches, and the British Army mandated moustaches for years. Many religions also either mandate the wearing of a beard or prohibit shaving, either for priests or for all of the faithful. For example, Sikhs do not cut their beards, Orthodox Christian priests were expected to grow beards, some Muslims feel that growing a beard is mandatory, and many Hasidic Jews also do not shave.

Shaving is probably the oldest style of hair removal, and is a form of depilation, which refers to removing the hair above the skin, usually with a razor blade, and is a temporary method of hair removal. The first razors were developed in Egypt around 3,000 BC, when copper tools were developed. Today, shaving can be done with an electric razor or a manual razor, and with or without lubricants. African American men have traditionally removed their facial hair with depilatory powders which remove the hair without a razor, and prevent razor bumps and ingrown hairs.

Today, other forms of hair removal include epilation methods which remove the entire hair shaft, such as waxing, plucking, and threading, all of which are temporary but which last longer than shaving, and electrolysis and lasers, which are permanent forms of hair removal. Transgendered people and male-to-female **transsexuals** will often opt for permanent hair removal methods for their face and bodies. Most men, however, still overwhelmingly favor shaving, although a few men in the West now use waxing and other methods to groom their eyebrows.

See also: Body Hair; Hair Cutting and Head Shaving; Hairstyles

Further Reading: Peterkin, Allan. *One Thousand Beards. A Cultural History of Facial Hair.* Vancouver: Arsenal Pulp Press, 2001; Reynolds, Reginald. *Beards: Their Social Standing, Religious Involvements, Decorative Possibilities, and Value in Offence and Defence Through the Ages.* New York: Doubleday, 1949.

FACIAL PIERCING

The most common facial **piercings**—both in contemporary society and historically—are **oral piercings**, or piercings of the mouth and lips, and **nose**

piercings. Today, however, there is a wide range of facial piercings that do not involve the nose or the mouth. Because new facial piercings (and indeed new piercings of all kinds) are being created constantly, this is not an exhaustive list.

One reason that there are more piercings available for the face today has to do with modern piercing techniques that allow for **surface piercings**. Another reason is the continuing mainstreaming of extreme body modification techniques; as previously "extreme" piercings move from the body modification community into mainstream youth culture, new, often more extreme, piercing methods and locations continue to be developed.

Other than nose (which includes nostril piercings as well as septum and bridge piercings), and the mouth (which includes tongue piercings, lip piercings, **lip plates,** and **labrets**), facial piercings can now be done in a wide variety of locations.

The area of the eye is one popular new location. Eyebrow piercings are generally vertical or angled piercings through the ridge of the eyebrow, and are typically found on the outer edge of the eyebrow. Jewelry for eyebrow piercings is usually a barbell or ring, both of which go through the eyebrow from bottom to top or top to bottom. An alternative to the vertical eyebrow piercing is the horizontal eyebrow piercing, which pierces horizontally along the upper brow ridge. Because this piercing goes through the surface of the skin, rather than using the extra flesh on the eybrow as in the traditional eyebrow piercing, it is a surface piercing and thus uses a surface bar rather than a barbell or ring. A much

> My piercings (lip and tongue) helped me test my strength and get over the fear of pain. My mom says these were mutilations of my body. They don't define me, but are a part of who I am and how I express myself.
>
> ANONYMOUS

rarer piercing is the eyelid piercing, which is a piercing done on the eyelid itself, generally with a ring.

Outside of the eye, there are a number of piercing choices. The temple piercing is a surface piercing to the area outside of the eye, on the temple of the face, and usually uses a surface bar. The anti-eyebrow is a facial surface piercing which pierces the upper cheek just below the eye. They are sometimes known as tears because of the location of the jewelry. The jewelry, usually a specifically bent surface bar or sometimes a curved barbell, has two beads that sit on the surface of the skin, the top of which generally sits closer to the eye, with the bottom angled away from the eye.

Cheek piercings are done on the fleshy part of the cheek, on the other hand, usually where a dimple would be found. It is not a surface piercing because the jewelry goes through the skin and emerges on the other side—inside of the mouth. Jewelry is usually a labret stud, so that just the stud of the jewelry appears on the surface of the cheek. People who are attempting to look like an animal often have multiple cheek piercings in the form of steel whiskers which emerge from the skin.

The nick piercing is another cheek piercing, but one that uses the highest point on the inside of the mouth, and then travels straight up under the skin and muscles of the mouth and exits underneath the eye, usually with a single stud appearing on the surface of the skin, although it is not a surface piercing. The end of the jewelry sits inside of the mouth, against the gums.

A chin piercing is a rare piercing that at first looks like a labret, with a stud sitting beneath the lower lip, but with additional studs emerging under the chin. It is a surface piercing in which the bar travels through flesh of the chin, and does not use the inside of the mouth at all. A horizontal philtrum is another rare piercing that uses the upper lip divet, just below the nose, to pass a barbell through. It does not go inside the mouth, yet is not a surface piercing, because it uses the flesh above the lip to pass through. The two beads of the jewelry sit on either side of the divet, below each nostril.

The forehead is a relatively recent spot for surface piercings. Forehead piercings are sometimes worn by people with loose skin, although they are difficult to heal without much excess skin. Sideburn piercings, done where a man's sideburns would grow, is another surface piercing on the face. Finally, a bindi piercing is a piercing using a vertical barbell above the bridge of the nose, in the spot where Hindu bindis are painted onto the skin.

See also: Labrets; Lip Plates; Nose Piercing; Oral Piercing; Surface Piercing

Further Reading: Pitts, Victoria. *In the Flesh: The Cultural Politics of Body Modification*. New York: Palgrave Macmillan, 2003; Vale, V., and Andrea Juno. *Modern Primitives*. San Francisco, CA: Re/Search Publications, 1989.

FACIAL TATTOOS

In the West, thanks to the tradition dating back to the Greeks and Romans of tattooing criminals on the face with a mark of their crime, facial tattoos are traditionally the mark of a convict. Even without that explicit connection, facial tattoos are extremely stigmatizing in the nontattooed world. Most tattooists do not want to contribute to marking an individual for life as an outcast, thus many tattooists will not tattoo on someone's face. For years, one could also not attend a **National Tattoo Association** convention with facial tattoos.

However, in recent years, facial tattoos have experienced a surge in popularity among the body modification community, especially among those who embrace **modern primitivism**, partly because of their extreme appearance, and partly because of their connection to "primitive" cultures.

Facial tattoos are most well known among Pacific Island cultures such as **New Zealand, the Marshall Islands, Tahiti,** and **Hawaii**, as well as some tribes in **New Guinea**. A great many **Native American** tribes also practiced facial tattooing. The most well known and classic of all facial tattoos is the *Moko*, the black curvilinear tattoo worn by Maori men and women as a sign of status as well as affiliation.

Besides the primitivist connection, though, modern wearers of facial tattoos often use their tattoos as a sign of rebellion against society, thanks to the continuing taboo against them. Another reason for the increasing popularity of facial tattoos has to do with the mainstreaming of tattooing in general. As tattoos (as well as piercings) become more popular and thus more acceptable, those within the body modification community feel that they need to use more extreme versions of tattoos and piercings, in order to stay ahead of the rest of society.

Finally, for those who embrace primitivism or just want an extreme sign of their individuality, getting one's face tattooed is one of the most public and permanent steps one can take, and represents a permanent commitment to one's beliefs, especially given the reluctance of most employers to hire a person with facial tattoos.

Facial tattoos are also popular with the small population of those who transform their bodies into animals, such as **Eric Sprague** (the Lizardman), the **Great Omi**, **Stalking Cat**, or Katzen.

See also: Animality; Criminality; Moko; Prison Tattooing

Further Reading: DeMello, Margo. *Bodies of Inscription: A Cultural History of the Modern Tattoo Community*. Durham, NC: Duke University Press, 2000; Simmons, D. R. *Ta Moko: The Art of Maori Tattoo*. Auckland, NZ: Reed Books, 1986; Spencer, Robert Francis, and Jesse David Jennings. *The Native Americans: Prehistory and Ethnology of the North American Indians*. New York: Harper and Row, 1965; Vale, V., and Andrea Juno. *Modern Primitives*. San Francisco, CA: Re/Search Publications, 1989.

FEMALE GENITAL MUTILATION *See* Clitoridectomy

FINGERNAILS

In Western culture, long, decorated or well-groomed fingernails are associated with women, whereas men are expected to have short nails. However, other cultures have not made this **gender** distinction, and today, some men are beginning to polish and decorate their nails, especially in the gay community, or among artists and musicians.

Fingernail decoration ranges from the simple (painting the nails with fingernail polish) to the sophisticated, involving a range of artificial nails and the application of a variety of nail art. Because women who work with their hands cannot maintain carefully decorated, long, or even very well groomed fingernails, fingernail length and grooming are a sign of status and wealth.

Fingernail painting is the most common form of fingernail decoration, and usually involves purchasing nail polish from a drug store, department store, or supermarket, and painting one's nails oneself. Nail polish colors, like makeup, change seasonally, with new colors becoming fashionable in a given season. However, many women, and some men, get their nails professionally painted, shaped, and cared for by manicurists at nail salons.

Even the shape of nails is dictated by fashion. While individual fingernails differ in shape and length of nail bed, nails themselves can be grown long or short and filed into shapes ranging from square to round to oval or even pointed. One popular fingernail look is the French manicure, which uses both "nude" and white polishes to achieve a "natural" look. The look is achieved by painting white polish to the white part of the nail that protrudes beyond the nail bed, and then painting a nude color along the entire nail.

Besides coloring fingernails, lengthening nails has been a concern for women whenever long nails are associated with beauty, status, sex appeal, or femininity. Artificial nails have become popular for women since the 1980s, and include plastic nail tips to glue onto the end of the nail, as well as acrylic nails which are formed directly on the nail, covering up the entire nail bed and creating a full false fingernail. Fiberglass or silk wraps are another way of either increasing nail length or strengthening nails by wrapping a small piece of fabric around the natural or artificial nail, and sealing it with glue. Inexpensive and temporary alternatives include artificial fingernails that can be purchased from the drug store and glued on at home. Most of the semipermanent options, however, are typically done at the nail salon.

Other options to lengthen nails include strengthening solutions which can be brushed onto the nail like nail polish. Many people also feel that drinking a gelatin solution strengthens the nails and thus makes them grow longer, however, it is most likely not true.

Another way of decorating the nails is by creating special effects on the nails. Some manicurists paint designs on nails, and today a variety of kits are available to purchase that include stencils, stickers, and glue on jewels and charms to decorate fingernails. Some artists also airbrush designs on fingernails, with or without stencils. Individuals can also paint images on their own nails, using just a toothpick dipped in nail polish. Some people paint the underside of the nail with a contrasting color when the nail is long enough. Temporary tattoos can also be applied to fingernails once they have been polished. In the last few years, new technologies have developed such as a printer that prints images directly onto fingernails; this technology is popular in some Asian countries but has not yet become well known in the United States.

Fingernails can also be pierced in order to accomodate jewelry, either using a needle or pin, or by purchasing a simple nail piercing tool. Some nail salons will also pierce nails.

Fingernail length and decoration often indicate social status or group membership. In **China**, for example, men and women have historically grown long fingernails, or only the nail on the the pinky finger, to show that they do not do manual labor. Indian fakirs have also grown their fingernails very long as part of **self-mortification** practices. Fingernails that are grown very long typically will not grow straight as short nails do, but will curve and sometimes spiral.

In the 1970s in the West, some men grew their pinky nail out in order to scoop cocaine with it. It has also been a common style for some American pimps. Members of the goth subculture wear their fingernails long, sometimes sharpened to a point, and typically painted black. Some classical guitar players will grow long nails in order to serve as guitar picks. Some men have a long nail fetish and enjoy looking at photos and videos of women with very long nails posing, smoking, in bondage scenes, or engaging in sexual activities. Similarly, some women and men enjoy seeing men with long fingernails, although this is not nearly as common.

See also: Makeup

FLASH

In traditional Western **tattooing**, tattoo customers picked tattoo designs from sheets called "flash" hanging on the walls of the tattoo shop. These designs are drawn in a highly formulaic manner, and the same images were often found on virtually all tattooists' walls, although often drawn in slightly different ways. Traditional designs included pinup style images of women, military insignia, ships, jokes, cartoons, fierce animals, knives, and skulls. Women sometimes had their own sheets of flash to choose from, which included flowers, less fierce animals, cute cartoons, and other "feminine" designs.

The tattooist credited by many with being the first to market sheets of flash was "Lew the Jew" Alberts, a wallpaper designer and tattooist in the early 1900s. Until the invention of flash, tattooists who wanted to reproduce another tattooist's design would have to copy that design off of a customer's body. Once Alberts began marketing flash, tattooists from around the country could buy these sheets and quickly set up a business.

While tattooists did sign their own sheets of flash, once a new design reached a tattooist he simply copied it, altering it slightly, and used it as his own. For this reason it is difficult to ascertain the origins of most tattoo designs. Since many tattooists used to cross off the name of the original creator of the flash and substitute their own, it was even harder to know who originally drew many classic designs.

Until the 1980s when tattoo shops moved toward custom designs, most tattoo shops had flash on every wall, the front windows, and sometimes the ceiling. Because flash composed the bread and butter of every tattooist's work, it was important to have a wide variety of flash designs and styles for customers to choose from. Flash sheets would sometimes be organized by theme (i.e., roses, or flowers, or animals), sometimes by artist, and sometimes by style, and other times, by color or the size or composition of the pieces. Other times, sheets would be organized by cost.

Acetate stencils were originally used to transfer the design to the body. Stencils were made by placing a piece of clear acetate or celluloid over the sheet of flash, and tracing the design directly onto the plastic, which would then be etched into the plastic using an exacto knife or similar blade. The tattooist would then rub carbon powder into the stencil design, and would transfer the design onto the body via the use of mentholatum. Most tattooists kept individual stencils for each flash design that they offered, often kept in a filing cabinet organized by name. (Today, tattooists who continue to use flash use rice paper, rather than cut acetate, to transfer the design to the body.)

Even when a tattooist had multiple sheets of flash, before the age of custom tattoos, design choices were still quite limited. Because of the highly standardized nature of the designs, and because the choice of designs was so limited, many tattoos became classics, worn by a majority of tattooees in a particular social group. These tattoos, like other fads, changed as the times changed, but certain classics, like the rose, remain popular today.

Most tattooists would have, in addition to their standard flash sheets, a "pork chop sheet," a sheet of cheap flash designs that sold for a dollar or less and provided a large part of the tattooist's daily income (and allowed the tattooist to eat pork chops, instead of hamburger). In the early days, before flash was mass marketed, and when what was being sold was often poor quality work, some tattooists would copy especially nice or new designs from customers' bodies in order to add to their own collection of designs.

See also: Tattoo Technology

Further Reading: Sanders, Clinton. *Customizing the Body: The Art and Culture of Tattooing.* Philadelphia, PA: Temple University Press, 1989.

FLESH COILS *See* Pocketing and Stapling

FLESH TUNNELS *See* Ear Spools and Earplugs; Ear Stretching

FOOT BINDING

Foot binding is the practice of binding a young girl's feet with cloth in order to restrict their size and control their appearance. Foot binding was practiced in **China** from the tenth century until the twentieth century.

Foot binding was initially reserved for the elites, particularly in north China, but by the twelfth century, it had become popular among women of all social classes, including the poor.

Like many other markers of **beauty** that are associated with the wealthy, bound feet were considered beautiful partly because a woman with bound feet could not work (and often could not walk), demonstrating her high status and wealth. In addition, in China, to have bound feet meant that a woman was disciplined, virtuous, and that she was brought up correctly. Parents looking for brides for their sons would find all of these traits attractive, so bound feet would not only be a sign of status but a marker of marriageability. The fact that a girl with bound feet could not walk also most likely meant that she was a virgin, making her even more attractive.

Girls' feet were typically bound at the age of 5 or 6, with tightly wound strips of cloth. Often the big toe was left unbound, but the other toes were folded down under the sole of the foot. Over a period of months and years, the bandages would be removed and the foot rewrapped. The result was that the feet would break and become more deformed as the girl reached adulthood, but would remain small and bent over. Many girls walked on their heels because the pain in the toes was so severe, leading to very hard heels. (Once the healing process was over, however, and the bones had healed into their new position, the pain was no longer a problem.)

Other results included infection, paralysis, and muscular atrophy. Different-sized feet were called different names with the lotus of gold (which measured 3 inches) being the most sought after.

Because of this intense attention on the feet, bound or lotus feet were fetishized, as were the lotus shoes made for them. There are questions today as to whether men were sexually aroused by the sight, touch, or smell of the feet. Some reports indicate that men fondled and licked the feet, while others indicate that the somewhat rotten smell had to be masked by perfume and that men would never see a woman's feet at all. In either case, prostitutes (both male and female) and concubines adopted the practice to make themselves more beautiful and sexually attractive.

Foot binding was prohibited in China in 1911 but continued in isolated regions well into the 1930s. When the Revolutionary Party, which banned foot binding, found women in vil-

Chinese woman with bound feet, 1899. Courtesy of Library of Congress Prints and Photographs Division, Washington, DC, No. LC-USZ62-97474.

lages with bound feet, they forced them to unbind them, which caused almost as much pain as the initial binding. Unbound feet were known as "liberated feet" and some grew as much as an inch after unbinding. In 1998, the last factory to manufacture shoes for women with bound feet ended production. Some effects of foot binding are permanent: some elderly Chinese women today suffer from disabilities related to bound feet.

See also: China; Corsets; Encumberments

Further Reading: Cummings, S. R., X. Ling, and K. Stone. "Consequences of Foot Binding among Older Women in Beijing, China." *Am J Public Health* 87 (1997): 1677–1679; Hong, Fan. *Foot Binding, Feminism and Freedom: The Liberation of Women's Bodies in Modern China*. London: Frank Cass & Co., 1997; Ko, Dorothy. *Cinderella's Sisters: A Revisionist History of Foot binding*. Los Angeles: University of California Press, 2005; Kunzle, David. *Fashion and Fetishism: A Social History of the Corset, Tight-Lacing and Other Forms of Body Sculpture in the West*. New York: Rowman & Littlefield, 1982; Levy, Howard. *Chinese Foot Binding: The History of a Curious Erotic Custom of Footbinding in China*. Buffalo, NY: Prometheus Books, 1992.

FOUCAULT, MICHEL

Michel Foucault (1926–1984) was a French philosopher who wrote extensively on sexuality, the body, psychiatry, medicine, power, and the prison system. His work is useful in understanding the modification and especially the control of the human body.

One of Foucault's concerns was with the physical body and the ways in which it is regulated. For Foucault noted that modern Western bodies are disciplined through various controlling mechanisms located throughout the social body, such as medicine, psychiatry, education, law, or social policy. But power is not just wielded by particular institutions—rather, it is a part of all social relations. Furthermore, the body is not simply the target of power; it is the source of power as well, because as Foucault demonstrated, with the multitude of regulatory agencies available throughout society, bodies begin to discipline themselves and each other.

Foucault's contribution to an understanding of the body in a culture has been tremendous, as can be seen by much of the late twentieth-century scholarship on the body, the gendered body, the tortured body, or the inscribed body. Using Foucault, for instance, allows scholars to look at the body as a canvas on which patterns of significance are inscribed and counterinscribed. Tattoos, **branding**, and **scarification**, for example, are examples of how culture, and sometimes the state, write on the body. Other scholars have focused on how fashion, for example, constructs the female body, or how the body is constituted through discourses of science. Some scholars of the body emphasize the ongoing struggle for control over the female body, as women challenge, through their bodies, dominant notions of beauty, femininity, or respectability, through the use of unconventional tattoos, **piercings**, or **bodybuilding**. Even obesity in this sense can be seen as a way that some women challenge conventional notions of beauty, health, and acceptability. For Foucault, however, as bodies resist control, power responds with an entirely new mode of control, and the struggle continues. Power is inscribed on the body, but power can also be exposed to counterattack from that same body.

See also: Class and Status

Further Reading: Foucault, M. *Discipline and Punish: The Birth of the Prison*. Harmondsworth, UK: Penguin, 1979; Foucault, M. *The History of Sexuality: Volume I, An Introduction*. New York: Pantheon Books, 1980; Foucault, M. *Power/Knowledge: Selected Interviews and Other Writings, 1972–1977*. Brighton, UK: Harvester, 1980; Sullivan, Nikki. *Tattooed Bodies: Subjectivity, Textuality, Ethics, and Pleasure*. Westport, CT: Praeger, 2001.

FRATERNITIES

Tattoos and **branding** are both used by fraternity members in the United States as a sign of group affiliation. While both are, in the West, historically associated with **criminality** and deviance, and both have been used punitively to mark criminals and slaves, both are now increasingly embraced by members of American fraternities as a way of marking both membership in the fraternity as well as creating a sense of individual identity.

Because tattoos are used as marks of affiliation by both mainstream and marginalized groups, fraternities lend themselves particularly to this use, and the tattooing of Greek letters are the most commonly seen fraternity tattoos. And even while many fraternity brothers see getting a tattoo as a **rite of passage** for entry into the fraternity, they do not however, embrace the modern primitivist ideologies that are used by much of the body modification community today. Most fraternity members also don't see themselves as belonging in any real way to the tattoo community or the larger body modification community.

Branding has been used as a fraternity initiation ritual in the United States for decades. Unlike livestock branding, branding is not seen in this context as a statement of ownership, but as a symbol of the person's commitment to the organization, not just for the duration of college, but for life.

At one time, many fraternities used branding as part of the formal initiation process, although today it is typically done outside of the formal rituals of entry. Today, many fraternity brothers will choose to voluntarily brand themselves with the fraternity letters after their formal initiation.

Branding in the United States is most associated with African American fraternities, some of whom have been practicing it since the 1920s. In the case of African Americans, branding is not just a sign of affiliation with and commitment to the fraternity, but has gone from being a mark of enslavement to a symbol of power. It is not coincidental that African Americans, whose ancestors were once branded as slaves, would embrace this practice, investing it with new meanings and disinvesting it of its original stigma.

See also: Branding; Slavery

Further Reading: Brown, Tamara, Gregory S. Parks, Clarenda M. Phillips, eds., *African American Fraternities and Sororities: The Legacy and the Vision*. Lexington: University Press of Kentucky, 2005; Mizumoto Posey, Sandra. "Burning Messages: Interpreting African American Fraternity Brands and Their Bearers." *Voices, the Journal of New York Folklore* 30 (Fall–Winter 2004): 42–44.

FREAK SHOWS

A freak show is an exhibition of physically and visually different people in order to shock, and sometimes educate, viewers.

Traveling shows in which human oddities were displayed alongside exotic animals, deformed animals, musicians, jugglers, and other attractions have been popular throughout the Western world, going back to the Middle Ages. In the mid-nineteenth century, human oddities joined what became known as the freak show or ten-in-one, in which multiple attractions were joined together into one show, as part of a stationary or traveling exhibit. In the United States, these exhibits were found primarily in the dime museums (named because admission cost 10 cents) popular in the nineteenth century.

These museums were a combination of educational enterprise and entertainment. In 1840, **P. T. Barnum** became the proprietor of the American Museum, bringing the freak show to prominence. Here the freak show joined the growing popular amusement industry. In the dime museum, tattooed people were exhibited alongside people with disabilities, natural wonders like wild animals, native people, and "gaffes," "hoaxes," or manufactured fakes. Since people had never before seen any of these curiosities, the managers and showmen were able to concoct bizarre explanations for their origins, stories which were morally and socially uplifting, as well as "educational."

The showman was an essential component of the freak show. The exhibit, of course, could not be seen before a show and therefore needed the showman to market their particular attractions to the curiosity-seeking public. An essential part of the telling of the tale consisted of wonderfully and medically impossible reasons to explain to the audience the history of the person they were going to see. The most popular attractions were oddities with extraordinary talents, who could do supposedly normal things despite their disabilities.

P. T. Barnum was the most well known and most successful of all showmen, and the stories he told about his **freaks**, including the a slave who was supposedly 160 years old, the tattooed Prince Constantine, the Fiji Mermaid, Chang and Eng, the original "Siamese twins," and the dwarf Tom Thumb, helped make him famous.

Although the human oddities—made up of both "made freaks" and "born freaks"—were not originally the main attractions in these early museums, they quickly became more popular than the stuffed birds and dusty artifacts and provided acceptable entertainment (disguised as education), in an era where the church frowned upon frivolous fun. From 1870 to 1890, the freak show was the king of dime museum attractions. At the end of the nineteenth century, the dime museum began to decline, as the forms of entertainment previously granted legitimacy by the scientific cover now expanded into other venues, like **circuses**, carnivals, street fairs, and World's Fairs. In 1880, the freak show appeared at Coney Island.

Dime museums were urban, but circuses went to rural areas where they, along with the county fair, were often the only entertainment. Single-freak attractions joined circuses in the early 1800s, but the organized sideshow didn't get started till mid-century. The earliest traveling freak shows were traveling museums, and some museums joined traveling circuses as concessions. By the 1840s, though, the museum part of the circus finally became the circus sideshow, no longer independently owned and operated. By 1870s, most circuses had a freak show, and they gradually faded out in the 1950s and 1960s.

Carnivals were the rural, and lower class, equivalent of amusement parks and they grew out of the Chicago Exposition of 1893. Early on, the freaks were exhibited as single-pit shows, and were often second rate like geeks (who bit the heads off of animals) and wild men (who were supposedly from dangerous countries like **Borneo** but were often just disabled Americans). Around 1904 carnival ten-in-ones developed.

In the twentieth century, with the rediscovery of Mendelian genetics, the rise of modern science, and the eugenics movement, born freaks began to be understood from a biological and cultural perspective and this began to adversely affect the attendance at the freak show. Notions of pity, humane impulses, and the desire to lock away all undesirables led to its decline, as well as the rising middle class and their aversion to corporeal entertainment such as this. The use of the physically disabled in freak shows finally ended in the 1960s when the American Civil Liberties Union brought attention to the situation of displaying the physically disabled in circus freak shows and caused their demise; many U.S. states now prohibit the exhibition of deformed or disabled people for entertainment. Many former sideshow freaks ended up in institutions or on welfare once the freak show had died. But even before that time, the display of freaks began to die out, as early as the 1930s, partly due to the effects of the Great Depression on America's spending habits.

In Germany, freak shows were restricted or banned as early as 1911, and especially after World War I when clean-cut showgirls emerged as a new form of entertainment. By the dawn of World War II, tattooed performers, the disabled, and most other freak show acts were banned. Some freaks fled the country, but others were most likely euthanized as part of the Nazis' program to clean up the country's hospitals from 1939 to 1941 when an estimated 100,000 physically and mentally disabled people were killed.

A modern version of the old circus and carnival freak show is the Jim Rose Circus Sideshow, which employed, during the 1990s, performers who took old sideshow acts like sword swallowing and fire eating and blended them with modern physical oddities like heavily pierced, tattooed, and implanted people. Many of the acts were geared to shock the audience, and included Mr. Lifto, who lifted heavy weights from his piercings, the **Enigma**, who ate slugs and could put a power drill up his nose, and the Tube, who swallowed tubes and pumped liquids into and out of his stomach. One modern freak show that still shows "born freaks," or people born with physical abnormalities, is the 999 Eyes of Endless Dream Sideshow, founded by Ward Hall, which includes a half girl, an elephant man, a giant, a lobster girl and a dwarf, as well as bug eaters, fire eaters, a man tattooed like a leopard, deformed animals, and the like. Finally, the Internet has created an entirely new audience for freaks, through Web sites that display (either for fetishistic purposes or for shock value) photos of human abnormalities.

See also: Freaks; Tattooed Attractions

Further Reading: Adams, Rachel. *Sideshow USA: Freaks and the American Cultural Imagination*. Chicago: University of Chicago Press, 2001; Audibert, Chris. "Gone Are the Days." *Tattoo Historian* 10 (1986): 12; Bogdan, Robert. *Freak Show*. Chicago: University of Chicago Press, 1988; Eldridge, Chuck. "American Circus 1793–1993." *Tattoo Archive* (Winter 1993): 17–19; Garland Thompson, Rosemary, ed., *Freakery: Cultural Spectacles of the Extraordinary Body*. New York: New York University Press, 1996; Haraway, Donna. *Primate Visions*. New York: Routledge, 1990; Hill, Dee J. *Freaks and Fire: The Underground Reinvention of Circus Art*. Brooklyn, NY: Soft Skull Press, 2005; Hollenbeck, Phil, and Dee J. Hill. *Freaks and Fire: The Underground Reinvention of Circus*. Brooklyn, NY: Soft Skull Press, 2005.

"The Peerless Prodigies of Physical Phenomena, including the Smallest Man Alive and the Congo Giant," the sideshow of Barnum and Bailey's Greatest Show on Earth, 1898. Courtesy of Library of Congress Prints and Photographs Division, Washington, DC, No. LC-USZC4-932.

FREAKS

The term freak refers to individuals who are physically and visually different from other people, and generally refers to those who are put on display. "Freak" doesn't just refer to a person with an unusual physical condition, however. A freak is also a performative concept, a way of thinking about and presenting oneself and others as a form of entertainment.

Freaks include "born freaks" (those with disfiguring diseases or disabilities, as well as, in the Western context, "native" people), "made freaks" (such as tattooed or heavily pierced people), as well as "novelty acts" which would include sword swallowers and fire eaters. Often known as monsters, those with different or extraordinary bodies have been ostracized, ridiculed, put on display, and sometimes killed for their physical appearance.

In the West, freaks were displayed as single attractions in inns, taverns, and at local fairs throughout medieval Europe. Early documented attractions included a woman from New Guinea displayed in Europe in 1738, a Feejee Mermaid (supposedly a mummified body of a mermaid but probably created from the bodies of a fish, monkey, and perhaps an orangutan) first displayed in 1822, and Chang and Eng, the first conjoined twins who were displayed starting in 1829.

The first freak to be displayed in the United States was Miss Emma Leach, a dwarf who was shown in Boston in 1771. One of the saddest and most notorious of the early freaks was the case of Saartjie Baartman, a Kung San woman with steatopygia, purchased for display as the Hottentot Venus. She was displayed in 1810 and 1811 in a cage in London where customers were invited to pinch her buttocks. After her death in 1815, her body was dissected, her body parts preserved for future study, and plaster molds of her body and genitals were displayed in a French museum until the 1980s.

Around 1840, however, human oddities became joined into what is now known as the **freak show**, the sideshow, or in **circus** and carnival parlance, the ten-in-one, meaning ten separate acts in one location, thanks especially to the endeavors of **P. T. Barnum** who established the American Museum in 1842 and brought a number of exotic attractions together into one place. Dime museums like the American Museum gave birth to the freak show as we know it, and later freak shows moved into World's Fairs, circuses, carnivals, and amusement parks.

When being displayed in a sideshow, freaks are what the talker or manager or showman makes them. Born freaks especially were rarely in charge of their own careers or destinies, and indeed, joined circuses or carnivals typically because it was the only way they could make a living for themselves. The "exotic" presentation is one form of displaying a freak, by appealing to people's interest in the exotic, the native, and the primitive. In this way, most freaks were also frauds or "gaffes," in that the showman created extraordinary stories that typically went well beyond the individual's personal history or capabilities. For example, Tom Thumb was displayed as an 11-year-old English boy, while he was actually a 4-year-old American, and the original Wild Men of **Borneo** were actually mentally disabled brothers from Ohio.

In cases like P. T. Barnum's long running "What is It?" attraction, the freak was played by two men; one who was born with very short legs, and one who was mentally retarded and also possessed a sharply sloping forehead. Both men portrayed wild men, or missing links between animals and humans.

Born freaks included hairy ladies, such as Leonine the Lion Faced Lady, Alice Bounds the Bear Lady, and Annie Jones; giants like Patrick O'Brien the Irish Giant, and Sam Taylor the Ilkeston Giant; fat men and women; dwarves and little people like Tom Thumb, Major Mite, Harold Pyott, and Anita the Living Doll; albinos; conjoined twins like Chang and Eng or Daisy and Violet Hilton, parasitic twins; animal–human wonders such as lobster boys, human torsos, pinheads, and hermaphrodites. Other types of born freaks include native people like the "Ubangi Savages" and the "Burmese Giraffe Neck Women," and "wild men" of Borneo, Australia, and Africa.

Made freaks and novelty acts (which often overlapped in the individual performers) included sword swallowers, tattooed men and women, fire eaters, contortionists, regurgitators, snake charmers, and other performers.

Human abnormalities were explained scientifically by a number of theories, including ideas that if a pregnant woman was scared, her child may be born with an abnormality relating to what scared her. Karma has also been used to explain the birth of abnormal children, and some cultures saw abnormal births as an omen, and those children were often killed. In the eighteenth century, the science of teratology developed, which was the scientific study of "monsters," or those born with disabilities. This led to a new understanding of freaks that saw them as part of God's natural order, a belief that was later discarded in favor of the missing link theory that developed after Darwinism, which saw freaks as being a literal half-human, half-animal creature, which gave rise to the freak known as the "wild man." But as modern genetic science developed which explained in simple terms the transmission of characteristics, freaks no longer were objects of awe and fascination, and became objects of pity, leading to the eventual disappearance of the freak show. Finally, the eugenics movement of the twentieth century which saw abnormal births in the same light as racial minorities, influenced the elimination of the physically disabled from the public eye in places like Germany, where freak shows were not only outlawed but their performers were often killed under Nazi rule. Today, the term "freak" is rarely used anymore to refer to people with disabilities, and the disability rights movement has created opportunities for the disabled that allow for a range of careers that do not depend on the display of one's condition for money.

Today, those born with disabilities often can undergo surgery to correct the conditions that would have at one time made them into freaks. Surgery to separate conjoined twins or to remove a parasitic twin is increasingly common and successful. Surgery can be used to repair deformed hands (that would have otherwise been known as lobster hands), and artificial limbs are available for those born without legs or arms.

On the other hand, there are still a number of people who willingly undergo multiple tattoo, **piercing**, implantation, and other body modification procedures in order to transform themselves into modern freaks. Katzen, **the Enigma**, the Leopard Man, and the Lizardman are all examples of modern freaks, many of whom perform in sideshows or other venues today.

See also: Freak Shows; Tattooed Attractions

Further Reading: Bogdan, Robert. *Freak Show*. Chicago: University of Chicago Press, 1988; Garland Thompson, Rosemary, ed., *Freakery: Cultural Spectacles of the Extraordinary Body*. New York: New York University Press, 1996; Hollenbeck, Phil, and Dee J. Hill. *Freaks and Fire: The Underground Reinvention of Circus*. Brooklyn, NY: Soft Skull Press, 2005.

G

GANG MEMBERS

Because tattoos have long been associated with **criminality** in the West, thanks to the practice, dating back to the **Greco-Roman world**, of **tattooing** criminals as a form of punishment and identification, it is not surprising that gang members in the United States and elsewhere would embrace tattooing as a sign of affiliation and a badge of rebellion and bravery.

While many people associate gangs today with inner city ethnic minorities such as African Americans, Latinos, and Asians, American urban gangs first formed in the nineteenth century in immigrant communities populated by Italians and Irish. As today, poor, alienated, and oppressed youth made up the original American gangs. While the Italian gangs eventually became what we now call the Mafia, newer immigrant groups, moving into inner city neighborhoods in New York, Los Angeles, Chicago, and San Francisco (and joined by African American youth) formed their own gangs which specialized in running drugs, and which continue unabated in most urban centers today.

Today, American gangs are estimated to have at least a million members, and are found not only in cities but in suburbs as well. Gangster style, as represented in rap videos, is pervasive among American youth who have adopted the clothing, language, and other stylistic markers of primarily African American gangsters. **Chicano** gangs in the 1940s on the West Coast also influenced mainstream Latino culture at that time, but never had the influence that African American gang style has today.

In the United States today, there are a variety of street gangs as well as prison gangs, with a great deal of crossover between the street and the prison context. Virtually all use tattooing as a way of marking their identity, just as they use grafitti to mark territory and communicate important information about the gang.

The most common gang tattoos are tattoos of the gang's name or symbol. Nuestra Familia tattoos may be either a NF, or NS, or a sombrero over a bloody machete, the New Mexican Mafia tattoos are often a circle with a skull and crossed blades within, the Norteños use a 14, and the Bloods often wear an upside down crab (which is an insult aimed at Crips) or the letters RBD or Blood. Crips will often have C or WS (for West Side) tattooed on them, and the Black Guerilla Family generally wears the letters BGF in Old English lettering.

Prison gangs will mark themselves with symbols associated with being incarcerated, such as barbed wire, spiderwebs, tears, and cell bars, and biker gangs like the Hell's Angels will wear tattoos associated with Harley Davidson motorcycles, gang names and symbols, as well as biker-style tattoos like Fuck the World.

One of the most popular gang tattoos, both within Chicano gangs as well as other types of gangs, is the *loca*, which identifies the neighborhood from which the gang comes from. Often tattooed in bold Old English letters across the stomach, chest, or back, the *loca* has been borrowed by nongang members, both inside and outside of the Chicano community. The *pachuco* cross, a small cross tattooed between the thumb and forefinger on the hand, is another common Chicano gang tattoo.

Asian gangs in the United States wear their own tattoos as well, symbolizing membership in gangs such as the Yakuza and Triad; Born To Kill; Dai Huen Jai, Kung Lok, Flying Dragons, and Ghost Shadows. Asian gang tattoos also represent gang names or symbols, and include as well animals like tigers, panthers, eagles, and cobras.

White gangs date back to the early Irish gangs in the United States, but are now commonly associated with white supremacist groups, and often overlap with bikers, which explains the popularity of biker tattoos such as Hell's Angels designs or designs from other biker clubs, Harley Davidson designs, and images and words associated with being an outlaw. White supremacist phrases are common in white gangs, as well as specific organizational logos and names such as the KKK or the Aryan Brotherhood, and swastikas and other images taken from the Nazis.

As with **prison tattooing**, urban criminal justice departments keep databases of gang tattoos in order to identify gang members and keep track of gang activities. Because gang tattoos, like the prison tattoos to which they are stylistically and thematically related, are often worn in public spots on the face, neck, and hands, former gang members who grow to regret their tattoos can take advantage of a number of city programs which provide free tattoo removal for gang members. On the other hand, some gang members are choosing today not to get tattooed, in order to make it more difficult for the police to identify them as gang members.

See also: Chicanos; Criminality; Prison Tattooing;

Further Reading: Govenar, Alan. "The Variable Context of Chicano Tattooing." In Arnold Rubin, ed., *Marks of Civilization: Artistic Transformations of the Human Body*. Los Angeles: Museum of Cultural History, UCLA, 1988.

GAUNTLET *See* Ward, Jim

GENDER

Gender assumptions, stereotypes, and roles play a major role in the types of body adornments that will be worn by men and women, and the types of body modifications that they will undergo, as well as the meanings associated with them.

In non-Western societies, the uses of body modifications and adornment are often very similar for men and women in that both men and women may receive **scarification,** or tattoos, or a **piercing** as part of an initiation ritual, which are sometimes very similar for men and women (or boys and girls). Men and women may also be similar in that their tattoos or scars convey important information about their rank, lineage, or geneology, regardless of gender. However, far more often than not, we find that where men's practices convey either social information about the man or his place in society, women's practices often serve primarily to beautify her, or to make her marriageable.

Men, as it has often been noted by feminists, are often defined by what they do and what they have achieved. Women, on the other hand, are often defined by how they look, as well as their reproductive abilities. Men's tattoos, **circumcisions**, scarrings, or piercings, then often signify an achievement: success in a hunt or in warfare, for example. Because so many of these practices are painful, they also serve as an important test of a man's strength and courage, which demonstrates his fitness as a man.

Women, on the other hand, often receive their marks to enhance their **beauty** and to make them marriageable. Many times those marks are thought to also enable their fertility, and when, as in the case of Yoruba scarification, the marks are painful, they are sometimes seen to measure whether the woman will be able to undergo the pain of childbirth. While childbirth is no doubt an achievement, it is not a cultural achievement the way that men's activities are.

In addition, a number of the beauty practices used by women today, such as **cosmetic surgery, makeup**, and dieting, are not only attempts to make a woman more beautiful, but ensure that her body conforms to other normative standards. Thus women cannot be too tall, too hairy, too muscular, too fat, too tattooed, or too much of anything. Their bodies must be disciplined and controlled.

Some practices are aimed exclusively at men or women. Men alone undergo circumcision, **subincision**, and **castration**. Circumcision and subincision both are important ritual activities that allow a boy to become a man (or in the case of **Judaism**, that mark one as a member of the tribe of Jews), and that, at the same time, test his strength and endurance, both important characteristics expected of men.

> When I was going through a very bad time in a marriage this [tattoo] became my shield. I became strong and I would have it re-colored in when I started to feel weak ... It was a sense of freedom.
>
> ANONYMOUS

Castration, on the other hand, is a punitive measure, but does not punish a person because he is a man, but because he is a criminal, a slave, or a prisoner of war.

Women, on the other hand, are unique in that they are the recipients of **female genital mutilation**, which involves the removal of the clitoris and an end to a woman's sexual pleasure. Unlike circumcision, female genital mutilation does not celebrate a woman's maturity, but ensures that her pleasure and her independence will be limited, in order to ensure fidelity to her husband. Some procedures, such as **infibulation** or recircumcision, are also geared to not only ensure faithfulness but to provide the man with extra sexual pleasure. **Foot binding** too is a practice that is only endured by women, in order to make them marriageable and keep them compliant. Many practices like foot binding or the wearing of **corsets** are not only worn by women to enhance their beauty, but often also restrict mobility, freedom, and even health.

In the West, too, we see that men and women have, traditionally, modified their bodies for very different reasons. Because normative standards of beauty demand that a woman appear youthful and fertile, diet and exercise are geared toward producing a very thin body which appears childlike. Makeup and cosmetic surgery, too, are aimed at keeping a woman looking as young and fertile as possible, regardless of the financial or physical costs. Even fashionable trends such as long **fingernails** or the wearing of high heels are geared to make women appear sexual and youthful, even while they make the woman less useful.

> Nice girls don't get tattooed.
>
> SAMUEL STEWARD (aka Phil Sparrow), tattooist

Men, on the other hand, are celebrated by their achievements, so physical appearance is not as important. When it is measured, men are expected to be strong and powerful, explaining the importance of sports like **bodybuilding** to men (and the ambivalent position women hold in that sport).

When we see men and women engaged in the same body modification practice, such as tattooing, it is still often done differently, based on gender ideologies and assumptions. Male and female **tattooed attractions** in **circus sideshows**, for example, traded on myths of the savage native for their success, but women were more popular because their myths also included a sexual element—that they were not only taken captive but possibly ravaged by their captors. Women also did not just display their bodies, but some engaged in a type of striptease to arouse the audience.

American women traditionally did not get tattooed, because tattoos were a mark of masculinity and the underclasses. When women did start becoming tattooed in large numbers in the 1970s, tattoos changed in many ways to accommodate them. More feminine designs were developed (dolphins, butterflies, rabbits, and kittens), and tattoos were placed on more "feminine" parts of the body (such as the ankle, lower back, or shoulder), in order to allow the tattooed woman to retain her femininity.

Yet some women resisted this redefinition, and embrace tattooing as a confrontational practice. Heavily tattooed women's bodies in the West still represent an assault to conventional notions about the female body. Yet many women use tattooing, and piercing, scarification, **branding,** and other more radical practices, to not only challenge normative conventions about femininity, but to reclaim their own bodies as well.

Western women, and especially middle-class women, often define their body practices in terms of healing, empowerment, or control. As feminist scholars have shown, the body is both the site for the inscription of power and the primary site of resistance to that power—the body entails the possibility of counterinscription, of being "self marked." One can argue that women, through marking their bodies with unconventional body practices, are working to erase the oppressive marks of a patriarchal society and to replace them with marks of their own choosing. These women can be said to control and subvert the ever-present "male gaze" by forcing men (and women) to look at their bodies in a manner that keeps them in control.

See also: Beauty; Cosmetic Surgery; Foot Binding; Makeup

Further Reading: Avis, K. *Reshaping the Female Body*. London: Routledge, 1995; DeMello, Margo. *Bodies of Inscription: A Cultural History of the Modern Tattoo Community*. Durham, NC: Duke University Press, 2000; Jeffreys, Sheila. *Beauty and Misogyny: Harmful Cultural Practices in the West*. London: Routledge, 2005; Mifflin, Margot. *Bodies of Subversion: A Secret History of Women and Tattoos*. New York: Juno Books, 1997; Pitts, V. "'Reclaiming' the Female Body: Embodied Identity Work, Resistance and the Grotesque." *Body & Society* 4(3) (1988): 67–84.

GENETIC ENGINEERING

Genetic engineering refers to the process of manipulating genes in humans, animals, or plants, in order to create an organism with new genetic characteristics, such as a crop that is resistant to pests or an animal which resists cancer.

Genetic engineering is being currently used today to genetically modify plants and animals for human benefit. Genetic engineering of livestock began in the 1970s. Changing the genetic makeup of an animal by manipulating and transferring selected genes from one animal to the next allows scientists to produce specific traits in animals to be used for food (such as tenderness of flesh, disease resistance and level of fat; it is even being used to produce meatier salmon). One company, for example, has discovered a gene marker which will allow scientists to breed pigs with leaner meat, while another has recently developed a way to test for genes for lean meat production ("double muscling") in cattle.

Cloning breeder livestock, and perhaps even animals to be consumed, is the wave of the future, since Dolly the sheep was successfully cloned in 1996. Cloning offers scientists the greatest level of control over offspring, promising higher yields by copying only very productive or disease-resistant animals (although the health of the clones is currently in question, since Dolly herself died at the relatively young age of 6, and for every healthy clone produced, a majority of deformed clones are born or miscarried). So far, the focus has been to clone only prized breeder animals as it is not yet legal to produce food animals themselves, although scientists involved in cloning have published studies maintaining that the cloned animals meet "industry standards" and compare to normal animals in most every respect.

Genetic engineering, too, is starting to take off in the pet-breeding world. Glofish—zebra fish modified with sea anemone genes to make them glow—were introduced in the United States as a novelty pet in 2004, unleashing a string of controversy and legal actions. But the primary focus in genetic engineering for the past few years has been to produce, via genetic modification, an allergen-free cat. An American biotech expects to offer the first genetically modified cat, or "lifestyle pet," for sale (for approximately $3,500) in 2007.

While human beings are not yet subject to genetic engineering, there is a movement called transhumanism which proposes that genetic engineering be used to enhance the human body and mind, and to eliminate negative aspects of the human condition such as aging or disease, resulting in a transformed human being that could be called post-human.

Further Reading: Agar, Nicholas. *Liberal Eugenics: In Defense of Human Enhancement.* New York: Blackwell Publishing, 2004; Dery, Mark. *Escape Velocity: Cyberculture at the End of the Century.* New York: Grove, 1996; Graham, Elaine. *Representations of the Post/Human: Monsters, Aliens and Others in Popular Culture.* New Brunswick, NJ: Rutgers University Press, 2002; Shanks, Peter. *Human Genetic Engineering: A Guide for Activists, Skeptics, and the Very Perplexed.* New York: Nation Books, 2005.

GENITAL MUTILATION

Genital mutilation refers to both the voluntary practices found within the body modification community (and which are themselves modeled after the traditional practices of "primitive" peoples) to radically modify the genitals, as well as a number of voluntary and involuntary practices, often performed during **rites of passage**, that result in the mutilation of the genitals.

In terms of voluntary practices, most genital mutilations are associated with the male genitals, and most involve the cutting of the penis as it is practiced in traditional societies in Australia, Africa, and other countries.

Circumcision, or the removal of the foreskin of the penis, is the most common practice that falls under the name genital mutilation. Widely practiced in cultures around the world to mark tribal membership and as part of initiation rituals into manhood, circumcision rituals generally occur sometime during a boy's adolescence. These rituals not only include the ritual cutting of the boy's penis without anesthesia (as a test of his courage and strength), but often involve the transmission of important cultural knowledge that is often only available to adult men.

Some groups, such as many Aboriginal Australian bands, practice a number of other genital mutilation rituals as well. The most common of these is **subincision**, in which the underside of the shaft of the penis is split lenghwise, and less commonly, **superincision**, in which the penis is split along the top of the shaft. A meatotomy is a procedure where the glans (or the head), rather than the shaft, of the penis is split. These practices have now been adopted by some members of the body modification community, and, while rare, are becoming more common within this subculture.

Far more rare are procedures that actually remove the penis, or destroy its functionality. As radical as subincision, superincision, and meatotomy are, they allow for urination, insertion into a vagina, orgasm, and ejaculation. A penectomy, on the other hand, is the total removal of the penis. While not practiced as part of most initiation rituals around the world, **Hijras**, a community of transgendered people in **India**, do have their penises (as well as their testicles) removed during their intitiation into the culture of Hijras. Male to female **transsexuals** also have their penises removed as part of **sex reassignment surgery**, although the procedure is not considered mutilation when performed in this context. Historically during wartime, victorious soldiers were known to remove the penises from the corpses of the enemy, as souvenirs and as a mark of humiliation and conquest.

On the other hand, some men do choose to have their penises removed in order to fulfill a sexual fetish, as part of a radical **BDSM** relationship, or for other personal reasons. Other men instead choose to have the glans of their penis removed, retaining the shaft, and still others in the modern body modification community have their glans surgically shaped. Trumpeting, for example, is a procedure whereby the urethral opening of the penis is flared, via removing the tip of the penis. Because most doctors will not perform these procedures, men often turn to underground or unlicensed doctors, friends, or they attempt the procedures themselves.

Castration is another surgery practiced by some men in the body modification community. It involves the removal of the testicles and generally the scrotum, and is performed sometimes to control the libido, for men in whom excessive sexual appetites are a problem. Other men do it for sexual masochism, and some feel sexually aroused at the thought of having their testicles, and sometimes penis, removed.

The results of castration include sterility, reduced or eliminated libido, sometimes a loss of body strength, feelings of calmness and sometimes depression, weight gain or fat redistribution, and softer body hair. Many early states castrated servants and slaves to reduce their sexual appetite, to destroy their reproductive ability, and to make them calmer. On the other hand, castration has often been used to punish criminals, especially those whose crimes were sexual in nature, as well as to emasculate vanquished enemies and prisoners of war. And finally, castration has been used by a number of religious groups as a form of **self-mortification** to deny the person sexual pleasure.

Male-to-female transsexuals, as well as some transgendered people such as Hijras, undergo physical castration as part of their transition from one gender to the other. Voluntary castration is also used today as an extreme body modification and for the purposes of sexual excitement. Men who seek voluntary castration today, like those who want to have their penises removed, often turn to underground doctors or cutters to perform the surgery.

The practice of removing the clitorises and otherwise mutilating the female genitals is an example of involuntary genital mutilation. Today, **clitoridectomies** and **infibulation**, in which the clitoris and labia minora are removed and the labia majora is sewn together, are commonly performed on young girls in many Arab, Muslim, and North African cultures, in order to ensure virginity upon marriage and sexual fidelity after marriage, by removing the source of a woman's sexual pleasure. It is also sometimes performed as part of a traditional initiation ritual for girls. Today, a very small number of women in the body modification community choose to have their clitorises removed, and sometimes their labia as well. More common is the practice of female circumcision, in which the clitoral hood, and sometimes the inner labia, is removed, but the clitoris is left intact. These procedures are said to increase sexual pleasure by uncovering the clitoris. Finally, some women today choose to undergo temporary infibulation, wherein the labia are temporarily sealed together with glue, **piercings**, or stitches, in order to deny oneself sexual pleasure for a set amount of time.

See also: Castration; Circumcision; Clitoridectomy; Subincision/Superincision

Further Reading: Momoh, Comfort. *Female Genital Mutilation*. Oxford: Radcliffe University Press, 2005; Myers, James. "Nonmainstream Body Modification: Genital Piercing, Branding, Burning and Cutting." *Journal of Contemporary Ethnography* 21(3) (October 1992): 267–306; Pitts, Victoria. "Body Modification, Self-Mutilation And Agency in Media Accounts of a Subculture." In Mike Featherstone, ed., *Body Modification*. London: Sage Publications, 2000.

GENITAL PIERCING

Genital piercings are one of the most popular types of piercings in the body modification culture. They are a decorative enhancement for many, and can enhance sexual stimulation and pleasure for the wearer and his or her partner. They are also often worn by members of the **BDSM** community as part of a slave/master relationship, or in non-BDSM relationships for partners to mark commitment to each other.

For women, many times receiving a genital piercing is a sign of empowerment; many women see the act of having one's genitals pierced as being a way that she takes her body back and claims ownership over it. Because genital piercings, unless performed as part of a play piercing ritual, involve the use of **jewelry**; many women see genital piercings as a way to celebrate and decorate the female genitalia, not generally seen as beautiful in Western culture.

Men also use genital piercings as a form of decoration, and see the various types of jewelry used on the penis and scrotum as an enhancement. In addition, most men report enhanced sexual pleasure with many of the piercings, and many men's partners also enjoy the sensation of a pierced penis.

Both men and women often choose to receive a genital piercing as a **rite of passage** to mark the transition from one life stage to another, or an important event. And for members of the **BDSM** community, the **pain** of the piercing is part of the pleasure, and is also a part of the transformative process for the wearer.

Male genital piercings include **penis piercings**, including the ampallang, which pierces the glans of the penis horizontally; the apadravya, which pierces the glans of the penis vertically; the Prince Albert, which is pierced underneath the penis behind the glans; and the Dydoe, which is a piercing around the edge of the glans. Frenum piercings are piercings that pierce the skin between the foreskin and the glans. Scrotal piercings are those that pierce the scrotum, and include the hafada piercing, which pierces the side of the scrotum, on the crease, and the Guiche, which pierces the base of the scrotum, through the perineum, while the transscrotal piercing is a piercing that goes through the entire scrotum, from front to back, or from side to side. Finally, a lorum is a piercing underneath the penis at its base, where the penis meets the scrotum. The jewelry used in male genital piercings are primarily the captive bead ring and the barbell.

Women's piercings include the clitoral hood piercing, which is perhaps the most common female genital piercing, and pierces the clitoral hood; labia piercings, which pierce the labia majora and/or labia minora; the fourchette piercing, which pierces the rim of the vagina; the Princess Albertina, which involves a ring which pierces the urethra and emerges from the top of the vagina; and the Christina piercing which is a surface piercing just below the pubic mound. Having the actual clitoris pierced via a **clitoral piercing** is quite rare, and is generally only found on women with a large enough clitoris to take the piercing and to not lose sensation.

See also: Clitoral Piercing, Penis Piercing

Further Reading: Myers, James. "Nonmainstream Body Modification: Genital Piercing, Branding, Burning and Cutting." *Journal of Contemporary Ethnography* 21(3) (October 1992): 267–306; Pitts, Victoria. "Body Modification, Self-Mutilation and Agency in Media Accounts of a Subculture." In Mike Featherstone, ed., *Body Modification*. London: Sage Publications, 2000.

GENITAL TATTOOING

While not common around the world, a number of cultures do have traditions in which the penis is tattooed, generally as part of a larger design. Among the people of the **Marshall Islands**, for example, many men were almost completely covered with tattoos, although certain tattoos, such as the neck and face tattoo, were limited to people of a chiefly rank. Penis tattoos were similar in that only chiefs could have their penises tattooed. The **pe'a**, which is the traditional Samoan tattoo that covers the torso from belly button to knees, also included the penis.

In the West, genital tattoos have not been very common, but have always been a topic around which jokes and stories circulated. Penis tattoos in particular, due to the difficulty in tattooing, the nature of the designs requested, and the effects on the person being tattooed, were (and are) a favorite topic in tattoo shops. Legendary designs included eyeballs or flies on the glans, and barber poles, lollipops and "YOUR NAME" on the shaft. One joke tells of a man who got a hundred-dollar bill tattooed on his penis: "He got it so that his wife could stretch their money and blow a hundred dollars just like that!" Another refers to the naval tradition of getting a rooster (cock) tattooed below the knee: If you put a chicken on one leg and a pig on the other, and if the ship sunk, you wouldn't go down with the ship. Additionally, the man can say to people, "my cock goes down to there," pointing to his lower leg. A related joke was to have a cherry tattooed on the body. A man could say to a woman, "here's my cherry, where's yours?"

One story that was told to me, but which may be yet another genital tattoo legend, goes as follows: This guy was getting tattooed by one of my coworkers in my shop. He wanted "Kosher" in Hebrew tattooed on his dick. So he goes to a store where they sell Kosher wine and he asks the guy who runs the store (who is Jewish) to write out "Kosher" in Hebrew, from a wine label, onto a piece of paper to take with him to the tattooist. So he does this. Then he's over here getting tattooed and I get this call for this guy. I say he can't talk right now, he's being tattooed. But the guy's real insistent and really wants to talk to him. So I say, OK, and I go get the guy. By this time, the tattoo's almost done. Turns out the guy had written the wrong Hebrew word down for him. What he actually wrote was "Boiled." So this guy's got "Boiled" tattooed on his dick! An older story which is most likely apocryphal, but which reflects the U.S. military practice of inspecting potential recruits' bodies for health and hygiene, goes like this: A guy in the service is getting his dick inspected for health, venereal diseases, etc. It's called the "short arm inspection." The sergeant comes along and sees his dick has a tattoo on it. "What's that?" "It's my girlfriend's name." "Oh, her name is Dot?" "No, when I have a hard-on it says Dorothy!"

On the other hand, gay men, and especially those involved with the leather or **BDSM** communities, have worn genital tattoos for years.

See also: BDSM

Further Reading: Featherstone, Mike, ed., *Body Modification*. London: Sage Publications, 2000; Vale, V., and Andrea Juno. *Modern Primitives*. San Francisco, CA: Re/Search Publications, 1989.

THE GREAT OMI

Born Horace Ridler (1886–1969), the Great Omi was a sideshow performer famous for his unique full-body tattoo, **piercings**, and sharpened teeth.

> To become a freak in order to earn a livelihood was a gamble which might not have come off. Fortunately it did and [Omi] was one of the most successful and highest paid showmen in both hemispheres.
>
> GEORGE BURCHETT, tattooist

Ridler grew up in an upper-class family outside of London, and joined the Army as an officer in the early years of the twentieth century, and again enlisted at the beginning of World War I. After the war, with little prospects and having spent an inheritance from his father, he decided to become a professional **sideshow** entertainer, getting a few tattoos and exhibiting himself at a dime museum called the Odditorium starting in 1922.

By that year, however, there was enough competition that his few tattoos were not spectacular enough to earn a decent living. So he wrote to English tattooist George Burchett in 1934, asking to be turned into a human zebra. His entire face and head and most of his body was ultimately covered with a heavy black curvilinear design, he had his earlobes pierced and stretched, he hired a dentist to file his teeth to sharp points and he had an ivory tusk inserted into a piercing in his septum (which he got from a veterinarian). He also acquired a number of elaborate costumes including tall gold boots. The Great Omi was born.

> Underneath it all, I'm really an ordinary man.
>
> THE GREAT OMI, circus freak

One of Omi's first gigs, however, did not go as well as he would have liked. He had been hired by a small **circus** in France, and found that he was billed as an animal and had to work next to the lions. In a letter to George Burchett dated September 1, 1935, he tells Burchett of his treatment: "I put in my resignation which they would not accept. When I was too ill to work they painted up a nigger with white paint and put him on in my place."

The Great Omi, sideshow performer. Courtesy of Tattoo Archive.

While the presentation of an African man (dressed in "native" clothes and exhibited in an "authentic" native village) was at one time exotic enough to bring in paying crowds, by this late date (the 1930s), it was not good enough. Nor was a simple tattooed man enough of a draw. It became necessary to present much greater oddities to the public, hence, Omi, and later his black substitute, was displayed as a man/beast. At other shows, however, he was displayed in a similar fashion to other **tattooed attractions** at the time, claiming in his show that he had been captured and forcibly tattooed in **New Guinea**.

Along with his wife Omette, he appeared at the World's Fair in New York in 1939, and ultimately became the longest running star attraction of Ripley's Odditorium Theatre, after which he moved to Ringling Brothers Barnum and Bailey Circus. Omi retired with his wife to a small village in England in 1950, and died at 77.

See also: Circus; Freak Shows; Freaks

Further Reading: Burchett, George, and Peter Leighton. *Memoirs of a Tattooist*. London: Oldbourne Book Company, 1958; Vale, V., and Andrea Juno. *Modern Primitives*. San Francisco, CA: Re/Search Publications, 1989.

GRECO-ROMAN WORLD

Tattooing was widely practiced among the civilizations of the ancient Mediterranean, primarily as a form of punishment for criminals, leading to the modern Western association of tattoos, **criminality**, and the underclass.

Originally, the Greeks did not use tattooing and saw it as a barbaric practice. Contempories of the Greeks who did use tattooing included the Thracians (of Bulgaria and western Turkey), the Egyptians, the Syrians, and the Persians. Tattooing for these groups probably served multiple purposes. The Syrians, for instance, wore tattoos on their wrists that had a sacred significance, and runaway slaves who received sacred designs were considered to now serve the divinity rather than their former masters and were freed of service. Thracian tattoo usage, found on both men and women, could have been decorative as well as serving social purposes. Egyptian tattoos were worn by women and were both decorative and used for ritual purposes. The Persians tattooed slaves and prisoners of war, and this was perhaps the source for later Greek tattooing.

The Greeks picked up the practice of tattooing in the fifth century BCE and began following the Persian practice of using tattoo marks for punitive purposes. The Greeks tattooed both prisoners and runaway slaves on the forehead, usually with a mark demonstrating their crime. The term **stigmata** was used to describe tattoo marks by the Greeks and later the Romans.

The Romans inherited punitive tattooing from the Greeks, and later began marking soldiers as well. They also used **branding** to mark animals (as did the Greeks) and human slaves, as did the Egyptians. Like the Persians, who often tattooed slaves and prisoners with the name of the king, the Romans sometimes marked slaves with the name of their owner. Prisoners of war and soldiers alike were tattooed with the name of the emperor (and soldiers were sometimes marked with a series of dots which may have represented their unit) and many criminals were marked with the sentence rather than the crime (such as being sent to the mines).

Because Christians were widely persecuted by the Romans, Christians were commonly marked with tattoos signifying the crime of being Christians, or, again, the punishment given to them. Eventually the stigma of being a persecuted Christian became a badge of honor among Christians, leading to the practice, starting about the fourth century, of Christians voluntarily tattooing themselves as a sign of faith and group membership. When the Roman Empire later converted to Christianity under Constantine, Constantine banned facial tattooing, but he allowed it on the hands and calves of criminals, although it was no longer forced upon Christians.

Both the Greeks and Romans also pierced the ears, and elites of both societies wore elaborate earrings and other **jewelry** made of fine metals and precious stones. Roman men pierced their nipples as well as a sign of virility, and Roman gladiators pierced their penises in order to tie them back as protection during their fights.

See also: Criminality; Christianity; Egypt; Slavery

Further Reading: Gustafson, Mark. "The Tattoo in the Later Roman Empire and Beyond." In Jane Caplan, ed., *Written on the Body: The Tattoo in European and American History*. Princeton, NJ: Princeton University Press, 2000; Jones, C. P. "Stigma and Tattoo." In Jane Caplan, ed., *Written on the Body: The Tattoo in European and American History*. Princeton: Princeton University Press, 2000.

H

HAIR CUTTING AND HEAD SHAVING

Because human head hair grows continuously throughout one's lifetime, humans have always had to cut their hair. Consequently, a number of rituals and styles associated with the cutting of hair have developed, with short hair, long hair, and a lack of hair all being socially and culturally significant.

Because hair is such a central aspect of human appearance, cutting the hair, especially in a significant way, often holds a great deal of importance. It's not surprising then, that hair cutting is often performed in a ritual fashion, and in particular, as part of **rites of passage** to mark a person's transition from one life stage to another. During a Greek Orthodox baptism, for example, the baby's hair is cut in three places in the shape of a cross, and Orthodox Jews celebrate a baby boy's first haircut at the age of three as a significant event in the child's life. During the ritual, all of his hair is removed except for a sidelock, to symbolize the baby becoming a boy. Brahmin children in **India** have their heads shaved before starting school, and Masai girls have their heads shaved at puberty. Among the Huli of **Papua New Guinea**, boys undergo a lengthy initiation period during which they grow their hair long; at the end of the iniation, they cut their hair off and make it into wigs which will be worn during ritual use.

Hair cutting can be functional, as in ancient **Egypt** when children as well as adults routinely kept their heads shaved as a way to cope with the heat as well as lice. Similarly, soldiers fighting in the First World War had to cope with lice and fleas, which led to the practice of soldiers wearing their hair very short, which continues today.

In many cultures, the heads of religious specialists are shaved, such as among Egyptian priests who not only shaved their heads but their entire bodies as a mark of purity. Buddhist and Christian monks usually have their heads shaved during their ordination; in **Thailand** monks shave their eyebrows as well. Usually, religious head shaving, or tonsure, is used to show the initiate's renunciation of vanity and other worldly concerns. Eastern Orthodox practices involved shaving the whole head; while Christian Celtic practices involved shaving the front of the head from ear to ear, while wearing hair longer in the back. During Roman times, Christian clerics shaved the top of the head, allowing the hair to form a crown around the head.

Hair cutting or head shaving is also associated with mourning in a number of cultures. Hindus, for instance, traditionally shaved a woman's head after her husband's death in order to prevent other men from being attracted to her. In

Tonga, it was customary for a woman to cut her hair as a sign of mourning for a person of higher status than herself. Hindu tradition states that men shave their heads when their father dies, and if a king or other respected male leader dies, often all men in the community will shave their heads.

Cutting or shaving the hair is often used as a punishment or a form of social control. For instance, the Han Chinese did not cut their hair, wearing it on top of their heads. When the Manchus conquered **China** in the seventeenth century, they forced the Han to shave their foreheads in order to look like the conquerors. During World War II, Jewish concentration camp prisoners had their heads shaved, and after the war, French Nazi collaborators had their heads shaved as punishment. In some Arab countries, the beards and eyebrows of prisoners are sometimes shaved off in order to humiliate the men. Finally, slaves in many countries often were forced to wear their hair short, as a way of stripping from them their identities as free men. In both the military and prison contexts, head shaving can also be seen as a form of social control, and as a way to reduce individual identity in favor of group identity and submission to authority.

In the West, voluntary head shaving did not become popular until British skinheads began shaving their heads, a practice which eventually moved into various youth subcultures in the United States. Today, while shaved heads are still not the norm in the West, some men do shave their heads, either as a fashion statement or to cover up male pattern baldness.

See also: Body Hair; Facial Hair; Hairstyles

Further Reading: Corson, Richard. *Fashions in Hair: The 1st 5,000 Years*. Chester Springs, PA: Dufour Editions, 2001; Hiltebeitel, Alf, and Barbara D. Miller, eds. *Hair: Its Power and Meaning in Asian Cultures*. Albany: State University of New York Press, 1998; Sherrow, Victoria. *Encyclopedia of Hair: A Cultural History*. Westport, CT: Greenwood Press, 2006.

HAIRSTYLES

Because humans are unique in having hair that continually grows on our heads, it's not surprising that humans would create such a wide variety of ways to style the hair. And while evolutionary psychologists propose that long hair is used to denote health, allowing people to easily gauge a potential mate's fitness as a partner, the fact that long hair is not universally found to be attractive makes this claim somewhat questionable. In fact, some cultures, like many African tribes, use mud, fat, or animal dung to style their hair, which would certainly mask the healthy appearance of the hair. We do know, however, that the way that hair is cut, styled, and colored indicates a great deal about cultural preferences, as well as an individual's social position and personal identity.

Gender, marital status, age, and group membership are all signified by hair in ways that are culturally and historically specific. For instance, while Masai warriors traditionally wear their hair long, with the front section braided and the back hair grown to waist length, Masai women and nonwarriors, on the other hand, shave their heads. Boys in ancient Greece wore their hair short, and Indian boys shaved their heads when they reached adolescence. In medieval Europe girls wore uncovered flowing hair, while matrons bound theirs under veils. As a sign of mourning the ancient Egyptians, whose heads were usually shaved, grew long hair, and widows in India cut off their hair when mourning. Chinese women combed their hair into a low knot, which might be decorated with jeweled combs, hairpins, or flowers, and unmarried girls wore long plaits. Hopi girls demonstrated their marriageable status by wearing their hair patterned into two squash blossoms over the ears, a style that they abandoned after marriage.

Starting in the seventeenth century, Japanese geisha have worn an elaborate chignon hairstyle known as the shimada. The type of shimada worn demonstrates the status or age of the geisha, with a high chignon worn by younger women, a flattened chignon worned by older women, and a style called the divided peach which is worn by geishas in training.

Gender, too, is marked through hairstyles, as men and women typically wear different hairstyles in most cultures, as a way of distinguishing the sexes. When men or women wear the hairstyles associated with the opposite gender, there is generally a great degree of social concern, as when, in the 1920s, women in the United States began wearing short hairstyles, or during the 1960s when men began wearing their hair long.

Historically, royalty and the wealthy have always worn more elaborate hairstyles than common people. Wealthy women in ancient Sumeria, for example, wore elaborate hairstyles of buns, rolls, and plaits, powdered with gold dust, and adorned with gold ornaments. The elites of Mayan culture practiced head shaping, shaved their heads in order to emphasize the noble shape, and wore high headdresses on top.

In ancient Greece and Rome, women visited hair salons or had slaves attend their hair, and wore their hair long, dyed with henna, and styled in a number of fancy styles. Greek and Roman elites often also wore wigs. Many men wore their hair long, but slaves wore theirs short or shaved. And while many Egyptians shaved their hair, Egyptian elites wore beautiful wigs made of human hair in a variety of hairstyles, and which were adorned with beautiful ornaments. Commoners later wore wigs as well, but could only afford those made of sheep's wool or vegetable fiber, or wore hair extensions.

In Europe, the wealthy also spent more time, effort, and resources on their hair in order to demonstrate status, conform to fashions, and appear beautiful. Women in the fifteenth century, for example, plucked their hairline to emphasize their forehead and wore their hair in an elaborate headdress, and as time went on, elite women's hairstyles only became more complicated, generally involving wigs and artificial frames on which the wig or hair would be piled. European (and later American) men, too, from the seventeenth century until the nineteenth century wore long hair or powdered wigs, generally worn curled, in a ponytail, or in plaits.

Sometimes hair is styled specifically for a religious ritual or other ceremonial purpose. For example, Fulani girls of West Africa celebrate the Diafarabe cattle crossing festival, during which their boyfriends return from months of herding cattle, by spending days to style and adorn their hair.

Some cultures abstain entirely from cutting the hair. Some conservative Pentecostal women do not cut their hair, just as Amish women do not. The Han Chinese saw hair cutting as mutilation, and Sikh men never cut their hair, covering their heads with turbans. Some Indian holy men also abstain from cutting their hair.

For some cultures, the display of the hair is problematic, and women (and sometimes men) are expected to cover their hair, either during worship services, or always. Orthodox Jewish women cover their heads with wigs or scarves, and Muslim women often cover their heads with scarves or veils. Sikh men and Amish women both keep their hair covered as well; unmarried Amish girls wear a black covering and married women a white one.

Hopi girl, Arizona, with her hair tied in swirls on the sides of her head. 1900, photo by Edward Curtis. Courtesy of Library of Congress Prints and Photographs Division, Washington, DC, No. LC-USZ62-106758.

Hair can demonstrate political motivations as well. The afro, for instance, is a hairstyle worn by some African Americans, in which very curly hair is grown long and worn in a helmet shape around the head. The afro became popular in the 1960s and 1970s as an extension of the Black Power movement, and as a rebellion against chemically straightened hair often worn by blacks such as the conk. The afro was a symbol of black pride, and was seen as threatening to much of mainstream America. Cornrows and other forms of braids now worn by African Americans can also be seen in the same light, as can dreadlocks.

In modern Western societies, hair remains an important sign of female beauty, and women spend millions of dollars per year on grooming products and hair treatments. As in classical times, regular hairdressing is a sign of wealth as the upper classes can afford to have more regular treatments, by higher status hairstylists.

The use of hair extensions is an example of this. While hair extensions are available to the general public, the cost of purchasing real hair extensions and having them professionally applied is prohibitively expensive for many, leaving extensions—and the ability to lengthen one's hair in the course of a couple of hours—is primarily available only to celebrities and the wealthy.

See also: Facial Hair; Hair Cutting and Head Shaving; Hair Treatments

Further Reading: Brain, Robert. *The Decorated Body*. New York: Harper and Row, 1979; Corson, Richard. *Fashions in Hair: The 1st 5,000 Years*. Chester Springs, PA: Dufour Editions, 2001; Fisher, Angela. *Africa Adorned*. New York: Harry Abrams, 1984; Hiltebeitel, Alf, and Barbara D. Miller, eds. *Hair: Its Power and Meaning in Asian Cultures*. Albany: State University of New York Press, 1998; Sherrow, Victoria. *Encyclopedia of Hair: A Cultural History*. Westport, CT: Greenwood Press, 2006.

HAIR TREATMENTS

Today, men and women not only get their hair professionally cut at hair salons, but get their hair colored, curled, and straightened as well.

Men and women have been coloring their hair for centuries. For instance, the ground leaves of the **henna** plant have been used to dye hair a reddish color in North Africa, the Middle East, and the Indian subcontinent for perhaps thousands of years. Hair dyes using henna and other plants were used as well by ancient Egyptians, Greeks, Romans, Babylonians, and Assyrians, and Africans, pre-Roman Europeans, and other peoples did this as well. Because hair loses its pigment and becomes gray as humans get older, covering up gray hair was probably an early motivation in the development of hair coloring techniques.

Today, hair coloring products include those that provide temporary, semipermanent, or permanent color. Temporary hair colors do not penetrate the hair cuticle, coating the hair with color that could last anywhere from a single shampoo to multiple shampoos. Semipermanent dyes deposit color on the hair shaft and penetrate the shaft, but do not lighten the hair. Semipermanent color usually lasts up to fourteen shampoos. Another type of semipermanent color is known as demipermanent. These dyes can last up to three months by penetrating the hair shaft more deeply than the semipermanent colors. Finally, permanent hair color penetrates the hair shaft completely, uses a bleaching agent to remove the natural hair color, and does not wash out. It can be used to darken hair, lighten hair, or cover gray.

Henna is one of the earliest known hair dyes, and is made of the ground-up leaves of the henna plant, mixed with coffee or tea to produce a paste that is applied to the hair. Henna is a permanent hair color, although it does not have a bleaching agent nor does it penetrate the hair shaft. Rather, it binds to the hair permanently.

Today, many women, and some men, use hair dye to create different effects on the hair, such as highlights, lowlights, or unusual hair colors.

Humans have, throughout history and across the world, modified the texture of their hair as well as the color. The ancient Egyptians covered their hair with mud and wrapped it around sticks until it dried, which created curls. Curlers and rollers of all kinds have been used around the world to create curls, and in the twentieth century, new methods developed such as the heated rollers or the curling iron, both of which use heat to (temporarily) curl the hair.

The permanent wave, a method of chemically curling the hair, was invented in 1906, and became popular with Americans as new techniques were developed and shorter hair became widely worn in the 1920s. The early permanents required heat, took six hours, and sometimes frizzed (or even burnt off) the hair. In the 1930s the cold wave, which used chemicals but no heat, simplified the process, although the earliest versions needed to be kept on the head overnight. In the modern cold wave the hair is wrapped around plastic rods and treated with a permanent wave soution. After a time the rods are removed and a neutralizer is applied to stop the waving action and lock in the new wave pattern. Today, people can get permanents at the beauty salon or at home with a home kit, although perms have lost popularity since the 1980s. Another type of permanent wave was the Jheri curl, worn by African Americans in the 1980s, which necessitated using a number of products every day that gave the style a distinctively glossy appearance.

While historically, curling straight hair has been much more popular than straightening curly hair, straight hair has been very popular in the West since the 1960s, leading to the modern phenemenon of either blowing out or ironing hair straight.

In the African American community, relaxing, or straightening, the hair with an alkaline lotion or crème product, has been popular since the ninteenth century, when African Americans realized that washing and combing hair with a lye soap helped to straighten it.

One of the reasons that African Americans have given for the use of relaxers is that it makes their hair more manageable. However, some scholars feel that racism is the underlying reason, given the low value associated with African American facial features and hair in American society. Starting from the time when African Americans served as slaves, those African Americans with lighter skin, straighter hair, or more Caucasian facial features were often granted more privileges than darker skinned blacks or blacks with tightly curled hair, leading many to straighten their hair. On the other hand, using relaxers allows African Americans the ability to create a number of hairstyles, such as the conk that are only possible on relaxed hair.

See also: Hairstyles; Hair Cutting and Head Shaving

Further Reading: Byrd, Ayana, and Lori L. Tharps. *Hair Story: Untangling the Roots of Black Hair in America*. New York: St. Martin's Press, 2002; Corson, Richard. *Fashions in Hair: The 1st 5,000 Years*. Chester Springs, PA: Dufour Editions, 2001; Hiltebeitel, Alf, and Barbara D. Miller, eds. *Hair: Its Power and Meaning in Asian Cultures*. Albany: State University of New York Press, 1998; Sherrow, Victoria. *Encyclopedia of Hair: A Cultural History*. Westport, CT: Greenwood Press, 2006.

HAND PIERCING

Hand piercing is one of the most unusual body piercings available today.

A hand or web **piercing** is a piercing that is in the skin between any two fingers of the hand. The most common places for these piercings include between the thumb and the forefinger, and between the forefinger and the middle finger. The jewelry used is usually a barbell or captive bead ring.

Hand piercings are **surface piercings** which mean they rest simply on the surface of the skin and don't actually pierce through two sides of skin tissue. This makes them somewhat problematic when it comes to healing. They are more prone to migration and infection than other piercings, and the fact that the piercing is on a part of the body that comes into contact with a great deal of bacteria makes them even more infection prone. In addition, they can be easily pulled out simply from the wear and tear of the hand in everyday usage.

See also: Body Piercing; Surface Piercing

HARDY, DON ED

Don Ed Hardy was born in 1945 in Corona del Mar, close to Long Beach, California. He was intrigued by tattoo designs as a child and drew **flash** and tattoos on his friends, and on his own body, in his home "studio." He met Bert Grimm in the mid-1950s and watched him work on the Pike in Long Beach. As he grew older, he moved from an interest in tattooing to other forms of art and went to the San Francisco Art Institute in the 1960s and ultimately received a BFA in printmaking. In the 1960s, Hardy first saw Japanese-style **tattooing** at the studio of Samuel Steward (who tattooed under the name Phil Sparrow) in 1966 and learned much of his early tattooing from him. Phil Sparrow's influence on contemporary tattooing cannot be understated.

After opening up his first shop, Hardy decided he needed to learn more about tattooing and later spent time with Zeke Owens in Seattle. From there he moved to Doc Webb's studio in San Diego in 1969, and later opened his own shop there, specializing in Japanese designs. By now Hardy was corresponding with **Sailor Jerry**, whom he had contacted through Don Nolan. Through Sailor Jerry, Hardy met Kazuo Oguri, and worked in Japan with him during 1973. In 1974 he opened Realistic Tattoo in San Francisco, the first custom-only, by-appointment studio in the United States. Realistic Tattoo was to serve as a model for aspiring tattooists all over the country who were interested in stretching the artistic borders of tattooing, as well as in reaching a new, more lucrative clientele.

Although Hardy is perhaps best known for his Japanese work, he also developed an eye for other kinds of tattoo styles that looked promising. In 1977, he met Jack Rudy and Charlie Cartright, two East Los Angeles tattooists who did Chicano-style tattooing and was so impressed by their work that he sponsored them. In 1978, he met **Leo Zulueta** and realized the power of the tribal work that Zulueta was doing, and sponsored him as well, making tribalism the focus of the first issue of his new magazine, *TattooTime*.

In 1982, Hardy, along with Ernie Carafa and Ed Nolte, staged the Tattoo Expo on the Queen Mary, and he also at that time launched *TattooTime*. *TattooTime* was the first tattoo magazine aimed at the middle class, published with the intent to correct the negative, overly sensationalistic view of tattooing held by most mainstream North Americans. Even though the **National Tattoo Association** was at that time sponsoring annual tattoo conventions, this was the first convention that included lectures and slide shows, and after that year, the association realized the potential inherent in offering an "educational" approach to tattooing and began offering lectures as well.

While Hardy's own tattoo work has been hugely influential in the history of North American tattooing, his larger influence has come from documenting the trends in tattooing in such a way as to make tattooing itself palatable to the middle class. The tribal style of tattooing that Leo Zulueta spearheaded is one example of this, as is Japanese tattooing. Both, after Hardy publicized them in *TattooTime*, became extremely popular among the new middle-class clientele, and served as a counterpoint to the traditional, sailor-style tattooing that was still being practiced in most U.S. shops. Japanese and tribal tattooing were seen as artistically sophisticated, visually powerful, and culturally and spiritually vibrant, while traditional U.S. tattooing was seen as outdated and ignorant.

The tattooists that Hardy trained or hired, too, have all gone on to be leaders in the field: Bill Salmon, Chuck Eldridge, the late Greg Irons, the late Jamie Summers, Bob Roberts, Leo Zulueta, Freddy Corbin, Dan Higgs, Eddy Deutsche, and others.

See also: Collins, Sailor Jerry; Tribalism; Zulueta, Leo

Further Reading: DeMello, Margo. *Bodies of Inscription: A Cultural History of the Modern Tattoo Community*. Durham, NC: Duke University Press, 2000; Vale, V., and Andrea Juno. *Modern Primitives*. San Francisco, CA: Re/Search Publications, 1989.

HAWAII

Hawaii, a group of Polynesian islands in the north Pacific Ocean, is well known for the traditional Polynesian **tattooing** found on the islands. The islands were most likely populated by people from the Marquesan Islands some time between AD 800 and 1000, who most likely brought their tattooing traditions with them. First visited by **Captain James Cook** in 1778, he named the islands the Sandwich Islands in honor of one of his expedition sponsors.

The Hawaiian word for tattoo, *kakau i ka uhi*, means to "strike on the black," which explains how it is done. Hawaiian tattooing as it was practiced in Cook's time was done by dipping a prepared tattooing implement—a comb made of sharpened bones or teeth, connected to a turtleshell or seashell and hafted to a handle—into a black dye. The tattoo artist placed the instrument on the skin, striking it with a mallet or other hammer-like implement. The dye used for tattooing was derived from the burnt remains of the kukui nut mixed with sugarcane juice.

Hawaiian tattoos, at the time of Cook's first visit, were primarily made up of lines, stars, cross-hatching, triangles, chevrons, arches, checkerboard patterns, and lizards. Tattoos probably served as protective devices for warriors, in that warriors' and chiefly tattoos were worn on the front of the body, the spear throwing arm, the legs, and the hands; areas which needed protection during fighting, because, unlike the rest of the body, they were not covered by a cloak or helmet. This protective function later disappeared as guns were introduced to the island through trade with Europeans. Tattoos also protected the wearer against other kinds of dangers such as shark bites. Women also wore tattoos on the hands, arms, chest, and other areas, primarily for decorative purposes.

Men's facial tattoos were made up of straight lines, rather than the curvilinear facial tattoos of the **Maori**, and chiefs did not wear facial tattoos.

European explorers often noted that Hawaiian tattoos were not as finely executed or aesthetically pleasing as those found on other Polynesian islands. Because of the protective function for warriors, Hawaiian tattoos were largely asymmetrical, unlike Maori, Marquesan, or Marshallese tattoos, in which the body is broken up into a series of symmetrical zones.

Tattoos were also used to note a person's geneology, and for mourning. This was especially seen when high-status members of the family or chiefs died, and men and women both got tattooed to commemorate the loss and to remember the person forever. (The Tongans, on the other hand, cut off a finger joint when a chief died.) Initially, mourning tattoos were done on the tip of the tongue, and the excessive pain was justified by comparing it to the love felt for the dead. Starting in the nineteenth century, Hawaiians began to tattoo the name of the chief and the date of his death in English characters on their bodies.

Tattoos also denoted the village a person came from, their ancestors, and the gods to whom they prayed.

As the traditional functions and meanings of tattooing disappeared, tattoos became more decorative, and also, probably, more symmetrical, although this may have also been due to the influence of European artists who were tattooing native people. Goats, for example, emerged as a decorative motif by at least 1816, and were found on both men and women. Also at that time, rifles, helmets, English names and dates began appearing as tattoos.

At least as far back as 1784, Cook's own crewmen started getting tattooed by the native people, and thus played a major part in bringing the tattoo to Europe. By at least 1816, ship artists on subsequent expeditions began tattooing the Hawaiians themselves, using native technology, introducing rifles and cannons and dates and words. Jacques Arago, who visited in 1819, even tattooed Ka'ahumanu, wife of the chief Kamehameha. It is interesting to note the relative ease with which the British sailors and explorers were willing to acquire Polynesian tattoos, and also the apparent enthusiasm of the Hawaiians to augment their own tattoos with British designs. Without this early cross-fertilization, it is doubtful that tattooing would have been reestablished in Europe or seen as anything more than a primitive oddity.

Tattooing in Hawaii began to disappear in the nineteenth century thanks to missionary efforts, although the process was slow and incomplete. For instance, travelers reported in the 1830s and 1840s that very few people were tattooed, yet by the 1880s, a new style of tattooing had developed of tattooing the outside of the legs with stripes and diamonds. Eventually, however, tattooing was eliminated.

Later, Hawaii became well known for tattooing when **Sailor Jerry Collins** settled in Hawaii, opening his first shop there after World War II. Collins was instrumental in bringing Japanese-style tattooing into the United States, changing the way tattooing was practiced in the West forever.

Like many other Polynesian communities, traditional tattooing has been experiencing a resurgence in popularity since the 1970s, as native Hawaiians want to embrace their Hawaiian heritage and culture. Because traditional Hawaiian tattooing was no longer practiced, Hawaiians who were involved in reviving the tradition needed to learn techniques from Samoans and other Polynesians who still tattooed in the traditional styles.

White artists working in Hawaii have also played a role in the Hawaiian tattoo revival. For instance, tattooist Mike Malone created a tattoo style in the 1970s called the "Hawaiian Band" which is a tribal-looking design made to wrap around an arm (there are now Hawaiian legband tattoos as well). While this tattoo is not an indigenous style, many Hawaiians have embraced the design as a native Hawaiian design, and it has even appeared in a painting depicting precontact Hawaiians.

See also: Collins, Sailor Jerry; Marquesas; Samoa; Tahiti

Further Reading: Allen, Tricia. *Tattoo Traditions of Hawaii*. Honolulu, HI: Mutual Publishing, 2006; Gell, Alfred. *Wrapping in Images: Tattooing in Polynesia*. Oxford: Oxford University Press, 1993; Green, Roger C. "Early Lapita Art from Polynesia and Island Melanesia: Continuities in Ceramic, Barkcloth, and Tattoo Decorations." In Sidney M. Mead, ed., *Exploring the Visual Art of Oceania*. Honolulu, HI: University Press of Hawaii, 1979; Kaeppler, Adrienne L. "Hawaiian Tattoo: A Conjunction of Genealogy and Aesthetics." In Arnold Rubin, ed., *Marks of Civilization: Artistic Transformations of the Human Body*. Los Angeles: Museum of Cultural History, UCLA, 1988.

HAWORTH, STEVE

Steve Haworth is one of the most well-known **piercing** and body art practitioners in the country. He designs piercing tools and **jewelry** and has pioneered a number of techniques now used in the body modification community like subdermal implants and laser **branding**. He considers himself a 3D artist whose medium is human flesh.

Haworth was first exposed to medical instruments when he spent summers as a child in his father's medical manufacturing company, and by the time he turned 18, he was designing **plastic surgery** equipment, later beginning his own medical manufacturing company in 1986. After that, he started making body piercing jewelry, began piercing, and opened HTC Body Adornments. While he began by creating conventional body piercing jewelry, he later got interested in the unconventional modifications that he calls 3D Body Art, designing tools, and experimenting on himself.

Haworth also is active in **suspensions**, beginning his own suspension group, but he is most well known for having created the implants for a number of famous people and **freak show** attractions including **Enigma, Stalking Cat**, Lifto, and Katzen.

Today, Haworth feels that body piercers, without specialized training, should not be performing implants, and has in fact stopped doing most piercings himself, so as not to give the idea that implants are the next logical step after piercing. He also does laser branding, subincisions, **ear shaping**, and other extreme modifications.

Besides the company that manufactures and sells jewelry and body modification tools, Haworth operates a number of piercing studios as well as two tattoo studios, and is currently trying to start a magazine about body modification.

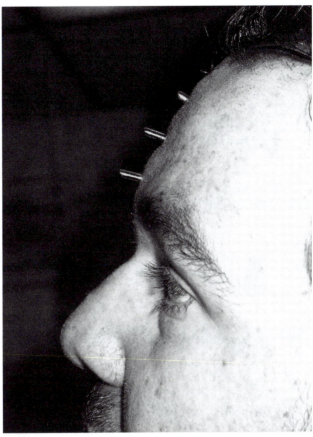

Steve Haworth pioneered the technique used to perform subdermal implants, now widely used in the extreme body modification world. Subdermal beading implants by Steve Truitt of Stay Gold Tattoo & Body Modification and Ascension Studios, Albuquerque, NM.

See also: The Enigma; Implants; Stalking Cat

Further Reading: Pitts, Victoria. *In the Flesh: The Cultural Politics of Body Modification*. New York: Palgrave Macmillan, 2003.

HEAD BINDING
Head binding refers to the deliberate reshaping of the human skull in order to make it flatter or sometimes cone-shaped. Usually performed on infants, because the skull bones are not yet fused, it has been practiced by a number of cultural groups who associate a flattened or otherwise shaped head with beauty or status. Head binding doesn't appear to cause any neurological or other damage to those who practice it.

The ancient Egyptians practiced head binding as early as 3000 BCE, but the cultures most well known for the practice were those of pre-Columbian **Meso-America** and South America.

For the Inca of Peru and the Maya of Central America, an artificially shaped head signified nobility. The Mayans wrapped infants tightly with cloth to a cradleboard, a process that could last for years until the head reached the right shape. Head binding has also been found in Venezuela, Colombia, Ecuador, Chile, Argentina, and Guyana.

Some **Native American** tribes also flattened the heads of their babies, or bound them in such a way as to create a pointed head. The Choctaw used the cradleboard method to flatten their babies' heads, as did the Chinookans, who associated round heads with slavery and flat heads with wealth.

Head binding was also practiced in **Papua New Guinea**, using barkcloth bandages and a vine to tie the bandage tightly around the head. Bandages were continuously reapplied but could be worn for a period of years until the head was elongated enough. Long heads were seen as attractive and girls' heads were generally longer than boys'. Aboriginal Australians also practiced head binding, who associated a long head with intelligence, spirituality, and high status.

In **Borneo**, among some Dayak tribes, flat foreheads were a sign of **beauty**, and were created with by strapping a cushion across the child's head, and gradually increasing the tightness of the straps.

Some African tribes such as the Mangbetu of the Congo also practiced head binding, using cloth to bind the head in order to create the desired long head, which was seen as beautiful, especially for women.

In the West, the French bound their babies' heads with bandages, replacing the bandage with a fitted basket, a practice which continued through the nineteenth century.

See also: Meso-America

Further Reading: Favazza, Armando. *Bodies under Siege: Self-Mutilation and Body Modification in Culture and Psychiatry*. Baltimore, MD: Johns Hopkins Press, 1987; Wesson, Cameron. *Historical Dictionary of Early North America*. Lanham, MD: Scarecrow Press, 2005.

HEALTH ISSUES

Both **tattooing** and **piercing**, because of the contact with blood, are associated with a number of important health issues.

Even though modern health and safety practices were unheard of in tattooing prior to the 1970s (and piercing and other body modifications were still confined to a very small, very private subculture), it wasn't until the 1950s that public officials began to show an interest in the health practices of tattooists, as tattooing became less associated with the military and more with the rising groups of underclasses now using tattoos such as bikers, prisoners, and **gang members**.

In fact, tattooing was a dirty business for much of the first half of the twentieth century. Sterilization was nonexistent; instead, many tattoo parlors had a bucket of dirty water with Lysol or Clorox in it for cleaning the machine between customers, and a dirty sponge or rag for wiping down a customer's arm prior to, during, and after tattooing. Sometimes the bucket would be changed daily, sometimes on a weekly basis. The ink for the tattoos came out of a community ink pot, and was not changed for each customer. Needles were not changed between customers, and were only changed when they got so sharp that they cut the skin.

After World War II, many municipal and state authorities began to take a closer look at tattooing, and newly tightened health and age regulations forced the closure of many shops across the country. By the 1960s, many areas began to ban tattooing altogether, based in part on outbreaks of hepatitis, including cities in New York, Oklahoma, Virginia, Massachusetts, Connecticut, Ohio, Arkansas, Wisconsin, Tennessee, and Michigan. (There has, as of this writing, been no cases of AIDS associated with either a tattoo or piercing.)

It was only in 1997 that New York City, for instance, once again allowed tattooing to be legally practiced in the city after a thirty-six-year ban that was precipitated by an outbreak of hepatitis (which health officials later admitted was never conclusively linked to tattooing). Today, however, thanks to the work of **Lyle Tuttle** and other tattooists who worked during the 1970s when tattooing became professionalized, as well as groups like the **Alliance of Professional Tattooists**, professional tattooing is conducted in the most modern and hygienic of conditions. Cities and states sometimes license tattooists, offering training and tests on bloodborne pathogens and other health and safety issues, and professional tattooists use modern, medical sterilization and cleaning procedures in their workspaces, on their machines and needles, and on their customers. Tattooists wear rubber gloves, changed between customers, and use single-use needles and inks for each customer. Machines and tubes are autoclaved after each use.

There are still risks associated with tattooing, however. Many young people tattoo out of their homes and often don't subscribe to the same health and hygiene practices observed in professional studios, and prison tattooists and other street tattooists don't practice modern sanitation techniques either. In 2006, for example, the CDC found six cases of methicillin-resistant Staphylococcus aureus (which can lead to flesh eating disease) associated with unlicensed and unhygenic tattooing in Kentucky, Ohio, and Vermont.

Body **piercing** is also not without its risks. Because piercing was popularized during the 1970s, at a time when tattooing was becoming professionalized, it benefited from many of the health and safety standards developed for tattooing, and today, those standards (which have been promoted by groups such as the **Association of Professional Piercers**) are observed in all professional piercing studios.

Still, piercing is a more risky procedure than tattooing, given the invasive nature of the procedures. Health risks include having an allergic reaction to the cleaning or postcare products used for piercing, or to the metals used in the **jewelry**; bacterial infections either from the piercing process itself or from exposure to elements during the healing process; parasitic or other infections from exposure post-piercing to parasites or protozoans while swimming; scar tissue or keloid tissue which can form from certain types of procedures, or procedures on already pierced skin, or certain types of skin; viral infections from inadequate hygiene practices; and trauma to the fresh piercing.

See also: Alliance of Professional Tattooists; Association of Professional Piercers; Legislation and Regulation; Piercing; Tattooing; Tuttle, Lyle

Further Reading: McCabe, Michael. *New York City Tattoo: The Oral History of an Urban Art*. Honolulu, HI: Hardy Marks Publications, 1997.

HENNA

The leaves of the henna plant, when ground up and mixed with water, coffee, or tea and made into a paste, are used by cultures around the world to dye the skin and the hair. In the hair, henna acts as a semipermanent hair dye, turning the hair a reddish color, and, when used on the skin, it is a form of temporary body adornment. Henna has been used as a hair dye for thousands of years in North Africa, the Middle East, and the Indian subcontinent as well by ancient Egyptians, Greeks, and **Romans**. It has also been used as a body decoration, known as *mehndi*, in **India**, Pakistan, and Bangladesh, as well as other Muslim and North African countries. Sometimes it is also used to stain the **fingernails**, as by the Egyptians.

When henna is used as body decoration, it is usually worn on the hands and feet, where the designs will last the longest. After creating the paste, it can be drawn on the skin with a stick or other implement.

Traditional Indian henna designs are quite intricate, and are often painted on brides' hands before their weddings, a process that can take hours. Muslims also use henna as decoration, but for medicinal purposes as well. It is said that Mohammad once said "there is no plant dearer to Allah than henna." In Muslim countries, henna is used for weddings as in India, and women will stay up late at night applying henna to each other's hands. The Fulani of West Africa also use henna on the hands, forearms, feet, and shins for special occasions like weddings and baptisms. Moroccan women will wear henna on many special occasions, and will use it as well during pregnancy and after childbirth to counteract evil spirits. Sudanese women also wear henna for weddings and other occasions.

Today, many Western women wear henna designs on the hands as a form of decoration.

See also: India; Islam

Further Reading: Van den Beukel, Dorine. *Traditional Mehndi Designs: A Treasury of Henna Body Art*. Berkeley, CA: Shambhala Publications, 2000.

HIJRAS

Hijras are transgendered men who live together in communities in **India**. Some hijras were born intersex, but others were born male and either decided that they did not want to be men, were impotent, or their parents decided that they should live as hijras.

Hijras usually refer to themselves as female and usually dress as women, and act in exaggerated feminine fashion. They are considered "almost women" or "man minus man." Most hijras choose to have their genitals removed, but they are not women, nor do they want to become women. Women are defined by their reproductive and sexual organs, which hijras do not have, therefore hijras can never become women.

In Hinduism, which has a tradition of androgenous gods, hijras belong to a special caste. They are usually devotees of the mother goddess Bahuchara Mata, who blesses them, and/or Shiva.

Hijras must renounce traditional kinship ties in order to join the family of hijras. Hijra initiates, or students, have a teacher or guru who teaches them how to behave and what their new life will be like. At the end of the period of initiation, the new hijra will often undergo a religious ritual that includes castration and the removal of the penis, which is performed by a hijra known as a midwife, and is seen as the individual's rebirth into the hijra community. After the surgery, the new hijra is treated during her recovery like a postpartum woman.

In the past, hijras were often hired as court eunuchs, a practice that continued until the 1950s. Today, many hijras work as prostitutes, engaging in receptive sex with (often married) Indian men. Others perform blessings at weddings and childbirths; while they are infertile themselves, they have the power to confer fertility onto others. Hijras are able to mock and expose cultural tensions in society, and are both feared, respected, and sometimes mocked by others. While hijras take a vow of celibacy, some have relationships with, and even marry, men.

See also: Castration; Intersexuality; Transgender

Further Reading: Balaji, Meena, as told to Ruth Lor Malloy. *Hijras: Who We Are.* Toronto: Think Asia Publisher, 1997; Nanda, Serena. *Neither Man Nor Woman: The Hijras of India.* New York: Wadsworth Publishing, 1998.

IMPLANTS

Implants are items that are surgically inserted into the body, sometimes for medical purposes but increasingly today, for aesthetic purposes. Medical implants include pacemakers and artificial joints, while the most common implant used for aesthetic purposes (and sometimes medical purposes as well) is the breast implant.

The oldest and most commonly used implant is the breast implant. Used since the end of the nineteenth century to augment the size of a woman's breasts, the earliest implants were made with a woman's own fat. Later substances included ivory, paraffin, rubber, polyester, and teflon. In the 1950s, silicone was injected directly into thousands of women's breasts in order to increase their size, resulting in granulomas and hardening of the breasts.

Modern breast implants are made with a silicone shell filled with either silicone gel or saline liquid. Almost 300,000 breast implant surgeries were performed in 2005, and they are becoming more common among women of all ages and socioe-conomic classes.

Today, cosmetic surgeons are using the technologies developed for breast implants to augment a number of other locations on the body on both men and women, including the buttocks, calves, pectoral muscles, and biceps.

In the body modification community, the term implant generally refers to a number of procedures, mostly performed by body modification practitioners rather than doctors, such as subdermal implants, transdermal implants, scrotal implants, and genital beading. These are still quite rare and are not accepted in mainstream society, and are often known as artistic implants.

A subdermal implant refers to the insertion of an object under the skin so that the shape of the implant is clearly visible through the skin itself. Most implants are made of teflon or silicon and are carved into decorative shapes such as stars or other simple designs. They are primarily used for decorative purposes. Body artist and piercer **Steve Haworth** is known to have popularized the use of such implants in the 1990s. The artist generally uses a scalpel to create an incision, then uses a spatula-like tool to open a pocket under the skin. The implant is then inserted into the pocket, and the wound is sutured together.

The horn implant, first performed by Steve Haworth, is a subdermal implant of (usually) two teflon bumps into the forehead, giving the appearance of a devil or goat or other animal. The first horn implants were inserted into **Enigma** in 1996. Subdermal implants can be stretched just like regular piercings, so, for example, a person can receive small horn implants, and once they have healed, have them removed and replaced with larger horns.

A transdermal implant is an item with one end implanted into the skin and the other end emerging from the body. The appearance after healing is a piece of jewelry, usually a spike or bead, that emerges straight from the body, often at a ninety degree angle. Common transdermal implants include "whiskers" emerging from the face, for those attempting an animalistic appearance, or spikes emerging from the crown of the head, often mimicking the appearance of a mohawk.

The procedure for transdermal implants involves using a scalpel to make an incision approximately an inch from the desired implant location, creating a pocket under the skin for the jewelry to reside in, and sliding the jewelry into the pocket until the end emerges from the hole. Besides the spike or visible part of the jewelry, the implant includes the part

A "mohawk" of transdermal implants on a man's head, by Steve Truitt of Stay Gold Tattoo & Body Modification and Ascension Studios, Albuquerque, NM.

that lies under the skin, which is flat and connects to the spike at a ninety degree angle. Because of the complicated process, success rates for this procedure are very low, and most implants never heal completely.

Scrotal implants are implants that are placed inside the scrotum. Scrotal implants can be artificial testicles used to replace a testicle removed during castration or cancer surgery, or damaged in an accident. Neuticals are artificial testicles used for neutered dogs, for example. Implants can also be used to increase the size of the testicles. Implants are typically made of stainless steel, titanium, or silicone.

Genital beading involves the implantation of stainless steel or silicone beads under the skin of the shaft of the penis in order to enhance sexual stimulation (for both the wearer and his partner), as well as for aesthetic reasons. Genital beads can also be inserted into the labia. The beads are inserted after first piercing the skin with a large piercing needle or a scalpel, then enlarging the hole with a taper, and inserting the beads with a rod. Alternatively, a spatula can be used to create a pocket under the skin into which the beads are inserted. After insertion, the wound is then closed.

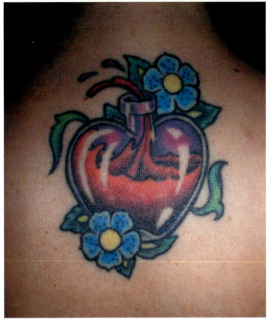

This couple chose to have similar images, a heart and flowers, tattooed on his arm and the back of her neck. By Fish, Photo Courtesy E. Williams.

Angel on shoulder. Jeff Hayes of Rival Tattoo Art Studios, Albuquerque, NM.

Flowers on a woman's shoulder. Jeff Hayes of Rival Tattoo Art Studios, Albuquerque, NM.

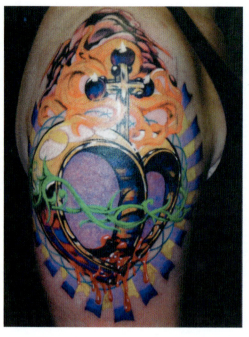

Sacred heart shoulder tattoo. Jeff Hayes of Rival Tattoo Art Studios, Albuquerque, NM.

1932 Ford with engine. Jeff Hayes of Rival Tattoo Art Studios, Albuquerque, NM.

Flower and rosary on hand. Jeff Hayes of Rival Tattoo Art Studios, Albuquerque, NM.

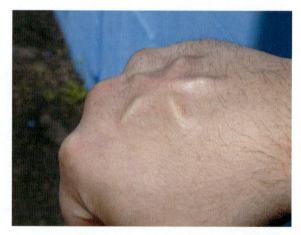

Subdermal implant in the shape of a star on a man's hand. Steve Truitt of Stay Gold Tattoo & Body Modification and Ascension Studios, Albuquerque, NM.

Role playing dice with "Critical Hit" on hand. Jeff Hayes of Rival Tattoo Art Studios, Albuquerque, NM.

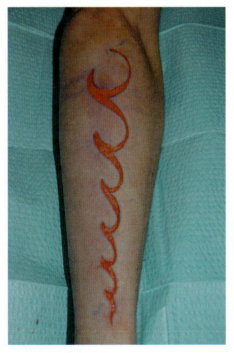

Monad symbol scar created through skin removal. Steve Truitt of Stay Gold Tattoo & Body Modification and Ascension Studios, Albuquerque, NM.

Abstract skin removal scar. Steve Truitt of Stay Gold Tattoo & Body Modification and Ascension Studios, Albuquerque, NM.

Skull on inner bicep. Jeff Hayes of Rival Tattoo Art Studios, Albuquerque, NM.

Skull with carrot on arm. By Jef Whitehead at Black Heart Tattoo, San Francisco, CA, Photo Courtesy E. Williams.

Dagger through skate wheel on forearm. Jeff Hayes of Rival Tattoo Art Studios, Albuquerque, NM.

Star Wars Sand Person on calf. Jeff Hayes of Rival Tattoo Art Studios, Albuquerque, NM.

Shield tattoo on arm. Jeff Hayes of Rival Tattoo Art Studios, Albuquerque, NM.

Fairy scene on a woman's back. Jeff Hayes of Rival Tattoo Art Studios, Albuquerque, NM.

"True Love Never Dies" in script across the back of a woman's shoulder. Jeff Hayes of Rival Tattoo Art Studios, Albuquerque, NM.

Black and white tattoo of wings on back. Jeff Hayes of Rival Tattoo Art Studios, Albuquerque, NM.

Cartoon bunnies on woman's chest. Jeff Hayes of Rival Tattoo Art Studios, Albuquerque, NM.

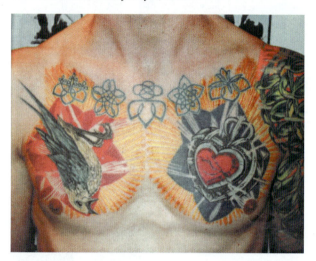

Swallow and heart chest piece. Jeff Hayes of Rival Tattoo Art Studios, Albuquerque, NM.

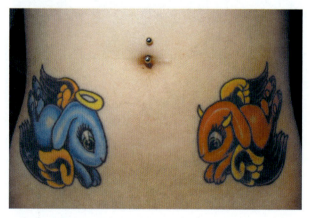

Angel and devil rabbits on woman's stomach. Designed by Anna Brahmstedt Akerlund, Photo Courtesy A. Page.

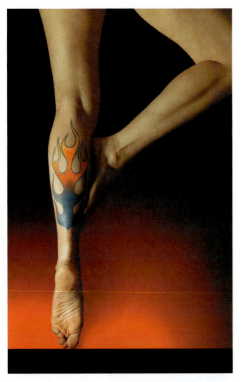

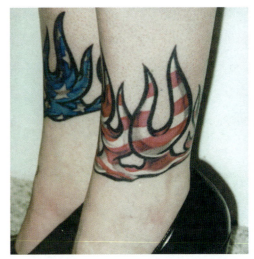

Red, white, and blue flame tattoo on woman's ankles. Jeff Hayes of Rival Tattoo Art Studios, Albuquerque, NM.

Abstract flames on leg. By Micheal Hanlin, Photo Courtesy Nels Akerlund.

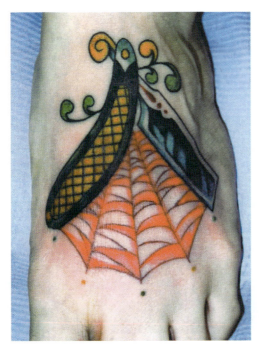

Straight razor tattoo on foot. Jeff Hayes of Rival Tattoo Art Studios, Albuquerque, NM.

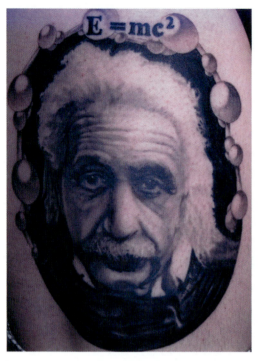

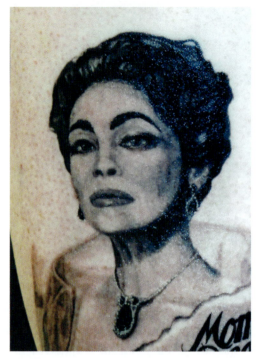

Photo-realistic tattoo of Albert Einstein. Jeff Hayes of Rival Tattoo Art Studios, Albuquerque, NM.

Faye Dunaway as Joan Crawford in *Mommie Dearest*. Jeff Hayes of Rival Tattoo Art Studios, Albuquerque, NM.

Orca whale tattoo. Jeff Hayes of Rival Tattoo Art Studios, Albuquerque, NM.

The legality of these procedures vary from region to region, but are often prohibited when practiced by nonmedical professionals because they are, in effect, surgical techniques. On the other hand, most doctors will not perform them, seeing them as self-mutilation. There are a number of practitioners who do specialize in these techniques, however.

Eyeball implants are the newest implant available today. Available in the Netherlands and offered by eye clinics, eyeball implants are jeweled implants in the shape of hearts, stars, clovers, and the like, that are inserted into the white part of the eye.

See also: Breast Augmentation and Reduction; The Enigma; Haworth, Steve; Silicone Injections

Further Reading: Galenorn, Yasmine. *Crafting the Body Divine: Ritual, Movement, and Body Art*. Berkeley, CA: Ten Speed Press, 2001; Rush, John A. *Spiritual Tattoo: A Cultural History of Tattooing, Piercing, Scarification, Branding, and Implants*. Berkeley, CA: North Atlantic Books/Frog, Ltd., 2005.

INDIA

Tattooing, piercing, and the use of **henna** are widely practiced on the Indian subcontinent, among tribal peoples as well as among caste Hindus.

Women in India have practiced tattooing since at least the fifteenth century and probably before. Indigenous tribal groups use tattoos to mark tribal identity, individual identity, marriageability, and sometimes ritual status. Designs include symmetrical patterns, birds, and animals, and tattooing was also seen as a purely decorative practice, used to beautify the individual. Men sometimes wore tattoos as well, but this is far more common today than it was in the past. Among the Mers, for example, girls are tattooed starting at seven or eight, starting with their forearms and hands. Later, their feet, calves, neck, and chest are tattooed. Dots and lines are used to create gods, animals, domestic images, and plants.

Among the Naga of Northeast India, women were tattooed on the back of the knee if they were married, and men wore facial tattoos that demonstrated their achievements in warfare and headhunting.

Tattoos are also used by some caste Hindus; this probably derives from Hinduism as both Krishna and Vishnu wore tattoos, and one theory explains women's facial tattoos as a way of identifying women who were captured by Muslims in the Middle Ages. Hindus also saw tattoos as evidence of earthly suffering, so wearing a tattoo could act as penance for one's sins and get one entry into heaven. The Bhils, on the other hand, saw tattoos as evidence of good deeds that also could ease entry into the afterworld. Women in the Gujarat region see the tattoo as the only items that stay on her body after her death, so her tattoos are used to identify her in heaven. Finally, Christian Indians had birds tattooed on their arms and thighs as symbols of the Holy Ghost.

In any case, tattoos for Hindus were certainly used to mark status, especially for women. Forehead tattoos were common, and higher caste women had fewer tattoos. Also, tattoos implied chastity and fidelity for a woman, and most women were tattooed prior to marriage, since tattoos were often a sign that she was marriageable.

Indian woman wearing court dress and Indian jewelry, 1890–1923. Courtesy of Library of Congress Prints and photographs Division, Washington, DC, No. LC-USZ62-88332.

Traditionally, tattoos were created on women by women, using three needles, wrapped together, and dipped in ink, and primarily utilized abstract designs. While they were not applied in a ritual context, they still were seen as an important **rite of passage** for a woman. Today, however, some men, often from the Waghari tribe, work as itinerant tattooists, traveling around the country tattooing at festivals and markets with an electric machine, and sheets of Indian **flash** with peacocks, gods, flowers, watches, and other local symbols.

The Newar of Nepal also practiced tattooing, and low-status women were both the principle wearers and artists. Women at one time did their own tattoos, or asked family or friends to help them. The technique was very simple and involved pricking the skin with a needle and rubbing pigment, made of ashes mixed with kerosene, directly into the wound. Tattoos were most commonly placed on the back of the calves, and the designs, made up of dots, included scrollwork, flowers, the peacock, and window screens. Gods like Krishna were also tattooed, but only on the right arm or forehand. While tattoos were not seen as a rite of passage or needed for marriage, most girls tattooed themselves prior to marriage, in order to beautify themselves, and also for luck.

In the nineteenth century, British colonial authorities saw that the tribal groups used tattooing, and because some of the groups were thought to be more criminal prone than others (during the nineteenth century a common theory in criminology was that **criminality** was inherent), officials began tracking which groups used which tattoos. They thought that by tracking the tattoos, they could keep track of crimes.

After 1797, criminals in some parts of India had their criminal status tattooed on them by the colonial authorities, a practice that was entirely new to India. The Hindi word for tattoo, *godna* (to prick, puncture, dot, or mark) came to mean the marking of criminals starting in the nineteenth century. Criminals were branded or tattooed, often with the word "thug" on their forehead. Since the forehead mark was so prominent, it precluded them from rejoining society, so some criminals wore their hair long or their turbans low to cover the marks. Punitive tattooing was not used in all localities, so authorities in some areas were frustrated that other areas, such as Bombay, did not tattoo, as they thought that criminals could move freely from province to province without the tattoo.

Henna, or mehndi, is a form of temporary body adornment like tattooing, used throughout India. The patterns of mehndi are typically quite intricate, including branches, flowers, and scrollwork, and are predominantly applied to brides before wedding ceremonies in India. The use of henna in this context acts as a prayer for a successful marriage. A common belief is that the deeper the color of the henna, the longer the love between the couple will last. In northwest India, the grooms wear henna too.

Nose piercings are very commonly worn by Indian women, a practice which was brought to the region by Muslim invaders in the sixteenth century. The most common location is the left nostril, which is associated with the female reproductive organs; this is supposed to make childbirth easier. Both studs and rings are worn in the nose, and sometimes the jewelry is joined to the ear by a chain. Occasionally, both nostrils are pierced. Nostril piercings are used to make a woman beautiful, and also to mark social status, and are still very popular in India, Pakistan, and Bangladesh. Tribal peoples in Nepal, Tibet, and some parts of India also have had their septums pierced.

See also: Criminality; Henna; Nose Piercing

Further Reading: Anderson, Clare."Godna: Inscribing Indian convicts in the Nineteenth Century." In Jane Caplan, ed., *Written on the Body: The Tattoo in European and American History*. Princeton, NJ: Princeton University Press, 2000; Rubin, Arnold. "Tattoo Trends in Gujarat." In Arnold Rubin, ed., *Marks of Civilization: Artistic Transformations of the Human Body*. Los Angeles: Museum of Cultural History, UCLA, 1988; Teilhet-Fisk, Jehanne. "Spiritual Significance of Newar Tattoos." In Arnold Rubin, ed., *Marks of Civilization: Artistic Transformations of the Human Body*. Los Angeles: Museum of Cultural History, UCLA, 1988.

INFIBULATION

Infibulation, also known as pharaonic circumcision, is a practice in which the labia minora of a girl or woman are removed and the labia majora are cut and sewn together, in order to prevent sexual intercourse. The labia will heal together, forming a smooth genital region broken only by a small hole through which urine and menstrual fluid can pass. Typically performed along with **clitoridectomy**, which refers to the removal of the clitoris, the practice is known as female genital mutilation by its opponents. Infibulation as well as clitoridectomy are commonly performed on young girls in many Arab, Muslim, and North African cultures. While infibulation is only practiced in 15–20 percent of all women who undergo clitoridectomies, in some countries such as Somalia and **Sudan**, the majority of all women undergo infibulation.

Girls typically receive the procedure during their early childhood, and always prior to the onset of puberty. By removing the clitoris, the women who traditionally performed the surgeries ensure that their daughters can experience no sexual pleasure and thus will be virgins upon marriage and will remain faithful to their husbands after marriage. In addition, by sewing together the labia, infibulation provides an even greater assurance that a girl will not attempt to have sexual intercourse, since her genitals will be inspected prior to marriage.

The sewn-together labia will then by opened with a knife by the girl's husband, and sometimes her female in-laws, so that intercourse can take place. Once the woman is ready to have her first child, the infibulation must be completely opened with a knife, a process known as defibulation, in order to allow a child to pass through the vaginal canal, but it will be sewn up once more after the birth.

As with clitoridectomies, this procedure is often carried out with unsanitary tools in unhygienic conditions, and often leads to infection, blood loss, and even infertility or death. Today, in some countries such as Somalia, infibulation is commonly practiced in a hospital, sometimes with anesthesia. Even in this case, however, intercourse is generally painful.

See also: Clitoridectomy; Female Genital Mutilation

Further Reading: Hicks, Esther Kremhilde. *Infibulation: Status through Mutilation*. Rotterdam: Erasmus University, 1987; Shell-Duncan, Bettina, and Ylva Hernlund, eds. *Female "Circumcision" in Africa: Culture, Controversy, and Change*. Boulder, CO: Lynn Rienner, 2000.

INTERSEXUALITY

Intersexuality refers to an individual who is born with ambiguous genitalia. This means that the genitals of the child do not clearly point to either male or female, or the child possesses reproductive organs that either do not match the genitals or the chromosomes. An older term for this condition is hermaphroditism, and hermaphrodites were once displayed as a human oddity in **freak shows**. Today, they are still considered to be a social and medical anomaly, and are generally surgically "corrected" during infancy or childhood.

Because the development of the sex in the fetus is created by a number of factors, including the chromosomes, the release of androgens and estrogens, the formation of the gonads, the creation of the internal reproductive organs, and the formation of the genitals, there are a number of stages in this process in which the gonads, reproductive organs, and/or the genitals can develop in a way that is not normative, and which may result in a child who is not completely male or completely female.

Another factor that leads to the relatively high number of people born with ambiguous genitalia (as many as one or two per thousand births) is the fact that, for the first seven weeks after conception, an embryo is sexually undifferentiated, with bud organs that will later, with the proper hormones, develop into either the ovaries or testes, the penis or clitoris, the scrotum or labia, and so forth. Men and women, then, are just deviations on the same basic pattern, rather than created entirely differently.

Intersex individuals can be born with mixed genitalia (male and female), or a larger than normal clitoris, or a smaller than normal penis. The external genitals may or may not match the internal organs, and in some cases, the internal organs are mixed, for instance, one testis and one ovary. Sometimes the sex chromosomes are not sorted correctly during meiosis, resulting in conditions like Turner syndrome, Triple X, or Klinefelter syndrome, none of which have the correct set of two chromosomes.

The most common cause of sexual ambiguity is congenital adrenal hyperplasia, an endocrine disorder in which the adrenal glands produce abnormally high levels of masculinizing hormones in a genetic female fetus. This leads to an appearance that may be slightly masculinized (such as having a large clitoris) but may also appear quite masculine, especially after puberty.

Another common condition is androgen insensitivity syndrome, which occurs in genetic male fetuses. In this case, there is an inability to respond to testosterone which leads to a genetic male with female external and sometimes internal organs.

How intersex people are treated depends on the culture in which they live. Many cultures that have a strict two-sex binary system, such as in the West, have no room for intersexuality, and see it as an abnormality that must be corrected. Other cultures that have a third gender category generally allow intersexuals to fit into that category, as in the case of the **Hijras** of **India**. Even in cultures that do not demand surgical intervention, typically an intersexed individual is asked to pick one sex and live within that sexual and gender role.

Today, most intersexuals have had their genitalia surgically modified as infants or children to resemble female genitals. Because these children do not consent to the surgeries, which are in effect **sex reassignment surgeries**, and many are emotionally and physically scarred, with impaired sexual functioning after the surgeries, there is a movement, led by the Intersex Society of North America, to end "normalizing" surgeries on infants and children. According to ISNA, the distress caused by the birth of intersex children should not be treated via surgery on the children, but therapy for parents and children, and tolerance in society and general.

In addition, in the intersex community, there are increasing calls for recognition of the various degrees of intersexuality as healthy variations on a sexual continuum which should not be subject to correction or stigmatization. Despite the attacks on the practice, most of the medical profession still supports it, and American society, like most societies, is still firmly committed to the idea that there are only two sexes, and that anything otherwise represents a deviation.

Interestingly, prior to the modern period, those who assigned gender to intersex persons did so in a more humane fashion than today, often waiting until puberty to observe the direction in which an intersex person was developing, only then assigning them their sex and gender identity. Today, physicians make this decision and typically do it right at birth, making a decision that will affect the child for his or her life based on functionality and expected fertility.

The modern medical practice of determining the sex of an intersex infant via medical intervention is notable in not only what it does to intersex people (making them one or the other sex without their knowledge or consent, and without an understanding of whether or not their own gender and sexual identity will conform to the choice that was made for them), but also in the fact that it effectively erases and suppresses intersexuality, and all forms of sex that do not conform to a male/female binary. This is a good example of **bio-power**: when the medical profession can control the very sex and identity of a person.

See also: Sex Reassignment Surgery; Transgender

Further Reading: Sytsma, Sharon. *Ethics and Intersex*. Heidelberg, Germany: Springer Press, 2006; Tine Cohen-Kettenis, Peggy. *Transgenderism and Intersexuality in Childhood and Adolescence: Making Choices*. Thousand Oaks, CA: Sage Publications, 2003.

INUIT

Inuit refers to the indigenous peoples who live along the Arctic coasts of Siberia, Alaska, Greenland, and Canada. These people practiced a unique form of **tattooing**. Some tattoos were individualistic, marking something important about the individual, and others were worn by all members of a clan or other subgroup. In either case, tattoos were used to convey important information about the individual as well as to act as a form of magical protection against a variety of ills.

Tattooing has been practiced among the Inuit for at least 3,500 years, according to archaeological evidence, and, as in the nearby Pacific Northwest, was primarily worn by women.

Elderly women did the tattooing, using bone or ivory needles threaded with needles blackened with soot. The women literally sewed the thread through the skin, leaving the black color in the skin, a skill that they developed through sewing clothing.

The first European descriptions and depictions of Inuit tattoos date to the mid-sixteenth century, and describe women's facial tattooing which partially covered the forehead, cheeks, and especially the chin, and which was made up of lines and geometric patterns. As with other tribes, chin tattoos, which were received after puberty, were used to show that a woman was marriageable, and were also thought to protect women from enemies. They also showed that she was able to endure pain, which was an attractive feature to look for in a wife. Women also sometimes received tattoos on the thighs, as a way to make childbirth easier and to show infants something of beauty when they emerged from the womb.

Men also wore tattoos, but, as with the tribes in the Pacific Northwest, they indicated success in hunting or warfare, with special tattoos for killing a man (such as two horizontal lines across the face) or killing a whale (a line extending from the mouth to each ear, or sometimes a simple dot on a joint).

Men and women both also wore small dot tattoos, on the joints of the body, for mourning and to protect them from evil during the funeral, since spirits often enter the body through the joints to cause sickness or death. Tattooing on the joints (which, interestingly, correspond to a number of **acupuncture** points) closed off the entryways for the spirits. Also common were tattoos that were worn in the spots in which other Northern Native people wore **labrets**, such as between the lower lip and the chin, and on both sides of the mouth. These circular tattoos may have also acted as a form of spiritual protection.

See also: Acupuncture; Labrets; Pacific Northwest Indians; Tattooing

Further Reading: Griffin, Joy. "Labrets and Tattooing in Native Alaska." In Arnold Rubin, ed., *Marks of Civilization: Artistic Transformations of the Human Body*. Los Angeles: Museum of Cultural History, UCLA, 1988; VanStone, James W. *An Early Archaeological Example of Tattooing from Northwestern Alaska*. Chicago: Field Museum of Natural History, 1974.

ISLAM

There are a number of body modification practices associated with Islam, including **circumcision, female genital mutilation**, and **henna**. While Islam forbids the practice of **tattooing, piercing**, and any other alteration or mutilation of the body, many Muslim cultures do have traditions of tattooing (which typically predate Islam), and Muslim women in India often have their nostrils pierced.

Many Muslim countries still have traditional tribal people who have long had tattoo traditions, such as Iraq (Saddam Hussain is said to have at least one protective tribal tattoo on his hand), Afghanistan, Morocco, and Algeria and Egypt. In addition, Iran now has a thriving underground movement in tattooing, in which women are getting secret tattoos. The Berbers of North Africa, for example, tattoo small symbols on the wrists of women, and traditional Tunisian tattoo designs included eagles which represented power; hand designs to protect the hand from sprain; a mirror for protection; fertility signs like the sun, moon, and stars, and the cardinal points.

In North African countries in which henna is widely used as a decoration, women also once tattooed the backs of their hands and arms with delicate designs alongside of their henna patterns. Women did the tattooing by pricking the skin with cactus needles dipped in ash, or simply needles, after which they would rub soot into the prick marks. Designs were both decorative and also magical, in that they could provide protection and fertility. Finally, as with so many other tattoos for women, these designs, which were given by the time a girl turned 16, marked her as marriageable.

Tattoos are not only frowned upon in Islam, in some countries, wearing a tattoo could put a person into danger. In 2006, for instance, a Pakistani immigrant in the United States who was arrested on drug charges and was about to be deported back to Pakistan told the courts that since he was a convert to **Christianity**, his tattoos would mark him as a non-Muslim, which could put his life in danger.

Using henna to decorate the hands and feet is very popular among Muslim women. Women typically paint the designs on freehand or use inexpensive stencils. Arabic designs include larger patterns and are more abstract than Indian designs. North African designs are simple and include geometric shapes as well as abstract symbols. In the Muslim world, henna is mostly associated with special occasions such as betrothals, weddings, childbirths, naming ceremonies, circumcisions, and the like. Henna is also worn to celebrate the end of Ramadan.

For the most part, however, body adornment in much of the Muslim world is generally achieved through **jewelry**, which can be decorative, can serve as a woman's dowry and wealth, and can serve as amulets to ward off evil.

Both circumcision and female genital mutilation are also associated with Islam, and reflect social and religious values.

Circumcision, or the removal of the foreskin of the penis, is performed as an initiation ritual for adolescent boys around the world, and predates Islam. Muslims, however, practice circumcision as well, although not as an intiation ritual and typically during infancy, although sometimes later. While not mandated by Islam, it is seen as a requirement for marriage and for Muslim converts. Some Muslim cultures do follow more traditional tribal practices, in that their boys are circumcised during or before adolescence as part of a **rite of passage**, followed by a major celebration. In other Muslim societies, however, especially in urban contexts, infants are circumcised in the hospital with no celebration or ritual at all.

Female genital mutilation, usually known by its proponents as female circumcision, refers to the partial or full removal of the clitoris, and may or may not include the removal of the labia minora and the sewing together of the labia majora. These practices are found throughout the Muslim world. It is most prominent in East and North Africa, as well as in some parts of the Arabian peninsula, and is also found in a handful of locations in the Middle East, as well as in Indonesia and Malaysia. Finally, female genital mutilation is now being seen in parts of Europe and the United States where Muslims from these countries have immigrated.

Female genital mutilation is performed in order to control female sexuality, which is seen as dangerous in Islam, and to ensure the purity and fidelity of daughters and wives. It is commonly performed on girls between the ages of 4 and 8, and results in the elimination of a woman's sexual pleasure, and for many, in scarring, infection, and pain as well.

See also: Circumcision; Female Genital Mutilation; Henna

Further Reading: Field, H. "Body Marking in Southwestern Asia," Papers of the Peabody Museum of Archaeology and Ethnology, Harvard University, Vol. XLV, No. 1, published by the Peabody Museum, Cambridge, MA, 1958; Searight, S. "The Use and Function of Tattooing on Moroccan Women." New Haven, CT: Human Relations Area Files, Inc., 1984.

IVORY COAST

The Ivory Coast, or Côte d'Ivoire, is a country located in West Africa that was colonized by the French in the nineteenth century. It is made up of dozens of ethnic groups, many of whom have traditionally practiced **scarification**, or decorative scarring, although it is less widely practiced today.

In most tribes, scarification was primarily a decorative practice in that it added to the beauty of the body. In addition, scarification in the Ivory Coast, as with other African countries, is seen as a critical way to demonstrate that a person is a cultural being; without scars, a person is not considered civilized.

The Senofo, who live in the northern part of the Ivory Coast and southern Mali, practiced facial scarification, with the most common pattern being lines that radiate outward from the mouth. Carved Senofo ancestor figures and ritual masks also show scarification, sometimes on the face and other times on the body.

The Baule, a neighboring tribe of the Senofo who migrated from Ghana in the eighteenth century, also practice scarification, known as *ngole*, as a way of beautifying themselves and pleasing others. In addition, scarification both orients an individual within society by marking tribal, clan, lineage, or other membership, and also denotes social information like marriageability or success in hunting. Finally, some scars were used to protect against magic and disease in that a small amount of poison as injected directly into the scar, known as a *kanga* mark. While scarification designs were like **hairstyles** in that they varied through place and time, with raised scars more common in the past and indented cuts more popular in recent years, one common pattern was a series of small scars on the forehead and at the base of the nose. Women often wore scars on their torsos and backs as well. The Baule also borrowed the Senofo pattern of lines radiating from the mouth, to protect young children from harm. Baule ceremonial masks and carved statues also show scarification patterns as well as the elaborate hairstyles favored by the Baule. Finally, the Baule also used body paint to protect newborns from disease, and as part of tribal rituals.

The Dan, who live in the western part of the country as well as Liberia, also wear facial scars. The patterns that the Dan favor emphasize bilateral symmetry, which is seen as beautiful. Dan dance masks also show scarification patterns.

See also: Scarification

Further Reading: Fisher, Angela. *Africa Adorned: A Panorama of Jewelry, Dress, Body Decoration, and Hair*. New York: Henry Abrams, 2000; Vogel, S. "Baule Scarification: The Mark of Civilisation." In Arnold Rubin, ed., *Marks of Civilization: Artistic Transformations of the Human Body*. Los Angeles: Museum of Cultural History, UCLA, 1988.

J

JAPAN

Not only is Japanese **tattooing** known to be one of the most sophisticated in terms of imagery, style, and technique in the world, but it is one of the oldest tattooing traditions in the world as well, dating back to the hunter-gatherers of the Jomon period (10,000 BC–300 BC). Archeologists have found clay human figures called *dogu* that have marks around the eyes, cheeks, forehead, and lips that may indicate tattooing, which was being practiced in other cultures during this period as well. In addition, the women of the Ainu, an ethnic group living on an island at the northernmost end of Japan, have worn upper lip tattoos for hundreds and perhaps thousands of years. Tattoos were worn as well by farmers in the Yayoi period (300 BC–AD 300), the period that saw the emergence of Japanese culture, as a marker of status, like many Polynesian cultures. In addition, the tattoos used religious symbols to ward off evil spirits. Again, clay figurines from the period show facial tattoos.

As in other stratified societies, such as in the **Greco-Roman world**, tattoos in the Kofun period (AD 300–600), during which modern Japanese political organizations emerged, became associated with **criminality** and were used not only to punish and identify criminals (often with the mark of their specific crime) but to identify untouchable classes as well. Chinese attitudes that associated tattooing with barbarism helped to further stigmatize tattoos during this period, given that China governed the region at this time. On the other hand, punitive tattooing may also be linked to the origins of decorative tattooing because, as in other states in which tattoos were used punitively, members of the underclass often modified those tattoos in order to disguise the original meanings, perhaps creating decorative markings in the process.

It wasn't until the late Edo period (1804–1868), however, that what we know of as modern decorative tattooing, or *horimono*, developed in Edo (now Tokyo), which was experiencing a cultural revolution of sorts. Prior to this time, lovers, courtesans, and prostitutes would often have the name of a lover written on the upper part of the arm, with the *kanji* or character for *inochi* (life), symbolizing a pledge of eternal love, added. These pledge tattoos probably derived from earlier "love dots" or small moles tattooed on the hand. But the major influence on the development of the sophisticated Japanese tattoo form were the wood-block print, or *ukiyo-e*, artists whose colorful and complex designs would later be seen in tattoos.

The most important of the ukiyo-artists in terms of the development of tattooing in Japan was Kuniyoshi, whose 1827 illustrations of the *Suikoden*, a Chinese novel translated into Japanese, included heavily tattooed warriors with mythical heroes, legendary battle scenes, and animals like koi, dragons, and tigers tattooed on their bodies. These images were surrounded by highly stylized waves, wind, and flowers, including cherry blossoms, chrysanthemums, and peonies. The pictures from this novel, and from the wood-block prints of nineteenth-century Ukiyo-e artists like Hokusai and Yoshitoshi, came to form the iconographic vocabulary for modern Japanese tattooing.

Furthermore, the ukiyo-e artists of the time became some of the first decorative tattooists of the period, who developed the technique still utilized by some Japanese masters today called *tebori* ("to carve by hand") in which bundles of steel needles at the end of bamboo rod are pushed into the skin, without the use of a mallet as in Polynesian techniques.

The modern Japanese full-body tattoo—encompassing the front and back of the torso (with an untattooed "river" down the front where an unbuttoned shirt or *happi* coat would hang open), and the arms and legs—finally developed at the end of the Edo period. This type of tattoo, called *irezumi*, took from two to five years to complete, and cost the equivalent of $20,000–50,000. Images ranged from traditional themes and heroic characters to stylized and symbolic images such as carp, dragons, floral designs, and religious icons, all of which had symbolic meaning in Japan.

Tattooing at this time was practiced by a large element of the lower classes, and in particular, firefighters, and was strongly disapproved by Japanese authorities. Firefighters used tattoos as signs of masculinity and group solidarity.

While tattooing was growing in sophistication and popularity (at least among the working classes), the government of Japan was cracking down on it. Partly because of its history going back to the Kofun period of being a mark of the underclasses, and partly because of the Chinese influence, tattooing was frequently banned by the government, although it continued to be practiced.

As Westerners started to arrive in Japan during the Meji era (from 1868 to present), tattooing was once again forbidden so that Japan would not seem backward to the outside world, although gamblers, outlaws, and the **Yakuza** (Japanese Mafia) continued to wear them. Ironically, it was also during this time that Japanese tattooing began to attract international attention, as Westerners—primarily sailors and other foreign travelers—began to receive Japanese tattoos, which were far more beautiful and finely executed than Western tattoos. It was also ironic that Japanese sailors, unlike sailors throughout the Western world, did not wear tattoos. Japanese artists were now being asked to give tattoos to the very foreigners whom the authorities sought to protect, and even European elite like King George V and Nicholas II of Russia got tattoos from Japanese artists.

In 1948, under the U.S. Occupation Forces, tattooing was finally legalized in Japan for Japanese citizens as well as for foreigners; yet by this time, it was so far underground that most decent Japanese citizens would not consider becoming tattooed. In fact, the law was changed largely due to the demand from U.S. military personnel. Many wanted souvenirs of the Far East, and because of this clientele, Japanese tattooists created smaller, badge-style designs unlike those that they gave to Japanese clients.

It was also this same time period, the postwar period, that saw the introduction of Japanese tattoo imagery, style, and use of the body into the United
States, changing American tattooing forever, largely thanks to the work of people like **Sailor Jerry Collins**. In 1960, Collins opened a tattoo shop in Honolulu's Chinatown and developed a strong interest in Asian tattoo styles. He developed a trade relationship with Japanese tattooist Horihide, and Hong Kong
tattooist Pinky Yun, whereby he would exchange American machines and needles for designs and advice. He was especially impressed by the Japanese use of
colors, shading, and their focus on the entire body as a canvas for sophisticated
artistic expression. Collins was one of the first Americans to borrow the Japanese
aesthetic style—a central image surrounded by clouds, wind bars, finger waves,
and rocks—as well as the use of full-body tattoos, and blend it with American
images.

The introduction of Japanese
tattoo aesthetics into U.S. tattooing is critical to the development of tattooing in the United
States. While Asian designs
like dragons, Chinese characters, cheongsam girls, and
tigers had long been popular in the West through the
naval practice of receiving tattoos in Eastern ports of call,
these tattoos were executed in
the Western style: as a series of
small, independent, badge-like
designs placed haphazardly on
the body. Before Sailor Jerry,
American tattooists had never
created tattoos that utilized the
full body and which were thematically and stylistically con-
sistent as well.

The second major reason
why Japanese tattooing has
been so influential in contemporary North American tattooing has to do with the fact that
it is seen as the polar opposite to U.S. tattooing. Unlike
traditional American tattooing,

**Japanese Koi tattoo by Jef Whitehead at Black Heart Tattoo,
San Francisco, CA. Courtesy of E. Williams.**

which is seen as folksy and primitive, Japanese tattooing is thought to be modern,
sophisticated, and linked to the more spiritual and refined East. At a time in the
United States when tattooing was at its lowest point in the public eye, interminably

linked with bikers, Skid Row, and criminals, the Japanese tattoo offered not only a new repertoire of images, but new hope.

Ironically, while Japanese tattooing was becoming popular in the United States and changing the face of American tattooing forever, it remained taboo in Japan. It wasn't until Japanese people began to catch on to the American tattoo trends that tattooing experienced a resurgence in Japan, for Japanese people.

Traditional Japanese tattooing is still not acceptable among the middle class in Japan, but many Japanese youth are now wearing Western (or what they call "one-point") tattoos, received by American tattooists or at the many one-point tattoo studios in Japan, as a part of a larger movement in favor of all things American. For the most part, however, tattooing has a long way to go before reaching mainstream status in Japan. Most Japanese people who do wear tattoos hide them under their clothing in order to escape the heavy stigma placed on them.

Today, partly because of the international interest in Japanese tattooing, the Japan Tattoo Institute is the first organization devoted to preserving and encouraging the traditional Japanese art of hand-tattooing. Established in 1981, the Tattoo Institute publishes books, videos, and CD-ROMs about Japanese tattooing and Japanese tattooists.

See also: Collins, Sailor Jerry; Criminality; Hardy, Don Ed

Further Reading: Burchett, George, and Peter Leighton. *Memoirs of a Tattooist*. London: Oldbourne Book Company, 1958; Fellman, Sandi. *The Japanese Tattoo*. New York: Abbeville Press, 1986; McCallum, Donald. "Historical and Cultural Dimensions of the Tattoo in Japan." In Arnold Rubin, ed., *Marks of Civilization: Artistic Transformations of the Human Body*. Los Angeles: Museum of Cultural History, UCLA, 1988; Richie, Donald, and Ian Buruma. *Japanese Tattoo* New York: Weatherhil, 1980; Sanders, Clinton. *Customizing the Body: The Art and Culture of Tattooing*. Philadelphia, PA: Temple University Press, 1989.

JEWELRY

Jewelry refers to the use of metals, beads, glass, bone, wood, shells, or stones to adorn the body, and has been worn by men or women (or both) in every known society throughout the world. Jewelry is typically created with a precious metal such as gold, platinum, silver, or bronze acting as the base and adding to that any number of stones, beads, or glass as further decoration. Other common bases include carved or molded wood, clay, bone (such as ivory) and today, plastic. Some jewelry doesn't use a base at all but instead is made from beads or shells or stones strung together on a string or animal sinew.

Jewelry is both decorative and functional. In many societies, the wearing of precious stones and metals was a way of storing and displaying wealth, and jewelry itself often served as a form of currency as well as dowry for women. Other practical functions include the use of some kinds of jewelry, such as buckles and brooches, to keep clothing together, and the use of jewelry to hold items, such as pendants which can carry a photo or perfume and rings which could hold snuff.

Around the world, many cultures have used jewelry as a form of protection against evil. Amulets, for example, are stones or metals, or sometimes a bag of herbs or other magical items, which are worn to protect the wearer from evil. Some Christians wear a medal belonging to a saint which provides protection and could bring good luck, and many Christians see the wearing of a crucifix as a form of protection. *Milagros* are small silver images used by Mexican and Southwest Catholics which were traditionally attached to statues of saints as a reminder of the person's prayer or request, although today they are often worn as jewelry. In this sense, jewelry and tattoos often perform the same religious function, although tattoos can provide the wearer with permanent protection.

Cameos, which include a carved likeness of a person, and lockets, which include a photo of a person, are often used as memorials of the dead or as commemorations of a loved one.

Finally, jewelry, like other adornments, often demonstrate social status and group membership. Religious icons such as the cross, pentagram, or Star of David mark one as a member of a particular religious tradition. The wearing of expensive jewelry demonstrates one's elevated status, and in some societies, such as ancient Rome, only the elites were allowed to wear certain items of jewelry.

The wearing of a particular piece of jewelry, such as a wedding ring, demonstrates one's status as a married person. Tiaras are associated with royalty. For a time period in the 1990s, it was common to associate men who wore earrings with homosexuality. Wealthy men in **China** wore hat buttons which demonstrated rank and Chinese women wore strips of gold decorated with gems on their foreheads, as a sign of status. The men of some Papuan tribes are allowed to wear specific headdresses once they have killed an enemy.

Most jewelry is used to temporarily adorn the surface of the body, and includes hairpins, headdresses, and barrettes for the hair, broaches and pins for clothing, necklaces and chokers for the neck, rings for the finger and toes, earrings for the ears, and bracelets for the arms. Other types of jewelry, however, are used to adorn temporary or permanent body modifications, and thus many are more adornments in the body rather than on the body. This includes a wide variety of jewelry used to adorn pierced ears, plus studs, rings, bones, and tusks for **facial piercings** and **body piercings**.

Some items of jewelry are used to modify the body itself. For instance, girls of the Padaung tribe in Myanmar (formerly known as Burma) traditionally had large golden rings placed around their necks and their calves from about 5 years old. Over the years, more rings are added, until an adult Padaung woman's neck carries over twenty pounds of rings and is extended by 10–15 inches.

Many African cultures use jewelry to stretch the earlobes, or enlarge ear piercings, while some African tribes as well as some South American tribes as well as ancient Meso-Americans have used **lip plates** or plugs to stretch the lips. A number of **Pacific Northwest Indian** groups also used **labrets** in their lips. Both of these practices have been incorporated into modern primitivist practices today.

Today, specialized jewelry is made specifically to be used in facial and body piercing. Much of today's piercing jewelry styles were created initially by **Jim Ward** of the **Gauntlet**. From the wide variety of earrings available around the world today to the studs, barbells, labrets, ear spirals, nipple shields, tusks, and other items of jewelry used in modern body piercings, piercing afficianados can choose from a wide variety of pieces made from surgical steel, gold, silver, bone, titanium, glass, and other materials.

See also: Body Piercing; Ear Piercing; Ear Spools and Earplugs; Ear Stretching; Facial Piercing; Labrets; Lip Plates; Nose Piercing

Further Reading: Evans, J. *A History of Jewellery 1100–1870*. London: British Museum Publications, 1989; Tait, H. *Seven Thousand Years of Jewellery*. London: British Museum Publications, 1986.

JUDAISM

Judaism takes a very strong position on a number of forms of body modification, especially **tattooing** and **circumcision**.

For example, tattooing is prohibited in the book of Leviticus, which reads: "You shall not make gashes in your flesh for the dead, or incise any marks on yourselves: I am the Lord" Leviticus 19:28.

Because the ancient Hebrews were concerned about differentiating themselves from neighboring tribes, many of whom practiced tattooing (which the Hebrews saw as idolatry), it makes sense that they chose to prohibit it for their own followers. Another explanation for the prohibition against tattooing sees many of the biblical taboos (such as food taboos) as reflecting a concern with hygiene and purity, both spiritual and physical.

Another reason why tattooing was thought to be prohibited in the **Bible** has to do with the Jewish concept of *b'tzelem Elokim*: man is created in the image of God, and the body is a gift from God, not personal property to be defaced according to one's personal preferences.

On the other hand, tattooing is mentioned in the Bible in a number of places, which suggests that not only did ancient Jews perhaps practice tattooing, but that certain nonidolatrous forms of tattooing—especially those in which the believer marks his status as a Jew—may have been acceptable to Judaism. In addition, it is well known that ancient Jews, like many in the **Greco-Roman world**, marked their slaves with tattoos as a sign of ownership.

Isaiah 44:23, for example, reads, "One shall say, "I am the Lord's," and another shall use the name of Jacob, and another shall mark his arm "of the Lord" and adopt the name of Israel." One interpretation of this passage is that the community of Jews would tattoo themselves (either literally or symbolically) as God's servants as a sign of their devotion to him.

In any case, since biblical times, rabbis have interpreted Leviticus to mean that tattooing is prohibited for all Jews, except for those who have been tattooed involuntarily or tattoos used for medical purposes, and Orthodox, Conservative, and Reform traditions all recognize this.

Today, because of the biblical prohibition on tattooing, many tattooed Jews wonder whether they can be buried in a Jewish cemetery or take part in other aspects of Jewish life. Some tattoo advocates, rabbis, and scholars feel that a tattooed Jew can still be buried in a Jewish cemetery and participate in synagogue rituals, since other body modifications intended to make the body more beautiful (such as **cosmetic surgery**) are allowable. In addition, many feel that if the wearer repents and shows regret that they were tattooed, they can still be buried according to Jewish law. Others take a more hard-lined approach, however, and many cemeteries and rabbis will not allow a tattooed person to be buried in a Jewish cemetery.

Since the end of the Holocaust, the biblical prohibition against tattooing was strengthened for many Jews, who now associate tattooing with the Nazi practices outlined here. On the other hand, some Jews today proudly wear tattoos, some with Jewish symbols, in order to display pride in their heritage or even as a reminder of the Holocaust.

Piercing is not prohibited in the Bible, although it is noted; ancient Jews as well as others of the time period pierced their noses and ears for decorative purposes, or to mark their profession or status. Slaves also had their ears pierced as a sign of servitude.

There is one body modification that is explicitly mandated for Jews. In Genesis 17:13, God tells Abraham that he must circumcise his slaves and his descendents as a bodily sign of his covenant with the Jewish people. "He that is born in thy house, and he that is bought with thy money, must needs be circumcised; and My covenant shall be in your flesh for an everlasting covenant."

Because circumcision differentiated the Jews from non-Jews, Jews who in ancient times did want to assimilate into other cultures (such as among the Greeks) found themselves in a difficult position, and many Jews at the time stopped circumcising their children. But since biblical times, it has been the consensus within the Jewish community that circumcision is required for all boys, except when precluded medically.

Jewish boys are circumcised in a ceremony called the *Bris*, which takes place on the eighth day of the child's life, traditionally by a man called a *Mohel*, although a non-Jewish doctor may, in some cases, perform the ceremony. Traditionally, after removing the foreskin, the Mohel will suck the blood from the wound in order to clean it. Today, most Mohels do not suck directly on the wound but use a glass tube between the wound and the Mohel's mouth, because of recent concerns about the spread of herpes during circumcision ceremonies.

Today, there is a small anticircumcision movement among some Jews who no longer want to circumcise their sons, and who have adopted alternative rituals to welcome their sons into Jewish life.

See also: Auschwitz; Bible; Circumcision; Piercing; Tattooing

Further Reading: Kolatch, Alfred. *Inside Judaism: The Concepts, Customs, and Celebrations of the Jewish People*. Middle Village, NY: Jonathan David Publishers, Inc., 2006.

L

LABRETS

A labret is a **piercing** that is attached below the lower lip, above the chin.

Also known as the "Mao" (because it looks like the mole above Mao Zedong's chin), the **jewelry** used in the labret is usually a labret stud, which consists of a metal shaft with a simple round stud protruding from the face; it is attached inside of the lip with a flat piece of backing metal. Also popular is the labret spike, which is structurally similar to the labret stud but looks more like an arrowhead protruding from the face. Captive bead rings (in which a bead bisects the ring and is held in place by the spring pressure of the metal) can also be used in labret piercings, but when a ring is worn, the piercing is generally referred to as a lip piercing, rather than a labret, because the ring encircles the lip; a typical labret looks like a bead or stud emerging from underneath the lip.

While the single stud underneath the lip is the most traditional and common form of the labret, a number of newer forms are worn today. A lowbret is a piercing placed as low as possible on the chin, but still accessible through the inside of the mouth. A Medusa is the opposite of a labret piercing, with the stud emerging from above the upper lip, below the nose, rather than below the lower lip. A Madonna or Monroe is a Medusa labret placed above and to the outside of the lip area, in order to simulate a beauty mark of the kind worn by Madonna and Marilyn Monroe. The jewelry used for these piercings is typically a labret stud or a jeweled stud.

Whereas normally labrets only show a single bead or stud, the vertical labret piercing is a piercing in which two studs are visible, one beneath the lip in the area in which a normal labret would be positioned, with the second positioned directly on top of the lower lip. A jestrum is very similar, but it's a vertical labret that pierces the upper lip and the area above the upper lip, with studs emerging from just below and just above the upper lip. Two labrets on each side of the lower lip are called snakebites or venom piercings, because the double holes look somewhat like snake bites.

Labrets have been commonly worn by cultures around the world, and in fact, the labret is one of the most commonly seen facial piercing in non-Western cultures. Traditional labrets were made of wood, ivory, metal, or quartz and other stones.

Labrets were worn, starting perhaps 3,000 to 4,000 years ago, among a number of **Native American** tribes, including many Northwest Coast Indians, such as the Tlingit, Haida, Chugach, **Inuit**, and Tsimshian, among whom the labret was often a sign of status. High-status Tlingit girls and women, for example, wore labrets as both decoration and to mark rank. Labrets would be inserted into the skin after an excision was made, usually as part of a rite of passage for girls who have just experienced their first menstruation. (Some observers, on the other hand, noted that infants were pierced.) In some groups, men also wore labrets, and men could wear single or double labrets, worn on either side of the mouth. (Different historical periods in the northwest are associated with either male or female wear, or both.) Like women, men received theirs as part of an initiation ritual. Labrets in this case, however, were not generally small studs inserted into a pierced opening below the lip, but were large plugs inserted below the lip, or sometimes in the lip itself, as with **lip plates**. Materials for labrets included walrus ivory, abalone shell, bone, obsidian, and wood.

Kenowun, Nunivak woman of the American Northwest coast wearing nose ornament and beaded labrets below her lower lip, 1929. Photo by Edward Curtis. Courtesy of Library of Congress Prints and Photographs Division, Washington, DC, No. LC-USZ62-74130.

Among **Pacific Northwest Indians**, labrets were commonly worn. In some tribes, both men and women wore labrets, but more commonly women wore them. Labrets were sometimes as wide as the lips, and were made of stone, bone, wood, and ivory. Beads were also sometimes strung from the labrets (into which holes had been drilled), creating the appearance of a beaded beard. The first labret was small, and would be replaced by increasingly larger labrets as the hole grew bigger. For that reason, labret size indicated both age and also status. Holes sometimes grew so large that without jewelry, the lip would hang down, exposing the teeth and gums. While most labrets were worn below the lip, between the lip and the jaw, some tribes wore labrets, which were typically round plugs, on both side of the lips.

Labrets were also commonly worn in pre-Columbian **Meso-America**. Among the ancient Aztecs and Mayans, labret piercings were only worn by elite men, who wore elaborately sculpted and jeweled labrets fashioned from pure gold in the shape of serpents, jaguars, and other animals.

Today, labrets are commonly worn in the body modification community, and especially among modern primitives and Goths. Labrets are considered piercings and are received at piercing studios, either via a normal piercing technique, or, in the case of larger labrets or lip plugs, through slicing the skin underneath the lip with a scalpel.

See also: Inuit; Lip Plate; Meso-America; Oral Piercing; Pacific Northwest Indians

Further Reading: Griffin, Joy. "Labrets and Tattooing in Native Alaska." In Arnold Rubin, ed., *Marks of Civilization: Artistic Transformations of the Human Body*. Los Angeles: Museum of Cultural History, UCLA, 1988; Jonaitis, Aldona."Women, Marriage, Mouths and Feasting: The Symbolism of Tlingit Labrets." In Arnold Rubin, ed., *Marks of Civilization: Artistic Transformations of the Human Body*. Los Angeles: Museum of Cultural History, UCLA, 1988.

LAZONGA, VYVYN

Vyvyn Lazonga (born Beverly Bean) is one of the most influential female tattoo artists in the United States, and played a major role in the transformation of tattooing in the 1970s and 1980s.

Lazonga had been an artist since childhood, and in the early 1970s saw a magazine article about a tattooist named Cliff Raven, then working in Los Angeles. Raven was one of the few tattooists at that time to use Japanese styles and imagery in his work, and, as a gay man, also incorporated very nontraditional imagery into his work for his West Hollywood clientele. Raven's work inspired Lazonga to try tattooing herself, and in 1972 she approached Seattle tattooist Danny Danzl, a retired merchant seaman who worked on Seattle's skid row, about an apprenticeship.

Lazonga has since noted that she learned a tremendous amount while working in Danzl's shop, but also experienced a great deal of sexism. She saw less experienced artists get promoted before her, was forced to use substandard equipment, and was not allowed to experiment artistically. Most of the clients at this time were sailors. But during her apprenticeship, she was able to see some of **Sailor Jerry Collins'** work through his correspondence with Danzl, which inspired her to continue to push the boundaries of what was typically accepted in American tattooing at that time.

After a few years, Lazonga opened her own shop in Seattle in 1979, where she began building a clientele interested in not only more artistic tattoos, but the uniquely feminine and spiritual perspective that Lazonga put into her work. Lazonga moved to San Francisco where she ran a shop in the Mission District, and later the Haight-Ashbury, where she continued to grow a dedicated clientele. It was in San Francisco that Lazonga met (and later got tattooed by) some of the most influential artists in the United States at that time, including **Don Ed Hardy**, **Lyle Tuttle**, Henry Goldfield, and Captain Don. In 1990, she moved back to Seattle where she still operates her studio at the Pike Place Market on the waterfront (and about two blocks from her original skid row location).

Lazonga's work is easily recognizable for its bold colors, beautiful lines, feminine imagery, and the way that she uses the female body. She is also notable for her personal attachment to the work that she does; she considers her tattoos to be a talisman on the skin that derives directly from the soul.

See also: Hardy, Don Ed; Tuttle, Lyle

Further Reading: Mifflin, Margot. *Bodies of Subversion: A Secret History of Women and Tattoos.* New York: Juno Books, 1997; Morse, Albert. *The Tattooists.* San Francisco, CA: Albert Morse, 1977.

LEGISLATION AND REGULATION

In the West, because of **tattooing**'s long association with the underclasses, as well as because of its ability to transmit disease, tattoos are the site of a great amount of regulation. **Piercing**, too, although much more recently a mainstream fashion, is also a target of a variety of laws and regulations, since, like tattooing, it involves the transmission of blood; and perhaps more importantly, has been associated with the gay community since the 1970s. And while **acupuncture** has never been associated with criminals, the underclasses, or nonnormative sexual practices, it too is becoming increasingly regulated in the West.

Laws regulating the various body modifications differ by country, and in the United States, they are found on a state-by-state basis. Acupuncture, for example, comes under state jurisdiction and the Departments of Health of most states have regulations on hygiene practices and licensing and training procedures, and waste disposal may come under the jurisdiction of the Department of Environmental Protection. A handful of states, however, have no regulations whatsoever.

Laws regulating tattooing and piercing are also located in the individual states, and in some cases, in cities or counties. Many state health departments regulate tattooing and piercing, again providing regulations on artist training, sanitation, sterilization, waste disposal, licensing, limitations on the customer (minimum age limits, signed consent forms, sobriety) and the like, although a great many states have no regulations whatsoever.

For years, tattooing was unregulated and, prior to the 1970s, there were no hygienic practices whatsoever: Tattooists reused needles, machines, and inks from one customer to the next, sometimes using bleach in between customers to clean needles. But the use of medical autoclaves and other sterilization devices, as well as all of the modern health techniques such as the use of rubber gloves, single-use needles, and the like, didn't develop until the 1970s and even later in many locations.

Because of the lack of attention to safety practices, there were a number of outbreaks of hepatitis in the 1950s that led to a number of states and municipalities outlawing tattooing, with two states—South Carolina and Oklahoma—only overturning their bans in 2005 and 2006, respectively. (The first recorded case, however, of legal action taken against a tattooist was in 1944 when **Charlie Wagner** was fined by the city of New York for failing to clean his needles; also in the 1940s tattooist William Irving was fined for tattooing a minor.) The drive to legalize tattooing in these states involved multiyear fights which dealt with issues of constitutional rights, safety issues, and morality. As is common when legislatures have legalized tattooing, both states have since adopted new health and safety regulations which include mandatory training in blood-borne pathogens, health and hygiene standards for studios, and procedures such as single-use needles and ink, as well as a minimum age and sobriety standards.

While there have been no cases of AIDS that can be traced to tattooing or piercing, since the 1980s, AIDS has become a great concern, leading to more regulations around the country. While many tattooists and piercers welcome many of these regulations, feeling that it improves the industry when all tattooists and piercers observe safe practices, some proposed regulations are seen as overly invasive. For example, Oklahoma's proposed new regulations may include a prohibition on body modification businesses operating within 1,000 feet of a church, school, or playground as well as a requirement for business owners to post a $100,000 bond in order to be licensed.

Because of these concerns, a new organization has formed known as the Coalition of Body Modification Associations. This informal coalition is made up of the **Alliance of Professional Tattooists**, the **Association of Professional Piercers**, and The Society of Permanent Cosmetic Professionals, and they are currently fighting a proposal by the National Interstate Council of State Boards of Cosmetology (NIC). The NIC oversees most cosmetic and beauty fields in this country (all of which, with the exception of cosmetic tattooing, involve noninvasive procedures), and is attempting to provide states with licensing exams to be used by the tattooing and piercing industries. Furthermore, the NIC is lobbying to allow boards of cosmetology to oversee tattooing and piercing, rather than the state boards of health, which is alarming to many piercers and tattooists.

Other issues of concern to the industries include a California lawsuit filed in 2004 (still active at the time of this writing) by the American Environmental Safety Institute against the major tattoo ink manufacturers, which claims that the inks expose customers to unsafe toxins such as lead and other heavy metals.

See also: Alliance of Professional Tattooists; Association of Professional Piercers; Health Issues

Further Reading: Sanders, Clinton. *Customizing the Body: The Art and Culture of Tattooing.* Philadelphia, PA: Temple University Press, 1989.

LIP PLATES

Lip plates, also known as lip plugs or lip discs, are items made of clay, wood, stone, bone, or metal that are inserted into a hole in the lower lip, or the area beneath the lip, above the chin. Small plates or plugs are generally inserted after slicing open a hole into the lower lip. After the hole heals around the plate, it is removed and larger ones are inserted, gradually stretching the hole. (In some cases a plate is also inserted into the upper lip.) Lip plates are usually no larger than 3 centimeters in width, but the women of southern Chad wear extremely large plates, often as large as 24 centimeters.

Woman from Sara Tribe of Chad with a lip plate. Courtesy of Library of Congress Prints and Photographs Division, Washington, DC.

Lip plates are generally worn by women as a form of decoration, status (with size serving as a marker of social or economical importance), and marriageability. Lip plugs are worn by men and women alike. Women with lip plates are seen as more beautiful than unadorned women.

Tribes that are known for their traditional lip plates include the Mursi and Surma of Ethiopia, the Suya of Brazil, the Mokolo of Malawai, and the Sara and Djinja of Chad. Among the Djinja, it is the young girl's fiance who will perform the procedure on her. Among the Makololo tribe of Malawi, lip plates are called *Pelele* and are used to arouse the men in the tribe. The Lobi women of Ghana and the Ivory Coast and the Kirdi of Cameroon wear lip plugs to protect the women from evil spirits who enter via the mouth. It is said that the lip plates worn by the women of Chad and Sudan look like the beaks of sacred birds, such as the spoonbill or broadbill.

In the West, while lip plates are not yet popular even among the most dedicated of modern primitives, lip plugs are sometimes worn in stretched holes in the lips.

See also: Labrets; Oral Piercings

Further Reading: Fisher, Angela. *Africa Adorned: A Panorama of Jewelry, Dress, Body Decoration, and Hair*. New York: Henry Abrams, 2000.

MAGIC AND THE OCCULT

Magic refers to the use and manipulation of supernatural forces in order to achieve a desired goal. In order for a society to believe in magic, there must exist a magical worldview in that society, that is, an idea that there are natural forces that people can access, and that people can control those forces and essentially shape the world to their liking through divination, curses, cures, luck charms, love spells, protection spells, and other magical means.

Magic is a part of religious systems around the world, in traditional societies in which spiritual forces (in the role of ancestors, spirits, gods, demons, and the like) are seen to exert a great deal of force over the lives of humans, as well as in contemporary Judeo–Christian contexts.

Tattooing has long been associated with the magical practices of a number of people. In many traditions, the use of magic words or magical symbols is said to have the power to command spirits or to enact change. These symbols can magically take on a physical quality of the phenomenon or object that they represent. Thus by tattooing magical symbols or words onto the body, practitioners hoped to be able to make something occur in life.

The practice of tattooing (or writing) magical symbols and words was common in Medieval Europe among occult practioners and lasted through the seventeenth century, when the tattooing of astrological symbols was common. This type of magic was seen as particularly useful because when it's difficult to get the rare ingredients needed for some magical spells, one can use the symbol of the ingredient or the symbol of the corresponding planet, and mark it on the body.

At the same time, European pilgrims were traveling to the Holy Land to pick up Christian tattoos, themselves seen as both souvenirs and magical forms of protection. European sailors, too, practiced magical tattooing, wearing certain tattoos for protection. For instance, a pig on one foot and a rooster on the other acted as a charm that would keep a man from drowning at sea and the words "hold" and "fast" could be

y tattoo is on my lower back and a half moon/half sun, with stars ound the outside. I am bipolar and me my tattoo is a symbol of living th such a difficult situation. Some ys are like night and day which symbolized by the sun and the oon. Stars to me are like blessings d it's been a blessing to learn to e with being bipolar.

ANONYMOUS

tattooed onto the knuckles of the hand to help the seaman to better hold the ship's riggings. Propellers on the buttocks would also "propel" the wearer to shore. British sailors also hoped that wearing a scene of the crucifixion of Jesus on their backs would either elicit sympathy during a whipping, or perhaps may protect them from undue pain. Coptic Christians often tattooed a cross on their foreheads, as both a sign of devotion and also to protect themselves from evil spirits.

Other cultures use tattooing for magical purposes as well. Burmese tattooists create love charms in the form of tattoos made with magical ink, and tattoo parrots on the shoulder for good luck. Tibetans use tattooing for magical and medicinal purposes, tattooing mantras to achieve inner harmony and tattooing acupuncture points with herbal dyes, and Hindus tattoo certain gods onto the body to relieve pain. Perhaps the culture with the best-known tradition of magical tattooing is Thailand.

In Thailand, tattoos are traditionally given by monks and those who were trained by monks, and the tattoos, once properly blessed, are said to be able to protect the wearer from harm, even making him invincible to guns or other weapons. Tattoos can also give the wearer special powers, and a person can even become possessed by the tiger, dragon, or other creature living on their body.

In the twentieth century, with the revival of magical beliefs in the West with **neo-paganism**, Wicca, and goddess religions, magical thinking and the use of magical symbols are once again incorporated into tattooing. On the other hand, some neo-pagans use tattoos not as spells but to express their religious values. Magical symbols popular today include runes, astrological symbols, symbols from alchemy, Egyptian symbols, and Masonic symbols. Some Western tattooists also specialize in what they call magical tattooing, or transformative tattooing, and feel that they are providing their customers with the power to transform themselves through their tattoos.

See also: Neo-Paganism

Further Reading: Rosecrans, Jennifer Allen. "Wearing the Universe: Symbolic Markings in Early Modern England." In Jane Caplan, ed., *Written on the Body: The Tattoo in European and American History*. Princeton, NJ: Princeton University Press, 2000.

MAKEUP *See* Cosmetics

MAORI *See* Moko

MARQUESAS

The Marquesas Islands are a group of Polynesian islands originally settled by Samoans between the first and fourth centuries. Like many other Polynesian islands, the Marquesas are known for their tattoo traditions, which were most likely brought to the islands by the first inhabitants. First explored in the late sixteenth century by Spanish navigator Álvaro de Mendaña de Neira, and later visited by **Captain Cook** in 1774, the islands were later claimed by France in the nineteenth century. Cook's visit, and his reports of tattooing traditions, were significant in that they played a major role in the exposure of Polynesian **tattooing** to the Western world, and also in the change and destruction of those same practices.

As with other Polynesian tattoo traditions, Marquesan tattooing was used to mark important features connected with status, wealth, and gender, but unlike other islands, the tradition was not restricted to chiefs and their families. Tattoos marked one's affiliation with any number of groups such as warriors, graded associations, or entertainers called *ka'ioi*, as well as his genealogical position. Because the tattoo recipient had to pay for the tattoo, wearing a tattoo demonstrated one's wealth, and for men, the ability to withstand **pain**. For women, tattoos were a sign of beauty, and for men and women they also served other purposes such as protection against evil and the marking of important events, and receiving a tattoo was a rite of passage for young men and women. Tattoos ultimately represented both individual and group identity, and allowed for the participation in important social and religious rituals.

Tattoo tools were similar to those on other Pacific islands, and included the primary tools, made out of wood, with sharpened bone combs of different widths protruding from the end. This tool would be tapped into the skin after being dipped into ink by a mallet, inserting the ink into the skin.

Tattoos were first given to boys and girls in their teens, but for men especially, could continue throughout their lives, as men were tattooed far more extensively than women. Women's tattoos were typically on the face, the lips, the ears, the feet, and the hands, while men's tattoos could eventually cover their entire bodies.

As in the **Marshall Islands** and among the **Maori** of New Zealand, the male body is divided into a number of zones, each of which is further subdivided. Tattoo designs are then created for each zone, with the result being an overall symmetry in design. Designs are primarily made up of straight and curved lines in a very abstract pattern, which together often gave the impression of fine black lace. Each individual had a different overall set of tattoos, and no two people looked the same.

Tattooing in the Marquesan Islands, as in the rest of Polynesia, was strongly influenced by European contact. For example, Marquesan tattooing at the time of first contact was based on abstract fine lines and other patterns, yet after European contact, lines became darker and broader, somewhat closer to the Maori style. Also, tattoos progressively became more a mark of prestige, losing some of their magical and religious connotations.

Marquesan tattoos also influenced Western tattooing, as well as Western understandings of "primtive man." The Frenchman Jean Baptiste Cabri and an Englishman named Edward Robarts were tattooed on the Marquesas after deserting a British whale hunting expedition at the end of the eighteenth century. Found by a Russian explorer in 1804, Cabri ended up traveling to Russia where he displayed himself as the first European **tattooed attraction**, ushering in a new career for many men and women, and bringing tattooing to people who had never before seen such a thing.

Starting in the 1840s, Protestant and Catholic missionaries arrived and began to stamp out tattooing, along with other cultural traditions, and while the tradition was not wiped out entirely, it changed forever. Today, some Marquesan Islanders still get tattooed, but with a tattoo machine and in a context entirely divorced from traditional practices.

See also: Cook, Captain James; Marshall Islands; Moko; Samoa; Tattooed Attractions

Further Reading: Allen, Tricia. "European Explorers and Marquesan Tattooing: The Wildest Island Style." *Tattootime* 5 (1991): 86–101; Handy, Willowdean. *Tattooing in the Marquesas*. Honolulu, HI: Bishop Museum, 1922.

MARSHALL ISLANDS

The Republic of the Marshall Islands is a group of Micronesian islands whose people are well known for their **tattooing**. Settled by other Micronesians between three and four thousand years ago, the first European to explore the Marshall Islands was English navigator John Marshall who arrived in 1788, after whom the islands are named. At the end of the nineteenth century, the islands came under the control of Germany, and was briefly also controlled by Japan and the United States. Early in the nineteenth century, the first descriptions and depictions of Marshallese tattooing were made by a Russian expedition, and later, German administrators and missionaries published a number of studies of the practice.

As with other Pacific Island tattoos, Marshallese tattoos were linked to status and rank, with chiefs being the only members of society to receive head and neck tattoos, which consisted of black horizontal bands running around the neck to the hairline, with tight vertical lines that run in a narrow band from the eyes to the jaw. Chiefs also exclusively wore the penis tattoo.

Tattoos also indicated rank in the sense that the tattoo needed to be paid for, both in gifts to the gods, from whom the tattoo was seen to come, as well as for the tattooist. Wealthier individuals could therefore afford more elaborate tattoos. Tattoos also served a protective function, and were used to beautify both men and women. In addition, as in many other cultures, tattooing especially for men was seen as a **rite of passage**, marking his initiation into manhood, as well as a test of his strength and endurance.

Tattoo motifs were abstract, as in many of the Pacific Islands, with lines serving as the primary design element. Because fishing was the major form of subsistence, and much of Marshallese culture revolved around sea travel and the exploitation of marine life, oceanic elements such as fish, shark's teeth, and shells, as well as canoe parts, were also represented symbolically in tattoos. It was said that because fish have stripes, humans should have stripes, linking even the omnipresent lines to fish. **Jewelry,** too, was derived from the sea and included armbands and necklaces made of shells, fish teeth, and the feathers of sea birds.

For the purpose of tattooing, men's bodies are broken into a number of zones, as we saw with Marquesan and **Maori** tattooing, and those zones are subdivided into a number of smaller zones. Each zone, such as the upper chest, stomach, or shoulder, would be tattooed with a different design. The entire torso, front and back, could be tattooed, as well as the arms and, less frequently, the legs, and many men were almost completely covered with tattoos, which from afar, looked to observers like a suit of chain mail. Arms were commonly tattooed with zigzag bands encircling the arm, and thighs and sometimes calves often had the same band patterns. Men also could be tattooed on their lower torso including the buttocks and genital areas, similar to the Samoan **pe'a**. The zigzag represented shark teeth.

Women were tattooed as well, and their bodies, like the men's, were divided into zones. As in Polynesian tattooing, women's tattoos were also less extensive than men's, and were primarily limited to the arms, legs, fingers, and shoulders. The most common configuration for a woman was to have both arms completely tattooed, along with both shoulders across the top of the back and across the top of the chest beneath the neck. Zigzag bands were common motifs for women as well as men, and finger tattoos, like neck and face tattoos for men, were only worn by women of chiefly status. The finger tattoos were perhaps influenced by the European practice of wearing rings on the fingers. Because both men and women kept their upper bodies unclothed, much of a man's tattoo, and all of women's tattoos, were exposed to the public.

Tattoo implements are similar to other Pacific island cultures. The main tool is a comb, either narrow or wide, made of fish or bird bones, lashed at right angles to a stick; the comb is dipped into pigment and tapped into the skin with a wooden mallet. Getting tattooed was an important ritual event, with the tattoo seen as a gift from the gods, for which gifts of food or woven mats were exchanged, and a prayer prior to the procedure would be uttered. The tattooing took place often in utter silence, in tattooing houses which were located in sacred locations on the islands. Men could take a month or longer (longer for chiefs) to be fully tattooed, although many men received their tattoos in stages, and during the tattooing, the man's face was covered with a mat.

Scarification was also practiced to a limited extent, a practice probably borrowed from other locations such as the Gilbert Islands.

Because of missionary activity, tattooing began to decline in the second half of the nineteenth century, although it was still practiced, primarily by women. However, by that time, foreign elements were appearing in Marshallese tattooing, both from other Micronesian islands, as well as, later, from European sources. During the Japanese occupation during World War II, it was banned entirely, and traditional tattooing is no longer practiced at all on the islands.

See also: Marquesas; Moko; Samoa

Further Reading: Spennemann, Dirk R. *Marshallese Tattoos*. Majuro Atoll: Republic of the Marshall Islands, Ministry of Internal Affairs, Historic Preservation Office, 1992.

MEDICAL TATTOOING

Tattooing has been used in the medical field since the early days of **plastic surgery**, when doctors realized that they could use tattoo techniques to cover scars or birthmarks and to camouflage the effects of injury or surgery on the body.

Today, the use of tattooing during reconstructive surgery is very common. Known as micropigmentation, it is essentially a form of **cosmetic tattooing** in which tattoo ink is tattooed into the skin to camouflage scars or recolor discolored skin, as in the case of vitiligo. In the case of breast reconstruction surgery, not only are the surgical scars covered by tattoos (using ink colors to match the patient's skin tone), but tattooing is used to color the reconstructed aureola. In addition, men and women experiencing alopecia can get their scalp tattooed to resemble hair, stretch marks that stem from childbirth or weight loss can be camouflaged, and burn damage can be corrected as well.

Medical tattooing is also used during radiation therapy for cancer. Because certain types of cancers must be very carefully irradiated, generally over a period of months, tattoos are sometimes used to mark the locations that the radiation needs to target, so that the same location can be precisely targeted during each treatment.

In 1955, the Assistant Secretary of Defense suggested that all U.S. citizens have their blood type tattooed onto their bodies in anticipation of a military attack on the United States, and many citizens evidently complied, getting their blood types tattooed on an arm or leg. Some Americans also got their social security number tattooed on them.

See also: Cosmetic Surgery

Further Reading: Baran, Robert, and Howard I. Maibach. *Textbook of Cosmetic Dermatology*. London: Taylor & Francis, 2004.

MESO-AMERICA

Prior to the arrival of Columbus in Central America, Meso-America refers to a number of cultures found throughout central Mexico, southern Mexico, and along the Yucatan Peninsula, including the Olmec, the Teotihuacan culture, the Mayans, and the Aztecs, all of whom used a number of forms of body adornment and modification.

The Olmec lived in the tropical lowlands of south-central Mexico from about 1200 BC to about 400 BC. The Mayan civilization thrived for almost three thousand years on the Yucatan Peninsula from about 1000 BC to AD 800. The Aztecs were primarily found in central Mexico and thrived from the fourteenth to the sixteenth centuries, until the arrival of the Spanish.

When Hernándo Cortés and his Conquistadors arrived in Mexico in 1519, they were shocked to find that the natives of the area not only worshipped what the Spanish considered devils, but also marked these images onto their skin. Because the Spanish had never seen nor heard of **tattooing**, they considered the practice to be the work of the devil.

The Aztecs, who the Spanish ultimately conquered, used tattooing to mark warriors, as both a sign of courage and also to commemorate his accomplishments. Early Aztec tattoos helped identify the rank of a warrior and the deeds he had accomplished. The tattoos may also have been thought to be important in guiding the dead to the afterworld.

We know from archaeological evidence that ancient Meso-Americans pierced their ears, noses, and lower lips, and such practices continue to be popular amongst indigenous peoples in these regions.

Jewelry-making developed five thousand years ago in Central and South America. Because gold was easily accessible, the Aztecs, Olmecs, and Mayans created bracelets, pendants, necklaces, earrings, nose ornaments, lip plugs, and ear spools using gold as well as materials like jade, silver, bronze, obsidian, and copper. Found materials like shell and jaguar teeth and claws were also utilized in jewelry.

Pierced lips and the wearing of **labrets**, or lip plugs, was reserved for male members of the higher castes of Meso-Americans. These elaborately designed pieces were inserted into the hole in the lip such that the decorated end, which could resemble a bird, serpent, or another animal, would emerge from the lip opening.

Among the Aztecs, only nobility wore gold jewelry, as it showed their rank, power, and wealth. The main purpose of Aztec jewelry was to draw attention to the wearer, with richer and more powerful Aztecs wearing brighter, more expensive clothing and jewelry made out of gold and precious stones. Commoners, on the other hand, had to wear plain clothing, and either no adornments, or simple adornments made out of bone, wood, shell, or stone. Aztec men and women also painted their bodies the color of the banner of their chief.

The Olmec and Mayans not only wore earrings in their pierced ears, but stretched their earlobes and wore gold, jade, shell, and obsidian ear spools in the enlarged holes. An ear spool is a large cylinder that fits through the ears with a large disk or decorative sheet on the front side. It is thought that ear spools were inserted into the ear by first slicing the ear open, inserting the spool, and as the wound heals, the spool is sealed into place. As with the labrets, only high-status Mayans could wear the larger ear spools. In fact, throughout the Americas, the elaborately large ear spools were used as a sign of high status.

Mayans also pierced their bodies for more than decoration. They practiced bloodletting as a form of religious sacrifice, in which Mayan rulers would cut or pierce their ears, cheeks, tongues, and genitals; each body part was cut for a specific reason. For example, a man would pierce his penis and let the blood drip out to symbolize and encourage fertility. Women participating in bloodletting rituals would often pull a rope covered with thorns through a piercing in her tongue.

The Mayans also practiced head shaping, by wrapping infants tightly with cloth to a cradleboard, a process which could last for years. Heads shaped like cones were thought to signify nobility, although it is clear that more than the nobles flattened their heads, since the majority of all skulls found from the period were flattened.

Upper-class Mayans also filed their teeth, and sometimes etched designs onto the surface of the teeth as well, a tradition that has also been found in Africa and contemporary Central America. They also drilled holes into the teeth for the purposes of inserting jewels, a practice which would have been limited to the elites.

See also: Cosmetic Dentistry; Earplugs and Ear Spools; Head Binding; Labrets

Further Reading: Bray, Warwick. *Everyday Life of the Aztecs*. New York: Dorset Press, 1968.

MILITARY TATTOOS

The rise of **tattooing** in the West can be directly traced to the influence of military men. Starting in the seventeenth century when English sailors were exploring the South Pacific, but possibly dating back to the colonization of the Americas and **India**, European sailors have picked up tattoos while traveling, bringing the tradition back to Europe, and later the United States, with them. It wasn't until the late twentieth century that military men were no longer the biggest customers of American tattooists.

In the United States, times of war, from the Civil War through the Korean War, were always good times for tattooists. Military personnel flocked to tattooists to get tattoos that established their patriotism (through military insignias, battle commemorations, etc.) and which could remind them of their loved ones back home ("mom," etc.). Consequently, most tattoo shops were located in port towns where sailors would not have to wander far to find one. Samuel O' Reilly, a famed tattooist in New York City, once stated, "A Sailor without a tattoo is like a ship without grog: not seaworthy." One of the great seaman-tattooists of all times was George Burchett-Davis who, in 1888 at the age of 16, shipped out on the H.M.S. Victory.

While sailors remained for many years the tattooist's best customer, the Navy did not always look favorably on all tattoos, and in 1909 prohibited "indecent" tattoos for sailors. While this ruling was ignored for many years, in the 1940s, sporting a naked lady tattoo would be enough to be refused entry into the Navy. Many tattooists took advantage of this rule by advertising to cover up obscene tattoos, and many sailors returned to the Navy with their formerly naked ladies clothed as nurses, hula dancers, or "Indian squaws."

The period between the two world wars saw tattooing at its most popular in the United States. It was at this time that tattooing had perhaps its highest level of social approval, due to its link with patriotism and Uncle Sam's fighting boys. This nationalist fervor can also be seen in the numbers of citizens, military, and nonmilitary, who acquire patriotic tattoos during these times. The link between soldiers and sailors and tattooing was so strong that it was assumed that a man with tattoos was serving in the armed forces, or had been at one time.

The tattoos popular among the nation's servicemen from the beginning of the twentieth century to the end of World War II comprise the system of traditional American tattooing which is both the most classic, and one of the most universally readable of all tattoo types. While it was not only military men who wore these tattoos, they were the most heavily tattooed population in the United States, and were the most influential in terms of setting trends in imagery, style, and placement. Sailors in particular were the best tattoo customers among the services due to their long history of getting tattooed, their travels to different parts of the world, and to the frequency of their paychecks: twice a month as opposed to once a month for the Army and Marines. Sailors were tattooed in the United States, Hong Kong, Japan, the Philippines, and Europe, and for most a collection of tattoos commemorating their journeys was a point of pride.

Sailors often visited tattoo shops in groups and competed with each other for the most, best, and biggest tattoos. The most popular designs for twentieth-century military men were patriotic themes (flags, eagles, American slogans), military emblems ("USN," ships, anchors), sea themes (mermaids, dolphins, whales), and "girlie tattoos" (nude women, hula dancers, harem girls, sailor girls, cowgirls, and geisha girls). The girls were patterned after many sources, including the Gibson girl, the "cheongsam girl" adapted from the movie *Suzy Wong*, as well as other stereotypical women of the period. The hula girl was placed on the upper arm so that by contraction of the muscles, the sailor could make her dance. Other classic designs popular in the military included the "rose of no man's land," depicting a military nurse's head emerging from a rose on a cross or anchor, "homeward bound," "rock of ages," and "sailor's grave" images dealing with a sailor's most anticipated and most feared final days at sea, and "death before dishonor," usually found on a snake encircled dagger or skull. Soldiers, too, had specific designs. Paratroopers had "chutes and boots" tattooed on them after they took their first jump out of an airplane.

Each war creates new designs; the Civil War gave us designs such as a woman wearing a "Liberty" cap; the Spanish American war provided the steam battleship; World War II provided tattoo slogans like "The Only Good Jap Is a Dead Jap"; the Vietnam War gave us tattoos caricaturing the Vietnamese. Tattoo artist **Sailor Jerry Collins** was skillful at the cartoon-style put-downs, creating a whole sheet of "Cong" designs in 1967, from the "Rice Paddy Daddy" to "Dead Cong = Good Cong."

Often a tattoo's reading is determined not only on the basis of the image used, but on its placement on the body as well. Again, the military, and especially the Navy, has the best tradition of this, with iconic tattoos such as a crying and laughing baby over the chest with the words "sweet and sour" under the babies—"sour," under the head of the crying baby, below the nipple, and "sweet," under the laughing baby above the nipple. Another popular chest piece was to have port and starboard ship lights tattooed on the left (port) and right (starboard) side of the chest.

When a sailor had traveled 5,000 miles at sea, he earned a bluebird on the chest; with 10,000 miles, a second bird could be added on the other side. When a soldier made his second cruise around the world, he earned a clothesline with girls' stockings and underwear between them. For crossing the equator, one could get a Neptune on the leg or a shellback turtle, and a golden dragon shows that a sailor crossed the international dateline. A full-rigged ship was proof that a sailor had sailed around Cape Horn, a dragon showed that he had served in **China**, and an anchor demonstrated that he had sailed the Atlantic. A pig on one foot and a rooster on the other acted as a charm that would keep a man from drowning at sea (since these animals cannot swim the seaman would quickly return to shore). The words "hold" and "fast" could be tattooed onto the knuckles of the hand to help the seaman to better hold the ship's riggings, and a rope tattooed around the wrist meant the sailor was a deckhand. British sailors at one time tattooed Jesus's crucifixion on their backs to ensure sympathy when being whipped.

Certain parts of the body were heavily favored as tattoo sites for U.S. servicemen, while certain spots were prohibited and others were simply ignored. The primary areas on the body to get tattooed were the back, chest (and/or stomach), biceps, forearms (front, side, and back), and both sides of the calves. Except for heavily tattooed people (primarily tattooists or circus and carnival freaks), the thighs, sides, and under the arms were usually ignored. Facial and hand tattooing was prohibited for servicemen.

"Mom" tattoos are in many ways akin to the patriotic tattoos in that both express deep love for the mother—both the biological mother as well as the motherland. Thus a sailor's choice of a "mom" tattoo is both an expression of personal affiliation/affection as well as a more nationalist mood. And finally, perhaps the most literal tattoo was the identification tattoo. Servicemen, for example, often had their names, service number, rate, and date of birth tattooed on them.

Tattooing changed after World War II. Not only had the price of tattoos gone up substantially, but the sailors, who were the bread and butter of the tattooist's trade, had changed. The Pacific Ocean was no longer a hub of North American military activity, and many of the new enlistees were not planning on a career in the military. In addition, in the 1950s as tattooing began to experience a downward turn in popularity among the mainstream population, even the Navy began to counsel the men to avoid tattoos. While with each new war after World War II, there would be another flight of enlisted men and patriotic citizens to the local tattoo parlor, between wars the demand largely dried up. In addition, soldiers and sailors, upon their return home, started to find that their wives or girlfriends, and even bosses, did not appreciate their tattoos. As the social pressure against tattooing increased, even military tattooing began to ebb.

Of course patriotic tattoos still come into fashion when we are either at war or are otherwise challenged as a nation. After 9/11, many Americans got tattoos commemorating the date.

See also: Cook, Captain James

Further Reading: Burchett, George, and Peter Leighton. *Memoirs of a Tattooist*. London: Oldbourne Book Company, 1958; Steward, Samuel. *Bad Boys and Tough Tattoos: A Social History of the Tattoo with Gangs, Sailors and Street-Corner Punks, 1950–1965*. New York: Harrington Park Press, 1990; Webb, Doc. *The Honest Skin Game*. San Diego, CA: Author, 1978.

MODERN PRIMITIVES

The **modern primitives** movement was brought to mainstream awareness through the publication of *Modern Primitives* in 1989. The twelfth book in the RE/Search series by Vale and Juno, *Modern Primitives* looks at **tattooing**, **piercing**, and other body modification practices, and links those practices to those of primitive peoples.

For many people who bought this book, it was the first time that they saw photos of a white man's bifurcated penis, Ndebeli women wearing collars around their necks, an Indian sadhu with coconuts sewed to his body, and **Fakir Musafar** hanging from meat hooks driven into his flesh.

While Musafar was already publicizing these practices for a limited audience through the publications *Body Play* and *PFIQ*, it wasn't until *Modern Primitives* was published that extreme body modification was brought into the public consciousness.

The term "modern primitives" was coined by Fakir Musafar, known as the father of the movement, and refers to people who modify their bodies in a ritualistic fashion, using symbols, philosophies, and practices borrowed from non-Western cultures in order to achieve not only physical but emotional transformation.

Modern Primitives includes chapters on over two dozen tattooists, piercers, and proponents and practioners of tattoing, piercing, and more extreme body modifications. Mainstream (but innovative) tattooists like **Don Ed Hardy, Leo Zulueta**, and Charlie Cartwright are featured alongside piercers **Jim Ward** and Raelyn Gallina, body modification pioneers like Fakir Musafar, and individuals like Tattoo Mike and Sailor Sid, whose bodies and stories illustrate the modern primitives movement.

The book introduces the concept of the modern primitive by explaining that for some Westerners, the contemporary Western way of life is unsatisfactory, life-thwarting, and emotionally and spiritually stifling. These individuals seek a "more ideal society," which they feel they can achieve by modeling their life and practices on an idealized notion of "primitive" people.

Modern primitivism does not just idealize the primitive, however. It assumes that primitive practices are somehow more essential and authentic than modern cultural practices, so by wearing tribal tattoos or an ampalang, one can tap into one's true nature and achieve a higher consciousness.

Modern primitivism also embraces **pain**, as something that cannot be simulated and thus is, again, a sign of that which is authentic, and which cannot be purchased.

Modern Primitives opens with a feature on Fakir Musafar, in which he discusses the motivations for his own practices, which include tattooing, fasting, self-piercing, waist cinching, lying on a bed of nails, suspending his body, wearing encumberments, stretching of the genitals, and various forms of body play.

Many of the artists and advocates interviewed in the book talk extensively about the body modification practices of non-Western peoples, as a justification for their own practices. Included are graphic photos of not only the tattoos, piercings, and other modifications of the interviewees' bodies and clients, but a variety of photos and drawings of "primitive" peoples and their practices. The links are made clear, throughout the book, between contemporary Western body modification practices and their primitive precursors, and demonstrate that these practices are authentic and legitimate ways for Westerners to challenge themselves mentally, physically, and spiritually.

See also: Musafar, Fakir; Primitivism

Further Reading: Klesse, Christian. "Modern Primitivism: Non-Mainstream Body Modification and Racialized Representation." In Mike Featherstone, ed., *Body Modification*. London: Sage Publications, 2000; Pitts, Victoria. *In the Flesh: The Cultural Politics of Body Modification*. New York: Palgrave Macmillan, 2003; Vale, V., and Andrea Juno. *Modern Primitives*. San Francisco, CA: Re/Search Publications, 1989.

MODERN PRIMITIVES *See* Primitivism

MOKO

The native people of New Zealand, called the Maori, are known around the world for their **tattooing**. Although their tattoos do not cover as much of the body as many South Pacific people such as the Samoans, the Maori developed their own unusual style of tattooing, covering the face and the buttocks. First described by **Captain James Cook** in 1769, Maori tattooing remains one of the most unique and beautiful of all tattoo traditions.

The *moko* is the curvilinear facial tattoo worn by Maori men and women as a sign of status as well as affiliation, and only high-status Maori and warriors at one time were tattooed. Women's tattoos were originally limited to the lips and sometime other parts of the body or forehead; in the nineteenth century, the spiral chin tattoo was developed. Men could wear the moko, or, if they had their bodies tattooed, the tattoo extended over the area between the waist and the knees, primarily covering the buttocks.

The tattoo design was first drawn onto the skin, and then carved into the skin with a tool known as *uhi whaka tataramoa*, which operated much like wood carving to which it can be related both in design and technique. The tattooist, who was always a man, literally carved the design into the skin. After cutting the skin, pigment was rubbed into the skin.

The procedure was said to be incredibly painful, and caused so much facial swelling that, after tattooing, the person could not eat normally, and had to be fed liquids through a funnel. (The person being tattooed was also asked to forgo sexual activities and solid food, so the funnel served two purposes.) A woman's moko, which covered the chin and lips, could take one or two days to complete. A man's moko, which covered the whole face, was done in stages over several years and was an important **rite of passage** for a Maori man; without the moko, a man was said to not be a complete person.

Unlike tattoos in Polynesia and elsewhere which have designs that are worn by everyone of the same tribe, clan, or rank, Maori tattoos were totally individual. While they did indicate a man's social and kinship position, marital status, and other information, each moko was like a fingerprint, and no two were alike. Maori chiefs even used drawings of their moko as their signature in the nineteenth century. Because the moko in part signified rank, different designs on both men and women could be read as relating to their family status, and each of the Maori social ranks carried different designs. In addition, some women who, due to their genealogical connections, were extremely high status, could wear part of the male moko.

As in Marquesan tattooing, Maori facial designs were divided into four zones (left forehead, right forehead, left lower face, and right lower face) and these further divided, giving an overall symmetry to the design. The right side of the face conveyed information abou the father's rank, tribal afflations, and position. The left side of a face, on the other hand, gave information about the mother's rank, tribal affiliations, and position. Each side of the face is also subdivided into eight sections, which contain information about rank, position in life, tribal identification, lineage, and more personal information, including occupation or skill.

Tattooing styles varied from tribe to tribe and region to region, as well as over time. Captain Cook, for example, noted during his expedition in 1769 that the men on one side of an inlet were tattooed all over their faces, whereas the men on the other side of the inlet were only tattooed on the lips. He also noted that some moko did not include the forehead but only extended from the chin to the eyes. Also, Cook's men noted that there was at least one man at that time who had straight vertical lines tattooed on his face, combined with spirals, as well as two elderly men with horizontal lines across their face. Tattoos of this sort were never again seen on subsequent visits. And by the nineteenth century, different styles of moko were seen, including both the classic curvilinear style as well as vertical and horizontal parallel lines.

The buttock tattoo, called *te marau*, is similar to the Samoan **pe'a** but was, like the moko, primarily composed of heavy black spirals, rather than the lines and dots of the pe'a. Like the Moko, the *te marau* is split into zones, each of which convey information about tribal descent, lineage, and so forth.

The Maori had a tradition of preserving the tattooed heads of deceased persons of nobility in order to, it was presumed, keep alive the memory of the dead. The heads were also held to be sacred, in that they continued to possess the deceased's tapu, or magical quality. But in 1770, just a year after initial contact, Europeans became interested in these tattooed heads, and initiated a heads-for-weapons trade that lasted until 1831, when it was banned by the colonial authorities.

> Not one great country can be named, from the polar regions in the north to New Zealand in the south, in which the aborigines do not tattoo themselves.
>
> CHARLES DARWIN,
> The Descent of Man, 1871

The first dried head to be possessed by a European was acquired on January 20, 1770. It was brought by Joseph Banks, who was with Captain Cook's expedition as a naturalist, and was one of four brought on board the Endeavour for inspection. It was the head of a tattooed youth of 14 or 15, who had been killed by a blow to the head.

The trade became especially scandalous because during the tribal wars of the 1820s, when European demand for the heads was at an all time high, war captives and slaves were probably tattooed, killed, and their decapitated heads sold to European traders. As the traffic in heads escalated, the Maori stopped preserving the heads of their friends, so that they wouldn't fall into the hands of the

Europeans. Evidently, it also became dangerous to even wear a moko, as one could be killed at any time and have one's head sold to traders. By the end of the head trade in the 1830s, the moko was dying out, thanks to missionary activity.

Tawaiho, Maori king with moko, 1900–1923. Courtesy of Library of Congress Prints and Photographs Division, Washington, DC, No. LC-USZ62-109768.

Like Hawaiian and Tahitian tattooing, Maori tattooing was also influenced by European contact. On Captain Cook's first visit to New Zealand, the ship artist, Sydney Parkinson, drew pictures of the moko, exposing Europeans for the first time to the Maori and their art, and, inciting the interest in tattooed heads that would follow. Tattoo techniques changed as well as a result of contact. Originally, the Maori applied their wood carving techniques to tattooing, literally carving the skin and rubbing ink into the open wounds. After European contact, sailors brought metal to the Maori, enabling them to adopt the puncture method found in other parts of Polynesia.

After European contact, the moko became associated with Maori culture as a way for the native people of New Zealand to distinguish themselves from the Europeans who had settled there, but by 1840, due to missionary activity, the male moko was falling out of fashion. It was revived briefly during the wars against Europe from 1864 to 1868, but by the turn of the century, there were only a handful of tattooed Maori alive. Ironically, it was during the period in which the male moko was declining that the female chin moko was gaining in popularity as a symbol of identity.

Since the late twentieth century, some Maori have begun wearing ta moko again as an assertion of their cultural identity. A few Maori tattoo artists are reviving traditional methods of applying ta moko, but most use electric machines.

See also: Cook, Captain James; Hawaii; Marquesas

Further Reading: Friedlander, Marti, and Michael King. *Moko: Maori Tattooing in the Twentieth Century.* Auckland, NZ: David Bateman, 1999; Gathercole, Peter. "Contexts of Maori

Moko," In Arnold Rubin, ed., *Marks of Civilization: Artistic Transformations of the Human Body*. Los Angeles: Museum of Cultural History, UCLA, 1988; Douglas, Bronwen, Nicholas Thomas, and Anna Cole, eds., *Tattoo: Bodies, Art and Exchange in the Pacific and the West*. Durham, NC: Duke University Press, 2005; Simmons, D. R. *Ta Moko: The Art of Maori Tattoo*. Auckland, NZ: Reed Books, 1986.

MUSAFAR, FAKIR

Fakir Musafar, born Roland Loomis in 1930, is considered to be the father of the **modern primitive** movement, and has not only pioneered a number of extreme body modification practices such as **branding,** play piercing, corsetting, **suspensions,** and the use of **encumberments,** but has been an influential promotor of such practices through the publications *Body Play* and **PFIQ**, his coverage in the Re/Search publication **Modern Primitives**, his role in the film **Dances Sacred and Profane**, and his lectures and performances around the world.

For many years a California advertising executive, Fakir first coined the phrase "modern primitive" in 1967, after decades of his own experimentation. He describes its meaning as "a non tribal person who responds to primal urges and does something with the body."

Fakir got involved in body modifications after seeing a man getting tattooed at a carnival sideshow as a child. He reported that from that moment he knew that he would have to mark and put holes into his body. Reading *National Geographic* as a child also inspired his interest in the practices of non-Western peoples. Fakir gave himself his first **body piercing** in his foreskin when he was thirteen and his first tattoo by high school, and over the next six decades continued to use innovative and extreme practices on his own body and on others' bodies, including the practice of play piercings, suspensions, and wearing weights on the body for emotional and physical transformation.

In 1977, he "came out" as Fakir with his first public performance at the first International Tattoo Convention in Reno, Nevada. (He found the name "Fakir Musafar" in an early Ripley's Believe It Or Not; ironically, he later performed at Ripley's in San Francisco by lying on a bed of swords.) Of his performance there— in which he hooked daggers in his chest, had bricks broken on his back, and dragged a belly dancer around by the holes in his chest—Fakir noted that the mainstream tattoo community was not at all receptive or ready for him and his extreme practices, demonstrating to him the shallowness of using tattoos or other "primitive" practices for superficial adornment.

It is difficult to quantify how great his role has been in the growth of the modern primitivist movement in the West, but it seems inarguable that without him, the idea that modifying one's body could extend well beyond the aesthetic and can be used for personal expression, spiritual exploration, and physical healing would not be as commonplace (although not yet mainstream) as it is now.

The **BDSM** movement also owes a great debt to Fakir. In the BDSM community, the term modern primitive refers to a host of sexual, sartorial, and cultural practices involving ritualistic body modifications like **cutting,** piercing, and **tattooing**. BDSM (with or without body modifications) is seen as a vehicle for personal transformation, a basis for greater spiritual awareness, and a way for participants to reconnect with their physical bodies, and again, Fakir played an enormous role in popularizing these practices, as well as refining some of the techniques used in them.

Perhaps his greatest contribution to the body modification movement is his work in body play. Fakir is perhaps the first white man to perform the O-Kee-Pa suspension in 1966 or 1967, a Mandan and Ogala Sioux ritual in which the participants hang from wooden pegs or flesh hooks pierced through the chest for up to twenty minutes. He is also the first person to have filmed a performance of his interpretation of a Native American Sun Dance ritual, in which he and Jim Ward attached themselves to a pole with skewers attached to the chest until the skewers were torn from their flesh. During this performance, captured on the film *Dances Sacred and Profane*, it took the two men four hours to rip their flesh free from the skewers. Other rituals Fakir has performed and made known to the public include the *Kavadi*, a trance-inducing dance ritual from **India** done while wearing a steel frame through which long weighted skewers are passed, which are then pierced into the skin of the back and chest. As the person "bearing Kavadi" walk and dance, the skewers pass further and further into the body, and are said to result in an ecstatic state.

Today, Fakir sees his life work involving writing, speaking, and teaching others what he has experienced and learned doing body play.

See also: BDSM; Body Piercing; Body Play; *Dances Sacred and Profane*; *Modern Primitives*; Primitivism; Suspensions

Further Reading: Klesse, Christian. "Modern Primitivism: Non-Mainstream Body Modification and Racialized Representation." In Mike Featherstone, ed., *Body Modification*. London: Sage Publications, 2000; Pitts, Victoria. *In the Flesh: The Cultural Politics of Body Modification*. New York: Palgrave Macmillan, 2003; Vale, V., and Andrea Juno. *Modern Primitives*. San Francisco, CA: Re/Search Publications, 1989.

N

NATIONAL TATTOO ASSOCIATION

The National Tattoo Association (NTA) is one of the oldest and perhaps the best-known tattoo association in the world. It was started by East Coast tattooist Eddie Funk as The National Tattoo Club of the World in 1976, and it was originally financed by Flo Makofske and Don Eaker at National Tattoo Supply.

NTA began as an equipment supplier, offering legal assistance, technical information, tattoo equipment, and a newsletter (since 1976) to members. It also offers members an ID card and a certificate—suitable for display in one's studio—thereby giving the tattooist a professional touch. And finally, NTA hosts what was at one time the largest annual tattoo convention in the world; their first convention was in 1979 in Denver. Membership costs $40 per year and is capped at 1,000, with a long waiting list of tattooists and enthusiasts who pay dues as "associate members" for up to three years until a member spot opens. Artists must be sponsored by another artist member in order to join.

Today NTA has shifted its focus from promoting tattooing as an art form to an audience largely suspicious of it to advancing professionalism and safety standards among tattoo artists.

See also: Alliance of Professional Tattooists; Tattoo Shows

Further Readings: Sanders, Clinton. *Customizing the Body: The Art and Culture of Tattooing*. Philadelphia, PA: Temple University Press, 1989.

NATIVE AMERICANS

Many Native American tribes used **tattooing, piercing, body painting,** and other forms of body modification and adornment to mark affiliation and identity, as parts of **rites of passage**, and as decoration.

A number of Native American tribes, for instance, used tattooing, and tattoos were typically associated with tribal membership, social status, gender, and specific roles. Tattoos were probably brought over with one of the groups of Asian immigrants who came to the Americas from the Bering Strait, possibly between 5000 and 1500 BCE. On the West coast, for example, women often wore chin tattoos that indicated group membership or marital status. Eastern Indians, such as those who lived in Virginia, the Carolinas, and Ontario, often wore tattoos that represented social status, and which were often representational, rather than abstract. Techniques ranged from using sharpened bones or rocks to carve the tattoo into the skin, rubbing into it ash to make a permanent mark, to using porcupine quills dipped in ink, to the use of needles made of fish bones.

Some tribes only tattooed women, while others only tattooed men. When men were tattooed, it was often given as a mark of adulthood or to commemorate an important event like a man's first time participating in a battle. Among other tribes, tattooing was used for spiritual, magical, or medicinal purposes.

The Ohlone Indians are Indians who lived on the Pacific Coast between Baja California and the San Francisco Bay Area. Tattooing was mainly done on women, and was mostly decorative. Ohlone tattoos were mostly found on the face but could also extend over the neck, breasts, and shoulders. Some tattoos had magical significance and some had practical uses. Unlike many tribes, Ohlone tattoos were not just black but incorporated the juice from a number of plants to create green and blue pigment as well, which they also used to paint their bodies. Ohlone women got their tattoos when they reached puberty; they noted the girl's tribal affiliation and lineage, and marked her as marriageable.

At the time of European contact, Cherokee men used body paint and also wore tattoos. Tattoo implements were made with needles made of fish bones, dipped into natural dyes, and pounded into the skin. In 1762, three tattooed Cherokee chiefs are said to have traveled to London as goodwill ambassadors for their people.

The Cree used tattoos as charms to prevent illness, which was seen as being of a spiritual nature; for example an image tattooed on the cheek could protect against toothaches, while a tattoo on the forehead would keep headaches away. Cree women wore chin tattoos made up of black lines reaching from the lower lip to the chin, similar to a number of other groups such as the Ojibwa and Inuit. Tattoo methods included dipping a sharpened stick into pigment and carving the design into the skin, and a later method included the use of steel needles wrapped around the stick.

The Haida, Iriquois, and Mic Mac were tattooed to mark clan membership and sometimes had their totems tattooed on the body; the Haida wore tribal crest designs. Haida tattoos, like those of many northwest coast Indian tribes, were typically more elaborate on higher status individuals.

Most native tribes also adorned themselves with **jewelry** made of seashells, semiprecious stones, pottery, and bone, and often wore elaborate headdresses made of feathers and other natural materials. Many tribes also used body painting during ritual events or for warfare.

A number of Native American tribes pierced their noses and ears, and some wore not only earrings and nostril and septum piercings, but lip plugs in stretched lip holes as well.

Piercing for spiritual reasons was practiced as well, as some tribes used **suspensions** or other ritual practices to test a man's strength, courage, and endurance, or as part of an initiation ritual, often combined with fasting, dancing, smoking, and other sacred activities. Suspension rituals included the O-Kee-Pa, which involve the temporary piercing and hanging of young men by hooks in their chest and back, so that the participants could achieve a trance and communicate with the spirits, or the Sun Dance, in which the participants are pierced in the chest, and the piercings are attached by rope to a pole from which the men strain until their flesh tears, again, achieving a state of ecstasy and communion.

See also: Dances Sacred and Profane

Further Reading: Mails, Thomas E. *The Great Sioux Piercing Tradition*. Tulsa, OK: Council Oak Books, 2003.

NAVEL PIERCING

A navel piercing is a **body piercing** that goes through the rim of the navel, or belly button, rather than the actual belly button. Most commonly, the piercing goes through the top of the belly button (an inverse navel piercing uses the bottom ridge). **Jewelry** worn in a navel piercing is either captive bead rings or curved or straight barbells.

Most navel piercings are worn by women, and are quite common in Western society today. Unlike many other body piercings, navel piercings are not borrowed from non-Western cultures, but have only been worn since perhaps the 1970s. Today, they are commonly seen on girls and young women thanks to the popularity of low-rise jeans and shirts that are worn above the belly button. Navel piercings are generally worn for decorative reasons and because they are considered sexy.

> When I first got my belly button pierced, I couldn't stop lifting my shirt up to look at it.
>
> ANONYMOUS

See also: Body Piercing

Further Reading: Gay, Kathlyn. *Body Marks: Tattooing, Piercing, and Scarification*. New York: Millbrook Press, 2002.

NEO-PAGANISM

Neo-paganism refers to a number of different religious movements that have become popular in Western countries in the last thirty years, which are derived from or based on pre-Christian religions. These traditions have both inspired the modern body modification movement, especially the practice of **tattooing**, and members of these groups are often drawn to tattooing and **piercing** as a means to express their philosophy.

While there are hundreds of types of neo-pagan philosophies and groups, both in the United States as well as Europe, most share a similar worldview that includes living in harmony with nature, a reverence for the earth and its creatures, polytheism, a distrust of modern society, and a focus on "ancient" rituals, myths, and symbols. Modern wiccans, for example, see themselves as continuing a religious tradition that was once worldwide, and dates back to Paleolithic times. The wiccan myth can be found in the writings of Gerald Gardner and especially Margaret Murray. Both of these writers claimed that European goddess-worshipping cults were part of an organized, worldwide fertility cult that has survived unchanged into modern times.

In the 1970s, Wicca experienced a second revival, with the publication of Starhawk's seminal book, *The Spiral Dance: A Rebirth of the Ancient Religion of the*

Great Goddess. This book linked the Murrayite view of the "Old Religion" to modern feminism. Like other witchcraft practitioners, Starhawk promoted a worldview that linked humanity with nature, and that drew heavily on Celtic symbols and rituals. But for the first time, Starhawk connected witchcraft to a uniquely feminine spirituality. Starhawk's Goddess religion draws heavily on the work of feminist "thealogists" such as Mary Daly (author of *Beyond God the Father,* 1973) and Mary Christ and Judith Plaskow (authors of *Womanspirit Rising: A Feminist Reader in Religion,* 1979) who discuss the political implications of embracing a spirituality centered on the feminine, nurturing power, rather than on a masculine, controlling one.

The philosophy that many tattooed people today embrace is neo-pagan in its view of modern society as repressive, alienating, and lacking in ritual. Contemporary uses of tattooing and piercing also resemble neo-pagan philosophies through their appropriation of non-Western symbols and rituals which are thought to be more meaningful than those found in our own culture. Although both tattooed men and women are drawn to the neo-pagan ideas and images, many women especially wear tattoos based on "goddess" images (Venus of Wellendorf, the ankh, the astrological symbol for Venus), acquire their tattoos in a ritualistic context, and see their tattoos as having a magical function.

Many neo-pagans use body modification to identify themselves, express their interests, and as part of their rituals. Many neo-pagans, just like many **modern primitives,** see in their tattoos and body modifications the possibility for self-transformation. For these practioners, tattoos can act as a talisman in times of crisis, they unify the body and spirit, and the process of tattooing is a **rite of passage** that counteracts the alienation around us. In addition, the symbols that are favored by many tattooed people today are themselves derived from the philosophies and religions that are incorporated into neo-pagan philosophies, such as yin/yang, the chakras, the signs of the zodiac, Sanskrit writing, Japanese bonji, feathers, and drums.

See also: Magic; Modern Primitives

Further Reading: DeMello, Margo. *Bodies of Inscription: A Cultural History of the Modern Tattoo Community.* Durham, NC: Duke University Press, 2000.

NEW GUINEA

New Guinea is a large Melanesian island, made up of the Indonesian provinces of Papua and West Irian Jaya, as well as the independent country of Papua New Guinea. The islanders practice a variety of body modifications and body adornments including **tattooing, scarification, circumcision,** and **body painting.**

Festivals were and are an important part of life for many highland tribes of Papua New Guinea. Many tribes wore elaborate headdresses made of shells, bark, wood, fiber, feathers, hair, and bones for ceremonial purposes, as well as body paint, in order to placate spirits and ensure prosperity. The types of decorations and body paint demonstrated clan membership as well as rank, and at large gatherings such as the annual Mount Hagen Festival, serve to let other tribes know one's tribal affiliation.

Papuan people also pierce their septums and their ears and men wear horns, bones, and tusks through the openings. The Kangi tribe wear bat bones and sweet potatoes in their noses, and other tribes favor pig tusks which make the men look fierce for warfare. Men and women also wear necklaces, armbands, and other types of **jewelry** as adornment and identification.

Some Papuan tribes also practice scarification as part of young men's initiation ceremonies. Like so many other **rites of passage** into manhood, Papuan scarification, in which the chest, back, and buttocks

Native New Guinea men with headdress, body painting, and nose ornaments, 1919. Courtesy of Library of Congress Prints and Photographs Division, Washington, DC, No. LC-USZ62-46886.

are cut with sharpened bamboo, test a boy's strength, courage, and self-discipline.

Tattooing is also a traditional Papuan practice, although it has been largely abandoned since the mid-twentieth century. Women were once tattooed with black geometric markings over their entire bodies including their faces. Girls were tattooed throughout their childhoods; at each stage of their lives they were tattooed on a different part of their bodies. The final tattoo, on the chest and belly, was added when a girl was ready to be married; without these tattoos, she was not marriageable. Men, on the other hand, just received chest tattoos as a demonstration of their participation in a headhunt.

Tattoo techniques were similar to those in Polynesia in which a wooden stick with one or more thorns sticking out of the end would be tapped into the skin with another stick. Tattooists were generally women and different women tattooed different parts of the body.

Unlike so many tribal societies that practice **circumcision** as a male initiation ritual, some tribes in Papua New Guinea instead practice **superincision**, the slicing open of the top side of the shaft of the penis. Only introduced in the 1950s, it fits into the initiation rituals of many Papuan tribes who see women as polluting. Men must undergo a form of ritual menstruation in order to be rid of the feminine essence, which may include superincision or simply ritual bloodletting in which the penis is cut so as to bleed out the feminine influence.

See also: Body Painting; Nose Piercing; Scarification; Superincision

Further Reading: Hogbin, Herbert Ian. *The Island of Menstruating Men: Religion in Wogeo, New Guinea*. Scranton, PA: Chandler, 1970; Kempf, Wolfgang. "The Politics of Incorporation: Masculinity, Spatiality and Modernity among the Ngaing of Papua New Guinea." *Oceania* (September 2002): 56–77; Kirk, Malcolm. *Man as Art: New Guinea Body Decoration*. London: Thames and Hudson, 1981; Strathern, Andrew and Marilyn Strathern. *Self Decoration in Mt. Hagen*. London: Backworth, 1971.

NEW ZEALAND *See* Moko

NIGERIA

Nigeria is a country in West Africa with a long tradition of body modification, including **scarification, body painting, female genital mutilation**, and **circumcision**.

Like many Sub-Saharan African tribes, most tribes in Nigera traditionally practiced scarification. The Tiv, for instance, view scarification as purely decorative although the designs also denote the wearer's generation since patterns change over the years, from flat, shiny scars to raised, lumpy scars, to flat, dull scars, to deep cuts rubbed with charcoal. The decorative function of the scars is most important because the Tiv consider scars necessary for a person to be beautiful. The Tiv also oil their skin, use elaborate forms of **jewelry** and **makeup**, and chip their teeth, all to beautify the body. Women are scarred on their back, neck, and stomachs, and because scars are tender to the touch for the first few years, this makes the stomach especially erotic. Men, too, are scarred, generally on the chest, face, arms, and legs. Scars can be geometric designs of animal representations.

The Ga'anda of northern Nigeria also use scarification, known as Hleeta, to make girls marriageable. The process begins at 5 or 6, with the final phase ending at 15 or 16 just before marriage, at which time the girl will also have her ears pierced for earrings and her lip pierced to insert a **labret**. Elderly women perform the procedure, which is done, like many other tribes, with a fishhook to raise the skin and a razor to slice the skin, leaving a raised welt. Girls are scarred on their forehead, shoulders, arms, belly, legs, back of neck, back, and buttocks, with an elaborate pattern of dots which form lines, curves, and diamonds. The Ga'anda, like a number of other African tribes, are seeing scarification disappear thanks to disapproval from authorities and a declining interest in arranged marriages.

Other tribes use scarification to mark status or clan membership, such as the Kaleri. The Yoruba is another tribe whose women are traditionally scarred, as a test of a woman's bravery and to ensure that she will be strong enough to withstand childbirth; she must be scarred prior to marriage. Yoruba scars, known as *kolo*, are carved with a y-shaped double-blade knife, followed by rubbing charcoal into the wounds to ensure a strong scar. The small scars are then combined into lines along the face, chest, arms, hands, back, calves, and thighs, and into elaborate images like the butterfly, moon, a king's crown, vulture, dove, and lizard. Some marks have a specific meaning, like the *osilumi* mark on the face that is worn for mourning. Men can be scarred too, but it's not as important culturally and they do not have the wide variety of designs that women have.

Other Nigerian tribes paint their bodies for special occasions. The Ibo, for example, use the seeds of uli plants to make a dye used in body painting known as *uli* designs. Girls are painted after leaving the fattening room in which they were fattened for a period of months prior to marriage. Because weight is a sign of health, status, and fertility, a fat bride is more valued than a thin bride. During fattening, the girl is also given much of the knowledge that she will need as a married adult woman, so the period of fattening serves as an important **rite of passage** into adulthood for girls. Upon emerging from her seclusion, she is painted to make her even more beautiful.

On the other hand, female genital mutilation is also practiced by a number of Nigerian tribes. Female genital mutilation is a form of involuntary genital modification that is used in many African and Arab societies to control a woman's sexuality and ensure her virginity upon marriage and fidelity after marriage. It usually involves the removal of the clitoris and may also involve **infibulation**, which is the sewing together of the labia in order to prevent sexual intercourse. While the Nigerian government has discussed banning the practice, it is still very common: one in four Nigerian women have experienced these procedures, generally as very young girls or infants, with the Edo, Ibo, Efik, and Yoruba tribes as being the most dominant.

Circumcision is not as common for boys in Nigeria as in other nations, and in many areas, boys are circumcised at infancy as a medical procedure rather than an initiation ritual (although it may have been different in the past). For example, the Yoruba and Igbo usually circumcise their sons as infants, and the procedure is not ritualized nor used as a mark of tribal membership.

See also: Circumcision; Clitoredectomy; Obesity; Scarification

Further Reading: Adams, Sarah. "Praise Her Beauty Well: Ùrì from the Body to Cloth." In *Call and Response: Journeys into African Art* (Exhibition Catalogue). New Haven, CT: Yale University Art Gallery, 2000: 9–44; Berns, Marla C. "Ga'Anda Scarification: A Model for Art & Identity." In Arnold Rubin, ed., *Marks of Civilization: Artistic Transformations of the Human Body*. Los Angeles: Museum of Cultural History, UCLA, 1988; Bohannon, Paul. "Beauty and Scarification amongst the Tiv." *Man* 56(129) (1956): 117–121; Drewal, Henry John. "Beauty and Being: Aesthetics and Ontology in Yoruba Body Art." In Arnold Rubin, ed., *Marks of Civilization: Artistic Transformations of the Human Body*. Los Angeles: Museum of Cultural History, University of California, 1988; Fisher, Angela. *Africa Adorned*. New York: Harry Abrams, 1984.

NIPPLE PIERCING

Nipple piercings are **piercings** through the erect tissue of the nipple. Nipple piercings can placed horizontally, vertically, or at any other angle, and are worn by both men and women. The **jewelry** worn in a nipple piercing is usually a barbell or a captive bead ring. When jewelry is worn, the nipple is larger and permanently erect, providing a great deal of satisfaction to many wearers.

My piercings helped me test my strength and get over the fear of pain. My mom says these were mutilations of my body. They don't define me, but are a part of who I am and how I express myself.

ANONYMOUS

Roman men, but especially warriors, pierced their nipples as a sign of strength and masculinity. Julius Caesar, for example, was said to have had pierced nipples.

Both American and British sailors are said to have traditions in which sailors would have their nipple pierced after they crossed an important latitude or longitude, but for the most part, the practice of men piercing their nipples is a relatively recent one. Female nipple piercing has a longer history, however, and may date back to the fourteenth century when wealthy women wore low-cut dresses and exposed their rouged and adorned nipples.

The end of the nineteenth century also saw a brief fashion trend of nipple rings known as the "bosom ring." After the 1890s, however, the nipple piercing disappeared, emerging only since the 1960s with the body modification and especially the gay and **BDSM** communities.

Since that time, nipple piercings have become far more common, however, and are worn by both men and women as a form of adornment and as an enhancement to sexual pleasure.

See also: Body Piercing

Further Reading: Zeeland, Steven. *Sailors and Sexual Identity: Crossing the Line Between "Straight" and "Gay" in the U.S. Navy*. Binghamton, NY: Haworth Press, 1995.

NOSE PIERCING

Nose piercing refers to the piercing of the skin or cartilage of the nose. Nose piercing types include the nostril piercing, septum piercing, and bridge piercing.

In a nostril piercing, the wearer has one side of their nostrils pierced. **Jewelry** is generally a ring, which encircles the nostril from the outside to the inside, or a nostril screw, which has a stud or bead on the outside and a narrow piece of metal in the shape of a curlicue hidden inside of the nose; this jewelry is literally "screwed" into the hole.

Nostril piercings were known in biblical times; Genesis 24:47 notes that Abraham's servant gave Rebekah a gift of a nostril ring when he realized she would be the wife of Abraham's son Isaac. The practice of piercing the nostril in order to wear jewelry probably spread from the Middle East to Asia in the sixteenth century by Moghul emporers. Since that time, it has become extremely common in **India** as both a marker of beauty and social standing for Indian girls. In more recent times, a Hindu girl often has her left nostril pierced on the night before her wedding. Both studs and rings are worn by Indian women, and sometimes the nose jewelry is joined to an earring by a chain. While some women do have both sides of their nose pierced, the left side is far more common, because the left nostril is associated in Indian medicine with the female reproductive organs. Having one's left nostril pierced is said to make childbirth easier and lessen menstrual pain. Some women in India also pierce their noses to induce a state of submissiveness, by placing the piercing in an acupuncture point. Some Indian tribes also enlarge their nostril piercings, such as the Apa Tani of northeastern India.

Nostril piercing was also practiced among the nomadic Berber and Beja tribes of Africa, and the Bedouins of the Middle East. In these cases, the size of the ring represents the wealth of the family. As jewelry, it is given by the husband to his wife at the marriage, and is her security if she is divorced. Nose piercing is still popular in Pakistan, India, and Bangladesh. It also remains popular in Middle Eastern and Arab countries.

In the United States, nostril piercing did not become popular until it was introduced by hippies in the late 1960s and 1970s. Afterward **punks** and other youth subcultures in the 1980s and 1990s adopted the nostril piercing, and today it is common with young people from a variety of backgrounds. Next to the earlobe piercing, it is the most popular form of piercing today. While some men have their nostrils pierced, it is far more common among women.

A nasal septum piercing, which is a piercing through the flesh that divides the nostrils, is less common in the West than nostril piercings. Septum piercings, like nostril piercings, can also be stretched to create a large hole.

Jewelry includes captive bead rings (in which the ring encircles the septum, entering both nostrils, and the bead sits just below the tip of the nose), circular barbells (which look a bit like a horseshoe with both ends of the jewelry emerging from the nostrils), a septum retainer (which is shaped like a staple and can be worn inside the nostrils, in order to hide it from view), and for those who want to make a statement, an artificial tusk (which necessitates a stretched piercing). The septum piercing in which a ring is worn is often referred to as a bull-ring piercing because they are sometimes used to control bulls.

> I was also told it wasn't very ladylike and I had to take it off, but I will take it off when I'm ready.
>
> ANONYMOUS

Septum piercings were worn by a number of traditional societies, but especially among men in warrior societies, probably because wearing a large bone or horn through the nose makes a person look very fierce. The use of septum tusks is common, for example on **Borneo, New Guinea**, and the Solomon Islands, as well as among some Australian Aboriginal groups. Typically septums were pierced in these cultures as part of initiation rituals for boys. Ancient Meso-Americans like the Aztecs and the Mayans as well as the Incans also had their septums pierced, and wore elaborate jade and gold jewelry. The Cuna Indians of Panama still wear gold rings in their septum.

Nakoaktok woman of the American Northwest coast with a septum piercing, 1914. Photo by Edward Curtis. Courtesy of Library of Congress Prints and Photographs Division, Washington, DC, No. LC-USZ62-52204.

Septum piercing was popular among some Native American tribes such as the Shawnee and many tribes of the Pacific Northwest Coast. Bones were often worn through the piercings, and sometimes beads were strung through the hole and hung in front of the mouth.

The next most common nose piercing is the bridge piercing. This piercing is a surface piercing through the small flap of skin at the top of the nose, between the eyes. Barbell-style jewelry is the most common jewellery worn in this piercing. This particular piercing is fairly rare, and can't usually be worn by people who wear glasses.

There are a number of newer and rarer nose piercings as well. For instance, the nasal tip piercing is a piercing through the nostril that emerges through the point of the nose. It is known as a rhino because the jewelry (usually a stud, but it could be a point) sticks out from the tip of the nose.

The Austin bar is also a nasal tip piercing, but does not begin in the nostril. Instead, this piercing pierces the entire tip of the nose horizontally from one side to the other with a barbell.

The nasallang is another rare piercing made up of a pair of nostril piercings (one in each nostril) with a septum piercing at the same level in between the two. A single piece of jewelry, usually a barbell is worn connecting all three—although from an outsider's view it will simply appear as a pair of nostril piercings assuming that the barbell sits flush with the skin.

Finally, the septril starts from a stretched septum piercing and emerges through the tip of the nose downward so that the stud of the jewelry pokes out from the bottom of the tip of the nose.

See also: India; New Guinea

Further Reading: Gay, Kathlyn. *Body Marks: Tattooing, Piercing, and Scarification*. New York: Millbrook Press, 2002.

O

OBESITY

Obesity refers to being clinically overweight, typically measured by one's body mass index (BMI). If a person's BMI is over 30, then that person is considered to be obese. While there are genetic factors that will determine one's weight in life (and diseases such as hypothyroidism can also be factors), obesity is generally thought to be caused by overeating and a lack of exercise. Obesity results in a body that is out of line with conventional standards of health and beauty in the West, and obese people face a great deal of discrimination.

Obesity can also be a sign of a psychological disorder. Binge eating disorder, for instance, is a condition in which individuals binge eat, often compulsively, in order to relieve stress or other unpleasant feelings. Like **cutting**, binge eating can be seen as a way that some people control pain, and thus, exercise control over their own lives. But like cutting, binge eating is viewed as unhealthy by most medical practitioners (as well as society at large), and results in a body that is often out of line with socially acceptable body standards.

While traditionally, obesity was combated by diet and exercise, increasingly, weight reduction surgery or **bariatric surgery** is used.

Obesity has not always been seen negatively, however. In a number of cultures around the world, obesity has been associated with physical attractiveness, strength, and fertility. For instance, obesity was often seen as a symbol of wealth and social status in cultures in which many people starve or suffer from undernourishment. Even today, there are a great many cultures which are traditionally more accepting of obesity, including some African, Arabic, Indian, and Pacific Island cultures.

Some tribal people still gauge female beauty by size and brides are often "fattened" before marriage. For example, girls in the Hima tribe of Uganda undergo a four-month fattening ritual prior to marriage, in which they eat and drink until they are suitably fat. The Efik of **Nigeria** have a similar ritual for girls between the ages of 15 and 18, in which girls first shave their heads and then spend time in a fattening room until they are ready for marriage. The Okrika of Nigeria also fatten girls from 14 to 16 to make their bodies "come out." While these practices are most commonly associated with Africa, Native American tribes like the Havasupai also fattened girls to make them more beautiful.

In modern Western culture, obese men and women—but especially women—are viewed with ridicule, scorn, and sometimes pity. Americans associate obesity with laziness, sloth, gluttony, and stupidity, and the obese suffer employment and other kinds of discrimination.

Today, obesity acceptance and advocacy groups have become prominent advocates for the acceptance of fat people, and have created public awareness campaigns to defend the rights of the obese and to make them socially acceptable.

Beyond the fat acceptance movement, however, there are other individuals in modern society who actively encourage obesity, and there are also those who are erotically attracted to overweight people. "Chubbies," for example, are gay men who are overweight or obese and the chubby community is made up of chubbies and "chubby chasers"—men who are attracted to them. In the straight community, "fat admirers" are men who are sexually attracted to overweight or obese women, known in this community as big beautiful women (BBW). These relationships may or may not be classified as fat fetishes, as the admirerers may simply appreciate larger men or women, while the fetish admirerers are sexually attracted to excess fat itself.

One specific fetishistic category includes "feeders" and "feedees"; feeders are people who overfeed their partner in order to see them gain weight, and feedees, or gainers, are the eaters. These relationships are sometimes associated with **BDSM**, as the feeder is generally the dominant partner and the feedee or gainer the submissive. ("Stuffing" is the temporary practice of overfeeding someone until their bellies are so full that they cannot move.)

Intentional obesity, whether through being a gainer or a feedee or simply an obese person, can be seen as a form of extreme body modification in that the person intentionally controls the size and shape of their body, in this case through food consumption.

See also: Bariatric Surgery; BDSM; Beauty

Further Reading: Bordo, Susan. "Reading the Slender Body." In Mary Jacobus, Evelyn Fox Keller, and Sally Shuttleworth, eds., *Body Politics: Women and the Discourses of Science*. New York: Routledge, 1990; Bordo, Susan. *Unbearable Weight: Feminism, Western Culture, and the Body*. Berkeley: University of California Press, 1993; Crossley, N. "Fat Is a Sociological Issue: Obesity in Late Modern, Body-conscious Societies." *Health and Social Theory* 2(3) (2004): 222–253; Fallon, P., M. Katzman, and S. Wooley, eds., *Feminist Perspectives on Eating Disorders*. New York: Guilford, 1994; Gremillion, Helen. "The Cultural Politics of Body Size." *Annual Review of Anthropology* 34 (2005): 13–32. Ritenbaugh, C. "Obesity as a Culture-Bound Syndrome." *Culture, Medicine, and Psychiatry* 6 (1982): 347–361.

ORAL PIERCING

Oral **piercings** are piercings in and around the mouth. Inside the mouth, these include tongue piercings, tongue web or frenulum piercings, and, rarely, uvula piercings. Inside and outside of the mouth would be lip piercings and **labret** piercings.

The most common oral piercing in the modern West is probably the tongue piercing. Tongue piercings are worn for decorative purposes and for sexual purposes. Women also often report feeling empowered by wearing a tongue piercing.

Tongues are usually pierced in the center of the tongue, and vertically, with the piercing going through the top and bottom of the tongue. Some people choose to get an off-center piercing, and very rarely is a horizontal, or side-to-side, piercing chosen. Other rare placements include tongue **surface piercings**. Related pierc-ings include the tongue web piercing, which is a piercing through the frenulum, or piece of tissue that connects the tongue to the bottom of the mouth. The edges of the tongue can be pierced as well with a tongue rim piercing, which generally uses a ring to encircle the edge of the tongue. **Jewelry** for tongue piercings is usually a barbell.

While tongue piercings for decorative purposes are not common outside of the body modification scene, tongue piercings did play a role in ancient Meso-American blood rituals. Mayan leaders in particular would cut or pierce a partic-ular part of the body, in order to give a blood sacrifice to the gods. For instance, women were known to pull a thorn-covered rope through a hole in their tongues. Members of a number of Northwest Indian tribes such as the Haida, Kwaikiutul, and Tlingit also pierced their tongues as an offering to the gods. In addition, Fakirs and Sufis from the Middle East practiced tongue piercing as a form of sacrifice and as proof of trance state.

Lip piercings are another common form of oral piercing. Lip piercings are either labrets, in which a stud or a spike is attached below the lower lip, above the chin, or are piercings any-where around the lip in which a ring encircles the lip. Labrets were com-monly worn among a number of North-west Native American tribes, as well as

> I have my tongue pierced and I was licking an envelope and my secretary came in and she just kind of spit her coffee across the room.
>
> ANONYMOUS

ancient Meso-Americans like the Mayans and the Aztecs. A number of African tribes also wear lip plates in large stretched lip holes. The Dogon of Mali and the Nuba of Ethiopia were two tribes which practiced lip piercing and wore rings, rather than labrets or lip plates.

Some Westerners have the tissue, or frenulum, that connects the upper or lower lips to the mouth pierced. Upper-lip frenulum piercings, also known as smiley piercings, pierce the web-bing underneath the upper lip, and can display the jewelry when the wearer smiles. Lower frenulum pierc-ings, known as frownies, pierce the webbing connecting the lower lip to the inside of the mouth, but the jewelry is not normally visible when the wearer smiles. Jewelry is usually a captive bead ring or a circular barbell.

> I pierced my tongue for intimate rea-sons. The tongue piercing was good for a while; the girls I dated got a kick out of it, especially because no one knew I had it. It was not a very obvious modification; I talked normally and even as I spoke you couldn't tell I had it. But after I got a chipped molar, the fun quickly fiz-zled out.
>
> ANONYMOUS

Finally, some people have the uvula, or the piece of tissue that hangs between the tonsils in the back of the throat, pierced. Because the uvula piercing cannot be seen as decorative (since it can not really be seen), motivations for getting such a piercing are generally much more personal. Because of the difficult to access location, and the tendency of most people to instinctively gag when an object is placed in the back of the throat, it is a difficult piercing to administer or receive. Jewelry is usually a captive bead or other type of ring.

See also: Labret; Lip Plate; Surface Piercing

ORCHIECTOMY *See* Castration

PACIFIC NORTHWEST INDIANS

The native people of the Pacific Northwest Coast, including Alaska, Washington, and Canada, includes such diverse groups as the Tlingit, Haida, Kwakiutl, Puyallup, Snohomish, Nez Perce, and the Makah. First populated by Asians who migrated over the Bering Land Bridge into North America starting about 18,000 years ago, the first Europeans to explore the region were Russians in the eighteenth century. Many of the tribes in the region practiced **tattooing**, lip piercing, and **nose piercing**.

Cheek plugs, **labrets**, and nose ornaments of all kinds have been found in archaeological sites throughout Alaska, the west coast of Canada, and the Pacific Northwest in the United States.

The first European reports in 1769 mentioned women with facial tattoos consisting of lines which radiated from the mouth to the jaw, similar to chin tattoos among other **Native American** tribes, as well as those which extended from the nose to the ears. Other tattoos included tattooed lines across the foreheads, as well as tattoos on the neck, arms, hands, and feet. Among all the groups, women are more commonly tattooed than men, and for women, the chin tattoo was the most common, received when a girl reached puberty. Transgendered boys, known as *schopans* in some tribes, were also tattooed with the chin tattoo, and were highly valued as wives. The tattoo technique in the Pacific Northwest Coast was to use a sharp tool to puncture the skin, followed by rubbing soot into the wounds. Certain tattoos were also associated with whaling, but for the most part, tattoos were used as part of **rites of passage** initiating young women and men into adulthood, protection, status, and identification.

In some tribes, both men and women wore labrets, or large plugs inserted into holes below the lower lip, and both men and women had their septum pierced. In some tribes, however, where women wore the chin tattoo, men wore the labret, while in others, only women wore the labret. Labrets were sometimes as wide as the lips, and were made of stone, bone, wood, and ivory. Sometimes bones were worn through the septum piercing and occasionally in the lip hole, and sometimes beads were strung from the septum piercing, hanging down in front of the mouth. Beads were also strung from the labrets (into which holes had been drilled), creating the appearance of a beaded beard.

Some tribes sliced open the lip in order to receive the first labret 20 days after birth; other tribes waited till puberty, or even till adulthood. For girls it was common to slice the lips during an initiation ritual which begins after her first menstruation. Among the Tlingit, for example, the girl would often be secluded from society for months at a time, initially fasting in darkness, during which time her lip would be sliced open and a bone or stick inserted into the hole. When she is reincorporated into society as a woman, her old clothes are burnt and a feast is held in her honor, at which time her first labret will be inserted into the lip hole. For the Tlingit, and for many other tribes, the labret marks her status as a marriageable woman, and she is generally married soon afterward.

In all cases, the first labret was small, and would be replaced by increasingly larger labrets as the hole grew bigger. For that reason, labret size indicated both age and also status. The material used to make the labret also could indicate status, with the highly valued blue beads only worn by the wealthiest people. While most labrets were worn below the lip, between the lip and the jaw, some tribes wore labrets, which were typically round plugs, on both sides of the lips.

The traditions of wearing labrets and tattoos started to disappear in the nineteenth century as missionary activity as well as commercial whaling disrupted cultural traditions. Among some groups, however, they simply replaced the large labret that was traditionally worn with a small silver pin, maintaining the tradition over time.

See also: Inuit; Labrets; Native Americans; Nose Piercing

Further Reading: Griffin, Joy. "Labrets and Tattooing in Native Alaska." In Arnold Rubin, ed., *Marks of Civilization: Artistic Transformations of the Human Body*. Los Angeles: Museum of Cultural History, UCLA, 1988; Jonaitis, Aldona. "Women, Marriage, Mouths and Feasting: The Symbolism of Tlingit Labrets." In Arnold Rubin, ed., *Marks of Civilization: Artistic Transformations of the Human Body*. Los Angeles: Museum of Cultural History, UCLA, 1988.

PAIN

The permanent body modifications discussed in this book, as well as a number of the **body play** practices, involve anywhere from a small amount to a considerable amount of pain.

Tattooing, piercing, branding, scarification, cutting, as well as practices like **circumcision**, when not conducted under anesthesia, can be quite painful. For most people getting these procedures, the pain is something to be endured in order to achieve the desired result. For others, enduring the pain is a badge of honor and strength, to be displayed proudly. For still others, however, the pain is a part of the process, to be experienced and overcome, rather than to be avoided.

Many practices in the body modification community are based on an acceptance of pain. Pain is seen as a tool for self-transformation, and many body modification practitioners follow the "no pain, no gain" motto in an effort to use pain in order to achieve growth. Being able to control pain, and turn it to one's advantage, is another benefit, as is testing oneself to see how far one can go, and how much pain one can endure.

For others, especially those who practice **BDSM**, the sensations associated with pain are felt to be pleasurable and even addictive. As endorphins are released during, for example, play piercing, the lines between pleasure and pain are blurred and are highly sought.

See also: BDSM; Body Play; Suspension

PAPUA NEW GUINEA *See* New Guinea

PE'A

The pe'a is the traditional Samoan body tattoo. Worn by men alone, it covers the body from the torso to the knees.

Young men receive the pe'a as a **rite of passage**, signaling his transition from boyhood to adulthood, and his intent to serve his family and community. Without the pe'a, a man will never truly be a man, and having a half-finished pe'a, known as a pe'a *mutu*, is considered shameful. A man who gets the full pe'a is a *soga'imiti*.

The process of being tattooed is an intense, painful ordeal which is done over five stages, and could take weeks to complete, given the level of pain and the time needed to recover between stages. It was also costly. Men could not receive the pe'a until they accumulated enough wealth to cover the cost of the woven mats or tapa cloths needed as payment to the tattooist.

The **tattooing** tools, known as *au*, are similar to those found in many other Polynesian cultures, and consisted of a comb of different sizes, made of sharpened teeth or tusks, lashed to a turtle shell, and attached at a right angle to a stick. The smallest is the *au fa'atala* which is used to tattoo points and dots. The largest is the *au tapulu* and is used to fill in the solid design. The comb is dipped into the pigment and is tapped into the skin using a separate mallet, known as a *iapalapa*.

The pe'a traditionally took five days to create, but often takes weeks, and began on the back and went around the torso, up the hips, down the legs, around the buttocks, and ended with a distinct design that went around the belly button.

The design is perfectly symmetrical, made up of lines, arrows, triangles, and other geometric patterns, and is created by the tattooist for the wearer, with each part of the design having its own meaning. The entire pe'a symbolizes a bat whose wings wrap around the man's legs.

Men still get the pe'a today, and it is still done in the traditional manner, although it is now entirely voluntary and no longer a part of contemporary culture.

See also: Samoa

Further Reading: D'Alleva, Anne. "Christian Skins: Tatau and the Evangelization of the Society Islands and Samoa." In Bronwen Douglas, Nicholas Thomas, and Anna Cole, eds., *Tattoo: Bodies, Art and Exchange in the Pacific and the West*. Durham, NC: Duke University Press, 2005; Handy, E. S. Craighill. *Samoan House Building, Cooking, and Tattooing*. Honolulu, HI, Hawaii: The Museum, 1924; Mallon, Sean. "Samoan Tatau as Global Practice." In Bronwen Douglas, Nicholas Thomas, and Anna Cole, eds., *Tattoo: Bodies, Art and Exchange in the Pacific and the West*. Durham, NC: Duke University Press, 2005; Sulu'ape, Petelo. "History of Samoan Tattooing." *TattooTime* 5 (1991): 102–109.

Samoan Pe'a tattoo. Courtesy of Tattoo Archive.

PENIS PIERCING

There are multiple types of penis piercings, and many types of reasons for getting one's penis pierced, although the most common reasons would be for decoration and to enhance sexual pleasure. Most genital piercings began in the United States within the gay community, and especially among **BDSM** practitioners.

An apadravya is a piercing which pierces the head of the penis vertically through the width of the head, rather than through the urethra. **Jewelry** is generally a straight barbell, with each bead of the barbell sitting on each side of the glans.

The ampallang is a piercing which pierces the glans or head of the penis horizontally. It is evidently the most painful male piercing. The initial jewelry is almost always barbell with each bead of the barbell sitting on each side of the glans. The ampallang was traditionally worn in various Polynesian cultures, and among a number of tribes in Borneo, from whom the term *palang* comes. The apadravya and the ampallang are exactly the same, except for the orientation of the piercing through the glans.

The Prince Albert piercing, named after the husband of Queen Victoria, is a piercing that enters the penis from underneath behind the head, and exits through the urethra. The reverse Prince Albert piercing enters through the urethra and exits through a hole pierced at the top of the head. In both cases, only one hole is pierced in the penis, because the piercing utilizes the urethral opening. Jewelry for both piercings can be either a ring or a barbell, and they are most commonly found on circumcised men as the foreskin would cover the jewelry.

The Dydoe is a piercing around the edge of the head of the penis, but not through the head, and is usually worn in multiples. When multiples are worn, the penis looks like it has a ring of studs encircling the head. Barbells or captive bead rings are the preferred jewelry. This piercing is only appropriate for a man who has been circumcised.

A frenum piercing is a piercing that pierces the skin between the foreskin and the glans, and does not enter the shaft of the penis at all, although the jewelry, either barbells or rings, sit on the shaft. Many men get multiple frenum piercings down the ridge of the penis which are known as a frenum ladder.

Finally, some men get their foreskin pierced, which is evidently an ancient practice.

See also: Genital Piercing

Further Reading: Vale, V., and Andrea Juno. *Modern Primitives*. San Francisco, CA: Re/Search Publications, 1989.

PERMANENT MAKEUP

Permanent makeup, also known as cosmetic **tattooing**, refers to the practice of using tattooing to create the permanent effect of **makeup**. Cosmetic tattooing is used to tattoo beauty marks, to create permanent eyeliner, lipstick, blush, eyeshadow or eyebrows, and can be used to correct scars or disfigurements.

Permanent makeup is used by women who don't want to have to apply makeup every day, or who are uncomfortable with the appearance of their eyes or lips without makeup. Some women get cosmetic tattooing if they are allergic to makeup, or have a physical condition that makes the application difficult. Others may have a loss of pigment in their skin or sparse or no eyebrows or eyeliners. In these cases, permanent makeup can create the illusion of facial hair and can correct pigmentation irregularities. Permanent makeup is also used to camoflage scars, birth defects, and other skin disfigurements, and tattooing the scalp is a way to simulate hair when a person suffers from premature hair loss.

The drawbacks to permanent makeup include the fact that colors will fade over time, especially when exposed to sunlight. In addition, makeup trends change, so the shape of one's eyebrows, the color of the lips or eyeshadow, or even the thickness and color of eyeliner, may go out of style well before the tattoos have faded.

Permanent makeup is done with a regular tattoo machine, although tattooists regularly offer it as a service. Instead, cosmetic technicians perform the procedures. Most states regulate cosmetic tattooing but in general, the training undertaken by cosmetic tattooists—often no more than forty hours—is far less than the training that professional tattooists have.

See also: Cosmetic Surgery; Medical Tattooing; Tattooing

Further Reading: Baran, Robert, and Howard I. Maibach. *Textbook of Cosmetic Dermatology*. London: Taylor & Francis, 2004; Baumann, Leslie S. *Cosmetic Dermatology: Principles and Practice*. New York: McGraw Hill Medical, 2002.

PFIQ

PFIQ, or *Piercing Fans International Quarterly*, was a magazine published by **Jim Ward** of Gauntlet Enterprises from September 1977 to the late 1990s.

After founding the Gauntlet, the first professional **piercing** studio and distributor of piercing jewelry, with funding and training from fellow piercer Doug Malloy, Malloy and Ward produced a flyer called "Body Piercing in Brief" which gave information and drawings on the different types of body piercings. The flyer drew a lot of correspondence from people interested in piercings from around the world, who wanted to get a piercing or wanted to learn how to pierce, and folks who wanted to meet other people with piercings. Because the Gauntlet at that point (which was located in Los Angeles only) was the only professional piercing studio in the country, most people with any interest in piercing were on their own. There was no readily available resource for information on piercing technique or to find the tools and materials to do it. Piercing enthusiasts were also widely scattered all over the globe and for the most part very closeted. *PFIQ* was created to fill that niche, even though Ward had no initial desire to produce a magazine.

Ward had the first issue printed in San Francisco and later found printers in Los Angeles, after finding that a number of printers as well as binderies would not handle it because of the "pornographic" content. Photographs were initially provided by Malloy and Ward, and later would be sent in by readers around the world, and a Los Angeles gay artist provided much of the early artwork. The first issue, which had an initial print run of 500, included an interview with Malloy, an article about male infibulation, and a number of photographs. Because one of the goals of the magazine was to allow pierced people to meet each other, *PFIQ* included in the first issue a classified section called Pin Pals, included as a separate insert with issued mailed directly to subscribers; later they offered a mail forwarding service for subscribers to contact each other instead of the classifieds.

Subsequent issues included interviews with and articles by **Fakir Musafar**, features on tattooists, in-depth articles on specific piercings and body play practices (which in the mid-1980s Ward decided to no longer include in the magazine, out of fear of censorship). *PFIQ* did not include articles or photos on modifications not related to piercing, such as castration.

The last issue of *PFIQ* was Issue #50; Issue #51 was never printed as the Gauntlet collapsed due to mismanagement in 1998. Since regaining control of Gauntlet Enterprises in 2004, Ward is deciding whether to reprint back issues of *PFIQ* or even restart the magazine.

See also: Body Piercing; Ward, Jim

Further Reading: Vale, V., and Andrea Juno. *Modern Primitives*. San Francisco, CA: Re/Search Publications, 1989.

PHILIPPINES

The Philippines is a group of islands located in Southeast Asia. Colonized by Spain in the sixteenth century, the island is populated by multiple indigenous groups, as well as by more recent immigrants from China, South Asia, and Spain. **Tattooing** has been practiced by tribal groups in the mountains of the Philippines for centuries, although the practice has been dying out even among the most isolated of groups. In fact, Spanish explorers called the islands "the islands of the painted ones."

Traditional mountain tattooing as it was practiced by the Mindanao, Kankanay, Ifugoa, Visayas, Kalinga, Isneg, and Luzon tribes were made up of straight lines and curves as well as representational images such as dogs, men, eagles, centipedes, and snakes. Men applied the tattoos by first smearing the skin with a mixture of ashes and the juice of sugarcane, and then pricked the skin with a needle or other sharpened instrument. Some tribes used multiple needles at the same time, but the basic method was the same. Tattoos were painful to receive and a great amount of time was needed to heal between tattoo sessions, so that a full tattoo could take months to complete. Once complete, however, the tattoo indicated that the man was strong and brave.

Tattoos were used to mark important achievements, such as headhunting among men, and also represented age, status, or other socially important features, and were usually started during childhood. Women's tattoos were primarily done as a decorative practice, to enhance their **beauty**. Tattoos can also have a magical significance and can be used to protect a person, and these tattoos often use animals like scorpions, snakes, and centipedes.

The amount of coverage on the body depends on **gender** as well as tribal affiliation. Visaya, Kankanay, and Ibaloi men, for example, tattooed their entire bodies, while Visaya women tattooed their hands, and Kankanay and Ibaloi women their arms. As with many Polynesian tribes, the level of coverage often decided how much clothing is worn; when tattoos cover much of the body, typically very little clothing is worn. Igarots tattooed their upper bodies, which resembled chain mail, and the men of the Ifugao tattooed most of the body except for the buttocks, face, and feet.

Today, traditional tattooing is rarely practiced as other cultural traditions, such as headhunting, have disappeared. During the annual Pintados-Kasadyaan Festival held every June in the Visayan Islands, the tribes participate in a religious festival that involves a simulation of traditional tattooing, in which dancers paint themselves to resemble no-longer-worn tattoo designs.

See also: Borneo; Tribalism

Further Reading: Kroeber, A. L. *Peoples of the Philippines*. New York: American Museum of Natural History, 1943.

PIERCING

The practice of using a needle or other sharp implement to insert a hole into the skin of the face or the body so that **jewelry** can be inserted has been practiced on every continent since ancient times. Piercing can also refer to the practice of play piercings, in which parts of the body are pierced for ritual or sexual purposes, or even bloodletting, which was practiced, for example, by the ancient Mayans as well as a number of **Pacific Northwest Indians**, as a form of sacrifice. Generally, though, piercing is most often performed as part of initiation rituals, and is used to mark an individual's social position or their transition from one life stage to another.

The areas that are the most commonly pierced around the world are the soft tissues of the face, including the lips, ears, and nose, but some people, past and present, have also pierced other areas of the body, such as the genitals or nipples. Jewelry for the ears, nose, and lips, as well as figures and other representations of piercings, have been found around the world, and include the ancient Hebrews, Egyptians, Greeks, Romans, and Chinese. Explorers who traveled around the world during the fifteenth to eighteenth centuries also reported seeing people wearing **labrets**, nostril jewels, septum piercings, **earplugs** and **ear spools, lip plates**, and penis piercings in people as diverse as the Pacific Northwest Indians, the Aztecs, Aboriginal Australians, East Indians, the **Inuit**, the Papuans, the people of **Borneo**, and many Native American and African peoples.

Piercing in the West today is typically practiced at piercing studios, and sometimes tattoo studios, and in the United States, most piercings are done with a hollow medical needle. The needle is partially inserted into the part of the body being pierced, and, while still in the body, the jewelry, usually stainless steel or titanium, is pushed through the opening and the needle is removed. In some parts of the world, the piercer uses a cannula, which is a hollow plastic tube placed at the end of the needle, into which the jewelry is inserted. Traditionally, however, piercings were done with any sort of a sharp implement, from a cactus needle to a piece of metal.

See also: Body Piercing; Clitoral Piercing; Ear Piercing; Facial Piercing; Genital Piercing; Hand Piercing; Navel Piercing; Nipple Piercing; Nose Piercing; Oral Piercing; Penis Piercing

Further Reading: Gans, Eric. "The Body Sacrificial." In Tobin Siebers, ed., *The Body Aesthetic: From Fine Art to Body Modification*. Ann Arbor: University of Michigan Press, 2000; Gay, Kathlyn. *Body Marks: Tattooing, Piercing, and Scarification*. New York: Millbrook Press, 2002; Myers, James. "Nonmainstream Body Modification: Genital Piercing, Branding, Burning and Cutting." *Journal of Contemporary Ethnography* 21(3) (October 1992): 267–306; Pitts, Victoria. *In the Flesh: The Cultural Politics of Body Modification*. New York: Palgrave Macmillan, 2003.

PLASTIC SURGERY *See* Cosmetic Surgery

POCKETING AND STAPLING

Pocketing is a procedure that borrows the technology of **surface piercing** but results in a look that is often described as "anti-piercing" in that the ends of the

jewelry do not emerge from the skin, but instead remain hidden beneath the skin. Instead, the middle of the jewelry, or the bar, is exposed on top of the skin. It is called pocketing because the jewelry is held in the skin by two small pockets created beneath the surface of the skin.

Jewelry for pocketing is custom-made for the procedure, and is a curved bar with rounded ends, and no beads or decorative motifs. The technique typically involves using a scalpel to slice two incisions into the skin, inserting a tube beneath the skin in each incision to create pockets, into which the jewelry ends are inserted, and the incisions are sutured or glued close. The ends of the jewelry just lie beneath the skin very close to the incisions, and often migrate back out of the skin.

Another attempt to achieve the same look is flesh stapling, which uses a piece of jewelry that, on the outside, looks exactly the same as the jewelry used in pocketing, but inside looks like a very simple paper clip or a closed staple. Because the jewelry is essentially wrapped onto itself beneath the skin, it has a much harder time coming out on its own than the jewelry used in pocketing. Stapling also utilizes a scalpel to make the incisions and another device to elevate the skin for the insertion of the jewelry.

Flesh plating is a more elaborate form of flesh stapling that uses jewelry in the shape of a flate plate rather than a thin staple. Many people prefer flesh plating over other forms of piercing because plating allows for larger sizes of jewelry, which can be decorated in a variety of ways.

Finally, a flesh coil utilizes the stapling technology but is a long bar that is coiled not only into the staple shape, which keeps it under the skin, but has an additional coil in it that results in two sections of parallel bars being present on the skin, creating, essentially, a double staple.

All of these techniques are relatively new, and most piercers still do not offer them.

See also: Surface Piercing

Further Reading: www.BMEZine.com.

PRIMITIVISM

Modern primitivism originated in the practices and ideologies of the sexually radical leather and **BDSM** scenes, and later moved into the straight, mainstream tattoo community with the publication of the Re/Search Volume, ***Modern Primitives*** in 1989, and the first issue of ***TattooTime*** in 1982. It is intimately connected with the modern **piercing** and body modification scene.

Fakir Musafar, a former advertising executive from South Dakota (he found the name "Fakir Musafar" in an early *Ripley's Believe It or Not*), is said to have originated the term "modern primitives" in 1967. He describes its meaning as follows: "a non tribal person who responds to primal urges and does something with the body." In the BDSM community, modern primitives refers to a host of sexual, sartorial, and cultural practices involving ritualistic body modifications like **cutting**, piercing, and **tattooing**.

Modern primitives, both in its original usage in BDSM, and in its more widespread usage today, also implies a critique of contemporary Western society, which is seen as an alienating, repressive, and technocratic place lacking in ritual, myth, or symbol. By rejecting modern society through participating in the primitive rituals of tattooing, piercing, or **scarification**, participants feel that they are aligning themselves with societies and worldviews that are more pure, more authentic, more spiritually advanced than our own. This view is seen in the central text for the BDSM body play community, *PFIQ*, as well as in other Web sites and publications produced by the community. Piercing and other forms of body modification are seen as emblematic of primitive life, used for **rites of passage**, status marking, and because many body modifications are permanent, they are seen as possessing more meaning than the accumulation of material possessions in "civilized life."

Musafar, for example, states: "Sometimes the tattoo artists in primitive cultures were shamans. They envisioned the marks, tattooed them on the body, and then the person who got the tattoo was whole, complete." As we have seen, many contemporary tattooists envision themselves as shamans too. For many readers, this ideology was the impetus to not only get tattooed, but to get tattooed with non-Western designs. Further, followers are encouraged to see in their tattoos a primal instinct, and even a magical force. As Musafar says, "The purpose of the tattoo is to do something for the person, to help them realize the individual **magic** latent within them."

Just as the men's movement promotes a return to the primordial masculine self through the adoption of initiation rituals derived from primitive tribes, members of the modern **tattoo community** who embrace this philosophy find this connection to primitivism as well. Tattooing has become for many a vision quest, an identity quest, an initiation ritual, a self-naming ritual, an act of magic, a spiritual healing, a connection to the God or Goddess, the Great Mother or the Wild Man. For members of the tattoo community who see their tattoos as connecting them to ancient or primitive cultures, the reality of those cultures is not important. Rather, it is the idealized version of primitive cultures—closer to nature, in harmony with the spiritual realm, egalitarian, nonrepressive—that provides the appropriate image.

One source for the modern primitivist movement, and the one most responsible for popularizing it within the mainstream, middle-class tattoo community, was the first issue of Ed Hardy's *TattooTime*. This issue, called "The New Tribalism" (1982), was devoted to the documentation of tattooing in "tribal" cultures such as **Borneo**, **Samoa**, **New Zealand**, **Hawaii**, and **Native America**, and included photographs of the tattoos that are being worn among people in the West in imitation of this style.

Today, even outside of the modern primitive circle, tattooing is aligned with primitive and "tribal" practices and this is seen in the language ("archetypal," "ritualistic," "primal," "instinctive," "pagan") used.

Of course tattooing and body piercing in modern societies recapture primitiveness, because they take place within a modern social context, where status and social position are gained through economic and educational achievement. Body marks in primitive society were markers of social membership in socially cohesive groups, wherein life-cycle changes were necessarily marked by tattooing and scarification. Tattoos and piercings today are commercial objects purchased in a capitalist marketplace and are personal and optional accessories for the self. They cannot serve as charismatic entrance points to the primitive.

See also: Modern Primitives; Musafar, Fakir; *PFIQ*; *TattooTime*

Further Readings: Atkinson, Michael, and Kevin Young. "Flesh Journeys: Neo Primitives and the Contemporary Rediscovery of Radical Body Art." *Deviant Behavior* 22 (2001): 117–146; Camphausen, Rufus C. *Return of the Tribal: A Celebration of Body Adornment: Piercing, Tattooing, Scarification, Body Painting*. Rochester, VT: Park Street Press, 1997; Gay, Kathlyn. *Body Marks: Tattooing, Piercing, and Scarification*. New York: Millbrook Press, 2002; Klesse, Christian. "Modern Primitivism: Non-Mainstream Body Modification And Racialized Representation." In Mike Featherstone, ed., *Body Modification*. London: Sage Publications, 2000; Myers, James. "Nonmainstream Body Modification: Genital Piercing, Branding, Burning and Cutting." *Journal of Contemporary Ethnography* 21(3) (October 1992): 267–306; Pitts, Victoria. *In the Flesh: The Cultural Politics of Body Modification*. New York: Palgrave Macmillan, 2003; Rosenblatt, Daniel. "The Antisocial Skin: Structure, Resistance, and 'Modern Primitive' Adornment in the United States." *Cultural Anthropology* 12(3) (1997): 287–334; Turner, B. "The Possibility of Primitiveness: Towards a Sociology of Body Marks in Cool Societies." *Body & Society* 5(2/3) (1999): 39–50; Vale, V., and Andrea Juno. *Modern Primitives*. San Francisco, CA: Re/Search Publications, 1989.

PRISON TATTOOING

While **tattooing** is prohibited in American prisons and in most prisons in the West, prisons have historically been a major site of tattooing, both voluntary and involuntary.

Punitive tattooing has been used in the West since the time of the Persians. The Persians, Thracians, ancient Greeks, and ancient Romans all marked criminals and runaway slaves with tattoo marks that often denoted the nature of their crime, or sometimes the punishment (i.e., going to the mines). If tattoos make the body culturally visible, then punitive tattoos, and particularly those on the face, neck, and hands (which were the most common locations historically for punitive tattoos), make the body especially obvious, and more importantly, express, to the criminal, other prisoners, and the outside world, the social position that that body occupies.

But at the same time that criminals were marked with punitive tattoos, many prisoners, beginning perhaps with Roman Christians, began marking themselves as well. Sometimes the convict would rework his punitive tattoo to erase the original sign, covering it with something else. But other times, prisoners would create their own systems of tattoos in order to demonstrate group affiliation or pride in their crime or social position.

In the West today, tattoos that are created in prison, because of the technology used to create them, the style in which they are worn, and the imagery portrayed, can be easily distinguished from professionally executed tattoos.

Prison tattoos can range from technologically simple to relatively advanced. The most primitive method of tattooing is known as hand plucking or hand picking. Here, the individual typically takes a sewing needle, wraps it in string, and dips it into ink. The needle is then stuck into the skin over and over until a line is achieved, and then the design is shaded in (the string acts as a reservoir for the ink). These tattoos usually look more primitive than tattoos created with a machine, because a continuous line is difficult to achieve with a handpicked tattoo. Whether this type of tattoo is done in prison or on the streets, the handpicked tattoo is the most maligned form of tattoo.

(There is some connection between street tattooing and prison tattooing. Street tattoos are tattoos that are created outside of a tattoo shop, usually by hand, and are found primarily among inner city **Chicanos, gang members**, and bikers. These forms often resemble prison tattoos due to, first, the similarities in technology, and second, because gang members and outlaw bikers bring their tattooing styles and images from the streets with them into prison. Both groups also carry their tattoos back out with them and influence their peers, who are tattooing on the street. Chicano street tattoos, in particular, are almost indistinguishable from tattoos produced on or by Chicanos in prison, because the technology, styles, and imagery are the same.)

Prison tattoos are clearly homemade, are usually self-inflicted, and are thus usually on a hand or lower arm. Thus not only does the method of execution signify that the wearer is of a low socioeconomic status in that he (or she) cannot afford, or has no access to, professional tattoos, but the tattoos themselves are usually on extremely public areas of the body where they can be easily read by others. In the Youth Authority system, by far the most common method of applying tattoos is by hand, and by the time an individual graduates from the juvenile justice system into adult prison, he usually graduates to machine-made tattoos as well, and often begins to cover up his old hand-plucked tattoos with better quality machine tattoos. (This same process occurs on the street, as Chicanos or bikers will often pay professionals, when they can afford it, to cover up the homemade tattoos of their youth with better designs.)

The second method of execution is the homemade rotary machine, and this too is found both in prison as well as on the streets. These machines are made up of a motor, taken from a cassette recorder, electric razor, electric toothbrush, or Walkman, connected to a guitar string or sewing needle which vibrates up and down in the barrel of a Bic pen. The whole machine is then hooked up to a 3- to 9-volt AC adapter, and it's ready to tattoo. Tattoos created with a machine afford the tattooist much better control, thus the tattoos are more sophisticated, with finer, smoother lines, and subtle shading. Even so, the use of a rotary machine marks the user (called a "scratcher") as being a member of a lower social position than the user of a professional machine.

Even the language used to describe the materials used in tattooing differs between the prison or street tattooist and the professional. For professionals, the machine is called a "tattoo machine," while in prison and on the street, it is called a "gun." Continuing with this symbolism, the cavity in which the tattoo needles vibrate is referred to as a "tube" by professionals, while for the convict it is a "barrel." The traditional designs used by tattooists to create tattoos are called "flash" by professionals while convicts refer to them as "patterns." And finally, convicts and bikers both refer to tattoos as "tats," a term which is rarely used by nonbiker professionals in this country, or just "ink."

While rotary machines are hand-built, generally with found parts, professional machines are purchased from professional supply houses, and run much smoother than the rotary machines. Additionally, professional machines can be outfitted with anywhere from one to fifteen needles at a time, making them more flexible than the rotary, which can only handle a single needle.

Stylistically, prison tattoos, as well as their counterparts on the streets, also differ sharply from professional tattoos. Prison and street tattoos are monochromatic, or black or blue only, because prisoners have no access to tattoo inks (which, like professional machines, must also be bought from a professional supply house): the black or blue ink in a ball point pen or from a bottle of India ink will work for a tattoo, while colored pen and drawing inks will not. Because of the single-needle format of the rotary machine, they tend to be fine lined as well, allowing for fairly intricate shading. Prior to the 1970s, any fine-lined, black-only tattoo would automatically be recognized as a prison or street tattoo, simply because professionals at that time used multiple-needle setups in their machines and preferred to use colors in their tattoos as well. However, this style has since been appropriated into the mainstream tattoo community and is now popular among professionals as well, blurring the boundaries between prison and mainstream tattooing.

The type of imagery that a convict will choose for a tattoo is based both on where the convict came from as well as on his present situation in prison. One of the most popular tattoos in prison is the *loca*, which gives the name of the convict's neighborhood of origin, or else his gang affiliation. These tattoos are extremely important in prison, as they serve as a reminder of the community to which the displaced convict belongs. They also identify him as a member of a certain group which has important social ramifications when he encounters members of rival groups. Likewise, having an ethnic affiliation ("White Power," etc.) tattooed on one's body is another means of identifying with a particular community as well as differentiating oneself from other groups in prison. Jailhouse iconography is also popular among convicts, and includes bars, the scales of justice, barbed wire, and other themes which echo the prisoner's own experiences behind bars, including the images from the convict's actual prisons.

The fact that prison tattoo imagery is so easily recognizable helps law enforcement to track members of gangs inside and outside of prison, via their tattoos. Each gang has its own distinctive tattoos, from the Mexican Mafia whose tattoos typically include the letters EME or MM, to the Aryan Brotherhood whose tattoos often include swastikas or the letters AB, to the Black Guerilla Family whose tattoos often include BGF.

Perhaps the most powerful prison tattoo in the United States is the tear, tattooed just below the outside corner of the eye. The tear immediately identifies an individual as a convict or ex-convict (each tear signifies a prison term served, or a man may wear a tear for each person he killed), and thus serves as a kind of self-inflicted brand, not unlike the marks which were forcibly tattooed on prisoners at one time in Japan, England, and Germany. The tear may also be seen as a symbolic expression of the convict's suffering at the hands of justice. Other popular prison designs include spiderwebs, clock faces (without hands), or tombstones, all of which indicate doing time or time served.

Christian imagery is also extremely popular in prison, due to the influence of Chicano prisoners who favor such imagery both in prison and on the street, and includes the Passion of Christ, the Virgin Mary, the Virgin of Guadelupe, praying hands, and crosses (such as the "Pachuco cross," tattooed on the hand between thumb and forefinger). Finally, tattoos of women, Harley Davidson imagery (wings, engines, bikes, etc.), skulls and fantasy images, as well as antisocial slogans such as FTW (Fuck the World), are also extremely popular.

Prison tattooing can also be distinguished from professional tattooing on the basis of economics. In prison, tattoos are paid for with drugs, money, or canteen. Because the amount of money available in prison is much less than on the outside, the costs are relatively low. For example, a full sleeve would cost between $150 and $200; a chest piece between $75 and $100; a back piece can cost $200 or a small color TV; and to get covered from the waist up can cost $500. Outside, on the street, tattoos are typically done for trade—one can purchase a tattoo for anything from a six-pack of beer to motorcycle parts. Semiprofessionals and professionals both charge cash for tattoos, although some may still offer trades. Tattooing is the second-best hustle in prison (next to drugs), thus the prisoner who does not want to hold a "straight" job can make a better-than-decent living through tattooing without the high risks involved in drug dealing. Some entrepreneurial convict tattooists not only tattoo, but sell designs, and other tattoo-related items as well. Some convict tattooists, particularly Chicanos, learned their trade on the streets, and brought it with them into prison. For others, however, tattooing is just a hustle, taken up out of boredom or economic need.

Who gets tattooed in prison? The answer depends first on the distinction between a convict and an inmate. An informant once told me: "Fuck the world, I'm a convict, not an inmate." The difference between a convict and an inmate is a question of respect. For the convict, after being locked up and stripped of everything he owns, respect is the one thing that cannot be taken away. An inmate has no respect. He is a model prisoner, one who bows to the authority of "The Man." A convict will not do this, he maintains his self-respect, and plays by his own rules. Since tattooing is illegal in prison, a convict gets tattooed, while an inmate does not. Prisoners generally begin to get tattooed in the Juvenile Justice system, between the ages of 14 and 19. The average age for prisoners who continue to get tattooed in the adult penal system seems to be between about 20 and 35 years. Blacks do get tattooed in prison, but because of their darker skin, the tattoos do not show up as well as on lighter skinned individuals.

Both whites and Chicanos perform the tattooing in prison, and it's been said that Chicanos make the best tattooists. While whites and Chicanos do tattoo each other, this will often invite danger.

There is, among convicts, a type of honor system related to who should be tattooed and who should not, which relates directly to the prisoner's age, and amount of time spent incarcerated. Older convicts feel that younger prisoners should not get tattooed if they don't already have any tattoos, and many tattooists in prison will simply refuse to be the first to tattoo a new prisoner.

An "honorable" prison tattooist doesn't want to be responsible for helping to screw up a young prisoner's life, particularly if that individual is going to be getting out of prison any time soon. If a man is only going to be imprisoned for a few years, and he hasn't spent his youth in the juvenile justice system—where a convict gets his first tattoos—he probably will not be a lifer, but by acquiring tattoos during his incarceration, he would be making concrete his identity as a convict, and may regret his decision to become tattooed. Ex-cons who try to make it in the "straight world" after prison often regret their prison tattoos. Because they are often so public, they are difficult to conceal, and many ex-convicts attempt to have them removed.

Once a convict has been in the system for a while, and knows that he will not be free for quite some time, he usually starts to cover up old work by getting newer, better looking tattoos. After a while, he will also begin to "fill in all the holes" (places on his body that are not yet tattooed), until he achieves complete coverage. Many convicts who get released will often continue to acquire tattoos on the outside, but they generally find that they cannot afford to purchase professional tattoos. These ex-convicts will either wait for the tattooist who did their work to be released, will find a buddy who will do the work cheaply, or will simply be rearrested within a short period of time, allowing the work to be completed.

Tattooing is illegal in prison, and the ramifications when caught tattooing include having one's equipment confiscated, having one's privileges removed, and being locked down in solitary. The work is carried out in secret, typically during the day when other inmates are exercising or playing cards. According to an informant, there have been numerous changes within the prison system since he was first incarcerated, leaving the environment for tattooing quite a bit less hospitable than it had previously been. The attitudes of the guards toward tattooing seem to be mixed. Some guards will look the other way, while others make a point of catching those convicts who tattoo. Some prisons, on the other hand, are considering creating a prison tattoo program in order to regulate prison tattooing and control disease.

The convict body, through its tattoos, incorporates both the context of imprisonment and the particular affiliations—gang, ethnic, personal—of the convict. Prison tattoos, then, mark the body wearing them as a convict or ex-convict, with important ramifications for the convict on the inside, and in the outside world.

At the same time, tattoos can also represent prisoners' differences from each other. Tattoos in this regard act as borders separating, not just prisoners from the outside world, but different communities within the institution, which are primarily based on ethnic differences. Prison can be seen as a cultural borderland—a site where multiple subordinate cultures press against the borders of dominant culture while at the same time competing among each other for power. Prison tattoos then serve to identify individuals as members of certain communities—via tattoos proclaiming ethnic or gang affiliations—in a context where loyalty to one group is often a life or death matter.

Tattooing in prison also creates a common culture. This process involves marking members as belonging to the same culture as much as it involves distinguishing members of one group from another. Tattooing in prison not only expresses social divisions, but it helps prisoners to produce meaning in their lives. The tattoo provides the new convict a means of joining the new community to which he now belongs (once he has convinced a tattooist to tattoo him). Without a tattoo, prisoners often feel isolated, both from their friends at home as well as from other convicts. The convict needs to identify with someone, as he is often abandoned by his friends and family on the outside, and the tattoo is a way of establishing or reaffirming community, either with those who were left outside (via tattooed names and pictures of loved ones, tattooed locas or gang names, etc.), with those who are inside, or both. This process of identity formation is particularly important in the prison context, where the prisoner experiences his identity being stripped from him, thus becoming tattooed is crucial in order for a convict to establish an identity vis-a-vis the prison establishment, as well as among other prisoners.

Finally, the convict body is itself counterhegemonic in that it incorporates both the system (prison) and the challenge (tattoos): through its bold markings on the face, hands, neck, and arms, it represents a willful defiance of the Man.

For convicts in prisons outside of the United States, tattoos are also a common and similar signal of group affiliation, resistance to authority, and a badge of honor. Prisoners in **Russia**, Mexico, and Europe all use tattooing in a similar way to the United States, although images will be drawn from individual countries' and cultures' symbolic repertoires, and will also, as in the United States, demonstrate the prisoner's specific rank within the class, racial, and prison system. Where barbed wire, skulls, and spiderwebs are common prison images around the world, for example, other designs are more culturally specific, such as the use of cathedrals in Russian prisons or the Virgin of Guadelupe for Mexican inmates.

See also: Australia; Biker Tattooing; Chicanos; Criminality, Gang Members; Greco-Roman World; Russia

Further Reading: DeMello, Margo. "The Convict Body: Tattooing among Male American prisoners." *Anthropology Today* 9 (1993): 10–13; DeMello, Margo. *Bodies of Inscription: A Cultural History of the Modern Tattoo Community*. Durham, NC: Duke University Press, 2000; Foucault, M. *Discipline and Punish*. Harmondsworth, UK: Penguin, 1979; Hall, Douglas Kent. *In Prison*. New York: Henry Holt and Company, 1988; Hall, Douglas Kent. *Prison Tattoos*. New York: St. Martin's Griffin, 1997; Sanders, Clinton, *Customizing the Body: The Art and Culture of Tattooing*. Philadelphia, PA: Temple University Press, 1989; Schrader, Abby M. "Branding the Other/Tattooing the Self: Bodily Inscription among Convicts in Russia and the Soviet Union." In Jane Caplan, ed., *Written on the Body: The Tattoo in European and American History*. London: Reaktion Books, 2000; Stewart, Hamish Maxwell, and Ian Duffield, "Skin Deep Devotions: Religious Tattoos and Convict Transportation to Australia." In Jane Caplan, ed., *Written on the Body: The Tattoo in European and American History*. London: Reaktion Books, 2000.

PUNK

The punk subculture in Europe and the United States has long been associated with body modifications, especially **tattooing** and **piercing**. In fact, the modern body modification movement can be said to have emerged from a number of different sources including the **BDSM** culture, but punk is certainly one major source as well.

Punk was born in the 1970s in Great Britain and spread to the United States and other countries, with a number of different subgenres. Punk refers to both a type of music, as well as a lifestyle and aesthetic style, which has since been copied and commodified through out mainstream culture.

Some of the most central aspects of the punk style is the outrageous use of clothing, hair, jewelry, makeup, and body modifications to challenge mainstream conventions and to shock observers. Punk was and is largely self-made, with members co-opting "normal" items and creatively transforming them into something entirely different. The classic example of this is the use of safety pins to not only hold together ripped and ragged clothing, but as an adornment through the ear, nose, or cheek.

Since punk is an oppositional subculture, punks have historically used forms of fashion and body adornment from the margins of mainstream culture, and that represent the ideology of freedom, nonconformity, antiauthoritarianism, and rebellion, thus the heavy use of ripped and defaced clothing, messy or crazy hair, ugly and loud **makeup**, and elaborately decorated jackets and jeans. These stylistic elements, when viewed as a whole, created a coherent style that was intended to shock society.

Punks have also drawn on the primitivist ideology in their critique of the excesses of Western civilization. For that reason, body modifications popular with the **modern primitives** scene are often used by punks, and the two movements often overlap significantly. Finally, because punks have typically spurned commercialization, they instead choose to express and reinvent themselves via their own artistic creations with respect to style. Piercings fit perfectly into this do-it-yourself ethos, since many can be done by oneself, at no cost, with simple (although perhaps not terribly hygenic) tools.

One of the most iconic punk **hairstyles** is the Mohawk, in which the hair, often dyed a brilliant color, is cut short on the side and very long on top, and then styled to stand straight up off the head through the use of products like egg whites, starch, glue, or hairspray. Punks also wear their hair in spikes, shaved patterns, and today, a shaved head is commonly associated with the punk scene.

Women in particular used their bodies as a form of rebellion, rebelling against conventional standards of female **beauty** with their use of makeup, hairstyling, clothing, and body modifications. Makeup was and is used by female punks as an antibeauty statement, either making the face look pallid or overly made up like a prostitute.

Piercing has been associated with punks since long before the mainstreaming of piercing in the West. And like the other elements of punk style, piercings were and often still are self-made, with punks sticking themselves with needles, pins, staples, and other sharp implements, as well as **cutting** themselves with razor blades and knives. Punk piercings also tend to be "louder" than piercings in other scenes, with jewelry utilizing knives, long chains, and bones are popular, as well as stretched piercings, and multiple piercings on the face.

Tattooing is and has been one of the most heavily used modifications in the punk scene. Because punks often drew indecent words or images on themselves, tattooing is the perfect medium for the expression of countercultural values. Punk tattoo styles were initially drawn from a number of other subcultures such as bikers, rockers, and teddy boys, and, like those other groups, marked the wearers as outsiders to mainstream culture, as well as insiders to the punk movement.

Thanks to the do-it-yourself ethos, many punks tattooed (and still tattoo) themselves or their friends, although as the punk style entered the tattoo scene in the 1990s, many punks began getting professionally tattooed at studios.

Since the 1980s, as tribal or neo-tribal tattooing became popularized, punks have been drawn to this type of tattoo, because of its primtivist origins and dramatic designs, and **Leo Zulueta**, the main proponent of tribal tattoing in the United States, found himself tattooing large numbers of punks in his West coast tattoo shop in the 1980s.

Ironically, tribal tattoos have, since that time, become the mark of the amateur tattooist, who tattoos tribal designs on his friends for no cost. This is one reason why punk tattoos were and are so heavily weighted toward tribalism. Given the strong impulse in the punk movement to create one's own style, including tattooing and piercing oneself, and the sense that tribal tattoos, with their heavy lines and black-only designs, were easy to execute, it is not surprising to see so many self-made tribal tattoos in the scene.

Other tattoo styles drew directly off of punk aesthetics and values, and included death motifs, anarchy symbols, and images and words directly related to punk music.

As tattooing, piercing, and styles derived directly from the punk movement such as the Mohawk move into mainstream culture, punks must continuously adopt more controversial and confrontational styles in order to retain their edge. Thus facial tattooing and highly unusual piercings are becoming more common for punks.

Subcultures that developed out of punk also tend to use body modifications or extreme body adornment, such as goths, psychobilly, riot grrrls, skinheads, and the straight edge movement, and indeed, every musical genre today that is oppositional, such as hip hop, whether or not it derived from punk, has borrowed the use of nonmainstream body modifications as well.

See also: Modern Primitives; Primitivism; Tribalism; Zulueta, Leo

Further Reading: Hebidge, Dick. *Subculture: The Meaning of Style*. London: Routledge, 1979; Wojcik, Daniel. *Punk and Neo-Tribal Body Art*. Jackson: University Press of Mississippi, 1995.

R

RITES OF PASSAGE

Rites of passage are rituals which mark and facilitate a person's movement from one social state to another, and include such religious rituals as the bar mitzvah, communion, baptism, and Native American vision quests, and secular rituals such as the quinceñera, wedding, and graduation ceremony, as well as many of the aspects of basic training for military conscripts and the process of joining a fraternity or sorority. Because rites of passage are used to mark the passage of life cycles, it is not surprising that around the world, there are a whole host of rituals marking birth, puberty, marriage, and death. One of the most common rites in traditional societies is the initiation ritual.

According to anthropologists Arnold van Gennep and Victor Turner, rites of passage have three disctinct phases: the separation phase, in which the person undergoing the ritual becomes separated from society; the liminal phase in which the person lies within an ambiguous state, betwixt and between the old and the new states; and the reincorporation stage in which the person is reincorporated into society in their new social position.

The liminal stage of the ritual is the most significant, as this is when the initiate experiences a temporary suspension or even reversal of everyday social distinctions and practices; no longer classified by their former social position, these people temporarily are without role, status, and position in the kinship system. All of the individuals undergoing the ritual will also experience at this stage a feeling known as "communitas" which refers to enhanced feelings of social solidarity, equality, and togetherness among people experiencing liminality together. And finally, the liminal stage is the stage during which the initiate learns all of the knowledge and skill that will allow him or her to proceed to the next stage.

In traditional societies, adolescent coming of age ceremonies often involve body modifications, especially during male rituals, either during the liminal phase or the reincorporation phase. Most involve a not inconsiderable amount of pain as well. **Circumcision** and other modifications of the genitals like **infibulation, subincision,** or **superincision**, are commonly found among male adolescent initiation ceremonies in Africa, Melanesia, and **Australia**. **Scarification** and **tattooing** are commonly found at both male and female rituals in Africa, Polynesia, Melanesia, and Micronesia, marking the initiate as either becoming a man or woman, or perhaps marking them as marriageable. Circumcision for Jews, on the other hand, is carried out soon after birth but as with other circumcision rituals, is an important rite of passage marking the boy as a member of his tribe.

Each one of my tattoos was made during a stage of my life that had great significance to how I was feeling at the time and for a memory of that time. When I look at them, I go back to the time I had them put on and my frame of mind. I remember how carefree I was and I'm reminded that I am still that person, only I have goals and more responsibility now in my 40s than I did in my 20s and 30s. They make me feel like it's okay to be carefree at my age.

ANONYMOUS

Girls in some African and Arab cultures also receive genital modifications, sometimes at puberty, and sometimes before. Female initiation rituals commonly include a **clitoridectomy** (also known as **female genital mutilation**), or the removal of the clitoris and sometimes the labia, sometimes also accompanied by the sewing up of the vaginal opening. Both adolescent boys and girls often receive a **facial piercing** as part of their initiation into adulthood and preparation for marriage.

While some of the outward circumstances of male and female genital rituals are similar (some people refer to them both by the generic term circumcision rituals, for example), the social and cultural meaning of them is typically quite different. Whereas male circumcision rituals involve the testing of a young male, via painful or difficult challenges, in order to see whether he can proceed to manhood, female surgeries are often done to establish social control over female sexuality, in order to ensure her virginity prior to marriage and her fidelity after marriage.

In the modern body modification community, many participants feel that modern Western society is lacking with respect to spirituality, and they see traditional rites of passage as being an antidote to the poverty of the Western experience. Many thus borrow rituals which involve body modifications from non-Western cultures in order to experience them in their own lives. Others, such as members of fraternities or the military, may undergo a modification like a tattoo or brand in order to mark themselves as a member of their new social group, even when no traditional ritual exists to do this.

See also: Circumcision; Female Genital Mutilation

Further Reading: Turner, Victor. *The Ritual Process*. Ithaca, NY: Cornell University Press, 1969; van Gennep, Arnold. *The Rites of Passage*. Chicago: University of Chicago Press, 1969.

ROMAN *See* Greco-Roman World

RUSSIA

Until the eighteenth century and the rule of Catherine the Great, Russian criminals were subject to corporal punishment of all kinds, including **tattooing**, **branding**, and whipping.

By the late eighteenth century, some forms of corporal punishment were abolished or left only to be used on the lower classes, but branding criminals continued, since it was not just punishment, but useful for identification and marking criminal status. Because the branding or stamping of property was common among all social classes in Russia as a way of marking ownership, this may be one reason why the state branded prisoners that they "owned" as well. In addition, Russian prisoners were often exiled to Sibera; those who committed very serious crimes were sentenced to hard labor, and those who committed less serious crimes were sent there as a form of exile.

Starting in the nineteenth century, tattooing also became a common form of marking prisoners. A "pricked" cross on the left hand, for example, was used to mark military deserters so it would be easy to recatch them if they escaped again. The use of tattoos probably began when officials rubbed gunpowder into the wounds left by branding to make them more permanent.

While government officials in Russia, as in **England**, **Australia,** and Europe, attempted to catalogue convict tattoos, they realized that it was futile since convicts kept retattooing themselves, and since authorities, then and now, often don't understand the real meaning of the designs.

Different classes of criminals also began to tattoo themselves, starting probably in the mid-nineteenth century, as a way to mark individual status and group membership. Vagrants, for example, were the highest class of prisoners in the Russian prison system, and developed a specific set of tattoo symbols for themselves. These nineteenth-century convicts served as the model for modern Russian convicts and outlaws. Tattoos for convicts in Russia today serve many of the same purposes as vagrant tattoos: they uphold traditions belonging to the group, signify group solidarity, and utilize a language kept secret from the authorities. Tattoos today, as in the past, are also given as a **rite of passage** for new convicts and serve as a calling card for other convicts. Today, tattoos are so common in Russian prisons that 75–85 percent of all Russian convicts are tattooed. As with tattoos in prisons around the world, prison tattoos were once primarily handpicked, but are now often give with homemade machines made from electric razor parts, using ink from pens or even made from ashes mixed with water or urine.

Symbols used by Russian prisoners, like prison tattoos around the world, signify the convict's position vis-a-vis the criminal justice system, and often express his or her contempt for the system. In addition, tattoos symbolize the convict's wish for freedom and suffering under intense confinement. Common images include barbed wire (tattooed across the forehead it signifies a life sentence), monasteries, cathedrals and fortresses (the number of spires can often represent the number of times a person has been imprisoned or the number of years), spiderwebs (common in the United States as well, this could signify drug addiction), skulls (which indicate murder), cats (which could mean that the convict was a thief), and white supremacist or Nazi imagery. Birds flying usually represent freedom and a cross can mean bondage or slavery. And while punitive tattooing is no longer Russian prison policy, some prisoners will forcibly tattoo others for certain transgressions.

Phrases are also often tattooed on the body that mention freedom, punishment, pain, and disdain for authority.

See also: Criminality; Prison Tattooing

Further Reading: Baldaev, Danzig, Sergei Vasiliev, and Alexei Plutser-Sarno. *Russian Criminal Tattoo Encyclopaedia*. London: Steidl Publishing, 2003; Lambert, Alix. *Russian Prison Tattoos: Codes of Authority, Domination, and Struggle*. Atglen, PA: Schiffer Publishing, 2003; Schrader, Abby M. "Branding the Other/Tattooing the Self: Bodily Inscription among Convicts in Russia and the Soviet Union." In Jane Caplan, ed., *Written on the Body: The Tattoo in European and American History*. Princeton, NJ: Princeton University Press, 2000.

S

SAMOA

The Samoan Islands are a group of Polynesian islands in the South Pacific, and may be the earliest of the Polynesian islands to have been occupied by humans. First visited by Dutch explorers led by Jacob Roggewein in 1722, and alternately controlled by the United States, Germany, Britain, and New Zealand, Samoa is well known for their distinctive torso tattoo known as a **pe'a**.

The pe'a was first described by members of Roggewein's crew, who noted that Samoans wore woven tights on their legs. It wasn't until other explorers visited the island later in the eighteenth century that it was noted that the tights were actually a distinctive form of tattoo, which covered a man's thighs, buttocks, and torso.

According to Samoan legend, at one time only women were supposed to be tattooed, because it was two sisters who received a tattoo tool from Fiji, who told the women that only women are tattooed. Unfortunately, the legend continues, the women, when presenting their gift to their people at home, told them that only men were tattooed, not women, reversing their previous instructions. From that time on, only men would receive the pe'a.

Receiving a pe'a is a critical event in a Samoan man's life, and marks an important transition from boyhood to adulthood. It signifies as well his intent to serve his family and community. Without the pe'a, a man will never truly be a man, and having a half-finished pe'a is considered shameful.

The process of being tattooed is an intense ordeal which is done over five stages, and could take weeks to complete, given the level of pain and the time needed to recover between stages. It was also costly. Men could not receive the pe'a until they accumulated enough wealth to cover the cost of the woven mats or tapa cloths needed as payment to the tattooist.

The tattooist, known as a *tufuga*, inherited his position—which gave him a high degree of rank—from his ancestors. Young tattooists act as apprentices to older artists until they are experienced enough to work on their own. The tattooist's wife assisted in the procedure.

The tattooing tools are similar to those found in many other Polynesian cultures, and consisted of a comb made of sharpened teeth or tusks, lashed to a turtle shell, and attached at a right angle to a stick. The comb is dipped into the pigment and is tapped into the skin using a separate mallet.

The process of getting a pe'a was highly ritualized, usually with at least two men being tattooed at once. The men, the tattooists, and the men's families and friends all present and participating. Songs were sung to commemorate the tattooing and to distract the men from the pain, and the process itself was carefully structured:

each part of the tattoo had a name, and each part was tattooed in order, starting at the waist, and ending with the belly button. The design is perfectly symmetrical, made up of lines, arrows, triangles, and other geometric patterns, and is created by the tattooist for the wearer, with each part of the design having its own meaning. The entire pe'a symbolizes a bat whose wings wrap around the man's legs.

Even though women do not receive the pe'a, there is a woman's tattoo known as the *malu*, which a woman receives during her adolescence or early adulthood. Like the pe'a, the malu covers the area from the waist to the knees, but is much finer and sparser than the pe'a, and appears much lighter. At one time it was said that only high-status women could receive the malu, but today any woman who chooses it can wear it, and it has never been seen as a necessity for marriage or adulthood.

Starting in the 1830s, English missionaries began to arrive in Samoa and attempted to ban tattooing, prohibiting the wearing of the pe'a in missionary schools. Ultimately, tattooing went underground, but was never completely eliminated. Unlike many Polynesian cultures, it has continued, although to a much lesser extent than in precontact times, to be practiced in Samoa, and in fact, Samoan tattooists have helped other cultures to regain their ancient traditions as well.

See also: Pe'a

Further Reading: D'Alleva, Anne. "Christian Skins: Tatau and the Evangelization of the Society Islands and Samoa." In Bronwen Douglas, Nicholas Thomas, and Anna Cole, eds., *Tattoo: Bodies, Art and Exchange in the Pacific and the West.* Durham, NC: Duke University Press, 2005; Handy, E. S. Craighill. *Samoan House Building, Cooking, and Tattooing.* Honolulu, Hawaii: The Museum, 1924; Mallon, Sean. "Samoan Tatau as Global Practice." In Bronwen Douglas, Nicholas Thomas, and Anna Cole, eds., *Tattoo: Bodies, Art and Exchange in the Pacific and the West.* Durham, NC: Duke University Press, 2005; Sulu'ape, Petelo. "History of Samoan Tattooing." *TattooTime* 5 (1991): 102–109.

SCALPELLING

Scalpelling refers to a way of creating modern body modifications such as large ear or lip holes with a scalpel.

Unlike **piercing**, which uses a small-gauge hollow needle to pierce a very small hole in the skin, scalpelling uses a surgical scalpel to slice a larger hole out of the skin. For people who would like to wear a **labret** or an **earplug**, scalpelling is a quicker way of creating a hole than could otherwise be created through piercing and gradual **stretching**. Scalpelling is also used for the insertion of subdermal and transdermal implants, and is also sometimes used to create **surface piercings**. Finally, scalpelling is also used to correct piercings that have been placed in the wrong area, that have migrated, or that have become infected.

Because it is such a new technique, many piercers are not experienced with scalpelling techniques, which involve much more blood loss than normal piercing, and scalpelling by piercers may not be legal in many jurisdictions. For these reasons, it may be difficult to find someone who can safely and legally perform these procedures in many areas.

See also: Earplugs; Labrets; Piercing; Stretching

Further Reading: www.BMEZine.com.

SCARIFICATION

In many African and Australian cultures, smooth skin is seen as naked and un-adorned. In these cultures, skin that has texture and design on it is much preferred.

Scarification refers to the practice of slicing the skin in order to create scars, which are typically joined together into decorative patterns. Also known as cicatrisation, scarification is an analogous practice to **tattooing**, in that both mark individuals with important social information such as rank, geneology, marital status, social status, and tribal or clan membership, and both are often performed as a part of a rite of passage, generally enabling the wearer to move from youth into adulthood. Because both practices are painful, wearing a tattoo or scar is a sign of one's strength and bravery, usually for a man, but sometimes also for women. Finally, both scarification and tattooing are often seen as a form of beautification, without which the individual would be less attractive. Tattooing, however, tends to be practiced by people with relatively light skin, through which the tattoos can show, while scarification, tends to be practiced by people with darker skin.

There are a number of different techniques used to create scars. Some techniques involve cutting the skin deeply, either in long lines or short ones, to create a scar. Indented scars are produced by slicing out a piece of skin, usually in a line. Others involve first pulling up a small amount of skin with a hook, and slicing off a piece of the elevated skin. This creates a raised welt, and, when multiple pieces of skin are raised and cut, it creates an overall design that can be quite stunning. Another method is to cut the skin, and afterward insert mud or ash in the cuts, which can leave the scars colored, or can leave raised bumps, known as keloids.

In many cultures, especially in Africa, women are more commonly scarred and wear more elaborate designs than men. Often, women's scars are seen as an indication that she can withstand the **pain** of childbearing, making her well suited to be a wife. Girls are generally first scarred at puberty, and the face, the shoulders, the chest, and the abdomen are the most common locations.

Tribes in Zaire, Nigeria, Sudan, the Ivory Coast, and Ethiopia use scarification, which was considered beautiful for women. For these tribes and other African groups, girls receive scars at puberty to demonstrate that they are ready to be married, and that they are strong enough to bear children. Of equal importance, the scars are seen as beautiful to touch and to look at.

Men in Africa often wear scars received during initiation, or sometimes after having killed an enemy, as a sign of bravery. Among the Barabaig of Tanzania, boys' heads are cut so deeply that they sometimes show up on the skulls. Because scars are considered attractive, they are often cut in such a way as to emphasize the contour of the face or body. The Tiv of Nigeria, for instance, mark along the cheekbones with long, linear scars as an emphasis to the cheekbones.

Among the Nuba of southern Sudan girls undergo scarification, usually from their breasts to their navel, a number of times during her life, in order to mark important events such as first menstruation or the birth of her first child, after which her back, legs, arms, and neck are scarred. Nuba men wear scars on their torsos and arms, usually as part of an initiation ritual. Men of the Dinka tribe of the south also scarify themselves, generally on the forehead during a boy's rite of passage into adulthood.

The Tabwa, who live in southwestern Zaire and northeastern Zambia, called their practice *Kulemba*, which means to inscribe or beautify a blank surface. Women were once scarred on the cheeks and forehead plus back and shoulders, but today scars are limited to small lines on the forehead, nose, and cheeks. As with most African tribes, girls without scars were not considered marriageable. Tabwa men also practiced facial scarification, with a pattern known as "face of the cross" in which tiny dots were patterned into lines that made up a cross across the face.

The Ga'anda of northern Nigeria also use scarification, known as *Hleeta*, to make girls marriageable. The process begins at 5 or 6, with the final phase ending at 15 or 16 just before marriage, once she has been engaged. Girls are scarred on their forehead, shoulders, arms, belly, legs, back of neck, back, and buttocks, with an elaborate pattern of dots which form lines, curves, and diamonds. Forehead scars are given when the girl's future husband pays her parents her brideprice. The Ga'anda, like a number of other African tribes, are seeing scarification disappear thanks to disapproval from authorities and a declining interest in arranged marriages.

The Tiv of Nigeria view scarification as purely decorative. Women are scarred on their back, neck, and stomachs, and because scars are tender to the touch for the first few years, this makes the stomach especially erotic. Men, too, are scarred, generally on the chest, face, arms, and legs. Scars can be geometric designs of animal representations. The Baule of the Ivory Coast also practice scarification, known as *ngole*, as a way of beautifying themselves and pleasing others. In addition, scarification both orients an individual within society by marking tribal, clan, lineage, or other membership, and also denotes social information like marriageability or success in hunting. Finally, some scars were used to protect against magic and disease in that a small amount of poison is injected directly into the scar, known as a kanga mark. Women often wore scars on their torsos and backs as well. The Baule also create patterns of lines radiating from the mouth, to protect young children from harm.

In Australia, scarring was once commonly practiced among a number of groups, but is very infrequent today. As with African scarification, Australian scars indicate strength, courage, endurance, social status, individual identity, and **beauty**. Both men and women were scarred, generally with lines, women between the breasts, men on the shoulders, chest, and belly. It was traditional that one needed to be scarred in order to engage in reciprocal trade relations, in order to marry, and in order to participate in rituals or didgeridoo playing. Nonscarred people were seen as unbranded, and if a person was unbranded, they were not allowed to do anything. Scarification begins when a man or woman is around 16 or 17, and is carried out with a sharpened rock, followed by burnt wood in the wounds to stop the bleeding.

In **Papua New Guinea**, young men receive scars as part of their initiation rituals. Using a piece of sharpened bamboo, boys are cut on their chest and back to test their physical strength and self-discipline, and to create scars which are said to represent crocodile teeth, since the boys have been symbolically swallowed by crocodiles and are reborn as crocodile-men.

Scarification also has a brief history in the West. In the early twentieth century, a scar received during dueling was popular among upper-class Austrians and Germans. Dueling was an important social practice and men who engaged in duels, and received a scar, wore the scar as a badge of courage, as well as a mark of upper-class status and honor. Because of the significance of the scar, some men cut themselves on the face with a razor in order to create their own scars.

Sudanese woman with scarification, 1890–1923. Courtesy of Library of Congress Prints and Photographs Division, Washington, DC.

In the **modern primitives** and body modification communities, scarification is also practiced, often as a rite of passage, although rarely as elaborately as we find it in Africa. Typically in the West, scarification is created by **cutting** lines in the skin, and sometimes removing narrow strips of flesh as well, rather than cutting small raised welts to form an overall pattern. However, raised scars are still typically the goal.

Methods for scarification today include cutting with a scalpel, using oxidizing agents to create the scar, cutting followed by the application of a chemical to create a more severe scar, the use of a dremel or other rotary tools to grind away the skin to create a scar; the injection of alcohol or other substances under the skin in order to cause a blister or other mark; the use of a tattoo machine (with or without ink) to overtattoo an area, creating a scar, and the use of a scalpel to slice away pieces of skin. After the scarification procedure, many of the above methods also involve rubbing ink or ashes into the wound to create a colored pattern.

See also: Australia; Ivory Coast; Nigeria; Sudan; Zaire

Further Reading: Bohannon, Paul. "Beauty and Scarification amongst the Tiv." *Man* 56(129) (1956): 117–121; Brain, Robert. *The Decorated Body.* New York: Harper and Row, 1979; Camphausen, Rufus C. *Return of the Tribal: A Celebration of Body Adornment: Piercing, Tattooing, Scarification, Body Painting.* Rochester, VT: Park Street Press, 1997; Drewal, Henry John. "Beauty and Being: Aesthetics and Ontology in Yoruba Body Art." In Arnold Rubin, ed., *Marks of Civilization: Artistic Transformations of the Human Body*, Los Angeles: Museum of Cultural History, UCLA, 1988; Fisher, Angela. *Africa Adorned: A Panorama of Jewelry, Dress, Body Decoration, and Hair.* New York: Henry Abrams, 2000; Gay, Kathlyn. *Body Marks: Tattooing, Piercing, and Scarification.* New York: Millbrook Press, 2002; Thevóz, Michel. *The Painted Body.* New York: Rizzoli International, 1984; Vogel, S. "Baule Scarification: The Mark of Civilisation." In Arnold Rubin, ed., *Marks of Civilization: Artistic Transformations of the Human Body.* Los Angeles: Museum of Cultural History, UCLA, 1988.

SELF-MORTIFICATION

Self-mortification refers to the practice of punishing oneself, either in a religious context or to atone for wrongdoing. Self-mortification can involve denying oneself bodily pleasures such as sex or meat, or it can involve adopting a simple or impoverished lifestyle. Self-mortification also refers to inflicting **pain** on one's own body by whipping, **branding, cutting,** or other means. Some people in the **BDSM** community practice self-denial as part of a dominant/submissive relationship, and others practice pain infliction because of an association of pain with sexual pleasure.

A number of different religious traditions encourage the practice of self-mortification either for their members or their priests, including Islam, Judaism, Hinduism, and **Christianity**. Various indigenous peoples also incorporate voluntary pain, suffering, and self-denial as part of their spiritual traditions as vehicles to the divine or rites of passage.

In Christianity, original sin necessitates that all Christians do penance for that sin as well as future sins to come, and in the **Bible**, God demanded that his faithful abstain from meat on Fridays, and later, the forty-day period of Lent (based on Jesus's fast for forty days) was instituted during which Christians are also asked to give up meat. The Bible also notes the practice of wearing rags, tearing clothes and hair, and fasting in order to humble oneself before God. During the early days of the church when the church was still preaching an imminent apocalypse, St. Paul counseled believers to renounce their earthly and bodily pleasures, since the present world was shortly to end.

Since the early years of the Christian church, though, many Christians have practiced voluntary, corporal penance as a way of imitating Christ's suffering. Some Christians take vows of poverty, others fast or deny themselves sexual pleasure, and still others wear hair shirts or flagellate themselves with whips, switches, or other tools, in imitation of Christ's suffering before his death. The goal of such practices could be to achieve union with God, to alleviate one's sins or the sins of others, or to secure a higher place in heaven. For others, suffering is critical to achieving salvation.

Ancient Meso-Americans also practiced ritual mortification. Mayan women pulled studded ropes through holes in their tongues, and Mayan kings used thorns and spines to draw blood from their penises, tongues, and earlobes.

Some Native American tribes also practiced self-mortification. For example, the Sun Dance included dancing, singing, drumming, fasting and culminated in a ritual in which participants attached themselves to a pole via ropes attached to bone or wood skewers, which are inserted into pre-pierced holes in the chest. Dancing around in a circle to the beat of drums and prayers, the particpants pull against the pole to tear the skewers out.

Indian holy men also engaged in self-mortification, including fasting, self-flagellation, lying on a bed of nails, and other practices. The *Kavadi*, for example, involves walking uphill while holding a steel frame through which weighted skewers are passed, which are then pierced into the skin of the back and chest as a form of penance.

Today, some people practice extreme forms of body mortification in order to obtain altered states of consciousness, such as to achieve ecstasy or visions. In the modern body modification community, **suspensions,** play piercings, and **body play** are ways in which this is attempted, and both the Sun Dance and the Kavadi are practiced now by Westerners who want to achieve some sort of personal or spiritual growth.

See also: Ascesticm; BDSM; Torture

Further Reading: Grimm, Veronika E. *From Feasting to Fasting, the Evolution of a Sin: The Development of Early Christian Ascetism.* New York: Routledge, 1996.

SELF-MUTILATION

Self-mutilation is the term doctors often use to describe **cutting** and other body modification practices that are not intended to be decorative, but that are used when the practioner is depressed or in **pain**. Other forms of self-mutilation or self-harm include burning, **branding**, biting, bruising, or picking of hair and skin.

Self-mutilation can be considered major, in which case it is associated with severe psychological disorders and can cause great injury such as in **amputations**. It can also be stereotypic, which could result from a mental disability, and results in repetitive and usually unconscious injury, such as through self-hitting. It can also be defined as superficial, which could result from a personality disorder and manifests itself in intentional acts like cutting or branding that one finds psychologically valuable. Superficial mutilation could also include certain eating disorders.

Emotional, physical, and sexual abuse can cause psychological trauma leading one to resort to self-mutilation. Many self-mutilators, for instance, have suffered abuse earlier in life.

In this case, individuals who are struggling with emotional, physical, or psychological problems will cut, burn, or otherwise harm themselves in order to feel pain, because self-created pain sometimes can relieve the other pain. In addition, making oneself feel pain can allow the person to feel a sense of control over their own body, if not their life. Unfortunately, self-mutilation in this sense rarely solves problems, and may create new ones as being a self-cutter is extremely stigmatized and may result in having even more independence and self-control taken away. Self-harm can also do more harm than the temporary pain, and can result in permanent damage.

On the other hand, self-mutilation is also used to refer to people who choose to pierce themselves, and especially to those who perform extreme body modifications on themselves, when they could not find a doctor or otherwise qualified person to do the procedure. For instance, having a body part amputated (by oneself or an unqualified practioner) in order to feel whole, is generally considered to be a form of self-mutilation, although the person doing it would not agree with that assessment.

Self-mutilation can also be used to label members of the body modification community who engage in practices that mainstream society view as frightening, shocking, or even just nonnormative. Here again, those practicing procedures like **subincision, tongue splitting**, or nullification would certainly disagree with any assessment that concludes that their practices are a sign of a disorder of any kind.

See also: Amputation; Cutting; Genital Mutilation; Health Issues

Further Reading: Favazza, Armando. *Bodies under Siege: Self-Mutilation and Body Modification in Culture and Psychiatry*. Baltimore, MD: Johns Hopkins Press, 1987; Hewitt, K. *Mutilating the Body: Identity in Blood and Ink*. Bowling Green, OH: Bowling Green State University Popular Press, 1997; Jeffreys, Sheila. *Beauty And Misogyny: Harmful Cultural Practices in the West*. London: Routledge, 2005; Myers, James. "Nonmainstream Body Modification: Genital Piercing, Branding, Burning and Cutting." *Journal of Contemporary Ethnography* 21(3) (October 1992): 267–306; Pitts, Victoria. *In the Flesh: The Cultural Politics of Body Modification*. New York: Palgrave Macmillan, 2003.

SEX REASSIGNMENT SURGERY

Sex reassignment surgery refers to the surgical procedures that a **transsexual** undertakes in order to change their body to the opposite sex. The term is sometimes also used to refer to the surgical "correction" of intersex individuals, which generally occurs during infancy and childhood. The first sex reassignment surgery was performed in the 1920s but it wasn't until the 1970s and 1980s that the techniques were modified to be as successful as they are today.

Those planning to undergo sex reassignment surgery must, in the United States, first receive psychological therapy (known as sex reassignment therapy), because the mental health profession does not consider surgery to be a cure for gender dysphoria or gender identity disorder.

Transsexuals who are planning to undergo surgery are known as preoperative (or preop) transsexuals and generally take hormones and dress and behave as their desired sex and gender during this period of time, which generally lasts at least a year.

Men transitioning into women, also known as transwomen, will undergo different surgical procedures than women transitioning to men, known as transmen, and both will typically undergo multiple procedures in order to achieve the desired results.

Surgical procedures for male to female transsexuals include the removal of the penis and testicles, a vaginoplasty, which is surgery to construct the vagina, the creation of a clitoris (out of the nervous endings in the penis), the insertion of breast implants, and facial feminization surgery.

A vaginoplasty involves creating a vaginal opening and vaginal space below the urethra and prostate gland, and taking the skin from the penis and inverting it to line the new vagina. Transwomen will also have a bilateral orchidectomy or **castration**, which involves the removal of both testes and the spermatic cord, and will also have most of their penis removed. The remainder of the penis will be used to create a clitoris during the clitoroplasty. Finally, the scrotal skin flaps are then converted into the outer labia, and the prepuce flaps from the penis are converted into the inner labia. The breasts will be created with breast implants of either saline or silicone in an identical procedure to female breast augmentation surgery.

Facial feminization surgery involves the surgical contouring of the bones of the forehead and the jaw, as well as the reduction of the Adam's apple via surgical shaving.

For female to male transsexuals, the most common surgery, and often the first surgery, is the removal of the breasts. Some individuals will elect to have a penis and scrotum constructed as well, although results are often unsatisfying, and some will also have their chests reshaped to appear more masculine. Those who do not choose to have a penis constructed will live out their postop lives with their breasts removed but fully functioning female genitalia.

During the period leading up to surgery, and often for the duration of one's life after surgery, many transsexuals will need to undergo hormone replacement therapy in order to first reverse the effects of their natural sex hormones on their bodies, and later, to maintain their new appearance.

Through taking testosterone, transmen, for example, will experience their voices getting deeper, the growth of facial and body hair, male pattern baldness, and a redistribution of body fat and muscles, conditions which could be reversed if they stop taking hormones. Transwomen, on the other hand, who take estrogen will see their breasts enlarge and their body fat and muscle redistributed, but they will not see their facial hair stop growing or their voice become higher.

Because sex reassignment surgery is sometimes difficult to obtain given the various physical and psychological criteria the patient needs to meet, many transsexuals travel to **Thailand** or other countries to receive their surgeries. Having surgery in a third world country is generally much less expensive and often doesn't involve the counseling and other requirements expected in the United States.

See also: Intersexuality; Transsexuals

Further Reading: Griggs, Claudine. *Journal of a Sex Change: Passage Through Trinidad*. Jefferson, NC: McFarland & Company, 2004.

SIDESHOW *See* Freak Shows

SILICONE INJECTIONS

Silicone injections are injections of silicone directly into the body in order to augment breasts, the penis, hips, and buttocks. Silicone has been injected in most parts of the body, but is most often used in the penis, the scrotum (but not in the testicles), the chest, and the buttocks, as well as the face. Known as "pumping," injecting silicone is illegal in the United States, and liquid silicone has not been approved by the FDA for use in this way.

Some transgendered men or male to female **transsexuals** in the United States as well as other countries inject themselves with silicone in order to feminize their faces or bodies. The practice is most popular among drag queens and beauty pageant contestants. Some men use silicone injections to increase the circumference of their penises, and women use silicone as a more permanent substitute for collagen injections in their lips, cheeks, and other areas of the face. People living with AIDS also sometimes use silicone injections to augment their faces and bodies after losing weight to the disease.

While silicone in sealed sacs has been used for years, with relative safety, to augment the breasts, buttocks, calves, pectoral areas, and other regions of the body, liquid, industrial-grade silicone is far more dangerous. Because it's not sterile, it can cause infections, particularly in the lungs, where it sometimes migrates.

Injected silicone can and does kill several people a year and disfigures many more, in states like New York, California, and Florida with large populations of transgenders. The most common causes of death immediately following a silicone injection are from an immune response that causes the lungs to fill with fluid, or from a pulmonary embolism. Silicone can migrate to the lungs or into the bloodstream, causing obstruction of the blood vessels, and can produce scar tissue that forms into hard lumps in the body.

While pumping is illegal in the United States, it is legal in some countries, leading many people to travel to have the work done overseas, or to seek out underground and often unlicensed doctors who perform the procedure in the United States.

See also: Cosmetic Surgery; Transgender; Transsexual

Further Reading: Kulick, Don. *Travesti: Sex, Gender, and Culture among Brazilian Transgendered Prostitutes.* Chicago: University of Chicago Press, 1998.

SKIN WHITENING

Skin whitening refers to using products, either internally or externally, to lighten dark skin temporarily or permanently.

In the West prior to the twentieth century, lighter skin was a sign of status for Europeans and Americans, since it indicated that they did not have to work outdoors. This goes back to classical times, when women of ancient Greece and Rome used lead paints and chalks to whiten their faces. During the Middle Ages, European women used arsenic to lighten their skins, and during the Renaissance, white face powder was worn to lighten the skin, and parasols were carried at all times when outdoors.

Light skin is a sign of status in non-Western countries as well, as in **India**, where higher castes are lighter skinned than the lower castes. Even today, actors and actresses in Bollywood films tend to be lighter skinned than most of the Indian population. In Eastern Asian countries as well, pale skin has typically represented nobility and status. In **Japan**, Geishas use thick white face powder to give the illusion of white skin, which represents beauty and sophistication. In **China** in the Middle Ages, women used skin whiteners made of mercury.

In parts of Latin America, the Arab world, and Africa, thanks to colonization, the lighter you are, the more beautiful. In former slave nations like Jamaica, for example, a brown complexion is often considered more beautiful than a black one. It's not surprising, then, that skin whiteners are very popular in these countries.

In the United States, women of color have also invested in skin-whitening products, not so that they could pass for white (although those with more Caucasian features sometimes could), but because going back to slavery, lighter skinned African Americans received better privileges than darker skinned blacks. Skin whiteners were also used by darker skinned Eastern and Southern European immigrants to help them blend into mainstream American society.

Even in the twentieth century, skin whiteners have been marketed which contain dangerous ingredients, like mercury and hydroquinone. While the Civil Rights and Black Pride movements made a dent in the skin-whitening industry by convincing many black women that dark skin was beautiful, skin whiteners are more popular than ever today, with hundreds of pills, soaps, creams, and lotions on the market in the United States, Asia, Latin America, Africa, and India. In Japan alone, the skin-whitening industry was worth $5.6 billion in 2001.

Skin whiteners generally work by breaking down the melanin in the skin, as well as providing sunscreen to protect the skin from the sun. Some whitening products are just bleaches, on the other hand, which temporarily lighten the skin. Exfoliants and lasers are more modern options.

While hydroquinone is considered the most popular and effective of the skin whiteners (often called a bleaching agent, it actually stops the production of melanin in the skin), its use has been banned in a number of countries, thanks to the damage that hydroquinone products have caused to skin. South Africa, for instance, banned products containing the chemical after countless black women were permanently disfigured. Other agents used are topical azelaic acid, tretinoin, kojic acid, glycolic acid, and a number of plant extracts.

Today, high-end skin whiteners are being marketed as antiaging products, and primarily target well-to-do women overseas, primarily in Asia. Cheap, often dangerous products are still being sold, often illegally, to minorities in the United States and poor women overseas, however.

See also: Beauty; Tanning

Further Reading: Allison, Kevin, and Dr. Faye Z. Belgrave. *African American Psychology: From Africa to America*. Thousand Oaks, CA: Sage Publications, 2005; Mullins, Paul R.

Race and Affluence: An Archaeology of African America and Consumer Culture. New York: Plenum Press, 1999; Russel, Kathy, Midge Wilson, and Ronald Hall. *The Color Complex: The Politics of Skin Color Among African Americans.* New York: First Anchor Books, 1993.

SLAVERY

Slavery refers to the practice of owning people as property. It is one of a number of forms of structured inequality found around the world, and has been practiced since antiquity and before, in a great many stratified societies.

Being a slave is both an acquired and an achieved position. Slaves are often born into slavery, but other slaves are acquired through warfare, as prisoners of war or war orphans. Colonization is another way that people could acquire the labor of other peoples for free, and debt bondage is a historical and modern way in which people become slaves. In debt bondage, a parent or relative typically loans a person, usually a child, to someone in exchange for a cash payment. The child then must work off the debt before they can return home, a prospect which is often impossible. In some cultures, people convicted of crimes or their families might be sold into slavery in order to compensate the victims.

In Western civilization, slavery may go back as far as the town of Jericho, an early farming community from around 10,000 BCE. Slavery was practiced in ancient Mesopotamia, **Egypt**, Greece, Israel, Persia, Rome, and Byzantium, as well as among the Chinese, Mayans, Aztecs, Indians, and among a number of African, Polynesian, and Melanesian peoples.

Because slaves are owned as property, it has often been common in slave-keeping societies for slave owners (or sometimes the state) to mark slaves with a brand or tattoo to demonstrate ownership.

Slaves in most societies could also be freely punished by their masters, via branding, whipping, **castration**, or even murder. Castration, on the other hand, was commonly used in some societies to control male slaves, such as in ancient Byzantium and in the Ottoman Empire. Slaves not only could be tortured, but in ancient Rome, slaves could not be trusted to confess to crimes voluntarily and were tortured for this purpose.

Today, members of the **BDSM** community who are dominant may tattoo or brand a mark of ownership onto their submissive or "slave" partner.

See also: Branding; Castration; Greco-Roman World; Tattooing

Further Reading: Davis, David Brion. *Inhuman Bondage: The Rise and Fall of Slavery in the New World.* Oxford: Oxford University Press, 2006; Hezser, Catherine. *Jewish Slavery in Antiquity.* Oxford: Oxford University Press, 2005; Wiedemann, Thomas E. J. *Greek and Roman Slavery.* Baltimore, MD: Johns Hopkins University Press, 1981.

SPANNER CASE

The Spanner case refers to a British court case in which sixteen gay men were prosecuted for engaging in consensual **BDSM** behavior.

The case began in 1987 when the Manchester, England police obtained what they thought was a snuff film in which a number of men were being tortured and, they thought, killed. The video was taken by some of the participants at a **body play** party in which the men were engaging in heavy BDSM activities including the beating of buttocks and genitals, the dripping of hot wax onto the genitals, genital bondage and manipulations, scrotal **stretching**, nipple and genital **branding**, play piercings, and other activities.

Because the men were easily identifiable in the video, the police investigation led to the arrests and prosecutions of all of the men for assault, even though BDSM practices are and were not themselves illegal in Great Britain, and all of the practices were between consenting adults.

In December 1990, the men pleaded guilty to a number of offences including assault with bodily harm, sending obscene materials through the mail, and using anesthetic without a license; some were fined, and others were sent to jail, with sentences up to four and a half years (many of which were later reduced). None of the men were acquitted based on the judge's interpretation of the law of assault.

A number of the defendants appealed against their convictions to the British Appeal Court, but their convictions were upheld. The case then went to the House of Lords, which in 1993 also upheld the original convictions. Finally, the case was appealed to the European Court of Human Rights in Strasbourg, France, which, like the courts before it, upheld the original judgment in 1997.

After the Spanner case was resolved, the British Law Commission published a Consultation Paper called "Consent in the Criminal Law" which questioned the notion of whether physical assault can take place between consenting parties. BDSM advocates as well as supporters of sexual freedom and the freedom to perform radical body modifications hope that the Consultation Paper can be used in future criminal cases on behalf of defendants like the men who became known as the Spannermen. Another result of the case was the formation of a British organization called the Spanner Trust which works to defend the rights of gay and straight participants in BDSM.

See also: BDMS; Body Play; Legislation and Regulation; Torture

Further Reading: Mottier, Veronique, and Terrell Carver. *Politics of Sexuality: Identity, Gender, Citizenship*. London: Routledge, 1999; Warburton, Nigel. *Freedom: An Introduction with Readings*. London: Routledge, 2001.

SPRAGUE, ERIC

Eric Sprague, who goes by the name of Lizardman, is a professional sideshow performer and **freak** who at one time worked with the Jim Rose **Circus**.

Performing for over a decade, Lizardman can swallow swords, lie on a bed of nails, hammer nails into his nose, eat and breathe fire, act as a human dartboard, escape from straight jackets and handcuffs, walk on broken glass, eat insects, and more. He is also active in public **suspensions**.

Lizardman is also well known for his extensive and extreme body modifications, which include 650 hours worth of **tattooing**—his body is covered with green scales mixed with black tribal designs, and his eyelids, fingertips, scalp, ears, tongue, and lips are tattooed; a split tongue, sharpened teeth, a large septum **piercing**, nipple piercings, a penis piercing, large **ear plugs**, and subdermal **implants** over his eyebrows.

A PhD candidate before he began performing, Sprague decided to modify his body for an art piece that would explore the idea of what it means to be human. He chose to transform himself into a reptile, and began his transformation in 1994.

Lizardman has been featured on "Ripley's Believe It or Not," and has appeared in a number of other television shows. He has toured with a number of bands and carnivals, and currently hosts the Jagermeister Music Tour, writes a column for BMEZine.com, and works as a solo artist.

See also: Animality; Freak Shows; Freaks; Primitivism

Further Reading: Potts, Annie. "The Mark of the Beast: Inscribing 'Animality' through Extreme Body Modification." In P. Armstrong and L. Simmons, eds., *Knowing Animals*. Leiden: Brill, 2007.

STALKING CAT

Born Dennis Avner in 1958, Stalking Cat has spent much of his life transforming himself into a tiger through a series of radical body modification procedures.

Avner, who is part Native American, says that he was told by an Indian chief to "follow the ways of the tiger," and decided to transform himself into his totem animal, like whom he already behaves, occasionally hunting his own food and eating raw meat.

He began his transformation in 1981 at the age of 23, and now has tiger stripes and fish scales tattooed on his body and face, a modified hairline, surgically pointed ears, surgically flattened nose, **silicone injections** in his lips, cheeks, and chin, six subdermal implants inserted into his brow, eighteen transdermal implants which act as whiskers above his lips, a bisected upper lip, and a full set of fangs. Most of Avner's work has been done by **Steve Haworth** although he has also traveled to Mexico to have some of the work performed by cosmetic surgeons there. He also wears green contact lenses with slits as irises, and detachable bionic ears, but hopes to get another set of transdermal implants, in his head, to act as permanent cat ears. He also plans to attach a permanent pelt to his skin.

Stalking Cat was featured on "Ripley's Believe it or Not!," "Larry King Live," the film *Animal Tragic*, and a number of other television and radio shows.

See also: Animality; Freak Shows; Freaks; Primitivism

Further Reading: Potts, Annie. "The Mark of the Beast: Inscribing 'Animality' through Extreme Body Modification." In P. Armstrong and L. Simmons, eds., *Knowing Animals*. Leiden: Brill, 2007.

STIGMATA

The term stigmata today refers to both the marks or bruises on the body of Jesus Christ from his crucifixion, as well as mystical marks or bruises on devout Christians, which are thought to correspond to the wounds of Jesus.

While reported cases of stigmata seen on other people are often on the hands or wrists and feet or ankles (which correspond to the areas on which Jesus was thought to be nailed to the cross), stigmata could also be seen on the forehead (where Jesus wore a crown of thorns), on the back (from scourging), or on other areas of the body. But the original Greco-Roman usage of the term actually means tattoo.

While cases of Christians reporting to bear the wounds of Christ did not develop until the thirteenth century, there are references to stigmata much earlier in Christian literature. For instance, Paul's letter in Galatians 6:17 reads "I carry the marks of Jesus tattooed on my body." The term stigmata was used in this case, and in much early Christian writing, both to refer to the visible wounds of Christ, as well to tattooing. Prior to the time of Jesus, however, the term "stigmata" was used almost exclusively by both the ancient Greeks and the ancient Romans to refer to tattooing.

While Paul's usage here was metaphorical (there is no reason to suggest that Paul was tattooed or that he was encouraging tattoos for the faithful), the usage demonstrates that the old term for tattooing common in the Roman world was giving way to a newer, Christ-centered term. It is also clear that there was a connection between the wounds of Christ and the practice of tattooing, commonly used in the ancient world as a form of punishment.

In fact, the Romans, like the Greeks before them, tattooed criminals (usually with a letter representing their crime, or sometimes their punishment) on the forehead, and until the rise of Constantine and the Christianization of the Roman Empire, Christians were commonly tattooed in this fashion. Thus the tattoo on the head of a faithful Roman Christian could be seen as a sign of faith and could be connected with the wounds of Christ.

Because the Romans found tattooing to be barbaric, and primarily used such stigmata to forcibly mark criminals and runaway slaves, the idea that one who wears a tattoo was somehow seen as socially unacceptable, became common, leading to the modern use of the term stigma to indicate a social stain.

See also: Christianity; Criminality; Greco-Roman World

Further Reading: Jones, C. P. "Stigma and Tattoo." In Jane Caplan, ed., *Written on the Body: The Tattoo in European and American History*. London: Reaktion Books, 2000.

STRETCHING

Stretching, in the context of **body piercing**, refers to the stretching of a hole in the skin in order to accommodate a large piece of **jewelry**. It can also refer to the stretching of holes for **suspensions** and other forms of **body play**. Ear piercings are the most commonly stretched piercings, with nasal septum piercings, and lip piercings following close behind.

In order to achieve a stretched piercing, typically one first receives a regular piercing in the ear, lip, or other part of the body, and allows that piercing to heal while wearing the starter jewelry. Once the piercing has healed, there are a number of ways of stretching the hole, which usually involve stretching it a little bit at a time in order to minimize tissue damage and **pain**.

Tapering is the most common technique used for stretching, and involves the use of a conical metal rod known as a taper, which is pushed through the hole until the widest part of the taper is even with the skin; larger jewelry is then pushed through, parallel to the back of the taper. Larger tapers, and then jewelry, will be substituted over time as the hole gets bigger. Another gradual method of stretching uses teflon tape. The existing jewelry is removed from the hole and a piece of tape is wrapped around it, forming a slightly larger diameter. As the hole stretches to accommodate the new size of jewelry, the jewelry is removed and more tape is applied.

Dead stretching is the practice of simply stretching a hole in the skin until it is big enough to accommodate the desired jewelry. This type of stretching often results in tearing as well as pain. A piercing can also be stretched via the hanging of weights onto the jewelry. This is a common way that people in traditional societies stretched ears in the past, although can result in tissue tearing and thinning. A more modern way of stretching is via **scalpelling**, or using a scalpel to cut a large hole around a piercing, removing a piece of flesh. Scalpelling can also be combined with tapering, which achieves a very large hole but can be quite painful. And finally, stretching can also be more easily accomplished by beginning with a larger gauged hole rather than a small hole.

Stretched piercings allow for a wider variety of jewelry than can be worn in many more conventional piercings, although the most commonly worn jewelry is known as a plug. A plug is a cylindrical piece of jewelry that fits into a large hole, and is sometimes flared at both ends to keep it in place. **Flesh tunnels** are a hollowed-out version of a plug, and resemble an empty spool of thread, and can be worn with another decorative item running through the middle. Ear spirals are another option, which are spiral-shaped coils that are inserted into the ear. Different kinds of materials can be used to make jewelry for stretched piercings because the larger hole allows for more delicate or brittle materials than would otherwise be found in a piercing. Plugs and spirals can be made of wood, bone, stone, or even glass.

Men and women have been stretching their piercings for thousands of years. Stretched lips into which **lip plates** or lip plugs are inserted have been worn in ancient **Meso-America**, South America, among the **Inuit** and other Northwest Coast Indians, and among a number of tribes in Africa. Stretched ears have been worn in ancient **Egypt** as well as a number of Asian countries.

In the West, many young people have stretched piercings, especially in the ears. While these practices began in the **modern primitive** community, they have expanded into much of mainstream society.

See also: Body Piercing; Ear Piercing; Ear Spools and Earplugs; Lip Plates

SUDAN

Like many Sub-Saharan African nations, the people of Sudan practice a variety of body modifications and adornments, including **scarification, body painting,** lip piercing and the wearing of **lip plates,** and **female genital mutilation.**

Among the Nuba of southern Sudan girls undergo scarification, usually from their breasts to their navel, a number of times during her life, in order to mark important events such as first menstruation or the birth of her first child, after which her back, legs, arms, and neck are scarred. Nuba men wear scars on their torsos and arms, usually as part of an initiation ritual. Men of the Dinka tribe of the south also scarify themselves, generally on the forehead during a boy's **rite of passage** into adulthood. As in other African societies, scarification involves the use of hooks or blades to raise and slice the skin, leaving a scar which is intensified by rubbing charcoal into the wounds.

Other Sudanese tribes practice scarification as well, sometimes on the face and other times on the body. Each tribe has its own mark, which distinguishes one group from another, and which include as well Muslims from the northern part of the country. Because of the ethnic warfare in Sudan, many refugees that have fled their homelands have discarded scarification, and it is rarely practiced in the cities.

Many Sudanese tribes also practice body painting. Nuba men, for example, paint their bodies at ceremonial events with yellow, red, white, and black ochre; the colors and designs, which include geometric patterns as well as dots and stripes to represent leopards or giraffes, represent clan membership and age grades. Some Sudanese women also wear **henna** designs on their hands.

Piercing is also practiced in Sudan. The Nuba traditionally wear rings in their septums, nostrils, and in their lips, and the women of the Sara tribe wear very large lip plates in their enlarged lip holes.

Female genital mutilation is a form of involuntary body modification that is practiced in Sudan, along with many other Sub-Saharan African countires. In Sudan, the practice generally involves a **clitoridectomy,** which is the removal of the clitoris, and recircumcision, and involves tightening the vaginal opening by suturing the labia minora together to leave a very small orifice, which is said to increase men's pleasure. Although Sudan outlawed female genital mutilation in 1946 and again in 1974, it continues to have one of the highest rates of this practice in the world.

See also: Clitoridectomy; Lip Plates; Scarification

Further Reading: Faris, James. "Significance of Differences in the Male and Female Personal Art of the Southeast Nuba." In Arnold Rubin, ed., *Marks of Civilization: Artistic Transformations of the Human Body*. Los Angeles: Museum of Cultural History, UCLA, 1988; Lienhardt, Godfrey. *Divinity and Experience: The Religion of the Dinka*. Oxford: Oxford University Press, 1961; Momoh, Comfort. *Female Genital Mutilation*. Oxford: Radcliffe University Press, 2005; Pitts, Victoria. "Body Modification, Self-Mutilation and Agency in Media Accounts of a Subculture." In Mike Featherstone, ed., *Body Modification*. London: Sage Publications, 2000.

SUPER/SUBINCISION

Subincision refers to the splitting of the underside of the penis through the urethra, whereas superincision is the bisection of the penis on the top, leaving the tissue below the urethra intact. Superincisions are far more invasive and dangerous than subincisions, and as a result are not only rare in the modern world of body modification, but on a historical level as well. A modified form of the subincision is the meatotomy in which the underside of just the glans is split.

Neither procedure results in two separate penises, like a bisection does (in which the penis is literally split into two, while remaining joined at the base). Instead, the penis is flayed open, but remains joined along one side. Both surgeries are very rare, extreme practices performed by some members of the body modification community, following traditional practices of non-Western peoples.

In the West, some men opt to undergo one of these procedures for sexual pleasure, as opening up the penis and exposing the nerves surrounding the urethra intensify sexual sensations. Partners of men with subincisions or superincisions also report greater pleasure because the penis is wider after the procedure. Others do it for aesthetic reasons or to experience a "primitive" **rite of passage**. Still others like the idea of removing urination from the shaft of the penis (because a super or subincised man will urinate from the base of the penis rather than the head), making the rest of the penis only an organ for sexual pleasure. Because men with one of these procedures will not urinate out of the glans anymore, the urine stream is no longer a stream but often comes out more like a shower head. Subincision and superincision also reduce the range of the ejaculate.

Many Australian Aboriginal groups, such as the Yiwara, Arrernte, Lardil, Luritja, and Pidjandara, traditionally used subincision. In some Australian groups subincisions were performed as a rite of passage for adolescent males. In other groups, subincision occured a few years after the initiation rituals during which a boy was circumcised. In either case, subincised men were allowed after the surgery to learn important aspects of adult male ceremonial life. Among the Lardil, for example, one can only learn the ceremonial language after being subincised, but because subincision is no longer practiced, the ceremonial language is no longer taught.

Many Australian groups see the subincised penis as symbolic of a woman's genitals, and the bleeding is likened to menstruation, enabling boys to menstruate out the polluting influence of women, helping them to become men. Ritual bloodlettings through the penis are often repeated throughout adult life. Subincision may also have been practiced in parts of Polynesia, Melanesia, Africa, and among the tribes of South America who live in the Amazon Basin.

See also: Circumcision; Genital Mutilation

Further Reading: Montagu, Ashley. *Coming into Being among the Australian Aborigines*. London: George Routledge & Sons Ltd., 1937.

SURFACE PIERCING

A surface piercing is a **piercing** in which the ends of a piece of jewelry sit on the surface of the skin while the body of the **jewelry** sits underneath the skin.

Surface piercings are relatively new and unusual piercings, and have a notoriously high failure rate. Because the body of the jewelry lies underneath a flat area of skin (rather than going through a piece of cartilage or flesh as with ear, nose, nipple, and genital piercings), there is a tremendous amount of stress placed on the skin above the piercing, which often causes the piercing to be rejected during healing. On the other hand, surface piercings that are done well and that heal well create often interesting or beautiful designs in which the beads of the jewelry appear to float on the surface of the skin.

Surface piercings are typically created with a regular piercing needle, but use a different type of jewelry from traditional **body piercing** jewelry. Jewelry is usually stainless steel or titanium surface bars, shaped to fit the anatomy of the particular area of the body to be pierced, with two beads that are screwed onto the ends. An alternative is a bar made with flexible plastic material that moves with the body. After piercing the skin, the jewelry is inserted into the hole at a ninety-degree angle, is then turned, and exits through the exit hole at ninety degrees. The result is a bar inserted directly beneath the skin at the same angle as the skin, with the two ends emerging from both holes.

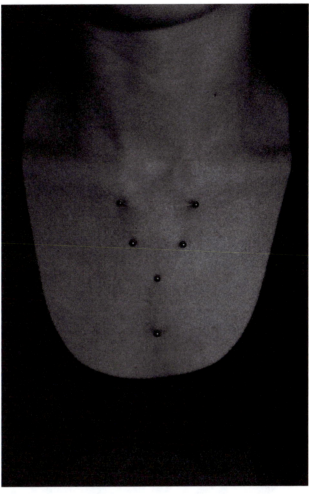

Chest surface piercing by Steve Truitt of Stay Gold Tattoo & Body Modification and Ascension Studios, Albuquerque, NM.

Another method of creating a surface piercing uses a dermal punch, which is a round needle that takes cookie-cutter bites out of the skin combined with a tapered steel rod to separate the skin from the connective tissue. An alternative method is to use two needles, rather than one, for the piercing.

Popular areas for surface piercings include the cleavage, the eyebrows, the navel, the back of the neck, the chest, and the base of the neck.

See also: Body Piercing

Further Reading: www.BMEZine.com.

SUSPENSIONS

Suspension is a ritualized form of **body play** in which a person hangs from flesh hooks put through holes in their body, often as a part of **modern primitive** practices.

Suspensions are done either privately or with a partner or small group of friends, or are public performances. One of the goals of participating in a suspension is to overcome the **pain** of the experience in order to achieve a feeling of euphoria, a trance-like state, or a heightened awareness of all senses. For many, participating in a suspension is a way to achieve a personal transformation. There are a number of professional suspension teams who perform public suspensions and provide private suspensions to individuals interested in experiencing one.

There are a variety of suspension types. Suicide suspensions are suspensions in which a person is hung vertically from piercings in their back; a vertical chest suspension is one in which the person hangs from hooks hung in their chest; a Superman suspension is one in which the body is suspended horizontally, face facing the ground, with hooks inserted through the back and legs; a coma suspension is also a horizontal suspension, but the face points upward; a lotus suspension is a suspension of a person in the lotus position, with hooks in the shoulders and legs; a resurrection suspension is a vertical suspension where the hooks are inserted into

Ogala Sioux Sun Dance. Illustration in Harper's Weekly, Jan 2, 1875, Jules Tavernier; Frenzeny. Courtesy of Library of Congress Prints and Photographs Division, Washington, DC, No. LC-USZ62-117138.

not only the chest but the stomach as well; and there are a number of suspensions in which only a certain appendage is hung, rather than the whole body. Generally, in all of these cases, a piercer first pierces the locations in the person's body where the hooks will be inserted (placement depends on the type of suspension and the number depends on the weight of the person and his or her experience), and then inserts large gauge steel fishing hooks into the holes, which are attached to a rope or cable, which is attached to the suspension apparatus which holds the body aloft. Suspensions can last minutes or hours, depending on the person's experience and desires.

Suspensions have been practiced as a religious ritual in a number of societies, and are typically associated with other practices such as fasting, dancing, meditating, chanting, or the use of hallucinogenic drugs, all of which are intended to induce an ecstatic state and to bring the participant closer to the spiritual realm. They have also been used as **rites of passage**, especially for young men or warriors in which their endurance, bravery, and strength are tested.

The Sun Dance is an example of a suspension ritual, and was a ceremony once practiced by several Native American tribes. In the suspension part of the dance, the dancers attach themselves to a vertical pole, via ropes attached to bone or wood skewers, which are inserted into pre-pierced holes in the chest. Then, dancing around in a circle to the beat of drums and prayers, the participants pull against the pole to tear the skewers out. Another Native American suspension ritual is the O-Kee-Pa, which involves the temporary piercing and hanging of young men by hooks in their chest and back, so that the participants could achieve a trance and communicate with the spirits.

Fakir Musafar, known as the father of the modern primitives movement, popularized suspensions for the body modification community (and in fact, performed on film the Sun Dance) and explains them as a transformative, life-altering event.

See also: Body Piercing; Body Play; *Dances Sacred and Profane*; Musafar, Fakir

Further Reading: Vale, V., and Andrea Juno. *Modern Primitives*. San Francisco, CA: Re/Search Publications, 1989.

T

TAHITI

Tahiti is a Polynesian island that was settled by inhabitants of **Tonga** and **Samoa** sometime during the first millennium CE. First encountered by the English explorer Samuel Wallis in 1767, it was visited by **Captain James Cook** on his second voyage in 1774, whose crew not only noted and drew the first pictures of the islanders' tattoo styles, but brought back (on Cook's second voyage) a tattooed Tahitian named Omai for display in Europe. Cook's first trip to Tahiti was also notable because it was from this trip that Westerners were first exposed to the Tahitian word *tatau*, which later became the English word tattoo. (Prior to that time, tattooing was referred to as pricking in the West.) Crew member and naturalist Joseph Banks wrote the very first account of Polynesian tattooing based on his visit to Tahiti, and illustrator Sydney Parks illustrated the first pictures of Polynesian tattoos seen in the West. The tattoos noted included lines, stars, and other geometric designs, as well as figures of animals and humans, and were worn by both men and women.

Tattooing was an important part of Tahitian society prior to the arrival of Europeans. Like other Polynesian tattoos, Tahitian tattoos marked rank, kinship, and, for girls, sexual maturity and marriageability.

The tattooing kit was known as a *tatatau*, and was made up of a comb with a number of sharpened bone needles joined onto a wooden handle. The tool is dipped into the dye which is made up of ashes mixed with water or oil, and then the needles are tapped into the skin via a mallet, which strikes the implement, pushing the ink into the skin. Prior to tattooing, the artist invoked the patron spirits of tattooing, Mata Mata Arahu and Tu Ra'i Po', to ensure the success of the procedure and the beauty of the final design.

> The woman must bear children and the man must be tattooed.
>
> Polynesian proverb

Men were tattooed all over their body, including on the neck and ears, although the face was untattooed for most men. Because tattoos signify rank, different tattoos were worn by priests, chiefs, warriors, and common people. Women were tattooed throughout their youth, first with designs on their arms indicating that they were free to eat food prepared by someone other than their mother, and next with tattoos on their buttocks to demonstrate their sexual maturity.

As with other traditional societies, tattooing was banned by the colonial authorities in the nineteenth century, but has been experiencing a renaissance since the

1980s, as Tahitian artists are once again practicing traditional tattoo styles on the island as a sign of their cultural identity. However, because the Ministry of Health has prohibited the use of the traditional tattoo kit because it is difficult to sterilize, tattoo artists are now using electric tattoo machines of their own designs, which use disposable steel needles.

See also: Cook, Captain James; Samoa

Further Reading: Allen, Tricia. "Tatau: The Tahitian Revival." 1998. www.tattoos.com/allen/TATAU.htm; Kuwahara, Makiko. "Multiple Skins: Space, Time and Tattooing in Tahiti." In Bronwen Douglas, Nicholas Thomas, and Anna Cole, eds., *Tattoo: Bodies, Art and Exchange in the Pacific and the West.* Durham, NC: Duke University Press, 2005; Kuwahara, Makiko. *Tattoo: An Anthropology.* New York: Berg, 2005.

TANNING

Suntanning describes the process of human skin darkening due to exposure to ultraviolet radiation from sunlight (or a tanning bed). While tanning is often inadvertent and can occur anytime someone is in the sun for an extended period of time, it can also be an intentional act in which a person deliberately exposes the body to the sun in the hopes of receiving a tan. In the West, this process is often called "lying out" or sunbathing.

The ancient Greeks sunbathed, calling the act of lying in the sun "heliotherapy"; they felt that natural sunlight could cure certain illnesses.

In the West prior to the modern era, however, light skin was preferred for Europeans and Americans, as light skin was seen as a sign that a person did not have to engage in outdoor labor. In ancient Rome, for example, women deliberately lightened their skin with **makeup** in order to appear well off, and throughout Europe during the Renaissance, elite women lightened their untanned skin even further with makeup and face powder. Having fair skin meant that one not only did not have to work outdoors, but that they were wealthy enough to hire other people to work for them. Elites in the United States prior to the twentieth century also worked to protect their skin from the sun and wore makeup to lighten their already-light skin.

In the twentieth century, however, with fewer people engaged in agricultural or other outdoor labor, most work moved indoors, and men and women of all classes were less exposed to the sun. In the 1920s, French fashion designer Coco Chanel acquired a suntan during a vacation on the French Riviera, and helped to popularize suntans among the wealthy; suntans at this point became a sign of status for men and women who could afford to travel to sunny or tropical climates for a holiday.

Starting in the mid-twentieth century, tanned skin also became associated with a new outdoor lifestyle—not of work, but of leisure. As clothing styles (especially for women) allowed for the display of more skin, and as many men and women began hiking, picnicking, or engaging in sports for relaxation, tanned skin became more popular still, as well as more available to the average American and European.

Sunbathing became a pastime in and of itself in Europe and America, and, by mid-century, cosmetic products were created to simulate the look of a suntan, and suntanning oils were marketed to encourage a better tan.

Another development in the twentieth century was the indoor tanning industry, first popularized in the 1970s and by the 1980s, tanning salons became ubiquitous in suburban America. Tanning salons, in which a person relaxes in a tanning bed that emits ultraviolet radiation, in order to achieve a suntan in minimal time regardless of the climate.

In the late 1970s, however, the link between exposure to ultraviolet radiation and skin cancer became apparent, and men and women who had sunbathed extensively began developing melanomas. In the late 1970s, the Federal Drug Administration developed the first sunscreen rating system that measured the product's sun protection factor or SPF. It wasn't until the 1980s, however, that the public became aware of the dangers of overexposure to the sun, either through sunbathing or lying in a tanning bed.

Today, artificial bronzers and sunless tanning products are popular with celebrities and the general public, which create the suntanned look without the associated dangers. These products can be applied at home, in the form of gels, lotions, mousses, sprays, and wipes, and airbrush spray tans are applied by professional technicians, who also operated sunlass tanning spray booths in which artificial bronzers are sprayed over the entire body.

Another reason for the popularity of sunless tanning products has to do with the time needed to receive a conventional tan. Because getting a tan requires a commitment of time (whether laying out in the sun or going to a tanning booth), and many modern Americans no longer have the time necessary for idle sunbathing, skin bronzers are also popular for that reason.

See also: Makeup

Further Reading: Sikes, Ruth G. "The History of Suntanning: A Love/Hate Affair." *Journal of Aesthetic Sciences* 1(2) (May 1998): 1–7.

TATTOO COMMUNITY

The term tattoo community refers to the virtual community comprised of tattooed people who share a strong interest in **tattooing**. Within this "community," there are broadly defined class and stylistic groups, and within each larger group there are also numerous subcommunities. The tattoo community is a real community in the sense that it is experienced by many tattooed people across the country; and yet it is differentiated, by class and status among other features, such that it often seems to exist in pieces more than as a whole.

Not all tattooed people consider themselves to be members of the tattoo community, and in fact, most would not. One becomes part of the community through participating in certain key rituals. These rituals would include, first, and obviously, becoming tattooed. After that however, one must have enough of an interest in tattooing to either read tattoo publications (including magazines, books, pamphlets, calendars, etc.), attend **tattoo shows**, or both. To be a member of the tattoo community involves more than just getting a tattoo—it involves a commitment to learning about tattoos, to meeting other people with tattoos, and a commitment to an entire lifestyle in which tattoos play an important role.

Conventions and magazines are important in terms of this commitment for a number of reasons. First, tattoo conventions constitute a space where individuals with common interests—tattoos—come together for a period of time. While tattoo shops are also places where tattooed individuals congregate, a different kind of community is created there. This type of community is more localized, more focused around a particular shop or tattooist, or style of tattoo (for example, a tattoo studio in San Francisco specializing in tribal tattooing will attract a small contingency of punks who identify strongly with that style and all that it represents). The sense of community that individuals find in the tattoo convention or reading a tattoo magazine has less to do with the physical congregation of bodies than with a feeling of "shared specialness." Tattooed people define themselves vis-a-vis nontattooed people and the dominant society in general. What makes tattooed people feel as if they are a part of a larger community, when at a convention or when reading (and writing to, sending in photographs, etc.) a tattoo magazine, is this feeling that "Here are some people who are like me, who are not like everyone else."

> I think that one of the saving graces of tattooing is that it goes beyond any kind of justification, you can't explain it, it goes beyond the rational, I think that's its virtue. Everything else in society is totally explained.
>
> ANONYMOUS

The second reason that conventions and magazines constitute community has to do with where and how the notion of community is defined within the movement. Without the organized structure of tattoo shows, tattoo magazines, Internet chat groups, and tattoo organizations (which often organize the shows), there would be no broader notion of community, because it is on the pages of tattoo magazines, and in the literature promoting tattoo organizations and their shows, that a broader idea of a community has taken shape. Prior to 1976 when the first big tattoo convention was held, the term "community" was unknown among mainstream tattooed people. In addition, while tattooists did communicate with each other about the best places to buy equipment and supplies, there was also a great deal of competition between tattooists, and many were suspicious that other tattooists might gain access to their secrets.

> I believe everyone is their own person, and they should be able to express themselves with body art, piercings, etc. It makes us happy, so we're not really worried about other people's thoughts or opinions.
>
> ANONYMOUS

Even with the rise of tattoo shows and magazines in the 1970s and 1980s, many older tattooists shunned these new developments, preferring to stay out of the limelight and keep to themselves. On the other hand, there did exist, prior to the development of conventions and magazines, a notion of community among other groups who practiced tattooing—bikers, convicts, sailors or members of the leather, and **BDSM** cultures, for example—but the community was not based on the tattoo, nor did the notion of community extend outside of each specific group to embrace others with tattoos. While the tattoos worn within each group, and especially those worn by convicts and bikers, did serve as important markers of group membership, the communities of bikers, convicts, or leatherboys, were based on much more than tattoos. But until the 1970s, there seems to be little evidence of a notion of community broader than that surrounding a particular shop.

For many tattoo fans, the tattoo community entails *communitas*, Victor Turner's term for a feeling of homogeneity, equality, camaraderie, and lack of hierarchy common among those who are marginalized or are undergoing a liminal transition from one state to the next. These assertions about the tattoo community as an example of *communitas* represent the idealized view of the tattoo community, one that is shared by not only tattoo organizations and tattoo magazine editors, but by a great many of the membership at large as well.

While the dominant discourse is one of family, equality, and sharing, the reality for many tattooists and fans, on the other hand, also includes stratification, differentiation, and competition. Furthermore, the idea that simply wearing a tattoo gives a person a deep connection with others who are tattooed is, to many, a ridiculous notion.

See also: Tattooing; Tattoo Magazines; Tattoo Shows

Further Reading: DeMello, Margo. *Bodies of Inscription: A Cultural History of the Modern Tattoo Community*. Durham, NC: Duke University Press, 2000.

TATTOOED ATTRACTIONS

For centuries, men (and later women) have been displayed as entertainment to paying customers in Europe and the United States. Tattooed attractions include both "**tattooed natives**" brought (voluntarily or involuntarily) to the West by Western explorers, as well as European and American men and women with extensive tattoos who displayed themselves for pay at carnivals, **circuses,** and fairs throughout the West.

By the end of the eighteenth century, a great many European seamen were becoming tattooed, some with small tattoos, and some with extensive body decorations. As tattooed natives became more popular attractions at carnivals and fairs in Europe, and it became clear that people were willing to pay to view such a thing, a new type of **freak** was created, and with it, a new occupation for a large number of people. Generally these first attractions were sailors who traveled inland to show themselves in inns and taverns. Later circus people stepped in to publicize and bring to the forefront this form of attraction. First they did this in a small single tent and then in larger tents as sideshows developed through the years.

The first Westerners displayed as tattooed attractions were viewed simply on the virtue of their tattoos. Because most Europeans (and later Ameicans) had never seen a tattooed person, especially one who was extensively tattooed, tattooed people were a popular attraction at carnivals and traveling fairs. The first Westerner displayed as a tattooed attraction was Jean Baptiste Cabris. Cabris was a French man who was working on an English whaling ship at the end of the eighteenth century, and got shipwrecked on the Marquesan Islands. He got tattooed while on the island, and married a chief's daughter. After his rescue in 1804, he worked as an attraction through Russia and Europe. Soon after, another French man, Joseph Cabri, was also tattooed while in the Marquesan Islands, and displayed himself until his death in 1818.

Later, as competition among attractions developed, the tale of "native capture" developed. Here the tattooed exhibit (or the manager of the show) would tell the crowd of the circumstances surrounding the acquisition of the attraction's tattoos. These stories centered around his capture and forcible tattooing by savage natives (they were often said to be cannibals), the **pain** involved in the tattooing, and his heroic escape from captivity. Perhaps the first white man to use such a ploy was the Englishman John Rutherford, who claimed that he had been captured and tattooed by the **Maori** in 1828, and was forced to marry a Maori princess. Rutherford was a popular display in the 1820s and 1830s, and while he probably did get some tattoos from the Maori, as well as Tahitian and Fijian tattoos, he was in all likelihood not the victim of kidnapping.

James O'Connell was the first tattooed white man exhibited in the United States. His story was that he was shipwrecked along with five shipmates on the island of Pohnpei in Micronesia in the late 1820s, married one of the chief's daughters, and was tattooed by natives. He had few tattoos but at that time (in 1833 he returned to the United States and began his circus career) there was still relatively little competition in this field, so he enjoyed a successful career that lasted until 1852. Like Rutherford, O'Connell may well have been tattooed in the South Seas, although probably not on the islands that he claimed to have been tattooed on, and his story is most certainly fabricated.

P.T. Barnum, of both the American Museum and Barnum & Bailey's Circus, was the most successful promoter of tattooed attractions of all time, and, thanks to him, being tattooed became a new profession. In 1873, Barnum brought Alexandrino from Greece to the United States where he was known as Prince Constantine. Constantine became the most flamboyant and best known of all tattooed attractions until he retired in the 1880s, traveling to Europe as well as through the United States. He had 388 tattoos, done in the "Burmese style," and he sold pamphlets describing them and his forced abduction by Chinese "tartars." Barnum even had doctors examine him, who pronounced that he was one of the most extraordinary specimens of genuine tattooing they had ever seen. Barnum boasted that he paid Constantine, a Greek "nobleman," $1,000 a week, although this was most likely an exaggeration. Constantine was displayed alongside a "leopard boy," and a number of other natural wonders, and, like other tattooed attractions, sold pitch cards with his photo and story. Another Barnum attraction, the brother and sister team of Annie and Frank Howard, claimed that they were forcibly tattooed after a shipwreck in the South Seas, although they were in fact tattooed by Martin

Hildebrandt and Samuel O'Reilly. Another popular attraction was John Hays, who had 780 tattoos which he said were forcibly tattooed on him by Indians; he too was tattooed by O'Reilly and traveled with Barnum.

Another way for these early entrepreneurs to make money off of their tattoos was to work as a tattooist in the traveling shows. Early tattooists offered their services both to normal people who wanted a single tattoo and to aspiring sideshow exhibits. **Charlie Wagner**, for example saw Prince Constantine in a New York dime museum and decided to get tattooed and be a tattooist (he later tattooed more than fifty freak show attractions). In the early part of the century, tattooists charged 50 cents to a dollar for a small tattoo. Bert Grimm, who joined the Buffalo Bill Wild West Show in 1916 (he told a story of being shipwrecked on a cannibal island and being forcibly tattooed by the natives) said that you could charge about $33 in those days for a total cover job, which took about six to eight weeks to complete, and could, in the early twentieth century, guarantee someone a job (paying anywhere from $25 to $30 per week) at a circus or carnival. Bert Grimm later tattooed Lady Viola and reworked **Betty Broadbent's** tattoos.

Generally, the circus and carnivals employed tattooists during the spring, summer, and fall, and during the off-season, they wintered in the South (primarily Florida), sometimes renting spaces in arcades and poolrooms. By 1932 there were approximately three hundred completely tattooed men and women who exhibited themselves in traveling shows and in urban dime museums. With these shows, tattooing moved inland from the port towns and was brought to areas where people had previously only heard or read about it. For instance, Artoria Gibbons was a poor girl born on a farm in Wisconsin who at 14 saw Red Gibbons tattooing at a carnival that traveled to her village; she later left home, joined the carnival, married Gibbons and became a tattooed lady.

Also beginning in the mid-nineteenth century, World's Fairs had tattooed attractions, such as the World's Fair in Queens, New York in 1939, where The Tattooed Venus (Betty Broadbent) was shown. Carnivals developed out of World's Fairs, but the early carnivals in the nineteenth century had no tattooed attractions. The sideshow (a string of ten in one or so freak acts, also known as the **freak show**) moved onto the carnival midway in 1908. The earliest record of a single tattooed person or tattooist on a carnival midway is Jack Stratt in 1908.

While in the late 1880s and early 1890s, tattooed attractions could command large salaries, up to $100–$200 per week, and could work wherever they wanted, this situation changed quickly. Competition began to increase and the proliferation of tattooed exhibits undermined the appeal of tattooed men altogether.

In the 1880s, however, tattooed women arrived on the scene, upstaging men completely. This was because they had to show their bodies (legs and thighs) to show their tattoos, and, during the Victorian period, to see a woman's thighs was considered quite racy (especially if she was performing what could be considered a strip show). Another aspect of their appeal was that tattooed women were seen as docile and chaste, which conflicted with the idea of tattoos, which had been up to now only seen on men. While men were tattooed on their hands and neck, tattooed women left their neck, hands, and heads free of tattoos, so that they could look modest when wearing clothes, and so that they could have an alternate career when they retired from show business. While both tattooed men and women had a hard time making a decent living after the 1930s, women could use their sexuality to sell tickets (and pitch cards and photos, a major moneymaker).

Female tattooed attractions told outrageous tales about how they acquired their tattoos, just like the men did. Irene "La Belle" Woodward, one of the first tattooed ladies who began in 1882 (after seeing Prince Constantine on display), said that her tattoos were required protection that she needed in the Wild West of Texas to escape the sexual attentions of hostile Red Indians. She worked in both the United States and Europe. Nora Hildebrandt, who also went on exhibit in the early 1880s, reported that her three hundred and sixty five tattoos were crafted by her father under the threat of death of his captor, Sitting Bull. (Hildebrandt was indeed tattooed by her father, but not under threat of death; her father Martin Hildebrandt owned the first professional tattoo shop in New York in the 1840s, and saw a business opportunity with his daughter.) Both Hildebrandt and Woodward, the pioneers of the tattooed ladies, were hand-tattooed in the days before the tattoo machine, making their extensive body coverage even more extraordinary.

One tattooed attraction, Olive Oatman, actually was tattooed by Native Americans. Captured by Yavapi Indians as a child and sold to the Mojave Indians, Oatman was found in 1856 with Mohave chin tattoos.

Pitch cards and handbills promoting female tattooed attractions use the native capture device to entice audiences as well. Most contrast a modestly attired lady in a Victorian gown with a scene of the same woman being forcibly tattooed by savages. This contrast—the ladylike demeanor of the women as against the story of their horrific encounter with natives (with its explicit sexual overtones)—was an integral part in selling these women to the customers. The stories on the pitch cards also emphasized their chastity, femininity, and vulnerability, and popular accounts of the performers accentuated the refined nature of their tattoos (such as the patriotic and religious tattoos worn by one attraction, Artoria Gibbons) and outside interests. These women, then, were feminine, classy "ladies" even though they wore tattoos.

For many women, being a tattooed lady was the only way for them to have an independent career. Bobby Libarry, for instance, was tattooed in 1902 by her husband, Andy, as a way to earn a living. Betty Broadbent was also tattooed in order to achieve financial independence, and she was one of the last working tattooed ladies, retiring from the Clyde Beatty Circus in 1967.

As the sideshow declined toward mid-century, tattooed ladies, like tattooed men, were old hat, and the salaries paid to tattooed attractions were becoming quite low. In fact, some circus and dime museums made the exhibits pay for the right to be in the show, their income deriving solely from the sale of pictures and from the fees from tattooing patrons. The last really successful tattooed attraction was the **Great Omi**, who was tattooed by George Burchett in the 1920s and exhibited himself in Europe and the United States in the 1930s and 1940s.

As competition increased, tattooed livestock and tattooed pets, tattooed dwarfs, tattooed fat ladies, and tattooed sword swallowers developed, and there was even a tattooed half man. The Frasers, for example, were a tattooed family who also

James O'Connell and George Keenan being forcibly tattooed, according to O'Connell's story, on the island of Pohnpei. Engraving by Henry Howe, 1865. Courtesy of Library of Congress Prints and Photographs Division, Washington, DC, No. LC-USZ62-82975.

worked as knife throwers during the 1919 Rice-Dorman Show. Madame Hall and Dainty Dotty were both tattooed fat ladies, and Dotty, at 600 pounds, was probably the largest female tattooist.

But the days of the freak show were numbered, and by the 1930s had largely died out. Today, there are a handful of modern freak shows with tattooed attractions such as Tattoo Mike, Jim Rose, and Enigma.

See also: Broadbent, Betty; Freak Shows; Freaks; The Great Omi; Tattooed Natives; Wagner, Charlie

Further Reading: Beard, Steve. "The Tattooed Lady: A Mythology." In Chris Wroblewski, *Tattooed Women*. New York: Carol Publishing Group, 1992; Bogdan, Robert. *Freak Show*. Chicago: University of Chicago Press, 1988; Burchett, George, and Peter Leighton. *Memoirs of a Tattooist*. London: Oldbourne Book Company, 1958; DeMello, Margo. *Bodies of Inscription: A Cultural History of the Modern Tattoo Community*. Durham, NC: Duke University Press, 2000. Mifflin, Margot. *Bodies of Subversion: A Secret History of Women and Tattoos*. New York: Juno Books, 1997; Oetterman, Stephan. "On Display: Tattooed Entertainers in America and Germany." In Jane Caplan, ed., *Written on the Body: The Tattoo in European and American History*. London: Reaktion Books, 2000; St. Clair, Leonard, and Alan Govenar. *Stoney Knows How: Life as a Tattoo Artist*. Lexington: University of Kentucky Press, 1981; White, Joanna. "Marks of Transgression: The Tattooing of Europeans in the Pacific Islands." In Bronwen Douglas, Nicholas Thomas, and Anna Cole, eds., *Tattoo: Bodies, Art and Exchange in the Pacific and the West*. Durham, NC: Duke University Press, 2005.

TATTOOED NATIVES

Long before European and American tattooed attractions became popular, European sailors and explorers had been bringing back native peoples to display in pubs as well as part of traveling displays. The purchase and display of native peoples in Europe had been going on since at least the early sixteenth century. Later, native peoples were shipped to America and displayed in dime museums, circuses, carnivals, and at the World's Fairs.

One of the first native people to be exhibited in London was a tattooed woman who Martin Frobisher brought back from the Pacific Northwest in 1578. Earlier, a family of tattooed people from the same region were displayed in France and Germany, possibly as early as 1560.

While tattoos and other forms of body modification have stood, since the earliest encounters with Polynesians as a hallmark of the primitive, the display of tattooed "natives" helped to solidify these notions of the primitive Other. This was particularly true within the context of the World's Fairs, where native exhibits were contrasted with the highest achievements of Western society to both accentuate the primitiveness of the natives and to emphasize the civilization of the Western world. While these displays were both reflective of, and contributed to, the colonial ideology, they were also influential in constructing a narrative about tattooed people as savages, a narrative that is later turned on its side when *white* tattooed people start to display themselves in sideshows.

Through the eighteenth and nineteenth centuries, the display of tattooed natives was a huge moneymaker for European businessmen. One of the first recorded tattooed native people was Prince Jeoly (or Giolo), originally from the Island of Meangis, just south of the Philippines. "The Painted Prince," as he came to be known, was acquired by ship's officer named Mr. Moody in 1691, and was eventually sold to the French explorer, William Dampier, who immediately sold him again to businessmen who exhibited him as a single attraction in pubs, and other public places. Jeoly's owners displayed and promoted him to both commoners as well as European elites, and had two full-length portraits engraved of him. Jeoly did not want to work as an attraction, but his owners told him that he would be paid handsomely and later returned to his home. Unfortunately, he died in England of smallpox not long after his arrival, disappointing his owners who had hoped to become rich.

Captain Cook's first and second expeditions to the South Seas in 1769 and 1774 brought back two tattooed Tahitians, Omai and Tupaia, who served as interpreters and guides for Cook. Later, Omai was, like Jeoly before him, seen to have financial potential as a human oddity, and he was ultimately put on public display by Joseph Banks, a member of Cook's crew. (Banks even compared keeping the exotic Omai to the keeping of lions and tigers by other travelers.) Omai was eventually returned to Tahiti on Cook's third voyage, bearing European gifts.

In the United States, the tradition of displaying tattooed natives did not begin until much later, and started with the display of "native villages." In 1876, with the Centennial Exhibition in Philadelphia, native people were for the first time exhibited in the United States. At this and other fairs, fairgoers could observe Alaskan, Hawaiian, or Samoan families in an "authentic" cultural environment, as well as peoples not within the American colonial system like the Japanese. Although they weren't displayed as a sideshow at this time, native villages paved the way for human oddities like tattooed people and freaks to be shown at World's Fairs, and later, on carnival midways. In 1893, the Colombian Exposition in Chicago had the first midway with exotic peoples from all over the colonized world on display, and by 1901, the first full **freak show** had arrived at the World's Fair in Buffalo at the Pan American Exposition.

The World Fair, with its twin poles of technology and primitivism, civilization and savagery, represented progress to the Western world. The natives displayed at these fairs, whether tattooed or not, were shown engaged in authentic— authenticated by anthropologists who participated in the construction of the other for public consumption—primitive activities which by their very nature could be contrasted with the more edifying activities of the civilized: architecture, imperialism, technology, science. They served to not only entertain fairgoers, but also to highlight the enormous progress achieved by the West through technological advancements and world conquest, and thus legitimate the imperialist agenda.

Tattooed native people were displayed in Europe and North America from the seventeenth century to the twentieth century. In the early twentieth century, as the practice of displaying what were essentially slaves fell out of favor, they began to be displaced by tattooed Westerners, who provided a different form of entertainment. But whether tattooed native or tattooed Westerner, both types of exhibits relied on the continuing association between tattooing and savagery in order to sell tickets.

See also: Freak Shows; Freaks; Tattooed Attractions

Further Reading: Allen, Tricia. "European Explorers and Marquesan Tattooing: The Wildest Island Style." *TattooTime* 5 (1991): 86–101; Bogdan, Robert. *Freak Show*. Chicago: University of Chicago Press, 1988; DeMello, Margo. *Bodies of Inscription: A Cultural History of the Modern Tattoo Community*. Durham, NC: Duke University Press, 2000; Oetterman, Stephan. "On Display: Tattooed Entertainers in America and Germany." In Jane Caplan, ed., *Written on the Body: The Tattoo in European and American History*. London: Reaktion Books, 2000.

TATTOOING

Tattooing refers to the insertion of pigment into the skin with needles, bone, knives, or other implements, in order to create a decorative design. Tattooing is a permanent form of body modification, and has been found on every continent of the world as well as among most island populations.

The earliest evidence for tattooing dates back to the Neolithic, mummies and other artificats dating from 6,000 BCE in Europe and 4,000 BCE in **Egypt**. Tattooing probably spread from the Middle East to the Pacific Islands, and later the Americas, by way of **India, China,** and **Japan**. By 1,000 BCE it was found virtually everywhere.

The word "tattoo" was brought to Europe by European sailors who encountered the practice of tattooing among Tahitians, Hawaiians, and Samoans. The Tahitian word *tatau*, meaning to mark or strike twice, was translated into the modern word for tattoo. Prior to that time, tattooing in Europe and America was known as pricking, because the tattoo was inserted by pricking a needle dipped in ink into the skin. Today, tattoos in most of the world are created through the use of electric tattoo machines.

Like many other forms of what might be called folk art, tattoos usually serve both aesthetic and functional purposes. They may be beautiful as designs in and of themselves, but they can also express a multitude of meanings about the wearer and his or her place within the social group. Whether used in an overt punitive fashion (as in the tattooing of slaves or prisoners) or to mark and communicate clan or cult membership, religious or tribal affiliation, social status, or marital position, tattoos have historically been a social sign. They serve as either a mark of inclusion or a mark of exclusion. They have long been one of the simplest ways of establishing humans as social beings—or, to use the language of French anthropologist Claude Levi-Strauss, transforming them from "raw" animals, into "cooked" cultural beings. In fact, tattooing is one of the most persistent and universal forms of body art.

> I don't think it's something great to be a tattooer.
>
> LEONARD "STONEY" ST. CLAIR,
> tattooist

Tattoos derive their communicative power from more than a simple sign-to-meaning correspondence: they also communicate through color, style, manner of execution, and location on the body. Traditionally inscribed on easily viewable parts of the body, tattoos were designed to be "read" by others. Today, however—at least in Western parts of the world such as the United States—tattoos have increasingly moved from the functional to the artistic, from the literal to the abstract, losing much of their traditional communicative power in the process. Tattoos for many middle-class North Americans have become a way to express personal rather than collective identity, as well as a more "sophisticated" artistic sensibility. For many, tattoos are now more about private statement than public sign, and these individuals, especially women, tend to favor smaller tattoos in private spots.

In traditional societies, tattoos were deeply embedded in social institutions, and were decorative and also functioned to communicate social status, rank, religious devotion or affiliation, marital status, and other social markers to the world at large. Often received during **rites of passage**, tattoos, like other forms of body modification, were and are critical features of society. In modern societies, too, tattoos are often used as a social marker, by marginalized members of society such as soldiers and sailors, **gang members** as well as fraternity members who use the tattoo as a sign of group affiliation.

In state-level societies like the **Greco-Roman world**, however, tattoos were often involuntary, and were used to mark slaves, prisoners, and sometimes soldiers, a tradition that continued into the twentieth century with the Nazi practice of tattooing Jews and other prisoners at **Auschwitz** with identifying numbers. Today, prisoners in European, Russian, and American prisons tattoo themselves, marking their own stigmatized status on their bodies as well as claiming ownership of those bodies.

While tattooing was a central aspect of many societies, in the West, thanks to the tradition of using tattoos to mark criminality or low status, tattooing has been stigmatized, used primarily by low-status groups but scorned by the middle and upper classes. Today, tattooing is experiencing a renaissance, as tattoo artists are drawn increasingly from the middle class (and come as well from fine art backgrounds), tattoo imagery has become increasingly sophisticated, and more and more middle-class people are now wearing tattoos. In addition, the meanings behind tattoos have changed as new wearers borrow not only designs and practices from non-Western cultures, but meaning systems as well, making modern tattooing truly a cultural pastiche. The stigma of tattoos as being a mark of the "class other" has begun to give way toward the appreciation of tattoos as the mark of the "ethnic other."

See also: Tattoo Technology

Further Reading: Atkinson, Michael. *Tattooed: The Sociogenesis of a Body Art*. Toronto: University of Toronto Press, 2003; DeMello, Margo. *Bodies of Inscription: A Cultural History of the Modern Tattoo Community*. Durham, NC: Duke University Press, 2000; Gell, Alfred. *Wrapping in Images: Tattooing in Polynesia*. Oxford: Oxford University Press, 1993; Hambly, H. D. *The History of Tattooing and Its Significance*. London: H. F. & G. Witherby, 1925; Sanders, Clinton. *Customizing the Body: The Art and Culture of Tattooing*. Philadelphia, PA: Temple University Press, 1989. In Jane Caplan, ed., *Written on the Body: The Tattoo in European and American History*. Princeton, NJ: Princeton University Press, 2000; Rubin, Arnold ed., *Marks of Civilization: Artistic Transformations of the Human Body*. Los Angeles: Museum of Cultural History, UCLA, 1988; Sullivan, Nikki. *Tattooed Bodies: Subjectivity, Textuality, Ethics, and Pleasure*. Westport, CT: Praeger, 2001.

TATTOO MAGAZINES

Since the mid-1980s when the tattoo magazine industry took off, tattoo magazines have been, next to the Internet, the most important location for members of the **tattoo community** to connect with each other, and for the general public and those interested in getting a tattoo to see what's available and what is going on in the world of **tattooing**.

Tattoo magazines include feature articles on tattooists and tattoo studios around the country or around the world, photo spreads of tattoos, reports on tattoo conventions, reviews of new books, videos, and products, **flash**, letters to the editor, historical articles, and more. The tattoo magazine caters primarily to tattooed people and creates for its readers a sense of *communitas* through its ability to make tattooed readers feel that they are both different from the mainstream society and a part of something larger than themselves. Particularly in the magazines' editorials and in their letters to the editor sections, this feeling that tattooed people form a community of brothers and sisters is demonstrated.

Tattoo magazines also contribute to and help to define the current public understanding of tattooing. This occurs through the magazines' editorial decisions about which artists or fans to showcase, whose letters to print, and what types of advertisements to run. Also, tattoo magazines debate with each other, illustrating and defining, the class-based borders within the community.

Editorial content notwithstanding, today's tattoo magazines (especially since the demise of **TattooTime**) are primarily picture books, and serve as a sort of source-book of design ideas for individuals planning their first (or next) tattoo. Prior to the rise of tattoo magazines, tattoo customers picked out a tattoo at a tattoo shop, from the flash on the tattooist's walls. Nowadays, tattoo magazines have become so prolific that many people pick their designs straight from tattoos represented in these magazines, and bring the magazines with them to tattoo shops for the artists to copy. This has led to a tremendous increase in the speed in which new designs are disseminated, both in the United States as well as globally, and it has led, as well, to a change in the way tattoos are chosen and executed. Especially today, as tattoos are moving increasingly toward custom-only work and away from flash, the idea of a "custom" tattoo taken from a magazine photo has certainly corrupted the idea of "custom" which once meant created and designed by one artist for a particular customer.

This commodification has led to tattoos becoming, ironically, more formalized, in that there are less choices and more orthodoxy in tattoo design, as individuals choose their tattoos from magazines (and off the Internet). This is ironic because while tattooists and their customers are promoting more customized work, tattoo magazines allow a reader to replicate *another person's* customized tattoo on their own body. Tattoo magazines claim that they exist to promote creativity, but in fact they play a part in stifling it, as tattoo magazines become, in essence, the new flash.

Tattoo, published since 1988, is one of the two leading magazines that derives from the biker world. It is published by Paisano Publications, the same company that publishes *Easyriders* magazine (the world's leading Harley Davidson magazine) as well as *Biker* and *In The Wind*. Like its parent magazine, *Tattoo* can only be purchased by adults, due to the photos of nude women. The features include coverage of conventions, fans or collectors, tattooists or tattoo shops, a section for reader's flash, and "In the Skin," which features black and white photos of tattoos sent in by readers. Along with the ubiquitous tattoo studios ads, it includes advertisements for tattoo equipment suppliers as well as cheap porn videos. *Tattoo* began as a biker magazine with a fairly limited readership but has now become much more mainstream, reaching out to nonbiker readers. In recent years, the quantity of nude female photos has been reduced, and the editors now try to include artists' credits with all of their photos in response to criticism from the highbrow magazines and their readers.

The other main biker magazine, *Tattoo Revue*, has been in print since 1990, and is published by Outlaw Biker Enterprises, which publishes the prominent *Outlaw Biker* magazine. It is a more upscale biker-oriented tattoo magazine, and it includes features on artists, interviews, articles on shops and conventions, materials from and about prison tattooing, and "Skin Stories," a newsprint feature that lets fans tell about their tattoos. Like *Tattoo, Tattoo Revue* also carries ads for porn videos and tattoo equipment ads.

Tattoo and *Tattoo Revue* and other biker-style magazines generally devote a section to photos of tattoos sent in by readers (sometimes with artist credit, sometimes without). Most include a feature on "fans," that is, nonartists with tattoos. Ads are both for tattoo machines and other tattoo-related products, as well as nontattoo ads, such as for sex services. Many of these magazines are criticized for including photos of attractive nude or nearly nude women, regardless of the number or quality of their tattoos.

Two newer magazines, *Skin and Ink* and *Tattoo Savage*, now compete for control of the tattoo magazine market. *Skin and Ink* was started in 1993 and is published by Larry Flynt of *Hustler* magazine fame. While *Skin and Ink* is not a biker magazine, it has a biker-style format in terms of its features (convention coverage, studio coverage, fans, and "Inked," a section devoted to photos of tattoos), tattoo supply advertisements, and pseudo-academic articles. On the other hand, the magazine reflects the movement, also seen in the biker magazines, toward more contemporary aesthetics and values, and aims at an audience who considers tattoos to be fine art.

Tattoo Savage, from Paisano Publications (publisher of *Easyriders*) started in 1994, and aims at a slightly different audience than the traditional biker publications. *Tattoo Savage* includes photographs and articles on piercing and other forms of body modification, S/M, alternative lifestyles, "fine art," "tattoo magic," as well as the usual collector and shop showcases. Like the biker magazines, it includes female nudity (like *Easyriders* and *Tattoo*, it can only be purchased by adults), flash sent in by readers, advertising for tattoo suppliers, and motorcycle paraphernalia ads. There are a number of other biker tattoo magazines with a much more narrow editorial focus, such as *Tattoo Flash*, *Tattoos for Men*, *Tattoos for Women*, and *Skin Art*. All of these magazines are dedicated to showcasing photos of tattoos, many sent in by readers, with little or no editorial content, and are primarily aimed at people who are looking for design inspiration for tattoos.

Among the tattoo magazines that attempted to move beyond the biker audience and aesthetic were *Tattoo Advocate* and *TattooTime*, both published by middle-class, professionally trained tattoo artists, and both now out of print. Other newer tattoo magazines include *International Tattoo Art*, which has always aimed at a middle-class audience. Other tattoo magazines aimed at the middle class, but which are no longer published, include *Tattoo World Quarterly* and *Tattoo Ink*.

TattooTime, published on an irregular basis from 1982 to 1993, was the first of the middle-class tattoo magazines to appear, and was aimed specifically at an educated audience. The editor and publisher, **Don Ed Hardy**, is a fine art tattooist with a Bachelors of Fine Art degree from the San Francisco Art Institute. *TattooTime* was not a "fan magazine" and included no ads, reader photos, flash (except in a historical content), letters to the editor or fan interviews. The emphasis in *TattooTime* was on the art, history, and cross-cultural perspectives of tattooing. Because of its in-depth pieces on the history of tattooing and the practices of tattooing around the world, *TattooTime* inadvertently kicked off the "tribal" tattoo craze which we still see today, as well as the practice of American and European customers drawing inspiration from non-Western tattoo styles and religious and cultural discourses.

The second highbrow tattoo magazine was *Tattoo Advocate*. This was a glossy magazine produced between 1988 and 1990 by Shotsie Gorman, a New Jersey tattoo artist. *Tattoo Advocate* promoted fine art tattoos and actively disparaged other, less sophisticated forms of tattoo, as well as the various biker magazines that display them. The language used in *Tattoo Advocate* had a strong New Age tone, and indeed, the magazine reads like a Bible for people seeking spiritual solace through tattoos. The articles focus on Buddhism, the occult, and tattoos from exotic cultures (i.e., those ostensibly more "spiritual" than our own) such as ancient Egypt. Some articles claim a healing potential for tattoos. Aside from the spiritual and healing realms, though, the range of themes in *Tattoo Advocate* was vast. There were articles on anthropology, on comic book art, on the forensic use of tattoos for identification—even one on Malcolm X, accompanied by a photorealistic tattoo portrait of him. *Tattoo Advocate* differed from other tattoo publications in that the editor openly discussed his progressive political and social beliefs, even though his were not the views of most members of the tattoo community. Gorman's liberal values were reflected in the editorials as well as in advertisements against nuclear testing and factory farming, and in support of animal rights.

International Tattoo Art (ITA) was the next highbrow tattoo magazine to appear; it was first released in 1992. Like *Tattoo Advocate*, ITA presents a picture of tattooing much different from the traditional image. For the editors of *ITA*, tattoos are spiritual, artistic, and deeply meaningful. *ITA* also represents itself as a source of scholarly material on tattooing. Unlike some of the other magazines, *International Tattoo Art* has a strongly international feel, although it is published in the United States.

These middle-class magazines differ from the original tattoo magazines, produced for bikers, in a number of important ways. There tends to be a heavy reliance on references to the fine arts (painting, drawing, sculpture, photography, as well as literature and poetry); to academic disciplines (specifically anthropology, philosophy, art history, and medicine); and to mainstream journalism. Many of these magazines include fiction, reviews of books and videos. Virtually all include "academic" articles—either written by scholars with known interests in tattooing or by nonscholars with an academic perspective. They include high-quality photos of "fine art" tattoos, and the names of the tattoo artists are listed. In fact, the policy of crediting artists represents a huge leap from the days when tattooing was seen as a folk art or trade, to today when tattooists are "artists" who claim personal authorship over their work. In another distinctive policy, the early middle-class tattoo magazines did not accept advertising from tattoo suppliers, because providing ads for suppliers which supply machines to people with no training has been long discouraged by the professional tattoo community (although this is no longer the case with current magazines).

Finally, there is a new magazine called *Tattoo Artist Magazine*, which is only available to tattooists. *Tattoo Artist Magazine* is aimed at a middle-class audience and eschews the normal convention reports, supplier ads, and nude photos found in some of the other magazines. *Tattoo Artist Magazine* includes the usual feature stories on artists and studios, but also includes technical articles, product reviews, stories on other types of art being produced by tattooists, flash, and articles on business concerns such as taxes or sanitation. Also in 2006, a new magazine hit the stands called *Tattoo Society Magazine*. Created by a tattoo artist, it too aims at a middle-class audience and includes features on fine artists, body modification practices, and elite tattooists and their work.

See also: Biker Tattooing; Hardy, Don Ed; Tattoo Community

Further Reading: DeMello, Margo. *Bodies of Inscription: A Cultural History of the Modern Tattoo Community*. Durham, NC: Duke University Press, 2000.

TATTOO REALITY SHOWS

In 2005, two new reality television shows were introduced which focus on **tattooing**; "Inked," which runs on the Arts & Entertainment Network, and "Miami Ink," which is shown on The Learning Channel.

"Inked" is set at the Hart & Huntington Tattoo Company inside the Palms Hotel and Casino (in fact, this is the first tattoo studio ever opened in a casino). Hart & Huntington was founded by motocross rider (and husband of rock star Pink) Carey Hart, and its clients include rock stars, celebrities, locals, and tourists. The show follows the workdays of the artists and the dramas created at the studio.

"Miami Ink" is filled at the Miami Ink tattoo studio, and, like "Inked," focuses on the relationships between the artists and the customers at this busy Miami studio, as well as some of the motivations of the customers for getting a tattoo.

Both shows are standard workplace reality series, and include dramatic stories about customers, the artists, as well as the shops' apprentices. Miami Ink also emphasizes the craft of tattooing and demonstrates how the process works.

See also: Tattooing

TATTOO REMOVAL

Tattoo removal refers to the process by which permanent tattoos are removed from the skin. People choose to have their tattoos removed for a variety of reasons, although the most common is regret. Many people got a tattoo without putting enough thought into it, or got a poorly thought-out design or a (now-ex) partner's name on their bodies. Other people feel that their lives have changed since they got their tattoo, and no longer want a reminder of their previous life or they feel that their tattoos will impede them in their new career or relationship. Former **gang members** and ex-convicts will often have their tattoos removed because the tattoo permanently marks their criminal past onto their bodies. Ironically, many tattooists now offer tattoo removal services to their customers who no longer want their old tattoos.

Tattoos are permanent because the ink is inserted into the secondary layer of skin just below the epidermis. Removing a tattoo involves getting beneath the epidermis to where the ink lies.

In the old days, some people removed their tattoos by rubbing the tattoo with salt or other abrasive substances, or by attempting to slice or burn the tattoo off. While these methods can be performed at home, they were (and are) painful and tend to leave horrible scars in place of the tattoos. Additionally, early in the twentieth century one could purchase "tattoo removers" which were made out of acid, and removed the tattoo as well as much of the skin. Tattooist and tattoo supplier **Milton Zeis** marketed a salve that he claimed removed large tattoos with very little scar tissue. This salve was tattooed directly over the tattoo.

There are several methods for tattoo removal which are in use today. In most cases, however, some scarring will occur, or at least a faint outline of the tattoo will remain. Larger and darker tattoos are more difficult to remove and some people's skin type will also affect the success of the procedure. In addition, how the tattoo was inserted, and how long it has been in the skin, will play a role in the ease of removal.

> I tell people every day that if this [tattoo] machine had an eraser, I'd be a millionaire.
>
> LEONARD "STONEY" ST. CLAIR, tattooist

One of the oldest methods of tattoo removal is to remove the tattoo via excision, or slicing off the part of the skin that contains the tattoo. While this has been practiced by desperate tattooed people probably for thousands of years, today it is performed by a surgeon with a local anesthetic applied, and the open wound is sutured together. A skin graft taken from another area of the body may also be used when the tattoo is very large.

Salabrasion refers to the use of salt, sandpaper, or other abrasive substances or materials to scrape off the tattoo. Like excision, people have used abrasian to remove tattoos for as long as tattoos have existed, but today, this can be done in a doctor's office with anesthesia. Dermabrasian is a similar process in which the tattooed skin is frozen and the skin is then sanded down to remove the tattoo.

Some companies also market tattoo removal creams, such as Inkbusters, TatB-Gone, or Wrecking Balm, which use skin lighteners and the ingredients used in chemical skin peels, but they are not known to be very effective.

Today, the most popular, albeit expensive, method of tattoo removal is laser surgery, performed by a doctor. Laser tattoo removal involves using light to break up the tattoo pigment. The process is somewhat painful and doctors will offer numbing cream to help dull the pain. The process takes several weeks of repeated treatments in order to completely or mostly remove the tattoo, although the length of time will differ based on the color and size of the design.

Some physicians, working with counseling or youth groups, offer tattoo removal services for free to ex-cons and ex-gang members who want to remove the stigma of their previous associations.

See also: Zeis, Milton

Further Reading: Zeis, Milton. *Tattooing the World Over*, Vol. 1. New York: Milton Zeis, 1947.

TATTOO SHOWS

Tattoo conventions are an important part of the **tattoo community**, in that they allow tattooists to solicit new customers, suppliers, and other vendors to advertise their wares, and tattoo "fans" to purchase books, magazines, and t-shirts, admire the artwork, or even get tattooed. But perhaps more importantly, tattoo conventions serve to allow tattooed people to come together a few times a year and enact important rituals of community.

The first major tattoo convention was held in 1979 in Denver, and was organized by the **National Tattoo Association**, who for years held the only, and later the major, tattoo conventions in the world. (There was also an independent show in Houston in 1976 organized by tattooist Dave Yurkew. There were previous tattoo parties as well, such as one in Hamburg, Germany in 1956, the Annual Bristol Tattoo Club Party hosted by Les Skuse, and get-togethers hosted by Milt Zeis in the 1940s. None of these, however, were conventions as defined above.) Today, tattoo shows are big business, and a number of conventions compete for biggest tattoo show or body art show in the world. During any given year in the United States, there are approximately three-dozen large conventions, and perhaps an additional dozen or so local shows (in addition to shows all around the world). These shows are held at convention centers and hotels and typically run for anywhere from two days to a week. There are also smaller, more exclusive shows, which are usually held for a few hours at a bar or nightclub. The tattoo show (with the exception of smaller, more focused shows like those exhibiting photos of tattoo art or displaying some aspect of tattoo history) has a three-fold structure: it is a commercial event where tattooists and vendors of tattoo-related materials rent booths and sell their products or advertise their services; there is a contest where people can enter their tattoos (or tattooists can enter their designs) to be voted on by the general audience or by a panel of judges; and it is a social event, where individuals show off their tattoos and meet other people with the same interests. Sometimes there are additional events, such as **piercing** demonstrations, dancing or live music, and some shows feature seminars on topics such as the history of American tattooing, Marquesan tattooing, Chicano script lettering, portrait drawing, and communicable diseases.

Tattoo conventions, in their commercial aspects, are similar to other kinds of trade shows held at hotels and convention centers across the country. Vendors rent booths to sell t-shirts, flash, tattoo-related items, and to tattoo. The sponsoring organization regulates activities on the floor of their conventions in that **tattooing** hours are limited and some shows don't allow tattoo equipment to be sold. Most shows cost anywhere from $10 to $30 to attend per day, and booths typically cost around $500 and up to rent.

There are basically two groups of fans who attend tattoo conventions. The first are those whose interest in tattooing is strong enough that they plan their vacations in order to travel to tattoo events. They have registered for the show in advance, have bought a ticket for the length of the show (up to a week), and often have made an appointment ahead of time to get tattooed by an artist outside of their own area. Next, there is the general public, that is, those who have an interest in tattooing but did not register in advance, usually only attend for a day, and live in the vicinity of the convention site. Within this division, however, there is a great deal of variation. Some shows are small shows which only attract local participants, and some of these shows, due to the geographic location and demographics of the area, primarily attract bikers, the middle-class elite, or the younger, avant garde members.

Because there are now so many tattoo shows to choose from, no tattooist attends every convention, even in the United States. Tattooists today will choose the shows they attend based on geographic area (whether the show is held in the artist's area or someplace the artist wants to visit), the organization or artist hosting the show, and the type of audience the show is aimed at.

Almost every tattoo convention or show includes a contest. The typical contest includes categories for best portrait, Asian, traditional, tribal, unique, cover-up, color, black and grey, leg, sleeve, back, and best tattooed male or tattooed female. Contestants must fill out an entry form for each tattoo (or region of the body) that they want to enter, which includes their name, the name of the tattooist, and a description of the tattoo. While the tattoo contest is geared toward celebrating the best tattoos, often the women with the best bodies and the individuals whose tattoos were created by the most elite artists take the best prizes.

The atmosphere of most tattoo conventions (even those that advertise that they are family-friendly events) is carnivalesque. Anything goes and conventional social rules are frowned upon. Men and women disrobe in public, showing off not only their tattoos but their **body piercings**, thongs, and pubic hair. They oil each other's bodies, and packs of men with cameras (both still and video) follow attractive women around the convention floor. Men hoot at the women parading on stage, and women shout encouragement to men as they undress.

The tattoo convention is both radical and conservative however, in that it challenges and subverts middle-class notions of propriety and taste, through its radical display of the grotesque body, yet it also reinforces mainstream society's class-based, and gender-based, divisions. Working-class tattooists from rural areas find their artistic contributions unwelcome in the face of the increasingly sophisticated artwork created by middle-class, fine art tattooists from the big cities.

And while it is thought by many that the presence of heavily tattooed women at the conventions (as elsewhere) disrupts conventional notions of the gendered body, in fact these women must continue to play by the same patriarchal rules in existence elsewhere in society. The women who enter their bodies in the tattoo contests are being judged as much for their physical appearance as for their tattoos, and the women who garner the most attention from photographers at the shows are generally the most attractive and/or have the most skin showing through their sexy outfits. It could be argued that, contrary to empowering women, tattoos, and the display of women's tattoos at the convention, contribute to women's further objectification. Just as many feminist scholars argue that fashion enslaves women, in the same way tattoos put the (female) body on display. Tattooed women—particularly those with extensive tattoos—cannot avoid being the object of voyeuristic looking. And while both male and female bodies are on display at the tattoo convention, and even though the objective of these events is to show off tattoos to an audience that appreciates them, it often looks like an excuse for men to gaze at, and photograph, women's scantily clad bodies.

For many individuals, and certainly for groups like the National Tattoo Association, tattoo conventions embody a spirit of fellowship and goodwill. For artists and fans who have been around for a number of years, it's an opportunity to see old friends. For others still, it's a commercial enterprise and an opportunity for vendors to sell their merchandise (some of which does not even relate to tattooing).

See also: Tattoo Community

Further Reading: DeMello, Margo. *Bodies of Inscription: A Cultural History of the Modern Tattoo Community*. Durham, NC: Duke University Press, 2000.

TATTOO TECHNOLOGY

Prior to the development of the electric tattoo machine at the end of the nineteenth century, tattoos around the world were created in much the same way: the skin is cut and pigment is inserted into the wound. In some cultures, tattoos were created in a similar fashion to **scarification**, where the design is cut into the skin with a knife or other sharp implement, and the wound is then rubbed with pigment created from ash or other substances.

More commonly, tattoo tools or kits are created via wrapping needles, teeth, pins, sharpened bones or sticks, or other needle-like implements together, and attaching the bundle of needles to a piece of wood which can be handled. Sometimes the resulting tool is then dipped into pigment and pushed into the skin, and sometimes, after dipping it into the ink, it is tapped into the skin with a mallet. Generally, the artist has different-sized with a different number of needles, or needles of different diameters, to create different designs. Sometimes the tattoo artist draws or transfers a design to the skin prior to the actual tattoo; other times, the artist creates the finished tattoo freestyle.

Pigments are traditionally created from mixing charcoal or ash with water. In the early days of commercial tattooing in the West, tattooists purchased their colors from pigment manufacturers and used word of mouth between tattooists to find out which inks were safe and permanent. Initially, black was the major color used, supplemented by red, green, brown, and yellow, but as the years went by and technology improved, tattooists experimented with pigments and brought in a far wider variety of hues that are used today. Today, most pigments are derived from iron, titanium, carbon, and other inorganic compounds, and are purchased from tattoo supply companies.

In 1891, a New York City tattooist named "Professor" Samuel O'Reilly patented the first electric tattoo machine, based on the perforating pen invented by Thomas Edison. He, like all other American tattooists, had been hand-pricking his tattoos but the method is slow-going and painful. The demand for more elaborate tattoos led O'Reilly to seek a faster method. He found a device called the "Electric Pen," invented by Thomas Edison in 1876, which was part of a document duplication system created to make painting and embroidery patterns. The handheld electric pen used a high-speed reciprocating motor, powered by a battery, to drive a single needle. It did not use any ink, but merely perforated holes in a master form.

The master form then became a stencil, and colored powder or ink would be distributed over the stencil, passing through the holes to transfer the design to the sheet below the stencil. O'Reilly took this invention, added multiple needles and an ink reservoir, and earned a U.S. patent in 1891.

In 1877, Edison received another patent on the electric pen, this time using two electromagnetic coils, with the coils set transversely to the tube assembly. In 1904, New York City tattooist **Charlie Wagner** patented a new tattoo machine, inspired by Edison's second electric pen. This new tattoo machine included an improved tube assembly with an ink chamber, an on and off switch, stroke adjustment, and a pin-vice-type needle bar. Finally, in 1929 tattooist Percy Waters of Detroit received a patent on the design that most people think of when they think of a tattooing machine. Waters' machine was the standard two-coil electromagnetic style, but the coils were set in line with the frame. Other modifications included fingertip on and off switch, spark shield, and a needle set up for cutting plastic stencils.

Since the early twentieth century, other tattoo machines have been patented, and tattooists around the world continue to tinker with their machines, personalizing them to their tastes and styles.

Today, the electric tattoo machine is the primary way that people tattoo the world over. The modern machine inserts ink into the skin via a group of needles that are soldered onto a bar, which is attached to a motor. Like a sewing machine, the machine drives the needles in and out of the skin. There are two kinds of tattoo machine: the liner, which has fewer needles (sometimes only one), and is used to create the outline for the design, and the shader, with a larger number of needles, used to shade and color the design. Machines are not directly plugged into the wall but are plugged into a transformer to cut the voltage down.

The process for getting a tattoo with a tattoo machine goes something like this. Once the client chooses a design, the tattooist must make a stencil for it. Typically, the tattooist will trace the image onto rice paper with a special pencil, and transfer the image to the body with soap, or often deodorant stick. Earlier in the century, when most tattoo designs were picked off of **flash** on the tattooists' wall, a tattooist would have permanent stencils, drawn with an exacto-knife on acetate, which is used to transfer the drawing to the body.

Once the design is on the body, the tattooist first uses a liner to outline the design (usually in black), and then switches to a shader to color the design in. Liner or shader, all tattoo machines consist of anywhere from one to twelve (or more) needles soldered to a needle bar; the motor causes the needle bar to vibrate up and down within a tube which is connected to the motor. The tattooist dips the tip of the machine into a small cup into which he or she has poured a small amount of ink. As the needles emerge from the tube, the machine works like a sewing machine, injecting small doses of pigment into the skin.

Further Reading: Eldridge, Chuck. "Tattoo Machine Patents and Related Ones." Berkeley, CA: *Tattoo Archive* (Winter 1991): 20–23; Hardy, Don Ed. "Tattooing as a Medium." In Don Ed Hardy, ed., *Pierced Hearts and True Love: A Century of Drawings for Tattoos.* Honolulu, HI: Hardy Marks Publications, 1995; McCabe, Michael. "Coney Island Tattoo: The Growth of Inclusive Culture in the Age of the Machine." In Don Ed Hardy, ed., *Pierced*

Hearts and True Love: A Century of Drawings for Tattoos. Honolulu, HI: Hardy Marks Publications, 1995.

TATTOOTIME

TattooTime was an extremely influential **tattoo magazine**, published from 1982 to 1993. Unlike the tattoo magazines before it, and many since then, *TattooTime* was aimed at an educated, middle-class audience. The editor and publisher, **Don Ed Hardy**, was a fine art tattooist with a fine arts degree from the San Francisco Art Institute, and published *TattooTime* for readers who took tattooing very seriously. The production quality of the magazine was extremely high, with high quality, professional photos, serious and scholarly articles, and no advertisements, letters to the editor, or fan interviews. The emphasis in *TattooTime* was on the art, history, and cross-cultural perspectives of **tattooing**.

TattooTime was a major contribution to the development of a middle-class interest in tattooing since the 1980s. The price of a single issue of *TattooTime*—$20—naturally narrowed its readership to those of an upscale socioeconomic status, and the production values, artists featured, and educational aspects clearly illustrate its middle-class appeal.

But beyond its highbrow aesthetic, *TattooTime* contributed to a middle-class discourse around tattooing in another respect: *TattooTime* was the first magazine to treat tattooing from a cross-cultural perspective, and thus it was the first to suggest that readers use non-Western images in their tattoos. Through its coverage of art and culture from **Borneo, Japan,** and **Samoa,** *TattooTime* conveyed—however unintentionally—to its readers that the values and mythologies of these cultures may be appropriated to provide meaning for their own tattoos. The first issue of *TattooTime*, "The New Tribalism," was the first publication to focus on a "new" type of tattooing which a few people were calling **tribalism**. Although *TattooTime* initially was not widely circulated, this issue became a point of convergence for many members of the new community. That single issue influenced a tremendous number of people to go out and create or receive "tribal" tattoos, and set the stage for the entire "tribalism" movement in tattooing. *TattooTime* was also influential in that a number of major tattooists of the 1980s and 1990s got involved in tattooing after seeing an issue of the magazine.

See also: Hardy, Don Ed; Tattoo Magazines; Tribalism

Further Reading: *TattooTime*, Volumes 1–5, Hardy Marks Publications, 1982–1993.

THAILAND

Tattooing has been practiced in Thailand for hundreds, and perhaps, thousands of years. Thailand's tattoo tradition is closely tied to Buddhism, and many designs are religious or magical in origin, worn and tattooed by monks.

In Thailand, tattoos are not traditionally seen as a decorative practice. Because of the long association with Buddhism, many people believe that tattoos can endow the wearer with special powers. Tattoos are sought in order to make the wearer more attractive, to attract love, to make the wearer more powerful, or to protect the wearer from harm. Some young men even believe that their tattoos will make them immortal. In this sense, tattoos are like amulets or other magical charms.

Popular tattoo images include heroes from the Thai epic *Ramayana*, fierce animals like lions, tigers, panthers, and snakes, and magical letters and symbols, as well as poems and spells. These images are surrounded by magical signs and the Pali script. Certain animals imbue the wearer with that animal's characteristics; lions make the wearer dignified and strong; boars fierce and dragons strong and wise. Tigers worn on the chest protect the wearer from injury.

The traditional Thai tattoo tool works like an electric tattoo machine, although it is powered by hand. It consists of a long brass or bamboo tube, with a long needle that runs down the inside, or sometimes is attached to the end of the tube. The tattooist, known as an *arjun*, dips the needle in ink, steads the tool with one hand, and the other hand pushes the needle into the skin, over and over, like a slow sewing machine, producing a series of dots which are turned into the final design. Inks are made from charcoal and other ashy substances mixed with a number of substances designed to give the tattoo its magical power, such as herbs or lizard skin. The tattooist also prays while tattooing in order to activate the tattoo and give it its power. After the tattoo is completed, many men report feeling energized and powerful.

Most Thai women don't wear tattoos, but some women will choose to get invisible, but still powerful, tattoos made with sesame oil rather than ink. Tattooists who tattoo in the traditional style work out of home studios in cities like Bangkok. *Arjun* are not only tattooists but respected community leaders, who offer spiritual protection and advice along with tattoos. Traditionally, also, the *arjun* did not charge for their tattoos, but often asked only for an offering of fruits or flowers.

Thailand is also known for an annual ritual known as *Wai Khru*, held at the Wat Bang Phra Buddhist temple. The temple is known for the magical tattoos that the monks create, and once a year, people wearing tattoos (usually from this temple) return to pay respect to their tattooist, and to also have their tattoos blessed so that the powers can be reactivated. Many participants at the festival become possessed by the spirit of the animal tattooed on their body: men wearing snakes will hiss and crawl while those wearing tigers growl and behave fiercely.

Today, many Thai youth, influenced by Western media and tourists, are interested in getting Western tattoos, rather than traditional Thai tattoos, but since visiting a typical tattoo studio is much more expensive than visiting an arjun, they are out of reach for many poor Thai youth. Still, many people do visit either modern studios or traditional tatttooists and request Western or tribal designs, rather than traditional Thai images.

See also: Magic and the Occult; Tattooing

Further Reading: McCabe, Mike. "Bangkok's Tattoo Arjan." http://tattoos.com/articles/mccabe/arjan/index.html(2006); McCabe, Mike. "Jimmy Wong—Bangkok Past and Present and the Tattoos of Indochina, Part I." http://tattoos.com/articles/mccabe/wong/index.html(2006); McCabe, Mike. "Jimmy Wong—The Changing Face of Bangkok Tattoo, Part II." http://tattoos.com/articles/mccabe/wong/index2.htm(2006).

TIGHTLACING *See* Corsets

TONGA

Tonga is a Polynesian island inhabited for perhaps 6,000 years. Explored in the seventeenth century by Dutch and English explorers, it was later visited by **Captain James Cook** in 1773, who named the islands the Friendly Islands, because of the friendliness of the people. Like many other Polynesian islands, tattooing was a very prominent part of Tongan culture prior to European arrival.

The first written account of a Tongan tattoo was made by the Dutch explorer Abel Tasman in 1643 who noted that the men's bodies were painted black from waist to thighs. Tasman was describing the Tongan version of the **pe'a**, the traditional tattoo worn by Samoan men, which covered the torso from the belly button down, buttocks, genitals, and thighs. The Tongan tattoo has been described, however, as thicker than the pe'a and with notched edges. Unlike Samoa, which is the only Polynesian island to have maintained their traditional tattoo tradition into modern times, Tongan tattoos were outlawed in 1838, and the tradition was wiped out.

The procedure for creating a tattoo in Tonga was very similar to the Samoan tattoo. First, the tattooist would draw the design onto the skin with a stick dipped in ink, and then the tattoo would be created. The tattoo tool was a sharpened comb, made of either bone or shell, with anywhere from six to sixty teeth, attached to a wooden handle. The comb was dipped into the ink and a mallet was used to tap the comb, inserting the ink into the skin. Ink was made from burnt candlenut ashes mixed with water or fat.

Men were tattooed at puberty as a **rite of passage** into adulthood. Tongan women were also tattooed, on the hands and fingers. Men's tattoos, because of their extensive coverage, took weeks or months to create, with periods in between each tattoo day to rest and heal. Even then, men often experienced intense **pain** and infections from the tattoo. Some men also chose to get tattooed on their arms and upper torso, although much later in life.

Within the basic design of the tattoo, the recipient could choose from a number of specific named designs, which needed to be applied in a specific sequence. Patterns were made up of a series of lines, dots, and triangles. Tattoos were used to mark adulthood in men, but also rank, as chiefs and warriors, for instance, wore different designs than commoners wore.

Tattooing was officially outlawed in 1838 with the arrival of Christian missionaries. (Ironically, it was around that time that a European named George Vason got tattooed on Tonga.) So successful was the prohibition that all knowledge of tattooing was lost from Samoa for two centuries. However, in the last few years, a handful of Tongans, working with traditional Samoan tattooists, are attempting to bring ancient Tongan tattooing back, although, unlike other Polynesian countries, most Tongans have so far resisted accepting this traditional part of their pre-Christian culture.

See also: Pe'a; Samoa

Further Reading: Allen, Tricia. "The Tongan Tattoo." http://tattoos.com/allen/Tongan.htm (1998).

TONGUE SPLITTING

Tongue splitting is an extreme body modification that involves the splitting of the tongue from the tip backward; the result is a literal forked tongue. While still rare, tongue splitting is growing in popularity within the body modification community. Reasons for having the procedure done include aesthetics as some people enjoy the way that they look, as well as sexual enhancement. Some people, with practice, can independently move and control the two halves of their tongue. For others, there is a personal or spiritual benefit from it, while for others, it simply looks and feels different. Like so many other modern body modifications, tongue splitting is also done because people simply want the ability to shape their bodies according to their own desires.

Tongue splitting is mentioned in a number of ancient Indian texts on yogic practices. *Khechari mudra* describes a practice in which the tongue is split like a serpent, washed with a mixture of milk, ashes, and clarified butter, and is flipped into the back of the throat where the two forks of the tongue block the nostril cavities. The yogi is encouraged to remain like this for several days in a semi-unconscious state.

In the West, tongue splitting was first documented in 1997, and is so far best associated with people who attempt to transform their bodies into animals, such as **Erik Sprague**, who goes by the name Lizardman.

Because tongue splitting is a surgical procedure, it is illegal in many localities for a nonlicensed doctor to perform it, so those who want a split tongue must either convince a surgeon to do it, or they do it themselves or with friends. Do-it-yourself surgeries pose substantial health risks including blood loss, nerve damage, and affected speech. Other than the risks, however, the process is relatively simple: the tongue is sliced down the middle with a scalpel, heated blade or laser, and allowed to heal in a split state. Other methods include using a tongue piercing in order to tie off the tongue with a piece of string, tightening it gradually until the tongue separates. This evidently is quite a painful procedure.

See also: Animality; Sprague, Erik

Further Reading: www.BMEZine.com.

TORTURE

Torture refers to using pain or the threat of **pain** to cause someone to give in to their captor or tormentor. It has historically been used by state and religious authorities to extract confessions or incriminating information from alleged criminals or prisoners of war who otherwise would not speak. It has also been used to convert unwilling participants to a new religion and to indoctrinate and "reeducate" political prisoners or political activists. Torture is also used to dehumanize those being tortured, and as a form of punishment for those accused of extremely serious crimes, such as heresy. During the European witch-hunts of the fifteenth to

Naked woman being tortured by Spanish Inquisition, 1901. Courtesy of Library of Congress Prints and Photographs Division, Washington, DC, No. LC-USZ62-65697.

eighteenth centuries, torture was also used to get the accused witches to confess, because authorities felt that a voluntary confession was invalid. Roman slaves, too, could not be trusted to confess voluntarily and were tortured for this purpose. Finally, torture has been used by sadistic killers, often serial killers, who take pleasure in watching their victims suffer before killing them.

Methods of torture have included forced exercise, the breaking of bones, removal of the nails or teeth, binding the body, roasting the soles of the feet over hot coals, branding, flogging, burning, castration, cutting, water torture, foot whipping, knee capping, the removal of limbs, rape, starvation, tongue removal, as well as various forms of psychological torture. In medieval Europe, a number of specialized tools were created to torture victims, including the rack, breaking wheel, lash, padlocks, stock, thumbscrew, boot, and iron maiden.

The term torture is also commonly used in the **BDSM** scene, where standard methods of torture are used to inflict pain on or to humiliate participants, although the levels of pain are generally much less severe in a BDSM context. Typically, the sadist or dominant partner will inflict pain on the masochist or submissive partner, as a form of sexual play for both partners. Forms of BDSM torture might include binding, **branding**, **cutting**, whipping, using fire or heated implements, as well as play **piercing** and **stretching**. Dripping hot wax onto the genitals is another common practice. In all of these cases, the infliction of pain causes the victim, as well as the perpetrator, to experience sexual pleasure. Part of the pleasure also derives from the ability to push one's own personal limits in terms of what one can endure.

Cock and ball torture refers to a form of sexual play wherein the penis and scrotum are manipulated in order to cause pain, such as through the use of needles, nails, clothespins, and hooks, or else by cutting off the circulation to the testicles with a band, partially crushing the testicles with a burdizzo, or hanging very heavy objects from the penis or scrotum in order to temporarily stretch the organs.

See also: Slavery

Further Reading: Foucault, M. *Discipline and Punish*. Harmondsworth, UK: Penguin, 1979.

TRANSGENDER

Transgender refers to men or women who adopt behaviors, roles, and appearances not typically associated with the gender roles assigned to their birth sex. Transgender people may also identify as both male and female or may adopt behaviors or characteristics of both genders.

Transgendered people include **transvestites** who cross-dress, those who choose to be androgynous in appearance and/or behavior, and biological men or women who identify with the opposite sex, or with neither sex. Some **transsexuals** and intersex people also could be considered, or may identify as, transgendered.

Being transgendered does not necessarily imply one's sexual orientation. Transgendered people can be attracted to people of the opposite sex, or may be attracted to individuals of the same sex, or both. For many transgendered people, sexual attraction is aimed at the individual of the opposite gender, while the sex may be the same.

One possible explanation for the existence of alternative genders is that the typical binary gender roles in many societies are very limiting, and people with unusual or special talents and skills may not fit into those roles: men or women who want to be more aggressive, nurturing, artistic, athletic, or beautiful than they are allowed to be may be able to express those talents through taking on the gender of the opposite sex. Also, if work is assigned by gender, and it is in most societies, then careers in certain fields may only be possible by taking on the appearance and status of another gender.

While in the United States, cross-dressers are the most commonly known form of a transgendered person, there are various forms of transgendered people around the world, many of whom have culturally defined roles available to them.

In **India**, for example, **Hijras** are a cultural category which includes those who were born intersex, men who have been defined as "impotent," or men who choose not to live as men. Because Hinduism embraces alternative genders and gender transformation, Hijras have a role in Indian society, and form a quasi-religious community, which worships the goddess Bahucharara Mata.

Hijras are considered "man minus man," "man plus woman," or "almost women," through ritual surgery, performed by a Hijra called a midwife, in which their penises are removed. Hijras are defined by their sexual impotence and liminal gender status, and adopt exaggerated female mannerisms and appearance. Because

Hijras cannot reproduce themselves, they can confer fertility on others, via blessings at childbirths and weddings. While they renounce sexual desire, many do work as prostitutes or even serve as wives to men.

Dozens of **Native American** societies also at one time had culturally defined roles for transgendered people known as "two spirits." Two spirits were biological men or women who adopted the roles, appearances, and behaviors of the opposite sex, forming a third or fourth gender. Men-women or women-men would have been recognized as different as children and allowed to grow up as the opposite gender, marrying into the opposite gender of their own (but same sex). Like Hijras, two spirits often had a special ritual function as well as their assigned gender role. Two spirits did not, however, receive any sort of surgery which modified their bodies, although they dressed, spoke, and behaved like the opposite sex.

See also: Castration; Genital Mutilation; Hijras; Intersexuality; Sex Reassignment Surgery; Transsexuals; Transvestites

Further Reading: Feinberg, Leslie. *Transgender Warriors: Making History from Joan of Arc to Dennis Rodman*. Boston, MA: Beacon Press, 1997; Kulick, Don. *Travesti: Sex, Gender, and Culture among Brazilian Transgendered Prostitutes*. Chicago: University of Chicago Press, 1998; Lang, Sabine, Sue-Ellen Jacobs, and Wesley Thomas. *Two Spirit People: Native American Gender Identity, Sexuality, and Spirituality*. Chicago: University of Illinois Press, 1997; Nanda, Serena. *Neither Man Nor Woman: The Hijras of India*. New York: Wadsworth Publishing, 1998.

TRANSSEXUALS

Transsexualism is a condition in which a person feels that they were born into the wrong sex, and not only want to adopt the behaviors, mannerisms, and roles associated with the opposite sex, but see their sexual identity as incorrect as well. Most transsexuals not only want to live as a member of the gender with which they identify, but want to surgically and chemically alter their bodies so that their bodies match their internal gender identity. Transsexualism is sometimes considered to be a type of transgendered behavior.

Transsexuals are thought by the psychiatric profession to suffer from gender dysphoria or gender identity disorder, both psychiatric conditions. Those who choose to change their bodies to match their gender identity must, in the United States, receive psychological therapy (known as sex reassignment therapy), because the mental health profession does not consider surgery to be the only necessary therapy for the condition. Transsexuals who are planning to undergo surgery are known as preoperative (or preop) transsexuals and generally take hormones and dress and behave as their desired sex and gender during this period of time, which generally lasts at least a year. These requirements are intended to prevent people who are not genuinely transsexual from changing their sex and later regretting having done so.

Once an individual has completed the requisite counseling, he or she moves to the next phase, which is receiving **sex reassignment surgery**. Once the surgery or surgeries are completed, these individuals are known as postoperative or postop transsexuals. Male-to-female transsexuals are those who have transitioned, or are transitioning, from biological male to biological female, and female-to-male transsexuals are those who have transitioned, or are transitioning, from biological female to biological male.

Some transsexuals, either because they cannot afford surgery in the United States or because they find the requirements of sex reassignment therapy too restrictive, instead choose to seek surgery in third world countries or by American doctors who are not properly licensed to perform the surgery. Many, including those who never do undergo surgery, will also order hormones on the black market.

Sex reassignment surgery consists of, in the case of male-to-female transsexuals, the removal of the penis and testicles, and the creation of a vagina. A clitoris is generally formed out of the nerve bundles remaining in the penis. For female-to-male transsexuals, the breasts are removed and a penis and scrotum are formed. The scrotum is formed through suturing together the labia and inserting prosthetic testicles, and the penis is usually formed with a skin graft from the patient's arm or leg rolled up to create a penis, with the original urethra lengthened and inserted into the new organ. Sometimes an additional prosthesis is inserted into the new penis to allow for sexual penetration.

Besides surgery, transsexuals must take hormones, often for the rest of their lives, to feminize or masculinize their appearance, and some male-to-female transsexuals will also require hair removal, facial feminization surgery, and voice surgery or voice training. Hormone replacement therapy will cause breasts to grow in male-to-female transsexuals, and facial hair to grow in female-to-male transsexuals, but will not cause breasts to disappear or facial hair to disappear.

While transsexuals probably exist in all cultures, in many they are considered to be sexual and social deviants. **Thailand** is an example of a country that assigns a special social category to transgenders and male-to-female transsexuals called kathoey. Kathoey dress and behave as women, occupy female gender roles, and many undergo hormone replacement therapy, sex reassignment surgery, and breast implants to become women. Many kathoey have achieved high-status careers as models or celebrities, but also like the transvestites, many work as prostitutes. Because of the high incidence of transsexuals in Thailand, sex reassignment surgery is a commonly performed surgery in the country, both for native Thai people as well as Westerners seeking low-cost surgery.

See also: Castration; Genital Mutilation; Intersexuality; Sex Reassignment Surgery; Transgender; Transvestites

Further Reading: Brown, Mildred L., and Chloe Ann Rounsley. *True Selves*. Hoboken, NJ: Jossey-Bass, 1996; Feinberg, Leslie. *Transgender Warriors: Making History from Joan of Arc to Dennis Rodman*. Boston, MA: Beacon Press, 1997.

TRANSVESTITES

Transvestites, also known as cross-dressers, are men who habitually or occasionally wear women's clothing. (The term can also apply to women, but because women can so easily wear men's clothing, especially in the West, the term is rarely used to refer to them.) Cross-dressing is a form of transgendered behavior.

Men who are sexually aroused by the wearing of women's clothing are known as transvestic fetishists. Straight men who wear women's clothing are generally known as cross-dressers, whereas gay men who wear women's clothing are usually called transvestites or drag queens.

Transitioning transsexuals cross-dress, generally as part of their preparation to take on the full roles and identity of the opposite gender. For a small community within the gay community, cross-dressing has been associated with a particular kind of performance art known as drag. But for some straight men, the wearing of women's clothing is not associated with sexuality or a gender identity issue, but can relieve stress or anxiety, or simply make the wearer feel more whole.

Historically, cross-dressing has been practiced by both men and women for a variety of reasons not necessarily related to sexuality or gender identity. Women, for instance, have been known throughout history to dress as men in order to serve in the military. Folklore and theater are rich with tales of men and women who cross-dress in order to pursue a lover, or escape from harm. Finally, the theater and operatic traditions of a number of societies required that men perform women's roles, since women were not allowed to act, leading to large numbers of cross-dressing actors.

Drag queens are men who wear women's clothing, generally in a performance context, and usually refers to gay men who perform in gay bars. In addition, the tradition of men dressing as women in order to perform remains a feature of modern society, outside of the homosexual context. Drag queens and other men performing as women, such as female impersonators in Las Vegas, wear not only women's clothing, but also wear makeup, wigs, prosthetic breasts, and shave or wax their bodies.

The practice of men wearing women's clothes has been found historically and around the world, and is generally associated with transgendered communities. One well-known example are the transvestite of Brazil, who not only wear women's clothing, but adopt female mannerisms and behaviors. Transvestite also take hormone pills in order to feminize their bodies, and inject themselves with silicone in order to create round feminine hips. Unlike transsexuals, or transgendered groups like Hijras, they do not have their penises or testicles removed. Transvestite date heterosexual men, and often work as prostitutes serving heterosexual and homosexual men.

See also: Transgender; Transsexuals

Further Reading: Garber, Marjorie. *Vested Interests: Cross Dressing & Cultural Anxiety*. New York: HarperCollins, 1992; Kulick, Don. *Travesti: Sex, Gender, and Culture among Brazilian Transgendered Prostitutes*. Chicago: University of Chicago Press, 1998.

TREPANATION

Trepanation is the practice of opening a hole in the skull via drilling, boring, scraping, or cutting. The word "trepanation" comes from the Greek trypanon, which means drill. It has been used historically to treat disorders of the brain such as migraines, seizures, and mental disorders, to relieve pressure on the brain from a cranial fracture, or to remove a damaged part of the skull. In addition, it has been used for mystical purposes in order to induce hallucinations, allow for clairvoyance or release evil spirits. For instance, the Kisii tribe of East Africa performs the surgery primarily to alleviate headache after a blow, whereas the nearby Lugbara tribe uses it to release evil spirits.

Healed holes in the skulls of human remains dating back to the Neolithic indicate that trepanation was practiced in prehistoric times, probably again both for spiritual and medical purposes, and in fact, it may have been one of the earliest forms of surgery. It was practiced in Europe and the Middle East from the Neolithic through the Renaissance, in North, Central, and South America, as well as in Africa, Asia, and Oceania. In the early twentieth century, it was still being performed in Africa, South America, and Oceania, and in Europe, and it wasn't until the sixteenth century that trepanation was no longer commonly performed.

The oldest examples of trepanation may be skulls found in North Africa, dating back to 10,000 BCE, and skulls have been found in excavations in the Middle East, Europe, and Asia from approximately 8000 to 6000 BCE.

Trepanation was practiced much more recently in the Americas, and drilled skulls have been found in Peru from 400 BCE, and later the practice appeared to move northward to Mexico and North America. Because of the prevalence of South American artifacts, it is thought that trepanation was very commonly practiced here. Amazingly, most of the skulls, perhaps as high as 80 percent, indicated that the patients survived the surgery.

Trepanation techniques varied from the simplest in which one would scrape or cut a hole in the skull with a piece of rock or shell. Another method uses a hammer and chisel to knock out a piece of the skull, but the method most well known uses a primitive form of drill in order to bore tiny holes into a circle on the skull; the circular piece of skull could then be knocked out. Most likely the patient was anesthetized with alcohol or drugs.

Today, there is a small subculture whose participants feel that opening a hole, or what they call a third eye, in the head gives one the power of clairvoyance, or enlightenment. By permanently relieving pressure on the brain, it is thought, one can increase the flow of blood to the brain, giving a sense of euphoria, and for some, an expanded consciousness. Still others feel that with more blood in the brain, more parts of the brain would work simultaneously allowing for a greater use of the brain, and, as some report, mental clarity and even brilliance.

Because most doctors in the West will not drill a hole into a healthy person's skull for the patient's own enlightenment, many advocates perform the procedures on each other, with tools purchased at medical supply stores and hardware stores, while others travel to Mexico for the procedure.

See also: Head Binding; Self-Mutilation

Further Reading: Arnott, Robert, Stanley Finger, and C. U. M. Smith. *Trepanation: History, Discovery, Theory.* Oxford: Oxbow Books, 2003.

William H. Egberts examining trepanned skulls in the Anthropology Laboratory at the National Museum, 1926. Courtesy of Library of Congress Prints and Photographs Division, Washington, DC, No. LC-USZ62-115187.

TRIBALISM

One of the biggest influences on modern tattooing is known as tribalism. Tattoo designs borrowed from places like **Samoa, Borneo, Hawaii,** and **New Zealand** have, since the 1970s, been extremely popular among members of the gay, **BDSM,** and leather communities, and in the 1980s, they became very fashionable among punks and middle-class youth as well. The man most responsible for the mainstream popularity of tribal tattooing is **Leo Zulueta**, a Hawaiian of Filipino descent, who began practicing tattooing under the tutelage of **Ed Hardy**, along with Cliff Raven and Dan Thomé, both of whom primarily practiced in the 1970s.

Tribalism also owes its huge popularity to the influence of *TattooTime*'s first issue, published in 1982, which was devoted to tribalism. It was this magazine, which ultimately went out to approximately 15,000 readers, which gave this movement and tattoo style a name and influenced a tremendous number of people to go out and create or receive "tribal" tattoos.

Tribal tattoos are usually black tattoos, made with heavy lines and heavy black shading, that mimic the abstract designs of tattoos from other cultures, primarily Polynesian tattoos.

Since the mid-1980s, young kids who want to start tattooing often execute their first pieces in the tribal style, because they think tribal tattoos are easy to tattoo. Thus tribal tattoos have, in many ways, now become the mark of the amateur tattooist, who tattoos Borneo- or Kwakiutl-inspired designs on his friends for no cost. This is one reason why **punk** tattoos are so heavily weighted toward tribalism.

While tribal tattoos were once the ultimate elite, non-Western tattoo, they have become for many who know how to read such tattoos, simply a relic of an earlier era, specifically, the 1980s. This is illustrative of how quickly tattoo trends become popular and then burn out.

Non-Western designs, technology, and styles have firmly uprooted traditional tattoo designs for most middle-class North Americans. There certainly are aesthetic reasons for this, in that many of these designs simply make good tattoos, but there are political reasons as well, which involve repudiating a working-class, white-bread past.

The irony here is that neither tribal tattoos, nor the **Chicano** tattoos that have recently become popular among whites, originated in the middle class—tribal tattoos were first worn by punks and kinky gays. Yet they have become popularized through middle-class wear, and the tribal tattoo, at least for a while, stood alongside the Japanese tattoo as the ultimate middle-class tattoo.

In addition to borrowing tattoo designs from other cultures, there are now a number of different tattoos that were created to *look like* non-Western, tribal tattooing. Tattooist Mike Malone designed a tattoo style in the 1970s called the "Hawaiian Band" which is a tribal-looking design made to wrap around an arm. While Malone's tattoo was not a traditional design, it looked enough like one that many people assumed it was. This is similar to the "Peace Corps tattoos" which developed in Samoa as souvenir tattoos for white Peace Corps volunteers but which later became popular with Samoans as well.

At the same time that middle-class North Americans are wearing tribal tattoos, the indigenous people of Hawaii, Australia, and New Zealand are experiencing their own tattoo revival. Sometimes the tattoos that they wear are in the tradition of their culture, and sometimes they are Western images. Quite often, they are tattooed with tribal tattoos as they have been recreated in the United States by Western tattooists.

See also: Borneo; Hardy, Don Ed; Moko; Punk; Samoa; *TattooTime*; Zulueta, Leo

Further Reading: Wojcik, Daniel. *Punk and Neo-Tribal Body Art*. Jackson: University Press of Mississippi, 1995.

TUTTLE, LYLE

San Francisco tattooist Lyle Tuttle was one of the most influential tattooists of the 1970s. The Vietnam War and the peace movement that it spawned, the civil rights movement, black power, Stonewall, and the new women's liberation movement all shook the foundations of middle-class stability, and all contributed as well to the changing face of **tattooing** in the United States. Tuttle, thanks to his vibrant personality, his quickness with language, his shop in San Francisco, and his status as a celebrity tattooist who tattooed Janis Joplin and a number of other rock stars and celebrities, gave tattooing in the 1970s a very public face. Tuttle was also a great spokesperson for the newly reviving art of tattooing because many tattooists at that time were leery of speaking to the press, given the negative association that tattooing had since the 1950s when tattooing was banned in many cities and states.

Lyle Tuttle, while never a leader in terms of artistic innovations, nevertheless played a major role in bringing mainstream media attention to tattooing. He opened his shop in San Francisco in 1957, and was for many years the only tattooist in town. During the Vietnam era, he found himself tattooing more and more hippies as well as celebrities, and he took advantage of the new media interest in tattooing to launch the biggest pro-tattooing publicity campaign that tattooing had ever experienced. Tuttle, his shop, and tattooing were featured in *Time* and *Life* magazines, as well as countless local papers, and Tuttle made appearances on television shows throughout the 1970s.

> Back then, tattooers were folk artists. There was open hostility between one another, almost. If there was a guy a few hundred miles away or a few thousand miles away, then that's where the communication was. But if they was fairly close, tattoo artists are like dogs—they run around pissin' on territory. There's less of that today.
>
> LYLE TUTTLE, tattooist

While younger tattooists were able to take advantage of the more relaxed social climate of the period and tattooing's emerging popularity thanks to Tuttle, many older tattooists resented Tuttle's influence. **Sailor Jerry Collins**, for example, felt that the publicity Tuttle brought to tattooing did the profession more harm than good. Today, Tuttle is himself ambiguous about the changes that he helped bring about, and once said that tattooing's skyrocketing popularity since the 1970s is not necessarily good for the art.

Because San Francisco was a major hub of antiwar and liberation activities, the tattoo designs that came out of Tuttle's shop were reflective of the changes in the social climate, and indeed, tattoo designs probably changed more during the 1970s than any period previously in

> Getting a tattoo is like joining a fraternal organization.
>
> LYLE TUTTLE, tattooist

U.S. history. Prior to this time, most of the tattoos found on the walls of tattoo parlors were masculine, both in terms of imagery (military icons, aggressive animals, biker insignia), style (bold lines), and placement (for example, the ubiquitous bicep tattoo). But with the peace, gay, and women's liberation movements came new designs, which were both more feminine, and at the same time, appealed to middle-class tastes more than the classic working-class designs. Peace symbols, the yin/yang image, astrological signs, and "feminine" animals like dolphins, butterflies, rabbits, and kittens, began showing up on women's shoulders, breasts, and ankles, and also on young middle-class men's bodies.

Tuttle was also instrumental in updating the health regulations governing tattooing in San Francisco, and this was a primary factor in the increasing professionalization of tattooing. He realized that one of the reasons that tattooing had such a bad reputation was the poor sanitation practices of most U.S. tattooists at mid-century. The ban on tattooing in New York City, for example, was linked to the incidence of hepatitis being transmitted via infected tattoo needles. Thus it was clear to many that in order for tattooing to survive, and to attract new customers, health regulations should be tightened.

Ultimately, Tuttle worked with the Department of Communicable Diseases to write the new health regulations on tattooing in San Francisco, and he pointed out the technological innovations in tattooing, including the development of the quick change machine which allows for the easy removal of the tube and needle bars for sterilization, and the use of individual pigment containers for each customer.

Tuttle's efforts to improve sanitation for San Francisco tattooists (like a similar effort by tattooer Doc Webb in San Diego) were important in bringing tattooing into the modern era, and to a middle-class audience.

See also: Legislation and Regulation

Further Reading: DeMello, Margo. *Bodies of Inscription: A Cultural History of the Modern Tattoo Community*. Durham, NC: Duke University Press, 2000; Gay, Kathlyn. *Body Marks: Tattooing, Piercing, and Scarification*. New York: Millbrook Press, 2002.

WAGNER, CHARLIE

Professor Charles Wagner (1875–1953) was one of the most influential tattooists of the early twentieth century. As a boy, he saw his first tattooed man—Prince Constantine—at a dime museum called the Grand Museum in the Bowery (lower Manhattan) in the 1880s, which influenced his decision to pursue tattooing as a career. Like many tattooists of the day, he began tattooing himself as well as sailors he met, with borrowed ink and a needle.

Once "Professor" Samuel O'Reilly patented the first tattoo machine, he began teaching other people how to use the new technology. One of his students was Charlie Wagner, and after Wagner mastered the technique, he earned the title of professor as well. Wagner later took over O'Reilly's original shop at 11 Chatham Square in the Bowery, which was both a tattoo shop and a barbershop, and worked there for fifty years, until his death in 1953.

During Wagner's time at Chatham Square, he patented his own tattoo machine in 1904, which involved a number of improvements over O'Reilly's design, including vertical coils in line with the tube assembly, an innovation that is still in use today. Wagner also had his own tattoo supply business, supplying machines, inks, flash, and the like to tattooists around the country, advertising in magazines like *Boy's Life* or *Popular Mechanics*.

Like most tattooists working in port towns, the military, especially sailors, were Wagner's biggest customers, especially during World War I and World War II. He also tattooed solders during the Spanish American War of 1898, at .25 cents per tattoo.

Also like his mentor O'Reilly, Wagner tattooed a number of **tattooed attractions**—perhaps up to fifty. With the electric machine, men and women could get full-body tattoos much faster and with less pain than in the old days, making the profession of tattooed attraction much more lucrative. He tattooed Mae Vandermark who later became Miss Artorio and worked in Coney Island and later with the Ringling Brothers Circus. Mildred Hull was another of Wagner's creations, who was one of the only women to work as a tattooist on the Bowery. He also, along with Joe Van Hart, tattooed **Betty Broadbent**, the most famous tattooed lady of all, who worked with Ringling Brothers, the New York World's Fair, the Cole Brothers Circus, and in Harry Carey's Wild West Show.

At the turn of the century when getting tattooed briefly became a fad for upper-class men and women in England and the United States, Wagner, one of the best-known tattooists of his day and the father of New York City tattooing, donned a tuxedo with tails and a stovepie hat to tattoo the elites of society.

Wagner said that he didn't use stencils and free-handed all of his work. He was known to decide in advance what type of tattoos he would apply on a particular day, and that would be the only design he would offer. One day it might be hearts; another, eagles. Stoney St. Clair, who worked with Wagner, reported that if a customer asked for a heart on an eagle day, he would find himself with an eagle tattoo anyway.

In 1943 Wagner was arrested for violating the Sanitary Code in New York but told the judge he was too busy doing essential war work (tattooing clothes on naked lady tattoos so the men could get into the Navy) to keep his needles clean; he was fined $10 and told to clean his shop up.

See also: Broadbent, Betty

Further Reading: McCabe, Michael. *New York City Tattoo: The Oral History of an Urban Art.* Honolulu, HI: Hardy Marks Publications, 1997; Parry, Albert. *Tattoo: Secrets of a Strange Art Practiced by the Natives of the United States.* New York: Collier, 1971; St. Clair, Leonard, and Alan Govenar. *Stoney Knows How: Life as a Tattoo Artist.* Lexington: University of Kentucky Press, 1981.

WARD, JIM

Jim Ward is one of the cofounders of the modern **body piercing** movement. He began piercing himself in 1968 when he was involved with the leather community in New York City, after reading about sailors who had received piercings to commemorate their travels. He opened the first professional piercing studio, The **Gauntlet**, in West Hollywood in 1978 (after having operated from a home studio for three years), originally catering primarily to the gay **BDSM** community, with funding provided by Doug Malloy, another early piercing innovator. The piercing practices and jewelry designs developed at the Gauntlet have since become standard industry practices, and, thanks to the Gauntlet's prominent Santa Monica Boulevard location and the publicity generated by Ward, body piercing began to attract new public attention and a new clientele.

Later, Ward opened three more Gauntlet studios in San Francisco, Seattle, and New York, attracting new customers and transforming piercing into a major phenomenon. In the 1990s, Ward sold his controlling interest of the company, and Gauntlet Enterprises went bankrupt in 1998. In 2004, Ward and his partner Drew Ward, with the help of an anonymous donor, were able to purchase back the business name, but, having retired from piercing—he now works as a graphic designer—he has not yet reopened the company.

Ward was also the founder and publisher of *Piercing Fans International Quarterly* (**PFIQ**), the first body piercing magazine, published from 1977 to the 1990s, in order to provide a forum for communication in the body modification community. As of this writing, there are plans to reprint back issues of the publication, and perhaps, to restart its publication.

See also: BDSM; Body Play; *PFIQ*; Piercing; Primitivism

Further Reading: Vale, V., and Andrea Juno. *Modern Primitives.* San Francisco, CA: Re/Search Publications, 1989.

WILDENSTEIN, JOCELYN

Jocelyn Wildenstein (born August 5, 1940) is a wealthy American socialite who underwent a series of plastic surgery procedures that have left her looking somewhat like a cat. She has been a staple of the New York City tabloids, which report on her activities when she is out in public, and is featured on www.awfulplasticsurgery.com. She has allegedly spent millions of dollars on plastic surgery over the years, and is known by the tabloids both as Catwoman and Bride of Wildenstein. Her last-known surgery was in 2004, according to reports.

The story of Wildenstein's surgeries explains that as a young wife and mother married to a billionaire art dealer, in the 1970s she caught him in bed with a 21-year-old Russian model. Hoping to keep him—he is also said to love large cats—she began a cycle of surgery to make herself look more like a cat. She is known to have received several silicone injections to the lips, cheek, and chin along with a face-lift and eye reconstruction, all of which have resulted in a strangely misshapen face. The story continues that her husband was horrified and immediately filed for divorce, leaving her for the other woman, with the divorce having been finalized in 1999. She currently resides in New York City and was often seen at social events and nightclubs throughout the city with celebrity friends. However, she has been largely absent from the tabloids since 2005.

See also: Animality; Cosmetic Surgery; Self-Mutilation

Further Reading: Potts, Annie. "The Mark of the Beast: Inscribing 'Animality' through Extreme Body Modification." In P. Armstrong, and L. Simmons, eds., *Knowing Animals*. Leiden: Brill, 2007.

YAKUZA

Yakuza refers to the Japanese mafia and its members, who make up one of the largest organized crime syndicates in the world.

The term "Yakuza" comes from a Japanese card game, *Oicho-Kabu*, which means "good for nothing," and refers to the manner in which the cards are counted. The worst hand in the game is a set of eight, nine, and three, which translate to Ya, Ku, and Sa in Japanese. Winning with a Ya-Ku-Sa hand requires the most skill and as well as bad luck, and the name now signifies bad fortune for anyone who tries to challenge the group.

Yakuza probably originated in the Edo period in the seventeenth century as *kabuki-mono* (crazy or raving ones), who were samurai who wore outlandish clothing and hairstyles, spoke in elaborate slang, and carried long swords in their belts. During the Tokugawa era, the samurai were no longer needed by the Emperor, and, without official service, they became criminals.

Modern Yakuza members instead feel that they are descendents of the *machi-yokko* (servants of the town) who protected villages from criminals and intruders, and stood up for the poor and defenseless against those who would exploit them.

More recently, Yakuza are linked to two groups which emerged in eighteenth century **Japan**: *tekiya* (peddlers) and *bakuto* (gamblers), and some modern gangs still identify with one group or the other. As industrialization led to urbanization, a third category of Yakuza called *gurentai* (hoodlums), who modeled themselves on 1940s-era American gangsters, developed.

At the time that the Yakuza were developing, during the Edo period, modern decorative tattooing was also developing. Decorative **tattooing** at this time was heavily influenced by the imagery of wood-block print, or ukiyo-e, artists, and in particular the illustrated novel *Suikoden* (*All Men Are Brothers*), about a band of outlaws who were folk heroes to the common people. The outlaws in the Kuniyoshi-illustrated versions had elaborate scenes, dangerous animals, stylized waves, wind, and flowers tattooed on their bodies, and it was these images that influenced the direction of Japanese tattooing and the types of tattoos favored by the Yakuza.

For the last century, the Yakuza have been known for their elaborate full-body tattoos, and one estimate places the number of Yakuza with tattoos at 73 percent. Japanese tattoos as worn by the Yakuza typically cover the entire torso, front and back, as well the arms to just below the elbow, and the legs to mid-calf. When wearing a *happi* coat, the tattoo is often invisible because of the untattooed "river" down the middle of the torso. While playing cards or at the bathhouse, however, the men often remove their clothes and show their tattoos to each other. Because of the extensive nature of the tattoos and the traditional Japanese tattoo techniques (known as *tebori*—to carve by hand), the tattoos are painful to receive and can take hundreds of hours to complete. As with tattooing among many tribal peoples, the pain is part of the process and is a measure of a man's strength and courage, as well as a sign of loyalty and group solidarity. During the Meji era (from 1868 to present), tattooing was forbidden for law-abiding Japanese citizens, although the Yakuza continued to wear them, making a clear link between tattooing and **criminality** in Japan. In recent years, however, tattooing has become less associated with the Yakuza thanks to the lessening influence of the group, the high cost of traditional tattoos, and the still-strong stigma against them in Japan. Some younger Yakuza now favor small, less expensive, Western-style tattoos rather than the full-body tattoos that so clearly demonstrated their ancestors' commitment to the Yakuza life.

See also: Criminality; Japan; Tattooing

Further Reading: Kaplan, D. E., and A. Dupro. *Yakuza: Expanded Edition*. Berkeley: University of California Press, 2003; Saga, Junichi. *Confessions of a Yakuza: A Life in Japan's Underworld*. Tokyo: Kodansha International, 1995.

Z

ZAIRE

Zaire is a central African nation (formerly known as the Democratic Republic of Congo) made up of over 200 tribal groups, most of whom are Bantu in origin. The main tribes in Zaire are the Kongo, Luba, Mongo, Bwaka, Lega, and Zande.

Like many other sub-Saharan African peoples, many of the tribes of Zaire use **scarification** to mark their bodies. Scarification is a long and painful process that many African girls go through when they reach puberty, as part of a **rite of passage** that also helps to make them marriageable. It is carried out through carving the skin with sharpened blades, and rubbing the wounds with ash. Scarification makes many African girls more attractive to men, who consider the patterns beautiful to look at and to touch. Because scarification is painful, a girl whose skin is scarred also demonstrates that she will be able to endure the pains of childbirth, making her an excellent candidate for a wife. Scarification patterns can also be seen on carved wooden sculptures made by a number of tribes.

The Lulua, for example, use scarification as a form of beautification and to attract benevolent spirits. The Yombe also use scarification to maximize feminine beauty, and to signal marriageability. For the Yombe, scarification begins for a girl at 10 and continues until she is married, and covers the front and back of the body. The abstract designs mimic traditional Yombe textile and basketry designs, which also convey the tribe's notion of beauty. Luba women often are scarred on their bellies and buttocks and scarification patterns can also reveal status.

The Tabwa, who live in southwestern Zaire and northeastern Zambia, called their practice *Kulemba*, which means to inscribe or beautify a blank surface. Women were once scarred on the cheeks and forehead plus back and shoulders, but today scars are limited to small lines on the forehead, nose, and cheeks. The method for scarification was to use a hook or thorn to pull up the skin, after which it is sliced off with a razor, and the incisions rubbed with soot. As with most African tribes, girls without scars were not considered marriageable.

Men in Zaire also undergo scarification. Kongo men, for example, undergo facial scarification, and women are scarred along their shoulders and backs. Tabwa men also practiced facial scarification, with a pattern known as "face of the cross" in which tiny dots were patterned into lines which made up a cross across the face. Lega men and women also used to be scarred.

Today, as clothing is worn by virtually all tribespeople in Africa, the practice of scarification is dwindling, and in some communities, such as among the Luba, scarification patterns are being transformed from the body to clothing via textile designs.

See also: Scarification

Further Reading: Cornet, J. *A Survey of Zairian Art*. Raleigh: North Carolina Museum of Art, 1978; Fisher, Angela. *Africa Adorned: A Panorama of Jewelry, Dress, Body Decoration, and Hair*. New York: Henry Abrams, 2000; Roberts, Allen F. "Tabwa Tegumentary Inscription." In Arnold Rubin, ed., *Marks of Civilization: Artistic Transformations of the Human Body*. Los Angeles: Museum of Cultural History, UCLA, 1988.

ZEIS, MILTON

Milton Zeis (1901–1972) was a tattooist, tattoo book publisher, and mail order tattoo equipment supplier. Zeis developed an interest in tattooing as a boy of 9 in Rockdale, Illinois, when he first saw **tattooing** on a riverboat show that played on the Mississippi. He tattooed a butterfly on his knee after that show, and he tattooed all the other neighborhood kids as well. Traveling through his teens and into his thirties, Zeis met tattooists and saw tattooing around the country. Upon his return to Illinois, he used what he saw and learned and opened the Zeis Studio, a tattoo studio and mail order business in his basement.

As a tattoo supply salesman, Zeis sold **flash**, machines, inks, and other supplies, and created a colorful catalog to advertise his wares. Zeis boasted that over his career, he created over 10,000 tattoo designs. During the 1940s and 1950s he evidently made and sold between 100 and 200 tattoo machines a month. Zeis wrote that he sold more tattoo equipment to plastic surgeons, "beauty operators," medical laboratories, fur ranchers, and animal breeders as he did to show people and others.

He offered the "Milton Zeis School of Tattooing," the first home-school course on tattooing starting in 1951, and promised that tattooing was so easy "even a child can do good tattooing." The course, which was accredited by the state of Illinois as a home study program, sold for $125 and included twenty lessons for home tattooists to practice on their own. He published "Tattooing the World Over," a tattoo history magazine, from the 1940s to the 1950s, and founded the International Tattoo Club.

Zeis was also a **circus** and carnival performer, creating the character "Uncle Miltie." Ironically, he died while performing Uncle Miltie for a charity event.

See also: Tattooing; Tattoo Technology

Further Reading: Zeis, Milton. *Tattooing the World Over*, Vol. 1. New York: Milton Zeis, 1947.

ZULUETA, LEO

The man most responsible for the mainstream popularity of tribal tattooing in the West is Leo Zulueta, a Hawaiian American of Filipino descent, who began practicing **tattooing** under the tutelage of **Ed Hardy**. Zulueta credits Hardy for supporting his interest in "pretechnological" tattooing, which in the late 1970s was almost unheard of among mainstream tattooists (with the exception of Cliff Raven and Dan Thome). Zulueta also credits Hardy's work with spreading Japanese tattoo styles on Western wearers as one justification for his own work, which has predominantly been worn by white Americans.

Zulueta began tattooing **punk** kids in Southern California in the 1970s, and also credits their interest in esoteric styles and imagery to helping him move into tribalism as his dominant tattoo aesthetic. Zulueta also saw one reason for his work being the disappearance of many Micronesian cultures and traditions; by preserving and continuing this style of tattooing, and embellishing it with his own creativity, he saw himself as continuing the culture. Finally, because Zulueta grew up in **Hawaii** at a time when native Hawaiians were no longer practicing their own indigenous tattoo traditions, he saw the need to resurrect traditions like this, both for native Hawaiians, and for others interested in this type of work.

See also: Hardy, Don Ed; Hawaii; Modern Primitives; Tribalism

Further Reading: Hardy, D. E. "The New Tribalism." *TattooTime* 1 (1982): 3–9.

Resource Guide

MAGAZINES

Body Painting Magazine
14 Jilloong Street
Mansfield
Queensland 4122
Australia
(07) 3349 1314
http://www.bodypaintmag.com/

Body Play
P.O. Box 2575
Menlo Park, CA 94026
(650) 324-0543
http://www.bodyplay.com/

International Tattoo Art
Butterfly Publications
462 Broadway, 4th Floor
New York, NY 10013
(212)-966-8400
http://www.internationaltattooart.com/

Skin and Ink
LFP Inc.
8484 Wilshire Blvd., Suite 900
Beverly Hills, CA 90211
(800)-251-2714
http://www.skinandink.com/

Skin Art
Art & Ink/Outlaw Biker Publications,
NC Music Factory
820 Hamilton Street #C6
Charlotte, NC 28206-2991
(704)-333-3331
http://www.skinart.com/

Tattoo
Paisano Publications
P.O. Box 3000
Agoura Hills, CA 91376
(800) 873-9110
http://www.easyriders.com/

Tattoo Flash
Paisano Publications
P.O. Box 3000
Agoura Hills, CA 91376
(800) 873-7896
http://www.easyriders.com/

Tattoo Revue
Outlaw Biker Enterprises,
820 Hamilton Street Suite C6
Charlotte, NC 28206-2991
(704)-333-3331
http://www.outlawbiker.com/

Tattoo Savage
Paisano Publications
P.O. Box 3000
Agoura Hills, CA 91376
(800) 873-8805
http://www.easyriders.com/

Tattoo Society Magazine
Hitman Publications
www.myspace.com/tattoosocietymagazine

ORGANIZATIONS

Alliance of Professional Tattooists, Inc.
http://www.safe-tattoos.com/
2108 S. Alvernon Way
Tucson, AZ 85711
(520) 514-5549

**American Academy of Cosmetic
Surgery**
http://www.cosmeticsurgery.org/
737 North Michigan Avenue, Suite 2100
Chicago, IL 60611-5405
(312) 981-6760

**American Association of Oriental
Medicine (AAOM)**
www.aaom.org
P.O. Box 162340
Sacramento, CA 95816
(916) 443-4770, (866) 455-7999

Association of Professional Piercers
http://www.safepiercing.org/
PMB 286
5456 Peachtree Industrial Blvd.
Chamblee, GA 30341
(888) 888-1APP or (505) 242-2144

Circumcision Resource Center
http://www.circumcision.org/
P.O. Box 232
Boston, MA 02133
(617) 523-0088

**Female Genital Cutting Education and
Networking Project**
http://www.fgmnetwork.org
P.O. Box 181077
Tallahassee, FL 32318

Intersex Society of North America
http://www.isna.org/
Intersex Society of North America
979 Golf Course Drive #282
Rohnert Park CA 94928

**National Association of Anorexia
Nervosa and Related Disorders**
http://www.anad.org/site/anadweb/
(847) 831-3438

**National Center for Transgender
Equality**
http://www.nctequality.org/
1325 Massachusetts Ave., Suite 700
Washington, DC 20005
(202)-903-0112

National Tattoo Association
http://www.nationaltattooassociation.com
485 Business Park Lane
Allentown, PA 18109
(610) 433 7261

The Society of Janus
http://www.soj.org/
The Society of Janus
P.O. Box 411523
San Francisco, CA 94141-1523

**The Society of Permanent Cosmetic
Professionals**
http://www.spcp.org/
69 North Broadway
Des Plaines, IL 60016
(847) 635-1330

WEB SITES

http://www.ampulove.com
http://www.bmezine.com
http://www.bodyplay.com
http://www.cirp.org/
http://www.modcon.org/
http://www.needled.com

http://www.piercing.com
http://www.rabbithole.org/oldindex.html
http://www.tattoos.com/
http://www.transgendercare.com/
http://www.trepan.com

MUSEUMS

Amsterdam Tattoo Museum
http://tattoos.com/xxx/mus01.htm
Oudezijds Achterburgwal 130
1012 DT, Amsterdam
The Netherlands

Baltimore Tattoo Museum
http://www.baltotat.com
1534 Eastern Ave.
Baltimore, MD
(410) 522-5800

British Tattoo History Museum
http://www.tattoo.co.uk/bthm.htm
389 Cowley Road
Oxford,
OX4 2BS
44 (0)1865 716877

Circus World Museum
http://www.wisconsinhistory.org/
circusworld/
550 Water Street (Highway 113)
Baraboo, WI 53913
866-693-1500

Mutter Museum
http://www.collphyphil.org/mutter.asp
19 South Twenty-Second Street
Philadelphia, PA 19103-3097
215-563-3737

**National Tattoo Museum of
New Zealand**
http://www.mokomuseum.org.nz
42 Abel Smith Street
Wellington,
New Zealand
(04) 385-6444

Tattoo Archive
http://www.tattooarchive.com
2804 San Pablo Avenue
Berkeley, CA 94702
(510) 548-5895

Thomas Lockhart's Tattoo Museum
http://www.westcoasttattoo.com/tattoo_
museum.htm
620 Davie Street
Vancouver, BC
Canada, V6B 2G5
(604)-681-2049

Triangle Tattoo & Museum
http://www.triangletattoo.com/
356 B North Main Street
Fort Bragg, CA 95437
707-964-8814

The Virtual Tattoo Art Museum
http://www.lyletuttle.com/

Bibliography

Adams, Bluford. *E Pluribus Barnum: The Great Showman and the Making of U.S. Popular Culture*. Minneapolis: University of Minnesota Press, 1997.

Adams, K. E. "What's 'Normal': Female Genital Mutilation, Psychology, and Body Image." *Journal of the American Medical Women's Association* 59 (2004): 168–170.

Adams, Sarah. "Praise Her Beauty Well: Ùrì from the Body to Cloth." In *Call and Response: Journeys into African Art* (Exhibition Catalogue). New Haven, CT: Yale University Art Gallery, 2000.

Agar, Nicholas. *Liberal Eugenics: In Defense of Human Enhancement*. New York: Blackwell Publishing, 2004.

Alam, M., and J. S. Dover. "On Beauty: Evolution, Psychosocial Considerations, and Surgical Enhancement." *Arch Dermatol* 137 (2001): 795–807.

Allen, Tricia. "European Explorers and Marquesan Tattooing: The Wildest Island Style." *TattooTime* 5 (1991): 86–101.

———. "Tatau: The Tahitian Revival." www.tattoos.com/allen/TATAU.htm (1998).

———. "The Tongan Tattoo." http://tattoos.com/allen/Tongan.htm (1998).

———. *Tattoo Traditions of Hawaii*. Honolulu, HI: Mutual Publishing, 2006.

Allison, Kevin, and Dr. Faye Z. Belgrave. *African American Psychology: From Africa to America*. Thousand Oaks, CA: Sage Publications, 2005.

Alt, K., and Pichler, S. "Artificial Modifications of Human Teeth." In K. Alt, F. Rosing, and M. Teschler-Nicola, eds., *Dental Anthropology Fundamentals, Limits and Prospects*. New York: SpringerWien, 1998.

Althaus, Frances A. "Female Circumcision: Rite of Passage or Violation of Rights?" *International Family Planning Perspectives* 23(3) (1997): 130–133.

Anderson, Clare. "Godna: Inscribing Indian Convicts in the Nineteenth Century." In Jane Caplan, ed., *Written on the Body: The Tattoo in European and American History*. Princeton, NJ: Princeton University Press, 2000.

Arnott, Robert, Stanley Finger, and C. U. M. Smith. *Trepanation: History, Discovery, Theory*. Oxford: Oxbow Books, 2003.

Atkinson, Michael. *Tattooed: The Sociogenesis of a Body Art*. Toronto: University of Toronto Press, 2003.

Atkinson, Michael, and Kevin Young. "Flesh Journeys: Neo Primitives and the Contemporary Rediscovery of Radical Body Art." *Deviant Behavior* 22 (2001): 117–146.

Audibert, Chris. "Gone Are the Days." *Tattoo Historian* 10 (1986): 12.

Aurre, Judy. "Meet Betty Broadbent." *Tattoo Historian* 1 (1982): 21–23.

Bakhtin, Mikhail. *Rabelais and His World*. Bloomington: Indiana University Press, 1984.

Balaji, Meena, as told to Ruth Lor Malloy. *Hijras: Who We Are*. Toronto: Think Asia Publisher, 1997.

Baldaev, Danzig, Sergei Vasiliev, and Alexei Plutser-Sarno. *Russian Criminal Tattoo Encyclopaedia*. London: Steidl Publishing, 2003.

Balsamo, Anne. "On the Cutting Edge: Cosmetic Surgery and the Technological Production of the Gendered Body." *Camera Obscura* 28 (1992): 206–237.

Banner, Lois. *American Beauty*. Chicago: University of Chicago Press, 1983.

Baran, Robert, and Howard I. Maibach. *Textbook of Cosmetic Dermatology*. London: Taylor & Francis, 2004.

Baumann, Leslie S. *Cosmetic Dermatology: Principles and Practice*. New York: McGraw Hill Medical, 2002.

Beal, George Brinton. "The Tattooed Lady." *Tattoo Archive* (Fall 1989): 44.

Beard, Steve. "The Tattooed Lady: A Mythology." In Chris Wroblewski, *Tattooed Women*. New York: Carol Publishing Group, 1992.

Beijing College of Traditional Chinese Medicine. *Essentials of Chinese Acupuncture*. New York: Pergamon Press, Inc., 1981.

Benson, John G. *The Well-Being of Farm Animals: Challenges and Solutions*. Oxford: Blackwell Publishers, 2004.

Benson, Susan. "Inscriptions of the Self: Reflections on Tattooing and Piercing in Contemporary Euro-America." In Jane Caplan, ed., *Written on the Body: The Tattoo in European and American History*. London: Reaktion Books, 2000.

Berger, Karen J., and John Bostwick Berger. *A Woman's Decision: Breast Care, Treatment & Reconstruction*. St. Louis, MO: Quality Medical Publishing, 1998.

Berns, Marla C. "Ga'Anda Scarification: A Model for Art & Identity." In Arnold Rubin, ed., *Marks of Civilization: Artistic Transformations of the Human Body*. Los Angeles: Museum of Cultural History, UCLA, 1988.

Bianchi, Robert. "Tattoo in Ancient Egypt." In Arnold Rubin, ed., *Marks of Civilization: Artistic Transformations of the Human Body*. Los Angeles: Museum of Cultural History, UCLA, 1988.

Bogdan, Robert. *Freak Show*. Chicago: University of Chicago Press, 1988.

Bohannon, Paul. "Beauty and Scarification amongst the Tiv." *Man* 56(129) (1956): 117–121.

Bolin, Anne, "Vandalized Vanity: Feminine Physiques Betrayed and Portrayed." In Frances Mascia-Lees and Patricia Sharpe, eds., *Tattoo, Torture, Mutilation, and Adornment: The Denaturalization of the Body in Culture and Text*. Albany: State University of New York Press, 1992.

Bordo, Susan. "Reading the Slender Body." In Mary Jacobus, Evelyn Fox Keller, and Sally Shuttleworth, eds., *Body Politics: Women and the Discourses of Science*. New York: Routledge, 1990.

———. *Unbearable Weight: Feminism, Western Culture, and the Body*. Berkeley: University of California Press, 1993.

Bourdieu, Pierre. *Distinction: A Social Critique of the Judgement of Taste*. London: Routledge, 1984.

Bradley, James. "Body Commodification? Class and Tattoos in Victorian Britain." In Jane Caplan, ed., *Written on the Body: The Tattoo in European and American History*. London: Reaktion Books, 2000.

Brain, Robert. *The Decorated Body*. New York: Harper and Row, 1979.

Brame, Gloria, William Brame, and Jon Jacobs. *Different Loving: An Exploration of the World of Sexual Dominance and Submission*. New York: Villard Books, 1993.

Bray, Warwick. *Everyday Life of the Aztecs*. New York: Dorset Press, 1968.

Brown, Mildred L., and Chloe Ann Rounsley. *True Selves*. Hoboken, NJ: Jossey-Bass, 1996.

Brown, Tamara, Gregory S. Parks, and Clarenda M. Phillips, eds. *African American Fraternities and Sororities: The Legacy and the Vision*. Lexington: University Press of Kentucky, 2005.

Browning, W.R.F. *A Dictionary of the Bible* (Oxford Paperback Reference). Oxford: Oxford University Press, 2004.

Bruno, Richard L. "Devotees, Pretenders and Wannabes: Two Cases of Factitious Disability Disorder." *Journal of Sexuality and Disability* 15 (1997): 243–260.

Brush, Pippa. "Metaphors of Inscription: Discipline, Plasticity and the Rhetoric of Choice." *Feminist Review* 58 (1998): 22–43.

Budge, E. A. *The Gods of the Egyptians*. New York: Dover Publications, 1969.

Burchett, George, and Peter Leighton. *Memoirs of a Tattooist*. London: Oldbourne Book Company, 1958.

Burma, John. "Self-Tattooing among Delinquents: A Research Note." In M. E. Roach and J. B. Eicher, eds., *Dress, Adornment and the Social Order*. New York: Wiley, 1965.

Byrd, Ayana, and Lori L. Tharps. *Hair Story: Untangling the Roots of Black Hair in America*. New York: St. Martin's Press, 2002.

Camphausen, Rufus C. *Return of the Tribal: A Celebration of Body Adornment: Piercing, Tattooing, Scarification, Body Painting*. Rochester, VT: Park Street Press, 1997.

Caplan, Jane, ed., *Written on the Body: The Tattoo in European and American History*. London: Reaktion Books, 2000.

Capozzi, Angelo. *Change of Face: What You Should Know if You Should Choose Cosmetic Surgery*. New York: Kampmann Publishing Company, 1984.

Carswell, John. *Coptic Tattoo Designs*. Beirut: American University of Beirut Press, 1957.

Clark, Katerina, and Michael Holquist. *Mikhail Bakhtin*. Cambridge: Harvard University Press, 1984.

Cohen, Shaye J. D. "Why Aren't Jewish Women Circumcised?" *Gender & History* 9(3) (1997): 560–578.

Cook, James W., ed. *The Colossal P.T. Barnum Reader: Nothing Else Like It in the Universe*. Champaign: University of Illinois Press, 2005.

Cornet, J. *A Survey of Zairian Art*. Raleigh: North Carolina Museum of Art, 1978.

Corson, Richard. *Fashions in Hair: The 1st 5,000 Years*. Chester Springs, PA: Dufour Editions, 2001.

Crocker, William H. "The Canela (Eastern Timbira), I: An Ethnographic Introduction." In *Smithsonian Contributions to Anthropology*, No. 33. Washington, DC: Smithsonian Institution Press, 1990.

Crossley, N. "Fat Is a Sociological Issue: Obesity in Late Modern, Body-Conscious Societies." *Health and Social Theory* 2(3) (2004): 222–253.

Cummings, S. R., X. Ling, and K. Stone. "Consequences of Foot Binding among Older Women in Beijing, China." *Am J Public Health* 87 (1997): 1677–1679.

Curry, Ginette, ed. *Awakening African Women: The Dynamics of Change*. Cambridge: Cambridge Scholars Press, Ltd., 2004.

D'Alleva, Anne. "Christian Skins: Tatau and the Evangelization of the Society Islands and Samoa." In Bronwen Douglas, Nicholas Thomas, and Anna Cole, eds. *Tattoo: Bodies, Art and Exchange in the Pacific and the West*. Durham, NC: Duke University Press, 2005.

Davis, David Brion. *Inhuman Bondage: The Rise and Fall of Slavery in the New World*. Oxford: Oxford University Press.

Davis, Geoffrey V., and Dieter Riemenschneider. *Aratjara: Aboriginal Culture and Literature in Australia*. Amsterdam: Rodopi, 1997.

Davis, Kathy. *Reshaping the Female Body: The Dilemma of Cosmetic Surgery*. London: Routledge, 1995.

———. "'My Body Is My Art.' Cosmetic Surgery as Feminist Utopia?" *The European Journal of Women's Studies* 4(1) (February 1997): 23–37.

DeMello, Margo. "The Convict Body: Tattooing among Male American Prisoners." *Anthropology Today* 9 (1993): 10–13.

———. *Bodies of Inscription: A Cultural History of the Modern Tattoo Community*. Durham, NC: Duke University Press, 2000.

Dery, Mark. *Escape Velocity: Cyberculture at the End of the Century*. New York: Grove, 1996.

Diamond, Jared. *Collapse: How Societies Choose to Fail or Succeed*. New York: Viking Press, 2004.

Douglas, Bronwen, Nicholas Thomas, and Anna Cole, eds. *Tattoo: Bodies, Art and Exchange in the Pacific and the West*. Durham, NC: Duke University Press, 2005.

Drewal, Henry John. "Beauty and Being: Aesthetics and Ontology in Yoruba Body Art." In Arnold Rubin, ed., *Marks of Civilization: Artistic Transformations of the Human Body*, Los Angeles: Museum of Cultural History, UCLA, 1988.

Ebenstein, Hanns. *Pierced Hearts and True Love: The History of Tattooing*. London: Derek Verschoyle, 1953.

Ebin, Victoria. *The Body Decorated*. London: Blacker Calmann Cooper Ltd., 1979.

Eldridge, Chuck. "TABC." *Tattoo Historian* 2 (1983): 9–10.

———. "American Circus 1793–1993." *Tattoo Archive* (Winter 1993): 17–19.

———. "Tattoo Machine Patents and Related Ones." *Tattoo Archive* (Winter 1991): 20–23

Ellis, Andrew, Nigel Wiseman, and Ken Boss. *Fundamentals of Chinese Acupuncture*. Brookline, MA: Paradigm Publications, 1991.

Elofson, Warren M. *Cowboys, Gentlemen and Cattle Thieves: Ranching on the Western Frontier*. Montreal: McGill-Queens University Press, 2000.

Emmett, Steven Wiley, ed., *Theory and Treatment of Anorexia Nervosa and Bulimia: Biomedical, Sociocultural and Psychological Perspectives*. New York: Brunner/Mazel Publishers, 1985.

Evans, J. *A History of Jewellery 1100–1870*. London: British Museum Publications, 1989.

Fallon, P., M. Katzman, and S. Wooley, eds. *Feminist Perspectives on Eating Disorders*. New York: Guilford, 1994.

Faris, James. "Significance of Differences in the Male and Female Personal Art of the Southeast Nuba." In Arnold Rubin, ed., *Marks of Civilization: Artistic Transformations of the Human Body*. Los Angeles: Museum of Cultural History, UCLA, 1988.

Favazza, Armando. *Bodies under Siege: Self-Mutilation and Body Modification in Culture and Psychiatry*. Baltimore, MD: Johns Hopkins Press, 1987.

Featherstone, Mike, ed. *Body Modification*. London: Sage Publications, 2000.

Featherstone, Mike, Mike Hepworth, and Bryan Turner, eds. *The Body: Social Process and Cultural Theory*. London: Sage Publications, 1991.

Fee, E., T. M. Brown, J. Lazarus, and P. Theerman. "The Effects of the Corset." *American Journal of Public Health* 92 (2002): 1085.

Feinberg, Leslie. *Transgender Warriors: Making History from Joan of Arc to Dennis Rodman*. Boston, MA: Beacon Press, 1997.

Fellman, Sandi. *The Japanese Tattoo*. New York: Abbeville Press, 1986.

Field, H. "Body Marking in Southwestern Asia," Papers of the Peabody Museum of Archaeology and Ethnology, Harvard University, Vol. XLV, No. 1, published by the Peabody Museum, Cambridge, MA, 1958.

Fisher, Angela. *Africa Adorned: A Panorama of Jewelry, Dress, Body Decoration, and Hair.* New York: Henry Abrams, 2000.

Foucault, M. *Discipline and Punish: The Birth of the Prison.* Harmondsworth, UK: Penguin, 1979.

———. *The History of Sexuality: Volume I, An Introduction.* New York: Pantheon Books, 1980.

———. *Power/Knowledge: Selected Interviews and Other Writings, 1972–1977.* Brighton, UK: Harvester, 1980.

Freud, Robert Michael, and Alex Van Dyne. *Cosmetic Breast Surgery: A Complete Guide to Making the Right Decision—From A to Double D.* New York: Marlow & Company, 2004.

Friedlander, Marti, and Michael King. *Moko: Maori Tattooing in the Twentieth Century.* Auckland, NZ: David Bateman, 1999.

Furth, G., and R. Smith. *Amputee Identity Disorder: Information, Questions, Answers and Recomendations about Self-Demand Amputation.* London: Authorhouse, 2000.

Galenorn, Yasmine. *Crafting the Body Divine: Ritual, Movement, and Body Art.* Berkeley, CA: Ten Speed Press, 2001.

Gans, Eric. "The Body Sacrificial." In Tobin Siebers, ed., *The Body Aesthetic: From Fine Art to Body Modification.* Ann Arbor: University of Michigan Press, 2000.

Garber, Marjorie. *Vested Interests: Cross Dressing & Cultural Anxiety.* New York: Harper-Collins, 1992.

Garland Thompson, Rosemary, ed., *Freakery: Cultural Spectacles of the Extraordinary Body.* New York: New York University Press, 1996.

Gathercole, Peter. "Contexts of Maori Moko." In Arnold Rubin, ed., *Marks of Civilization: Artistic Transformations of the Human Body.* Los Angeles: Museum of Cultural History, UCLA, 1988.

Gay, Kathlyn. *Body Marks: Tattooing, Piercing, and Scarification.* New York: Millbrook Press, 2002.

Gell, Alfred. *Wrapping in Images: Tattooing in Polynesia.* Oxford: Oxford University Press, 1993.

Gilman, Sander. "Imagined Ugliness." In Tobin Siebers, ed., *The Body Aesthetic: From Fine Art to Body Modification.* Ann Arbor: University of Michigan Press, 2000.

Girard, Rene. "Hunger Artists." In Tobin Siebers, ed., *The Body Aesthetic: From Fine Art to Body Modification.* Ann Arbor: University of Michigan Press, 2000.

Govenar, Alan. "The Variable Context of Chicano Tattooing." In Arnold Rubin, ed., *Marks of Civilization: Artistic Transformations of the Human Body.* Los Angeles: Museum of Cultural History, UCLA, 1988.

———. "The Changing Image of Tattooing in American Culture." In Jane Caplan, ed., *Written on the Body: The Tattoo in European and American History.* Princeton, NJ: Princeton University Press, 2000.

Graham, Elaine. *Representations of the Post/Human: Monsters, Aliens and Others in Popular Culture.* New Brunswick, NJ: Rutgers University Press, 2002.

Graham, P. *Iban Shamanism: An Analysis of the Ethnographic Literature.* Canberra: Research School in Pacific Studies, Australian National University, 1987.

Graves, Bonnie. *Tattooing and Body Piercing: Perspectives on Physical Health.* Mankato, Minnesota: Life Matters Press, 2000.

Green, Roger C. "Early Lapita Art from Polynesia and Island Melanesia: Continuities in Ceramic, Barkcloth, and Tattoo Decorations." In Sidney M. Mead, ed., *Exploring the Visual Art of Oceania..* Honolulu, HI: University Press of Hawaii, 1979.

Gremillion, Helen. *Feeding Anorexia: Gender and Power at a Treatment Center.* Durham, NC: Duke University Press, 2003.

———. "The Cultural Politics of Body Size." *Annual Review of Anthropology* 34 (2005): 13–32.

Griffin, Joy. "Labrets and Tattooing in Native Alaska." In Arnold Rubin, ed., *Marks of Civilization: Artistic Transformations of the Human Body.* Los Angeles: Museum of Cultural History, UCLA, 1988.

Griggs, Claudine. *Journal of a Sex Change: Passage through Trinidad.* Jefferson, NC: McFarland & Company, 2004.

Grimm, Veronika E. *From Feasting to Fasting, the Evolution of a Sin: The Development of Early Christian Asceticism.* New York: Routledge, 1996.

Groning, Karl. *Decorated Skin: A World Survey of Body Art.* London: Thames and Hudson, 1997.

Gurney, C. "Accommodating Bodies." In L. McKie and N. Watson, eds., *Organising Bodies*, pp. 55–80. London: Macmillan, 2000.

Gustafson, Mark. "The Tattoo in the Later Roman Empire and Beyond." In Jane Caplan, ed., *Written on the Body: The Tattoo in European and American History.* Princeton, NJ: Princeton University Press, 2000.

Hall, Douglas Kent. *In Prison.* New York: Henry Holt and Company, 1988.

———. *Prison Tattoos.* New York: St. Martin's Griffin, 1997.

Hambly, H. D. *The History of Tattooing and Its Significance.* London: H. F. & G. Witherby, 1925.

Handy, E. S. Craighill. *Samoan House Building, Cooking, and Tattooing.* Honolulu, HI: The Museum, 1924.

Handy, Willowdean. *Tattooing in the Marquesas.* Honolulu, HI: Bishop Museum, 1922.

Haraway, Donna. *Primate Visions.* New York: Routledge, 1990.

Hardy, Don Ed. "The New Tribalism." *TattooTime* 1 (1982): 3–9.

———. *Rocks of Ages.* Honolulu, HI: Hardy Marks Publications, 1992.

———. *Sailor Jerry Collins: American Tattoo Master.* Honolulu, HI: Hardy Marks Publications, 1994.

———, ed. *Pierced Hearts and True Love: A Century of Drawings for Tattoos.* Honolulu, HI: Hardy Marks Publications, 1995.

———. "Tattooing as a Medium." *Pierced Hearts and True Love: A Century of Drawings for Tattoos.* Honolulu, HI: Hardy Marks Publications, 1995.

Hebidge, Dick. *Subculture: The Meaning of Style.* London: Routledge, 1979.

Hewitt, K. *Mutilating the Body: Identity in Blood and Ink.* Bowling Green, OH: Bowling Green State University Popular Press, 1997.

Heywood, Leslie. *Bodymakers: A Cultural Anatomy of Women's Body Building.* New Brunswick, NJ: Rutgers University Press, 1998.

Hezser, Catherine. *Jewish Slavery in Antiquity.* Oxford: Oxford University Press, 2005.

Hicks, Esther Kremhilde. *Infibulation: Status through Mutilation.* Rotterdam: Erasmus University, 1987.

Hillson, S. *Dental Anthropology.* New York: Cambridge University Press, 1996.

Hiltebeitel, Alf, and Barbara D. Miller, eds. *Hair: Its Power and Meaning in Asian Cultures.* Albany: State University of New York Press, 1998.

Hogbin, Herbert Ian. *The Island of Menstruating Men: Religion in Wogeo, New Guinea.* Scranton, PA: Chandler, 1970.

Hollenbeck, Phil, and Dee J. Hill. *Freaks and Fire: The Underground Reinvention of Circus*. Brooklyn, NY: Soft Skull Press, 2005.

Hong, Fan. *Foot Binding, Feminism and Freedom: The Liberation of Women's Bodies in Modern China*. London: Frank Cass & Co., 1997.

Jeffreys, Sheila. *Beauty and Misogyny: Harmful Cultural Practices in the West*. London: Routledge, 2005.

Jonaitis, Aldona. "Women, Marriage, Mouths and Feasting: The Symbolism of Tlingit Labrets." In Arnold Rubin, ed., *Marks of Civilization: Artistic Transformations of the Human Body*. Los Angeles: Museum of Cultural History, UCLA, 1988.

Jones, C.P. "Stigma and Tattoo." In Jane Caplan, ed., *Written on the Body: The Tattoo in European and American History*. Princeton, NJ: Princeton University Press, 2000.

Kaelber, Walter. *Tapta Marga: Asceticism and Initiation in Vedic India*. Albany: State University of New York Press, 1989.

Kaeppler, Adrienne L. 1988. "Hawaiian Tattoo: A Conjunction of Genealogy and Aesthetics." In Arnold Rubin, ed., *Marks of Civilization: Artistic Transformations of the Human Body*. Los Angeles: Museum of Cultural History, UCLA, 1988.

Kaplan, D. E., and A. Dupro. *Yakuza: Expanded Edition*. Berkeley: University of California Press, 2003.

Kempf, Wolfgang. "The Politics of Incorporation: Masculinity, Spatiality and Modernity among the Ngaing of Papua New Guinea." *Oceania* (September 2002): 56–77.

Kirk, Malcolm. *Man as Art: New Guinea Body Decoration*. London: Thames and Hudson, 1981.

Kitamura, Takahiro, and Katie Takahiro. *Bushido: Legacies of the Japanese Tattoo*. Atglen, PA: Schiffer Publishing, 2001.

Klein, Alan. *Little Big Men: Bodybuilding Subculture and Gender Construction*. Albany: State University of New York Press, 1993.

Klesse, Christian. "Modern Primitivism: Non-Mainstream Body Modification and Racialized Representation." In Mike Featherstone, ed., *Body Modification*. London: Sage Publications, 2000.

Ko, Dorothy. *Cinderella's Sisters: A Revisionist History of Foot Binding*. Los Angeles: University of California Press, 2005.

Kolatch, Alfred. *Inside Judaism: The Concepts, Customs, and Celebrations of the Jewish People*. Middle Village, NY: Jonathan David Publishers, Inc., 2006.

Kroeber, A. L. *Peoples of the Philippines*. New York: American Museum of Natural History, 1943.

Kulick, Don. *Travesti: Sex, Gender, and Culture among Brazilian Transgendered Prostitutes*. Chicago: University of Chicago Press, 1998.

Kunzle, David. *Fashion and Fetishism: A Social History of the Corset, Tight-Lacing and Other Forms of Body Sculpture in the West*. New York: Rowman & Littlefield, 1982.

Kupka, Karel. *Dawn of Art: Painting and Sculpture of Australian Aborigines*. Sydney: Angus and Robertson, 1965.

Kuwahara, Makiko. "Multiple Skins: Space, Time and Tattooing in Tahiti." In Bronwen Douglas, Nicholas Thomas, and Anna Cole, eds., *Tattoo: Bodies, Art and Exchange in the Pacific and the West*. Durham, NC: Duke University Press, 2005.

Kuwahara, Makiko. *Tattoo: An Anthropology*. New York: Berg, 2005.

Lambert, Alix. *Russian Prison Tattoos: Codes of Authority, Domination, and Struggle*. Atglen, PA: Schiffer Publishing, 2003.

Lang, Sabine, Sue-Ellen Jacobs, and Wesley Thomas. *Two Spirit People: Native American Gender Identity, Sexuality, and Spirituality.* Chicago: University of Illinois Press, 1997.

Levenkron, Steven. *Anatomy of Anorexia.* New York: W.W. Norton & Co., 2001.

Levi, Primo. *Survival in Auschwitz: The Nazi Assault on Humanity.* New York: Pocket Books, 1995.

Levy, Howard. *Chinese Foot Binding: The History of a Curious Erotic Custom of Footbinding in China.* Buffalo, NY: Prometheus Books, 1992.

Lienhardt, Godfrey. *Divinity and Experience: the Religion of the Dinka.* Oxford: Oxford University Press, 1961.

Lindsay, Cecile. "Body Building: A Postmodern Freak Show." In Rosemary Garland Thompson, ed., *Freakery: Cultural Spectacles of the Extraordinary Body.* New York: New York University Press, 1996.

Lombroso, Cesare. *Criminal Man.* Raleigh, NC: Duke University Press, May 2006.

Lowe, Maria R. *Women of Steel: Female Bodybuilders and the Struggle for Self-Definition.* New York: New York University Press, 1998.

Lynch, Wilfred. *Implants: Reconstructing the Human Body.* New York: Van Nostrand Reinhold Company, 1982.

Maciocia, Giovanni. *The Foundations of Chinese Medicine: A Comprehensive Text for Acupuncturists and Herbalists.* Oxford: Churchill Livingstone, 2005.

MacQuarrie, Charles. "Insular Celtic Tattooing: History, Myth and Metaphor." In Jane Caplan, ed., *Written on the Body: The Tattoo in European and American History.* London: Reaktion Books, 2000.

Mails, Thomas E. *The Great Sioux Piercing Tradition.* Tulsa, OK: Council Oak Books, 2003.

Mallon, Sean. "Samoan Tatau as Global Practice." In Bronwen Douglas, Nicholas Thomas, and Anna Cole, eds., *Tattoo: Bodies, Art and Exchange in the Pacific and the West.* Durham, NC: Duke University Press, 2005.

Mansfield, Alan, and Barbara McGinn. "Pumping Irony: The Muscular and the Feminine." In S. Scott and D. Morgan, eds., *Body Matters.* London: Falmer Press, 1993.

Martin, Louis F. *Obesity Surgery.* New York: McGraw-Hill, 2004.

Mascetti, Daniela, and Amanda Triossi. *Earrings: From Antiquity to the Present.* London: Thames and Hudson, 1999.

Mascia-Lees, Francis, and Patricia Sharpe, eds., *Tattoo, Torture, Mutilation, and Adornment: The Denaturalization of the Body in Culture and Text.* Albany: State University of New York Press, 1992.

McCabe, Michael. "Coney Island Tattoo: The Growth of Inclusive Culture in the Age of the Machine." In Don Ed Hardy, ed., *Pierced Hearts and True Love: A Century of Drawings for Tattoos.* Honolulu, HI: Hardy Marks Publications, 1995.

———. *New York City Tattoo: The Oral History of an Urban Art.* Honolulu, HI: Hardy Marks Publications, 1997.

———. "Bangkok's Tattoo Arjan." http://tattoos.com/articles/mccabe/arjan/index.html (2006).

———. "Jimmy Wong—Bangkok Past and Present and the Tattoos of Indochina, Part I." http://tattoos.com/articles/mccabe/wong/index.html (2006).

———. "Jimmy Wong—The Changing Face of Bangkok Tattoo, Part II." http://tattoos.com/articles/mccabe/wong/index2.htm (2006).

McCallum, Donald. "Historical and Cultural Dimensions of the Tattoo in Japan." In Arnold Rubin, ed., *Marks of Civilization: Artistic Transformations of the Human Body.* Los Angeles: Museum of Cultural History, UCLA, 1988.

McNab, Nan. *Body Bizarre Body Beautiful*. Old Tappan, NJ: Fireside, 2001.

Meggitt, M. J. *Desert People: A Study of the Walbiri Aborigines of Central Australia*. Sydney: Angus and Robertson, 1986.

Meskell, Lynn, and Rosemary Joyce. *Embodied Lives: Figuring Ancient Maya and Egyptian Experience*. London: Routledge, 2003.

Métraux, Alfred. *Ethnology of Easter Island*. Bulletin 160. Honolulu, HI: Bernice Bishop Museum, 1940.

Mifflin, Margot. *Bodies of Subversion: A Secret History of Women and Tattoos*. New York: Juno Books, 1997.

Miller, Lila, and Stephen Zawistowski, eds., *Shelter Medicine for Veterinarians and Staff*. London: Blackwell Publishing, 2004.

Milner, G., and Larsen, C. "Teeth as Artifacts of Human Behavior: Intentional Mutilation and Accidental Modification." In Marc Kelley and Clark Spencer Larson, eds., *Advances in Dental Anthropology*. New York: Wiley-Liss, 1991.

Mizumoto Posey, Sandra. "Burning Messages: Interpreting African American Fraternity Brands and their Bearers." *Voices, the Journal of New York Folklore* 30 (Fall–Winter 2004): 42–44.

Momoh, Comfort. *Female Genital Mutilation*. Oxford: Radcliffe University Press, 2005.

Money, J., R. Jobaris, and G. Furth. "Apotemnophilia: Two Cases of Self-Demand Amputation as a Paraphilia." *The Journal of Sex Research* 13(2) (1977): 115–125.

Montagu, Ashley. *Coming into Being among the Australian Aborigines*. London: George Routledge & Sons Ltd., 1937.

Morini, Simona. *Body Sculpture: Plastic Surgery From Head to Toe*. New York: Delacorte Press, 1972.

Morse, Albert. *The Tattooists*. San Francisco, CA: Albert Morse, 1977.

Mottier, Veronique, and Terrell Carver. *Politics of Sexuality: Identity, Gender, Citizenship*. London: Routledge, 1999.

Mullins, Paul R. *Race and Affluence: An Archaeology of African America and Consumer Culture*. New York: Plenum Press, 1999.

Musafar, Fakir. "Kiss of Fire: The Abc's of Branding." *Body Play* (1) (1992).

Myers, James. "Nonmainstream Body Modification: Genital Piercing, Branding, Burning and Cutting." *Journal of Contemporary Ethnography* 21(3) (October 1992): 267–306.

Nanda, Serena. *Neither Man Nor Woman: The Hijras of India*. New York: Wadsworth Publishing, 1998.

Oetterman, Stephan. "On Display: Tattooed Entertainers in America and Germany." In Jane Caplan, ed., *Written on the Body: The Tattoo in European and American History*. London: Reaktion Books, 2000.

Ostier, Marianne. *Jewels and Women; The Romance, Magic and Art of Feminine Adornment*. New York: Horizon Press, 1958.

Parry, Albert. *Tattoo: Secrets of a Strange Art Practiced by the Natives of the United States*. New York: Colier, 1971.

Peers, C.J., and Michael Perry (illustrator). *Imperial Chinese Armies: 200 BC–589 AD (Men-At-Arms Series, 284)*. Oxford: Osprey Publishing, 1995.

Peterkin, Allan. *One Thousand Beards. A Cultural History of Facial Hair*. Vancouver, WA: Arsenal Pulp Press, 2001.

Phillips, Anita. *A Defence of Masochism*. London: Faber & Faber, 1999.

Phillips, Katharine A. *The Broken Mirror: Understanding and Treating Body Dysmorphic Disorder*. Oxford: Oxford University Press, 2005.

Pitts, Victoria. "'Reclaiming' the Female Body: Embodied Identity Work, Resistance and the Grotesque." *Body & Society* 4(3) (1988): 67–84.

———. "Body Modification, Self-Mutilation and Agency in Media Accounts of a Subculture." In Mike Featherstone, ed., *Body Modification*. London: Sage Publications, 2000.

———. *In the Flesh: The Cultural Politics of Body Modification*. New York: Palgrave Macmillan, 2003.

Polhemus, Ted, and Randall Housk. *The Customized Body*. London: Serpent's Tail, 1996.

Potts, Annie. "The Mark of the Beast: Inscribing 'Animality' through Extreme Body Modification." In P. Armstrong and L. Simmons, eds., *Knowing Animals*. Leiden: Brill, 2007.

Rees, Laurence. *Auschwitz: A New History*. New York: Public Affair, 2006.

Reiss, Benjamin. *The Showman and the Slave: Race, Death, and Memory in Barnum's America*. Cambridge: Harvard University Press, 2001.

Reynolds, Reginald. *Beards: Their Social Standing, Religious Involvements, Decorative Possibilities, and Value in Offence and Defence through the Ages*. New York: Doubleday, 1949.

Richie, Donald, and Ian Buruma. *Japanese Tattoo*. New York: Weatherhill, 1980.

Ritenbaugh, C. "Obesity as a Culture-Bound Syndrome." *Culture, Medicine, and Psychiatry*. 6 (1982): 347–361.

Roberts, Allen F. "Tabwa Tegumentary Inscription." In Arnold Rubin, ed., *Marks of Civilization: Artistic Transformations of the Human Body*. Los Angeles: Museum of Cultural History, UCLA, 1988.

Roberts, T. A., and S. A. Ryan. "Tattooing and High-Risk Behavior in Adolescents." *Pediatrics* 110 (2002): 1058–1063.

Rosecrans, Jennifer Allen. "Wearing the Universe: Symbolic Markings in Early Modern England." In Jane Caplan, ed., *Written on the Body: The Tattoo in European and American History*. Princeton, NJ: Princeton University Press, 2000.

Rosen, Christine. "The Democratization of Beauty." *The New Atlantis* No. 5 (Spring 2004): 19–35.

Rosenblatt, Daniel. "The Antisocial Skin: Structure, Resistance, and 'Modern Primitive' Adornment in the United States." *Cultural Anthropology* 12(3) (1997): 287–334.

Rosenthal, M. Sara. *Women and Unwanted Hair*. Toronto: Your Health Press, 2001.

Rubin, Arnold. "Tattoo Renaissance." In Arnold Rubin, ed., *Marks of Civilization: Artistic Transformations of the Human Body*. Los Angeles: Museum of Cultural History, UCLA, 1988.

———. "Tattoo Trends in Gujarat." In Arnold Rubin, ed., *Marks of Civilization: Artistic Transformations of the Human Body*. Los Angeles: Museum of Cultural History, UCLA, 1988.

Rush, John A. *Spiritual Tattoo: A Cultural History of Tattooing, Piercing, Scarification, Branding, and Implants*. Berkeley, CA: North Atlantic Books/Frog, Ltd., 2005.

Russel, Kathy, Midge Wilson, and Ronald Hall. *The Color Complex: The Politics of Skin Color Among African Americans*. New York: First Anchor Books, 1993.

Saga, Junichi. *Confessions of a Yakuza: A Life in Japan's Underworld*. Tokyo: Kodansha International, 1995.

Salecl, Renata. "Cut in the Body: From Clitoridectomy to Body Art." In S. Ahmed, J. Stacey, eds., *Thinking through the Skin*. New York: Routledge, 2001.

Sanders, Clinton. *Customizing the Body: The Art and Culture of Tattooing*. Philadelphia, PA: Temple University Press, 1989.

Saxon, Arthur H. *P.T. Barnum: The Legend and the Man*. New York: Columbia University Press, 1995.

Scharer, H. *Ngaju Religion: The Conception of God among a South Borneo People.* The Hague: Martinus Nijhoff, 1963.

Schrader, Abby M. "Branding the Other/Tattooing the Self: Bodily Inscription among Convicts in Russia and the Soviet Union." In Jane Caplan, ed., *Written on the Body: The Tattoo in European and American History.* Princeton, NJ: Princeton University Press, 2000.

Scott, Sue, and David Morgan, eds., *Body Matters.* London: The Falmer Press, 1993.

Scutt, R. W. B., and Christopher Gotch. *Art, Sex and Symbol: The Mystery of Tattooing.* New York: Cornwall Books, 1974.

Searight, S. "The Use and Function of Tattooing on Moroccan Women." New Haven, CT: Human Relations Area Files, Inc., 1984.

Shanks, Peter. *Human Genetic Engineering: A Guide for Activists, Skeptics, and the Very Perplexed.* New York: Nation Books, 2005.

Sheils, W. J., ed., *Monks, Hermits and the Ascetic Tradition.* London: Basil Blackwell, 1985.

Shell-Duncan, Bettina, and Ylva Hernlund, eds., *Female "Circumcision" in Africa: Culture, Controversy, and Change.* Boulder, CO: Lynn Rienner, 2000.

Sherrow, Victoria. *Encyclopedia of Hair: A Cultural History.* Westport, CT: Greenwood Press, 2006.

Siebers, Tobin, ed., *The Body Aesthetic: From Fine Art to Body Modification.* Ann Arbor: University of Michigan Press, 2000.

Sikes, Ruth G. "The History of Suntanning: A Love/Hate Affair." *Journal of Aesthetic Sciences* 1(2) (May 1998): 1–7.

Simmons, D. R. *Ta Moko: The Art of Maori Tattoo.* Auckland, NZ: Reed Books, 1986.

Smith, R. and Furth, G. *Amputee Identity Disorder.* Bloomington, IN: IstBooks Library.

Spencer, Robert Francis, and Jesse David Jennings. *The Native Americans: Prehistory and Ethnology of the North American Indians.* New York: Harper and Row, 1965.

Spennemann, Dirk R. *Marshallese Tattoos.* Majuro Atoll: Republic of the Marshall Islands, Ministry of Internal Affairs, Historic Preservation Office, 1992.

Spitzack, Carole. "The Confession Mirror: Plastic Images for Surgery." *Canadian Journal of Political and Social Theory* 12(1/2) (1988): 38–50.

St. Clair, Leonard, and Alan Govenar. *Stoney Knows How: Life as a Tattoo Artist.* Lexington: University of Kentucky Press, 1981.

St. Martin, L., and N. Gavey. "Women's Bodybuilding: Feminist Resistance and/or Femininity's Recuperation." *Body & Society* 2(4) (1996): 45–57.

Stark, Richard B. *Aesthetic Plastic Surgery.* Boston, MA: Little, Brown and Company, 1992.

Steele, Christy. *Cattle Ranching in the American West.* Milwaukee, WI: World Almanac Library, 2005.

Steele, Valerie. *Fashion and Eroticism.* New York: Oxford University Press, 1985.

———. *The Corset: A Cultural History.* New Haven, CT: Yale University Press, 2001.

Steward, Samuel. *Bad Boys and Tough Tattoos: A Social History of the Tattoo with Gangs, Sailors and Street-Corner Punks, 1950–1965.* New York: Harrington Park Press, 1990.

Stewart, Hamish Maxwell, and Ian Duffield. "Skin Deep Devotions: Religious Tattoos and Convict Transportation to Australia." In Jane Caplan, ed., *Written on the Body: The Tattoo in European and American History.* London: Reaktion Books, 2000.

Strathern, Andrew, and Marilyn Strathern. *Self Decoration in Mt. Hagen.* London: Backworth, 1971.

Strouhal, Eugen. *Life of the Ancient Egyptians.* Norman: University of Oklahoma Press, 1992.

Sullivan, Deborah. *Cosmetic Surgery: The Cutting Edge of Commercial Medicine in America.* New Brunswick, NJ: Rutgers University Press, 2001.

Sullivan, Nikki. *Tattooed Bodies: Subjectivity, Textuality, Ethics, and Pleasure.* Westport, CT: Praeger, 2001.

Sulu'ape, Petelo. "History of Samoan Tattooing." *TattooTime* 5 (1991): 102–109.

Sweetman, Paul. "Anchoring the (Postmodern) Self? Body Modification, Fashion and Identity." In Mike Featherstone, ed., *Body Modification.* London: Sage Publications, 2000.

Swift, B. "Body Art and Modification." In Guy N. Rutty, ed., *Essentials of Autopsy Practice: Current Methods and Modern Trends.* New York: Spring Publishing, 2001.

Sytsma, Sharon. *Ethics and Intersex.* Heidelberg, Germany: Springer Press, 2006.

Tait, H. *Seven Thousand Years of Jewellery.* London: British Museum Publications, 1986.

Taylor, Gary. *Castration: An Abbreviated History of Western Manhood.* New York: Routledge, 2000.

Teilhet-Fisk, Jehanne. "Spiritual Significance of Newar Tattoos." In Arnold Rubin, ed., *Marks of Civilization: Artistic Transformations of the Human Body.* Los Angeles: Museum of Cultural History, UCLA, 1988.

Thevóz, Michel. *The Painted Body.* New York: Rizzoli International, 1984.

Thomas, C. "The 'Disabled' Body." In Mary Evans and Ellie Lee, eds., *Real Bodies: A Sociological Introduction.* Basingstoke: Palgrave, 2002.

Thompson, Mark. *Leatherfolk: Radical Sex, People, Politics, and Practice.* Los Angeles, CA: Daedalus Publishing, 1992.

Tine Cohen-Kettenis, Peggy.*Transgenderism and Intersexuality in Childhood and Adolescence: Making Choices.* Thousand Oaks, CA: Sage Publications, 2003.

Turner, B. "The Possibility of Primitiveness: Towards a Sociology of Body Marks in Cool Societies." *Body & Society* 5(2–3) (1999): 39–50.

Turner, Terence S. "The Social Skin." In Jeremy Cherfas and Roger Lewin, eds., *Not Work Alone: A Cross-Cultural View of Activities Superfluous to Survival.* Beverly Hills, CA: Sage Publications, 1980.

Turner, Terence. "Social Body and Embodied Subject: Bodiliness, Subjectivity and Sociality among the Kayapo." *Current Anthropology* 10(2) (1995): 143–170.

Turner, Victor. "Three Symbols of Passage in Ndembu Circumcision Ritual: An Interpretation." In Max Gluckman, ed., *Essays on the Ritual of Social Relations.* New York: The Humanities Press, 1962.

———. *The Ritual Process.* Ithaca, NY: Cornell University Press 1969.

United States Congress, House Committee on Agriculture, Subcommittee on Livestock and Horticulture. The Development of USDA's National Animal Identification Program: Hearings Before the Committee on Agriculture. United States Congress, 2004.

Vale, V., and Andrea Juno. *Modern Primitives.* San Francisco, CA: Re/Search Publications, 1989.

Van Cutsem, Anne. *A World of Earrings: Africa, Asia, America.* New York: Skira International, 2001.

Van den Beukel, Dorine. *Traditional Mehndi Designs: A Treasury of Henna Body Art.* Berkeley, CA: Shambhala Publications, 2000.

van Gennep, Arnold. *The Rites of Passage.* Chicago: University of Chicago Press, 1969.

Van Stone, James W. *An Early Archaeological Example of Tattooing from Northwestern Alaska.* Chicago: Field Museum of Natural History, 1974.

Virel, Andre. *Decorated Man. The Human Body as Art/Text.* New York: Henry Abrams, 1979.

Vogel, S. "Baule Scarification: The Mark of Civilisation." In Arnold Rubin, ed., *Marks of Civilization: Artistic Transformations of the Human Body*. Los Angeles: Museum of Cultural History, UCLA, 1988.

Wallerstein, Edward. *Circumcision: An American Health Fallacy*. New York: Springer Publishing Company, 1980.

Warburton, Nigel. *Freedom: An Introduction with Readings*. London: Routledge, 2001.

Webb, Doc. *The Honest Skin Game*. San Diego, CA: Author, 1978.

Weinberg, Thomas S. *S&M: Studies in Dominance & Submission*. New York: Prometheus Books, 1995.

Wesson, Cameron. *Historical Dictionary of Early North America*. Lanham, MD: Scarecrow Press, 2005.

White, Joanna. "Marks of Transgression: The Tattooing of Europeans in the Pacific Islands." Bronwen Douglas, Nicholas Thomas, and Anna Cole, eds., *Tattoo: Bodies, Art and Exchange in the Pacific and the West*. Durham, NC: Duke University Press, 2005.

Wiedemann, Thomas E. J. *Greek and Roman Slavery*. Baltimore, MD: Johns Hopkins University Press, 1981.

Wiseman, Jay. *SM 101: A Realistic Introduction*. Emeryville, CA: Greenery Press, 2000.

Wojcik, Daniel. *Punk and Neo-Tribal Body Art*. Jackson: University Press of Mississippi, 1995.

Wolf, Naomi. *The Beauty Myth: How Images of Beauty Are Used against Women*. New York: Harper Perennial, 2002.

Wykes-Joyce, Max. *Cosmetics and Adornment: Ancient and Contemporary Usage*. New York: Philosopical Library Inc., 1961.

Younger, John G. *Sex in the Ancient World from A to Z*. London: Routledge, 2005.

Zeeland, Steven. *Sailors and Sexual Identity: Crossing the Line between "Straight" and "Gay" in the U.S. Navy*. Binghamton, NY: Haworth Press, 1995.

Zeis, Milton. *Tattooing the World Over*, Vol. 1. New York: Milton Zeis, 1947.

Zysk, Kenneth G. *Asceticism and Healing in Ancient India*. New York: Oxford University Press, 1991.

Index

About the Author

MARGO DeMELLO has a BA in Religious Studies from U.C. Berkeley and earned her PhD in Cultural Anthropology in 1995 from U.C. Davis. She currently lectures at Central New Mexico Community College, teaching sociology, cultural studies, and anthropology. Her books include *Bodies of Inscription: A Cultural History of the Modern Tattoo Community* (Duke University Press, 2000), *Stories Rabbits Tell: A Natural and Cultural History of a Misunderstood Beast* (with Susan Davis, Lantern Press, 2003), *Low-Carb Cookbook* (Book Publishing Company, 2004), and *Why Animals Matter: The Case for Animal Protection* (with Erin Williams, Prometheus, 2007). She has had her work published in journals such as *Anthropology Today*, *Journal of Popular Culture*, and *Anthrozöos*, and contributed essays and chapters to *Pierced Hearts and True Love: A Century of Drawings for Tattoos* (Don Ed Hardy, ed., The Drawing Center, 1995), *Cultural Anthropology: The Human Challenge* (William Haviland, Wadsworth Publishing, 2004), *Encyclopedia of Human–Animal Relationships* (Marc Bekoff, ed., Greenwood Publishing, 2007), and *A Cultural History of Animals: The Modern Age* (Randy Malamud, ed., Berg Publishing, 2007).